GOD'S WORD
and
GOD'S PEOPLE

GOD'S WORD
and
GOD'S PEOPLE

by

Lucien Deiss, C. S. Sp.

Translated by
Matthew J. O'Connell

THE LITURGICAL PRESS
Collegeville, Minnesota

GOD'S WORD AND GOD'S PEOPLE is the authorized English version of *Vivre la parole en communaute*, published by Desclee de Brouwer, 1974.

Nihil obstat: William G. Heidt, O.S.B., S.T.D., *Censor deputatus. Imprimatur*: ✝ George H. Speltz, D.D., Bishop of Saint Cloud. June 15, 1976.

Excerpts from the text of *The New American Bible*, copyright © 1970 by the Confraternity of Christian Doctrine, Washington, D.C., are reproduced herein by permission of said Confraternity of Christian Doctrine. All rights reserved.

References to the pronouncements of Vatican Council II have been made according to translation given in *Vatican Council* II, the Conciliar and Post Conciliar Documents, edited by Austin Flannery, O.P.

Printed by The North Central Publishing Company, St. Paul, Minnesota, U.S.A. ISBN 0-8146-0904-X.

Abbreviations

ANET   *Ancient Near Eastern Texts*, ed. J. B. Pritchard. 3rd. ed. Princeton, 1969.

CCL   *Corpus Christianorum Latinorum*. Turnhout, 1953–

DB   *Dictionnaire de la Bible*. Paris, 1895–1912.

DBS   *Dictionnaire de la Bible: Supplément*. Paris, 1928–

DS   H. Denzinger, *Enchiridion Symbolorum*. 32nd ed. by A. Schönmetzer. Freiburg, 1963.

DTS   *Dictionnaire de théologie catholique*. Paris, 1902–50.

JB   *Jerusalem Bible*. New York, 1966.

PG   *Patrologia Graeca*, ed. J. P. Migne. Paris, 1857–66.

PL   *Patrologia Latina*, ed. J. P. Migne. Paris, 1844–64.

SV   *Sacramentum Verbi: An Encyclopedia of Biblical Theology*, ed. J. B. Bauer. New York, 1970.

TDNT   *Theological Dictionary of the New Testament*, ed. G. Kittel, tr. G. W. Bromiley. Grand Rapids, 1964–74.

CONTENTS

Part Two

FROM THE RETURN FROM CAPTIVITY TO THE NEW TESTAMENT

Part Three
THE MESSIANIC AGE

INTRODUCTION

The word of God plays an extraordinarily important role in the history of Israel. In fact, we may even say that it is the foundation of the very existence of the people of God; without it there would have been no Israel. It is as important for the people of God under the old covenant as the Incarnation of Jesus Christ is for the people of God in the new covenant. In the last analysis, we are dealing in both cases with one and the same mystery. Just as in the Old Testament God gathers his people by means of his word, which created both the world and the history of Israel, so in the New Testament he continues to gather his messianic people by means of Jesus Christ, his incarnate Word, who creates both a new world and a history which opens into eternal life.

The acknowledgment of this fact — or, better, the reality itself — imposes an immensely important conclusion on the Church of today: The Church can grow and renew its life only if it is built (in the strongest sense of this word) on the word of God. Just as the community of the old covenant came into existence through dialogue with God, so the messianic community established by Jesus will be "fitted together and take[s] shape as a holy temple" (Eph. 2:21) only if it continues to be built upon the word. The Church must constantly look at itself in the mirror of the word, see its pristine face as Spouse of Christ, and scour away the threatening wrinkles of sin. It must constantly take new root in the word so as to produce blossoms and fruit. Amid the surrounding darkness it must constantly radiate the splendid light of the word.

We are speaking here not of a condition for greater vitality, but of a condition for life itself. Being grounded and rooted in the word is absolutely necessary if the people of God is to be one and united, if the temple of the Spirit is to be built on rock, if the Spouse of Jesus Christ is to be capable of loving. The Church may have a thousand languages in which to sing the praises of Jesus, but it has only one voice for doing so. It may have a thousand beautiful faces, but it has only one mirror in which to see them. It may have countless tender ways, but it has only one love to inspire them. Its voice, its mirror, its love, is the word of Jesus Christ, the incarnate God.

Purpose and Plan of the Book

If we wish to understand correctly how the word of God brought into existence the ecclesial community of the Old and New Testaments and how the community continues to grow today, it will not be enough to reflect at length on the nature of God and of his word, as if everything of importance were simply a deduction from our idea of God. The God of Christian revelation is to be discovered through his action, and not first and foremost by philosophical or theological reflection on his nature. He is not reducible to the God of Aristotle or Plato. He reveals himself as "God, the Father of our Lord Jesus Christ" (2 Cor. 1:3) and manifests himself most strikingly in what St. Paul, in a splendid phrase, calls "the message of the cross" (1 Cor. 1:18). When compared with the mystery of Jesus and the message of the Cross, all human wisdom, even that of Aristotle or Plato, is but a child's stammering. We must therefore attempt to discern the path God has followed and to hear the lesson history teaches us. Only thus will we be able to understand correctly the mystery of the Church and its word.

The Bible has preserved the memory of the chief moments in which God called men together by means of his word and thus created his people. These were also the moments in which the people listened to God, stored up in its memory the words of its dialogue with him, and celebrated the covenant.

In our study of the memories of God's people, as collected in what we call the "Sacred Scriptures," we shall consider first of all the period from the Exodus to the return from captivity (Part One). In this Part we shall reflect on the community of Sinai, the community of Shechem, the community led by Josiah, and, finally, the community established under Ezra at the return from captivity.

We shall consider next the period from the return from captivity to the beginning of New Testament times (Part Two). Here we shall be more directly interested in the word, or, specifically, in the formation of the canon of Scripture and in the celebration of synagogal worship, which was based on the reading of the Law and the prophets, on the homily, and on the praying of the Psalms.

Finally, we shall consider the new situation brought about by the coming of Jesus, the incarnate Word (Part Three).[1]

Before launching into Part One, we shall discuss two points of general interest in this Introduction. The first has to do with the power and efficacy of the word according to the biblical tradition, the second with the initiative which God always retains in his loving dialogue with man.

POWER AND EFFICACY OF THE WORD OF GOD

The word of God is all-powerful and possesses a sovereign efficacy. God speaks and the universe exists; he commands and all things come into being. Wherever he sends his word, it acts as a messenger empowered by him and everywhere accomplishes its mission in an irresistible way.

> For just as from the heavens
>   the rain and snow come down
> And do not return there
>   until they have watered the earth,
>   making it fertile and fruitful,
> Giving seed to him who sows
>   and bread to him who eats,
> So shall my word be
>   that goes forth from my mouth;
> It shall not return to me void,
>   but shall do my will,
>   achieving the end for which I sent it (Is. 55:10-11).

When God's word comes to man and enters into his heart, it wounds like a sword and pierces like a rapier. It causes those strange wounds, at once sweet and searing, that lay the heart bare and enable life to enter it: "Indeed, God's word is living and effective, sharper than any two-edged sword. It penetrates and divides soul and spirit, joints and marrow; it judges the reflections and thoughts of the heart" (Heb. 4:12).

If we are to understand correctly the full meaning of these statements, we must situate the expression "word of God" in the Old Testament context in which it originates and has its roots.[2] "Word of God" is a translation of the Hebrew *debar Yahweh*. But in fact there is no single word in English that adequately translates the Hebrew *dabar*. Certainly the term "word" is too limited to do justice to all the values and nuances of the Hebrew word. If, then, we are to be faithful to the biblical term and grasp the realities to which it points, we must try to enrich our hackneyed term "word" by attaching to it the far richer significance of the Hebrew *dabar*.

To the Semite, a word is not simply the exteriorization of a thought that "arises" in a man's mind nor an insubstantial breath that issues from his mouth and, though it expresses what is in his soul, vanishes as soon as it is pronounced. On the contrary, every word is freighted with the mystery and personality of the one who utters it; it shares in his very life: "Deep waters, such are the words of man: a swelling torrent, a fountain of life" (Prov. 18:4 JB).

The mysterious power of the word was something that fascinated people in the ancient East, who attributed a dynamism and almost magical power to it. The formulas for charms that are found in Sumerian literature, as well as the exorcisms for expelling demons, counteracting charms, and neutralizing spells, bear witness to popular belief.[3] It is true enough, of course, that magical practices were always put down in Israel in a forcible, sometimes even brutal way, for they were too much of a threat to the pure Yahwist faith. But the very fact that the prohibition had to be renewed over and over again[4] shows that necromancers and soothsayers never disappeared entirely from the land. The unreasoning belief of people in the mysterious power of magical formulas has deep roots indeed in the human soul! And what a thrill it gives to make the gods dance to the tune we call by using cabalistic words and thus to take revenge on them for the way they have used their powers!

When the *dabar* is uttered before the Lord, its power is further augmented. This is true especially of curses and blessings and of oaths.

Curses, it was thought, might have a truly terrifying power. Thus, the curse which Joshua uttered against Jericho[5] still weighed heavily on the city centuries later, so that when Hiel of Bethel rebuilt it, he did so at the price of his two sons, Abiram and Segub.[6] Elsewhere, in Egypt and Phoenicia,[7] curses were incised on tombs to keep them from being broken into and to assure the dead of a peaceful final rest; it is true that these curses did not deter those who wished to rob the corpses, but these people really needed the courage of highwaymen if they were to ignore the curses.

Blessings also possessed extraordinary efficacy.[8] The blessing of a father on his child, for example that of Isaac on Jacob, was infallibly beneficial; it was also irreversible in its effects, even if it had been coaxed from a blind father by trickery and fraud (Gen. 27:1-45). Sirach seems to reflect the current belief of Israel when he writes: "A father's blesssing gives a family firm roots" (3:9). The recipient of a blessing has not received a mere set of words; a cloak of favor now enwraps him.

The idea that words are identical with what they signify is still to be found in the New Testament. In his missionary discourse to the seventy-two disciples Jesus says: "On entering any house, first say, 'Peace to this house.' If there is a peaceable man there, your peace will rest on him; if not, it will come back to you" (Luke 10:5-6). The peace the disciples are to wish is thought of as a reality that must come to rest on someone. If there is no one to receive it, it will return to the wisher.

Such is the power of the human word. But if the word comes from God, it is a divine word. The following ancient Sumerian poem on the power of the god Marduk's word sounds to us like an old hymn that got mislaid from the Psalter:

> Your word is spread like a sublime net over heaven and earth.
> It falls upon the sea, and the sea grows stormy,
> It falls upon the canebrake, and the canebrake moans,
> It falls upon the waters of the Euphrates:
> The word of Marduk stirs them to their depths. [9]

Israel will devoutly gather up these images created for Sumerian prayer: the voice of Yahweh wakes the morning stars and shows the dawn its place as the chorus of the Pleiades dances; [10] it digs out the oceans to make room for the deep waters or dries the rivers up and silences their roaring; [11] it summons the light which trembles and obeys, it calls the stars and they answer "Here we are!" (Bar. 3:34-35); [12] it burns like a devouring fire and crushes rocks like a hammer; [13] it breaks the cedars on the mountains, makes Lebanon leap like a calf and Sirion like a young bull, shakes the wilderness of Kadesh and sets the terebinths trembling. [14]

All these sparkling images are gathered up, as it were, in the story of creation as told in the Priestly document: By his word God creates all the splendor of heaven and earth. [15] This creation, in God's judgment, is but an image of the new creation which is initiated in the heart of every believer by the coming of the eternal Word, Jesus Christ, the Word of God. The Book of Genesis opens with the words: "*In the beginning*, when God created the heavens and the earth" (Gen. 1:1); to them correspond the opening words of St. John's Gospel: "*In the beginning* was the Word. . . . Through him all things came into being" (1:1-3). [16]

So real is the power of the word that in the Hebrew language and

in the biblical outlook *dabar*[17] can be in some way identified with
the reality which it signifies. The term *dabar* can be used for a case
at law (Exod. 22:8), a miracle God does for his people (Ps. 105:27),
the story of Abram and Melchizedek (Gen. 14:18), the incident of
Saul and his father's asses (1 Sam. 10:2), the forced labor of the
Israelites in Egypt (Exod. 5:13) — in short, anything that we could
describe in English with such words as "thing" or "affair." In Gen.
15:1 and 22:1, there is a phrase which reads literally "after these
words," but we must translate it as "after these events." Another
example: in 1 Kings 11:41 the writer mentions deeds recorded "in
the book of the words of Solomon," but the sense is "in the book of
the chronicles of Solomon." Such a use of *dabar*, or "word," is also
found in the New Testament. Thus, when the angels told the
shepherds in the fields at Bethlehem of the birth of Jesus, the
shepherds said to one another: "Let us go over to Bethlehem and
see the *word* [= event, i.e. the birth of Jesus] which the Lord has
made known to us" (Luke 2:15).[18] Then when the shepherds had
found Mary, Joseph, and the newborn Jesus, "they repeated what
[literally: the word] they had been told about him" (Luke 2:17 JB).

This usage of *dabar*, closely linking the noetic aspect with the
dynamic aspect and the reality signified, is very important for
understanding the word of God. We today like to distinguish between the word and action indicated by it, between the name and
the person named. We usually contrast the weak, insubstantial
character of the word with the reality of the object. The Semitic
mind, on the contrary, saw the one with the other, even the one in
the other, and thus ennobled the tenuous word by associating it
with the substantiality of the thing signified.[19] Seen in this perspective, the *debar Yahweh* displays an extraordinary breadth of meaning, for it includes not only the word that narrates the history which
God shapes, across the centuries, for his people but also, in a certain
fashion, that history itself.

The word of God is not simply the word spoken by his servants
the prophets but also the word proclaimed by the events of history,
the word that becomes perceptible in the din of war, the glad shouts
of victory, and the lamentations of the Exile. For Israel's sacred
history too is God's word and the revelation of his name. As Lord of
history and Master of the word, God is constantly conversing with
his people. The dialogue goes on as he guides them through the
reeds of the Red Sea, no less than when, in the sacred Book, he
reminds them of this rescue; in the action of the warlike Jael as she

crushes Sisera's head out of love for her God, no less than in the
canticle of Deborah with its enthusiastic celebration of this victory;[20] in the words of the Book of Deuteronomy which Josiah
discovered in 622, and in the arrow that pierced the young king at
Megiddo; in the cries of Jeremiah as he prophesies concerning
Jerusalem, and in the sword of the Chaldeans and the burnt walls of
the Holy City.

For its part, Israel became the people of God through this uninterrupted dialogue with the Lord of history and Master of the word.
It answered him in the prayers of its Psalms, in its sacred dances to
the rhythm of the sounding cymbals,[21] in its muffled sobs by the
banks of the "rivers of Babylon," in the sighs of love and the lan-
guishings of the dark-skinned betrothed in the Song of Songs, in the
forced marches across the desert to Babylon or Jerusalem (Israel was
well acquainted with the road in both directions, and each direction
has a profound significance in the Bible), in the rebellion of Job, in
the disillusioned questions of Qoheleth, and in the blood of the
Maccabean martyrs. The sacred history of Israel was the cradle of
the word, and the word was the soul that gave unity to the history
and passed judgment upon it. Edmond Jacob writes: "It is impossible to study the theology of the word without relating it to the
revelation of God in history. Whilst in Babylon and Egypt the divine
word intervenes in isolated events which have no connection with
one another, the word of God in the Old Testament directs and
inspires a single history which begins with the word of God pronounced at the creation and which is completed by the word made
flesh (John 1:14)."[22]

By making the connection between the word and history a vital
part of its life, Israel set out to achieve the ideal achieved by Enoch
of old, an ideal which undoubtedly embodies one of the best definitions of "biblical man" or the man who lives according to the word:
"Enoch walked with God" (Gen. 5:22).

THE INITIATIVE IN THE DIALOGUE

God takes the whole initiative in the call he utters and the
dialogue that ensues. His word is not a response to a cry of human
distress reaching his ears. Still less is it a reward or salary earned by
our human works, for he calls us "not because of any merit of ours
but according to his own design" (2 Tim. 1:9; cf. Rom. 9:12). His
word is essentially a call that issues from the depths of the divine

silence; it addresses itself to men, creates the ecclesial community, and makes messianic salvation a reality.

Does this mean that man does not have to cry out to God and to open his empty heart to him? By no means. But when he does cry out to God, he does so because God has already touched his heart. God's act always comes first: "God . . . calls into being those things which had not been" (Rom. 4:17); his love always anticipates ours: "He first loved us" (1 John 4:19). Man's action can only be a response and an acceptance: "I am the servant of the Lord. Let it be done to me as you say" (Luke 1:38).

How could man have gained access to the riches of God if God's word had not first invited him to do so? How could he have passed from death to eternal life and the glorious kingdom if God had not brought him there? [23] How could he have traversed the darkness and reached God's "marvelous light" if God had not taken him by the hand and taught him to sing the praises of his name? [24] Could he use trickery or violence to force his way through the gates of heaven, or manage by deception to be present as a hidden, uninvited guest at the wedding feast of the Lamb? [25] And could any woman have become the mother of Jesus if God had not begun the dialogue of the Annunciation? Yes, God has the complete initiative in the great adventure of salvation; he alone can begin the dialogue between heaven and earth, and he alone can lead it to a happy conclusion: "Those he predestined he likewise called; those he called he also justified; and those he justified he in turn glorified" (Rom. 8:30).

The prophets remain bound by the law of divine initiative. The hand of the Lord lays hold of them, and despite their panic and their efforts to escape, hurls them into the midst of the unending battle in which light and darkness, grace and sin, confront each other. Their protests are useless. Moses beseeches God: "If you please, Lord, I have never been eloquent, neither in the past, nor recently, nor now that you have spoken to your servant; but I am slow of speech and tongue." In his timidity he begs: "If you please, Lord, send someone else!" (Exod. 4:10, 13). Jeremiah plays the child, hoping thus to discourage his Master: "Ah, Lord God! I know not how to speak; I am too young" (Jer. 1:6). But God laughs at these objections and continues his demands on his spokesmen.

So transcendent is the divine action that the word even addresses those who do not invoke God:

> I was ready to respond to those who asked me not,
> to be found by those who sought me not.

> I said: Here I am! Here I am!
>> to a nation that did not call upon my name
>>> (Is. 65:1; cf. Rom. 10:20).

Sometimes the word intervenes with turbulent power in the peaceful life of a believer, like a clap of thunder on a calm summer evening. That was what happened to Amos, a shepherd from Tekoa, who was taken from the midst of his flock[26] and sent by God to roar like a lion on the mountains of Samaria: "Prepare to meet your God, O Israel" (Amos 4:12). It was also what happened to Ezekiel, who was seized by God while with the exiles by the river Chebar; confused and bewildered, he was snatched up into an ecstasy and saw the heavens opened before him![27] How could anyone resist? When God's word forces its way into a man's heart, how can he contain and muffle it? Jeremiah had made the attempt:

> I say to myself, I will not mention him,
>> I will speak his name no more.
> But then it becomes like fire burning in my heart,
>> imprisoned in my bones;
> I grow weary holding it in,
>> I cannot endure it. . . .
> My breast! my breast! how I suffer!
>> The walls of my heart!
> My heart beats wildly,
>> I cannot be still (Jer. 20:9; 4:19).

In other cases, the prophet begs for light so that he can speak to his brothers, but God seems to remain silent. Thus, when the refugees who were fleeing with Johanan toward Egypt asked Jeremiah to seek advice from the Lord, the prophet had to wait ten days for an answer.[28] On another occasion, in a dispute with the false prophet Hananiah, Jeremiah got in over his head and stammered a lame answer because Yahweh did not immediately enlighten him.[29]

The situation was quite different with the soothsayers and magicians of the Sumerian-Akkadian and Egyptian worlds.[30] There one could meet with a god through oracles; thanks to a repertory of magical formulas, one had the gods at one's own disposal; when one questioned the pantheon, it was sure to reply. Dreams were sold, oracles bought, and gods tailored to man's measure. Israel, on the contrary, knew only a transcendent God:

> As high as the heavens are above the earth,
>> so high are my ways above your ways
>> and my thoughts above your thoughts (Is. 55:7).

How often, when confronted with the transcendent divine control of things, the prophets were forced, amid smiles or tears, to reflect on the great Yahwist rule:

> Our God is in heaven;
> whatever he wills, he does (Ps. 115:3)!

God acts as he pleases — not whimsically but as his love bids him act.

If we reflect on this initiative of God in speaking his word and in entering into dialogue with man, we find ourselves faced with one of the central affirmations of the Bible and one of the great themes that left an indelible impress on the heart of Israel: the transcendence of God over man and the transcendence of his action over man's activity and bustling restlessness. "As the Lord of hosts lives, whom I serve . . ." (1 Kings 18:15): this cry of Elijah, the prophet with the fiery heart, is a good summation of the believer's situation before his God. The believer serves God with humble love and, like the young Samuel, stammers: "Speak, Lord, for your servant is listening" (1 Sam. 3:10).

"Biblical" man, formed as he was by the piety embodied in the Scriptures, avoided any word or action that could, as it were, compromise God's freedom of speech and action. He acted indeed energetically and tenaciously, but always in a spirit of joyful submission that inspired to all kinds of bold action. When he read the book of creation, he found the name of God written in it, and when he meditated on history, he was in wonder at God's interventions in it. But he also knew that God infinitely transcended both creation and history, even though he manifested himself in both: he was master of creation and shaper of history. Even when God would become immanent in mankind, at the time of his Incarnation in human history, when he would be so intimately present in the heart of a man and body forth his tenderness in the smile of a little child at Bethlehem, when the invisible God would let himself be bound like a thief in the olive garden and crucified like a criminal on a gallows, even then he would lose nothing of his transcendence. Jesus, while adored as man, remains nonetheless God. His *transcendence* itself is *immanent* in mankind. He is master of the events which seem to hold him prisoner and retains the complete initiative with regard both to his life and to his death.[31]

The scriptural idea of God's transcendence is important for our understanding of the mystery of the Church and its liturgy. The Church does not exist because men take the initiative in gathering to praise God, but because God takes the initiative in calling them together through his word so that they may praise him. God creates the Church as he creates everything else: by calling things into being out of nothingness. And when the Church, once gathered, undertakes to praise God in its liturgy, its first prayer must be to listen to God's word.

According to the Christian revelation (the situation may be different in other religions), prayer is not first and foremost a cry from the heart of man, but a response to a word. It is not an appeal forcing its way through the thick darkness and leaping upward to the light, but a light blazing out in the darkness. It is not human poverty begging for a share of God's wealth, but the infinite riches of God freely offering themselves to meet man's need. In this respect, we may well say that the Church and its liturgy must constantly be learning to pray, since they are always in need of learning to hear God's word. It is also clear that for us as individuals the most important moment in our prayer is not when we begin to speak to God, but when we begin to be silent within so that we may hear his word.

There is need of a real conversion here. Perhaps the Church of Vatican II will become the Church of hunger for God's word, thus fulfilling the prophecy of Amos:

> Yes, days are coming, says the Lord God,
> when I will send famine upon the land:
> Not a famine of bread, or thirst for water,
> but for hearing the word of the Lord (Amos 8:11).

---

[1] This chronological division into three parts squares only imperfectly with the subjects treated. For example, the Palestinian canon was fixed only in the first century A.D. for the "Writings," but the prehistory of the canon for the Law begins well before the Exile. Nonetheless, we shall keep the division because it is a handy one.

[2] On the meaning of "word of God," cf. A. Debrunner *et al.*, "legō," *TDNT* 4:69–143; A. Robert, "La parole divine dans l'Ancien Testament," *DBS* 5:442–65; P. van Imschoot, *Theology of the Old Testament* 1: *God*, translated by K. Sullivan and F. Buck (New York, 1965), pp. 188–95; W. Eichrodt, *Theology of the Old Testament* 2, translated by J. A. Baker (Philadelphia, 1967), pp. 40–45; E. Jacob, *Theology of the Old Testament*, translated by A. W. Heathcote and P. J. Allcock (New York, 1958), pp. 127–35; G. Ziener, "Word," *SV* 3:991–95; C. Larcher, "La parole de Dieu en tant que révélation dans l'Ancien Testament," in *La Parole de Dieu en Jésus-Christ* (Cahiers de l'actualité religieuse 15; Tournai, 1961), pp. 35–67.

[3] Cf. R.-J. Tournay, "Logos," *DBS* 5:426.

[4] Cf. Exod. 22:17; Lev. 20:6, 27; Deut. 18:9-12; 1 Sam. 15:23; 28:3; Micah 5:11; Jer. 27:9; Ezek. 13:18-20; Mal. 3:5.

[5] According to Josh. 6:26.

[6] Cf. 1 Kings 16:34.

[7] Cf. Van Imschoot, *op. cit.*, p. 189.

[8] Cf. H. Beyer, "eulogeō," *TDNT* 2:755.

[9] R.-J. Tournay, *art. cit.*, col. 427. See the similar hymn to the god Sin in R. Labat, "Les grands textes de la pensée babylonienne," in *Les religions du Proche Orient Asiatique* (Paris, 1970), p. 283.

[10] Cf. Job 38:7-12, 31.

[11] Cf. Is. 44:27.

[12] Cf. Is. 40:26.

[13] Cf. Jer. 23:28; cf. 5:14.

[14] Cf. Ps. 29:5-9.

[15] Gen. 1:1–2:4.

[16] On the relationship between the account of creation and the prologue of the Fourth Gospel, cf. M.-E. Boismard, O.P., *St. John's Prologue*, translated by Carisbrooke Dominicans (Westminster, Md., 1957), especially pp. 102–13.

[17] Cf. O. Procksch, in "legō," *TDNT* 4:92. Of the etymology of the term *dabar*, A. Robert writes: "In Hebrew the verb *dabar* means simply 'to speak,' but derivatives from the same root, apart from the noun *dabar* (which means 'word, affair, event, thing'), have quite divergent meanings. Philologists have frequently tried to find a unity behind the diversity. Recently, O. Procksch ('logos,' *TDNT* 4:92) compares the Hebrew word with the corresponding Arabic, Aramean, and Ethiopic words, and concludes that *dabar* is properly the rear of a thing, that is, its intelligibility or dynamism. . . . The safest course here, as so often, is to suppose that there were two parallel roots, one meaning simply 'to speak,' the other meaning 'to be in the rear' " (*art cit.*, col. 442).

[18] Cf. L. Deiss, *Synopse de Matthieu, Marc et Luc, avec les parallèles de Jean* 1 (Paris, 1963), p. 173.

[19] Cf. O. Procksch, *Theologie des Alten Testaments* (Gütersloh, 1950), pp. 450–54 ("The significance of the name"). — A.-M. Besnard, *Le mystère du nom* (Lectio divina 35; Paris, 1962). — This aspect of the matter is not peculiar to Yahwism but is found in the other religions of the Middle East: "For the Egyptians the name of a thing is identical with the thing itself; to pronounce a name aloud is to call to life the being or thing the name represents" (L. Desroches-Noblecourt, "La religion égyptienne," in *Histoire générale des religions* 1 [Paris, 1960], p. 195).

[20] Cf. Judg. 4–5. On the connection between word and history, see below, Chapter 14.

[21] Cf. Ps. 150:4-5.

[22] Cf. Jacob, *op. cit.*, p. 129.

[23] Cf. 1 Tim. 6:12: "Take firm hold on the everlasting life to which you *were called*."

[24] Cf. 1 Peter 2:9: ". . . to proclaim the glorious works of the One who *called* you from darkness into his marvelous light"; and 1 Thess. 2:12: "the God who *calls* you to his kingship and glory." Cf. also 2 Thess. 2:14; 1 Peter 5:10; 2 Peter 1:3.

[25] Cf. Apoc. 19:9: "Happy are they who have been *invited* to the wedding feast of the Lamb."

[26] Amos 1:1; cf. especially 3:3-8: "The lion roars — who will not be afraid? The Lord God speaks — who will not prophesy?" (v. 8).

[27] Cf. Ezek. 1:1-3.

[28] Jer. 42:1-7. Cf. J. Steinmann, *Le prophète Jérémie* (Lectio divina 9; Paris, 1952), p. 265.

[29] Jer. 28.

[30] Cf. R. Largement and A. Massart, "Magie," *DBS* 5:706–32.

[31] Cf. John 10:18: "No one takes it [my life] from me; I lay it down freely. I have power to lay it down, and I have power to take it up again. This command I received from my Father."

GOD'S WORD
and
GOD'S PEOPLE

Part One

FROM THE EXODUS TO THE
RETURN FROM CAPTIVITY

Chapter 1

THE ASSEMBLY OF THE
EXODUS AND SINAI

INTRODUCTION

1. Importance of the Exodus theme in the biblical tradition

We are all aware of the great importance the Israelites attributed to the events that made up the departure from Egypt, the journey through the desert, and the entry into the Promised Land. "The Exodus is the decisive event in the history of Israel. In the consciousness of the people, the march through the desert, between the miracle of the Red Sea and the miracle of the Jordan, holds the place which is occupied in the Christian consciousness by the life of Jesus."[1] Just as Jesus is "our Passover" (1 Cor. 5:7), that is, has made us pass from death to life, from darkness to light, from the sadness of sin to the joy of salvation, so the God of Israel brought his chosen people out of Egypt and established them in the Promised Land. This first liberation, from the penal colony of Egypt, became a type of all future liberations, and especially of the Messiah's act of ransoming. It is, in the supreme sense, the "glorious deed" which God is constantly repeating and which always retains its newness:

> Thus says the Lord,
>   who opens a way in the sea
>   and a path in the mighty waters. . . .
> Remember not the events of the past,
>   the things of long ago consider not;
> See, I am doing something new!
>   Now it springs forth, do you not perceive it?
> In the desert I make a way,
>   in the wasteland, rivers (Is. 43:16-19).

The formula "Yahweh brought out of Egypt" is thus equivalent to

3

a profession of faith. It occurs both in the earliest creeds, that of Deuteronomy, for example,[2] and in the most recent texts.[3]

Throughout its history, Israel would meditate with predilection on the great events that accompanied its birth at the Exodus. And as history is never more beautiful than when time has allowed tears to dry and wounds to heal, the piety of the people would attach to the Exodus all the happy memories that had marked its life and all the tender associations that had soothed its heart over the years. A good number of traditions — some of them possessing only local interest, all of them moving freely like desert nomads through the oral tradition — would readily become part of the great Exodus story and attract to themselves some of its radiance.

The period of the Exodus would thus become the object of nostalgic longing, a blessed time when God, as it were, had checked the trite flow of history, heaped miracles upon his people, carried them in his arms, and saved them "with mighty hand and outstretched arm." The hurried journeying of a group of refugees through the lonely deserts of Sinai and the migrations of sheepherding tribes in search of watering holes would become the triumphal march of a people of priests and kings on their way to the Promised Land; all the elements of such a march would be there — the procession of the Levites, the blare of royal trumpets, the ark with its retinue.[4]

There, amid the sand and boulders of Sinai, God would set a table for his people[5] and feed them "with the best of wheat, and with honey from the rock" (Ps. 81:17); the sweet delight of this heaven-sent "food of angels" would show the Father's tender love for his children (Wis. 16:20–21). There, too, God would quench his people's thirst by turning "the rock into pools of water, the flint into flowing springs" (Ps. 114:8); scorning the stagnant water in the desert watering-holes, he would delight in bringing new springs of living water forth from the rocks at each stage in the journey. St. Paul explains that this wonderful rock, always ready to produce a miracle, faithfully advanced with the children of Israel.[6] So great a fascination did the desert have for the prophets that they would never tire of returning to this privileged theme. The conversion of Israel would be seen as a new Exodus taking the people through a desert that bursts into blossom as they pass; flowers will drape the arid waste in a mantel of joy and will cry out for gladness as God brings his people back to Jerusalem:

> The desert and the parched land will exult;
> the steppe will rejoice and bloom.

They will bloom with abundant flowers,
    and rejoice with joyful song. . . .
They will see the glory of the Lord,
    the splendor of our God. . . .
Streams will burst forth in the desert,
    and rivers in the steppe. . . .
Those whom the Lord has ransomed will return
    and enter Zion singing,
    crowned with everlasting joy (Is. 35:1-10).

The return from exile (to which this prophecy refers) was undoubtedly in reality a less lyrical affair; undoubtedly, too, the desert between Babylon and Jerusalem was not the same as that between Egypt and the Promised Land. No matter — from the viewpoint of God's word there is always a desert to be crossed before reaching Jerusalem and always an exodus to be undertaken before entering the country of God. The desert had been the place of espousal between God and Israel, a marvelous, idyllic place, and it would forever carry the connotation of this divine tender love:

I will allure her,
    I will lead her into the desert
    and speak to her heart. . . .
She shall respond there as in the days of her youth,
    when she came up from the land of Egypt (Hos. 2:16-17).

Like a lover, the Exodus will draw into its orbit the three ancient festivals in the Israelite calendar[7] and enrich them with historical memories.

The first, the Feast of Unleavened Bread,[8] was originally a festival celebrated by farmers when they offered the first fruits of the barley harvest. It later fused with the Feast of Passover, a festival celebrated by nomadic shepherds when they offered the first fruits of their flocks.[9] Both were celebrated at the first full moon of the springtime. Exodus connects the memory of the passage out of Egypt with this Feast of Passover and of Unleavened Bread.

The second feast was the Harvest festival.[10] It marked the end of the wheat harvest,[11] and at it people offered "the first of the crop that you have sown in the field" (Exod. 23:16). It was also called the Feast of Weeks (Deut. 16:9–12, 16; Num. 28:26–31; Exod. 34:22) or Pentecost,[12] because it took place seven weeks, or fifty days, after the offering of the first sheaf of barley. The Priestly tradition links to this feast the memory of the gift of the Law at Mount Sinai fifty days after the escape from Egypt.[13]

The third great festival was the Feast of Ingathering, "when you gather in the produce from the fields" (Exod. 23:16). This was the most popular and joyous of the festivals. It was also called the Feast of Huts or Tents,[14] an allusion, it would seem, to the custom of sleeping amid the vines, in shelters made of branches, throughout the period of the grape harvest.[15] But, as we might expect, this explanation did not satisfy the piety of the Levites, and the latter preferred to think back to the encampments in the desert: "During this week every native Israelite among you shall dwell in booths, that your descendants may realize that, when I led the Israelites out of the land of Egypt, I made them dwell in booths" (Lev. 23:42-43).

Thus, thanks to the Exodus, the three festivals mentioned in the calendar of the Covenant Code (Exod. 23:14–17), namely, that of Unleavened Bread and Passover, that of the first fruits of the Harvest, and that of the Ingathering, all received a new meaning and a historical dimension. The exclusive connection was broken between these festivals and the rhythm of agricultural or nomadic life, a self-enclosed rhythm constantly repeated without any novelty; instead, the festivals became marked by the great rhythm of the Exodus, where hope and openness to the future were the distinguishing traits. A cyclical religion became an eschatological religion. In celebrating these feasts, Israel no longer celebrated the dying seasons but a living sacred history. It now worshiped, not the God of the spring season, but the eternal God who was guiding Israel to a time that had no end. The whole Israelite liturgy became simply a memorial of the Exodus. .

2. History and faith

At this point, there is a question we must face. If we think of the various "histories" that intermingle and make up the one "history" of the Exodus, and if we think of the various sources which contributed through the centuries to the formation of the Pentateuch or Hexateuch,[16] we must inevitably raise the question of the historicity of the facts therein related. Are we dealing here with legend or history? The question is a legitimate and healthy one, and the Christian is glad to face it, because he knows that dealing with it will purify his faith.

The faith of Israel undoubtedly embellished the narratives. Each generation projected both its present experiences and its expectations for the future onto the past events. Poring over the ancient memories like waves covering a beach, each age in its meditation on the events deposited in the narrative a bit of its own rich faith. "He allows us to commemorate his marvels" (Ps. 111:4 JB). Israel had excellent powers of memory. In meditation enlivened by fervent love and enlightened by a penetrating faith, the facts took on grandiose proportions; they became mysterious and majestic. The trite becomes solemn; the ordinary, hieratic. Moreover, in relating the events, Israel used lyrical, sometimes deeply moving, language, and sang of them with great enthusiasm. Its laments were there for all to hear, and so were its cries of joy; it showed it knew from experience the heavy burdens of both love and hate. It had taken Yahweh's side and could not now stand off from itself and judge itself impartially. Amid this Semitic civilization where the burning wind of the desert blew everywhere, how could Israel narrate its own history with the objectivity (and sometimes the tediousness) of an exegete in his book-lined study?

Biblical criticism, especially during the last one hundred and fifty years, has faced up to this situation and tried to separate historical fact from literary dress and to shed a clear light on the originality and active role of Israel's faith. It has analyzed the documents, sifted their sources, and uncovered literary modifications.

> As this process took shape, the old picture of Israel's history which the Church had derived and accepted from the Old Testament was bit by bit destroyed. Upon this process there is no going back, nor has it yet indeed come to an end. Critical historical scholarship regards it as impossible that the whole of Israel was present at Sinai, or that Israel crossed the Red Sea and achieved the Conquest *en bloc* — it holds the picture of Moses and his leadership drawn in the traditions of the Book of Exodus to be . . . unhistorical.[17]

These, then, are the elements of the problem. The resultant situation is evidently a somewhat uncomfortable one. But truth is always a liberating force, for it leads us to the light.

a) Authentic history

Even if faith has tended to inflate the facts so as to have greater reason for wonder, and even if, on the other hand, biblical criticism has sought to minimize the facts so as to follow a surer path, the story of the Exodus will always have a historical nucleus which no exegete can or wants to challenge: a decisive intervention of God in favor of his people. M. Noth writes:

> In the last resort that was all that really mattered, even if there was no authentic tradition about the actual course of events. There can be no

doubt, however, that this was a real event; we can discern to some
extent the conditions and circumstances which led to it and can fit it
into a historical situation of which we have quite reasonable knowledge. The incident itself, which the Israelites experienced as an un-
expected and mighty act of deliverance of their God, remains veiled
from our sight.[18]

The ancients did not share our somewhat fetishistic respect for the
supposedly objective literal account of events;[19] in their view,
poetry did not necessarily do violence to history but, on the contrary,
could enrich it with a greater degree of human truth.[20] The ancients
did not panic when the miraculous suddenly made its appearance in
our world. For these reasons, the historian relies on the biblical
documents and asserts that God intervened directly in the life
of his people — this, even though we have no literal account of
the Exodus events, even though we know that the narratives have
reached us in the form of splendid poetry, and even though we judge
that a taste for the miraculous has played an important role in the
interpretation of the facts.

b) Authentic interpretation

In the accounts of the Exodus, then, we have authentic history;
but we also have authentic interpretation. On the one hand, there
are the events, the unadorned facts; on the other, there is their
spiritual significance. With regard to both, God helps his people.
He is close to them when they emerge from Egypt and struggle to
conquer Canaan. He is equally close to them when they reflect on
these facts in the light of their faith. Moreover, the help the Spirit
gives is all the greater, the more Israel in its meditation is concerned
to find God. This spiritual discovery of history's supernatural dimension is more important than history in the sense of a set of
material facts. For the spiritual significance is the soul; it is to the
events what joy is to a smile on a person's lips, what sadness is to
tears, and the heart to the face. At the same time, however, none of
these interior realities can manifest itself without the aid of the
external.

I. GOD CALLS AND GATHERS HIS PEOPLE

"Out of Egypt I called my son" (Hos. 11:1)

1. The historical facts according to the biblical tradition

In one of the most ancient professions of faith, quoted by
Deuteronomy, the original historical nucleus of the Exodus events

is presented thus: "We cried to the Lord, the God of our fathers, and he heard our cry and saw our affliction, our toil and our oppression. He brought us out of Egypt with his strong hand and outstretched arm, with terrifying power, with signs and wonders" (Deut. 26:7-8).[21]

The content of the Yahwist faith is here summed up in the simple affirmation of a historical fact. No theological reflection accompanies the statement; the only thing that is important is the proclamation of God's mighty intervention in the exodus from Egypt.

As the years and then the centuries passed, however, the narrative became more and more extensive under the irresistible impulse of faith. The simple melody of the early text became a polyphony of countless voices; strange and marvelous harmonies were created to seduce the pious ears of the faithful and rejoice their hearts. The great biblical traditions took shape chiefly in the ancient sanctuaries, for it was there that the heartbeat of Israel could be felt most clearly: at Shechem,[22] near the sacred Oak of Moreh, where heaven had opened to Abraham; at Bethel, "abode of God" and "gateway to heaven";[23] at Beer-sheba, where the patriarch had called upon Yahweh, God the Eternal, and planted a tamarisk;[24] at Gilgal, the most celebrated of all, where, according to tradition, the ark rested after the crossing of the Jordan, the people were circumcised, the first Passover in Canaan was celebrated, and the manna ceased to fall;[25] at Shiloh, where people came to marvel at the Lord's "palace"[26] and where the young girls danced in the vineyards at the annual pilgrimages;[27] at Gibeon, "the most renowned high place" in Solomon's time, where the king, we are told, offered a thousand holocausts;[28] at Mizpah in Benjamin, at Ophrah, at Dan, and, of course, at Jerusalem.[29] It was in these sanctuaries that the inspired storytellers glorified the great deeds of the Exodus. They celebrated the arm of Yahweh which, in the amusing old formula, had never proved too short,[30] and they recited their epics at the feasts where the people were gathered. These narratives came directly from the heart of God. The Spirit had inspired them, and they fed the great Yahwist, Elohist, Priestly, and Deuteronomic traditions, those immense streams that flowed together in the Pentateuch.[31]

The profession of faith in Deuteronomy spoke of "signs and wonders." The profession in the Book of Joshua (Josh. 24) saw the beginnings of a description of these signs and wonders: hastening after the Israelites, the Egyptians in their chariots drove them into the Sea of Reeds, but Yahweh wove a curtain of thick fog to hide his people and then sent the sea to engulf the enemy chariots (Josh. 24:6-7).

The narrative in Exodus 14 uses Yahwist and Priestly elements to create a brilliant mosaic.[32] According to the Yahwist tradition, Pharaoh assembled six hundred of his best chariots, manned by elite teams, and went in pursuit of the fugitives (v. 7). The angel of the Lord, who till now had been advancing in front of the people, moved to the rear and faced the enemy (v. 19). The column of cloud did the same and shed darkness over the no man's land between the two armies (vv. 19–20). Simply by his divine glance, the Lord threw the enemy ranks into confusion, in a mysterious fashion clogged the wheels of the Egyptian chariots (v. 25), and finally overturned "horse and chariot" (as Miriam would later sing: Exod. 15:21) into the midst of the sea (14:27). All that was left for Israel to do was to gaze on the corpses tossed on the shore by the sea (14:30).

This narrative, with its brilliant reflection of popular faith and joy, must have seemed somewhat confused to the Priestly author. At any rate, he is careful to tell an orderly story; it is an order worthy of a splendid liturgical procession. Moses presides over this cosmic celebration in which desert, darkness, and sea all come to the help of the chosen people. He extends his rod — his pastoral staff, we might almost say — over the waves, and they divide (vv. 16, 21a), and over the sea, and it "fled" (Ps. 114:3).[33] The children of Israel enter the immense cathedral, with its walls of water (v. 22). At daybreak Moses extends his hand once again and the walls collapse; the sea closes in and covers chariots and charioteers (vv. 26-27a). Then a canticle of thanksgiving is sung.[34]

2. Significance of the Exodus for the Bible

Such are the historical facts according to the biblical tradition. How are they interpreted, and what do they mean?

In Israel's view, the call that caused them to leave Egypt and cross the Sea of Reeds constituted them God's people. It was a creative call that summoned and gathered what the tradition would later call the "desert assembly" (Acts 7:38). Liberated from the penal colony of Egypt, the tribes became a unity; they gather around God as around a standard, and their cry was *Yahweh-nissi*, "The Lord is my banner" (Exod. 17:15 RSV). A pack of undisciplined, quarrelsome Bedouins became a kingdom of priests and a holy nation:

> You have seen for yourselves how I treated the Egyptians and how I

bore you on eagle wings and brought you here to myself. Therefore, if you hearken to my voice and keep my covenant, you shall be my special possession, dearer to me than all other people, though all the earth is mine. You shall be to me a kingdom of priests, a holy nation (Exod. 19:4-6).[35]

The departure from Egypt, then, was more than a simple liberation from slavery, more than a rescue from prison. It gathered the anonymous multitude of Israelites into a single people, a single kingdom, and made them a holy nation of priests and kings. In calling them out of Egypt, God summoned them to exist as a nation.

In trying to bring out the real meaning of what had happened, Israel used all the words in the language of human tenderness. The emergence from Egypt was a mysterious birth for Israel, and the period of the Exodus was its childhood, the time when it was still a nurseling. There, in the howling chaos of the desert, Israel was "adopted" (Deut. 32:10 JB). God's word had called Israel out of Egypt as a father calls his son in order to embrace him and touch his cheek with his own:

> When Israel was a child I loved him,
>   out of Egypt I called my son. . . .
> It was I who taught Ephraim to walk,
>   who took them in my arms;
> I drew them with human cords,
>   with bands of love;
> I fostered them like one
>   who raises an infant to his cheeks; . . .
> I stooped to feed my child (Hos. 11:1-3).[36]

The nuptial theme, which is especially prominent in the prophet Hosea, conveys the same message of tenderness: The covenant uniting Israel to its God is a bond of love; God chooses his people for himself and loves them as a man chooses his bride from among countless others and loves her; and the people belong to God as a bride to her husband.[37] Ezekiel develops this theme in a lengthy parable: formerly Israel had been a young girl, a foreigner born of an Amorite father and a Hittite mother; at birth, she was thrown out to die. While she weltered in her blood, the Lord passed by, sheltered her with the edge of his robe, covered her nakedness, and raised her up; then when she was old enough for love and marriage, he adorned her with jewels and splendid garments (Ezek. 16). The period of espousals and love, according to Jeremiah, was the time of the Exodus, when Israel "followed" the Lord in the desert:

> I remember the devotion of your youth,
> how you loved me as a bride,
> following me in the desert, in a land unsown (Jer. 2:2).

It was in the desert of the Exodus that Israel, the virgin, found favor and that the young bride was loved "with an age-old love" (Jer. 31:3).

The Exodus theme acquires its greatest splendor when explained in the light of the creation theme. There is a relationship between these two "splendid works" of God, between the day when he created the world and the day when he created Israel.[38] Creation is, we might say, the birth of the universe, which God by the power of his word wrests from primordial chaos and establishes in the splendid light of being; the Exodus is the birth of the chosen people, whom God by the power of his word calls from the chaos of Egypt and establishes in the beauty of the Promised Land. God creates the Church as he creates everything else: "He speaks, and it comes to be." For this reason the professions of faith, based as they are on the narrative of the events of sacred history, pass without a break from the acclamation of the God of Genesis to the acclamation of the God of the Exodus. The Creator God is also the Savior God. He who establishes the earth upon the waters and hangs the great sources of light in the vault of heaven is also the God who divides the Sea of Reeds and lays a path for Israel through the sea.[39] In the course of a single prayer, Second-Isaiah asks that the arm of the Lord would awake and put on strength, as it did long ago when it crushed Rahab, the monster in the abyss of chaos, and pierced the dragon of the deep, dried up the sea and the waters of the ocean, and in the depths of the sea made a road by which the redeemed might return to Zion, singing their songs of praise (Is. 51:9-11).

II. GOD GIVES HIS LAW TO HIS PEOPLE

*"Hear, O Israel, the statutes and decrees which
I proclaim in your hearing this day"* (Deut. 5:1)

1. Hear, O Israel

After calling and gathering his people, God gives them his law. In a discourse in which Yahweh sums up the history of Israel, Ezekiel shows us very clearly these two saving acts of God: "I led them out of the land of Egypt and brought them into the desert. Then I gave them my statutes and made known to them my ordinances, which everyone must keep to have life through them" (Ezek. 20:10-11).

In the assembly of Sinai this life-giving law is summed up in the Decalogue.[40]

In fact, however, the legislation set down in the Pentateuch is far from fitting within the framework of the Decalogue. The collection of laws, along with the account of the events during the stay in Sinai, is "a complex of tradition of quite abnormal size,"[41] stretching as it does from Exod. 19:1 to Num. 10:10, and including the whole of Leviticus. Very divergent traditions come together at the foot of the sacred mountain; they are juxtaposed or intermingled in a carefree literary disorder, and all seek in one way or another a link with the great festival of Sinai. So great was the veneration which the tradition had for Moses that it attempted to cover with his mantle as legislator traditions which evidently come from other sources. The Torah, or law, people said, was the marriage contract between Israel and the Lord, and Moses was the bride's attendant;[42] with the passage of the years and the centuries, every possible prescription would be written into the contract, and the bride's attendant would find himself at the head of an immense cortege. To introduce a law with the sacrosanct phrase "Moses has said" (found even in the Gospels[43]) was automatically to guarantee its authenticity. Consequently, we find the following attributed to Moses:

The Covenant Code: Exod. 20:22–23:19 (called "the book of the covenant" in Exod. 24:7). It contains a collection of religious laws cast in the style of the Decalogue, as well as ancient customs (*mišpatim*) which had acquired normative value.[44]

The Cultic Decalogue: Exod. 34:11–26, which contains ritual prescriptions for feasts, offerings of firstlings, and sacrifices.[45]

The priestly laws, such as the Holiness Code of Lev. 17–26, so called because it is dominated by the ideal of holiness proper to Leviticus;[46] the Torah or ritual for sacrifices, Lev. 1–7, which codifies the various sacrificial rites; the law of legal purity, Lev. 11–16, which contains prescriptions for legal purity and impurity and is based on very ancient prohibitions.

The Deuteronomic Code, Deut. 12–26, which gathers together a number of ancient legislations, renews them, and infuses them with new life from the Deuteronomic ideal.[47]

The Decalogue, of which we shall be speaking at greater length.

2. Early Yahwism

We must observe that all these laws are "Mosaic," in the sense
that they conform to the Yahwist ideal which the tradition attributes
to Moses. On the other hand, none of these laws, in their present
literary form, can claim to stem from the great events at Sinai. Even
if they transmit the archaic laws which may date from the time of the
Exodus, they have recast these laws and given them a dress tailored
to the fashion of a later time or to the needs of the period at which
they became part of a "code." Pinpointing dates for the laws is often
a more fruitless task than trying to paint on vapor or light up a fog.
In these circumstances, is it still possible to maintain that on Mount
Sinai God gave his "law" to his people, when the law is evidently
much more recent?

Yes, it is possible, in the sense that there is a "Mosaic religion"
which can be identified with early Yahwism and is the content of the
revelation God gave to the people of the Exodus. "When Moses
died before the entry into the Promised Land, Yahwism was as yet
only the religion of a semi-nomadic group, and would become a
world religion only through a slow development that would involve
the labor both of other men of God and of God himself. But Moses
was the source; he planted this extraordinarily fruitful seed. He was
the first 'servant of the Lord.'"[48]

The central factor in this early Yahwism was monolatry; that is,
Yahweh alone had a right to the adoration of the people of the
Exodus. In this respect the religion of Moses was the heir to the
religion of the patriarchs. But exclusivism, intolerance, and the
"jealousy" of Yahweh burned so intensely at the heart of Yahwism
that they brought on the death-throes of the false gods and hastened
the monotheist revolution. It is doubtless not possible on the basis
simply of a few texts to maintain that Moses himself was a
monotheist.[49] Early Yahwism in fact admitted a plurality of gods.
Thus, the canticle in Exodus 15 sings of Yahweh as having no like
among the other gods; and Jethro, Moses' father-in-law, says on
hearing the news of the deliverance from Egypt: "Now I know that
the Lord is a deity great beyond any other" (Exod. 18:11). The
dynamism proper to the religion of Sinai would topple the Canaanite pantheon. Religious meditation, aided by the teaching which
history affords, would in the course of time link the following statements into a logical series: *Yahweh alone is to be adored* by the
people of the Exodus; this people may not worship other gods; these

other gods are powerless to help; they are even powerless to help their own devotees; they are "nothings" and do not exist; *Yahweh alone is God.*

Whatever be the date at which Israel reached the final affirmation, the religion of Moses certainly was a decisive stage in the journey toward monotheism.

In the Mosaic period, worship took the form chiefly of the sanctification of the *sabbath*;[50] the offering of bloody *sacrifices*,[51] which came quite naturally to a religion of shepherds and were an element in the conclusion of the covenant at Mount Sinai (Exod. 24:5-8); the *prohibition of images*[52] representing Yahweh (Exod. 20:4), a prohibition intended to emphasize the mysteriousness and transcendence of the God of Sinai; the desert sanctuary or *tent*[53] of meeting, which was the place of encounter with Yahweh and contained the *ark*[54] of the covenant, the symbol of God's presence (both tent and ark date from the nomadic period).

As first "servant of Yahweh," Moses was also chief servant of Yahwism: "This organizer who enjoyed no proper political power, this national leader who boasted no prowess in war, this man who directed the worship of God without ever having received the status of priest, who established and mediated a new understanding of God without any of the credentials of prophetic powers of prediction. . . ."[55] Moses transcends all the categories of prophetism, priesthood, and kingship: he is "the messenger who should proclaim God's will for social, political, and cultic life."[56] The law God gives the people of the Exodus is, first and foremost, the Yahwism he communicates to them through Moses.

3. The Decalogue

Like the other laws, the Decalogue bears the mark of a long history.[57] It has reached us through a twofold literary tradition.

One of these is found in Exod. 20:2-17. The promulgation of the Decalogue here takes place as part of a cosmic liturgy in which the storms shout the praises of the "God of the mountains" and the eternal hills (1 Kings 20:23). The people had pitched camp facing Mount Sinai and prepared itself by ritual purifications for its solemn meeting with God. On the third day the celebration of the theophany was held. While the mountain was shaken by violent tremors, Yahweh manifested himself in the form of fire in the midst of lightning and thunder,[58] and promulgated the Decalogue (Elohist version).[59]

The other tradition is found in Deut. 5:6-18. Moses calls the
people together and passes the law on to them. The form of the
Decalogue seems less ancient than that in Exod. 20:2-17; it cannot
be taken as a simple reformulation of the latter.[60]

Both traditions undoubtedly derive from the same original which,
in lapidary formulas, stated the basic requirements of the covenant.
It was proclaimed to the people during the festivals when the covenant was renewed.[61] Attempts to reconstruct the original Decalogue
yield the following text:

> I am the Lord your God:
> you shall not prostrate yourself before other gods.
> You shall not make idols.
> You shall not call upon the Lord your God to witness to a lie.
> You shall not work on the sabbath.
> Honor your father and your mother.
> You shall not commit adultery with your neighbor's wife.
> You shall not shed your neighbor's blood.
> You shall not steal from your neighbor.
> You shall not bear false witness against your neighbor.
> You shall not covet your neighbor's house.[62]

In the course of time the text was augmented, especially by explanations and motivations.[63] "The present redaction seems,
therefore, to be the result of a rather lengthy development."[64] The
precepts of the Decalogue may be found in other codes, but their
grouping in the form of the "Decalogue" took on an increasingly
important spiritual meaning as time passed, especially under the
influence of Deuteronomy.

a) The ten words of the covenant

We should note, to begin with, that Israel never thought of the
Decalogue as a set of ten "commandments," that is, an anonymous
collection of prohibitions and taboos, but rather as "words of
God,"[65] or, better still, as "the ten words of the covenant."[66] The
Decalogue is part of the covenant dialogue which God enters into
with his people. It is as if God were saying to this people: "If you
want to enter upon the covenant, here are the words for your
dialogue with me. By keeping them you will become my people and
I shall remain your God." Consequently, when Israel thinks of "the
ten words of the covenant," it does not start sighing as though it
were contemplating a burden, or groaning as though it were
weighed down by them; its attitude is one of gratitude and praise.

God's word is refreshment for the soul, joy for the heart, light for the eyes; it is more desirable than purest gold, sweeter than syrup or honey from the comb (Ps. 19:8-15). In receiving it, Israel did not receive a set of police regulations, but its own freedom; not chains, but the bonds that tenderness creates. In carrying God's word, it was not rendering forced labor, but proving itself to be God's kingly people: "Be silent, O Israel, and listen! This day you have become the people of the Lord, your God. You shall therefore hearken to the voice of the Lord your God" (Deut. 27:9-10).

The law is the voice of God calling his people as a father calls his child. It bestows an abundance of wisdom and understanding on those whom God acknowledges as his own. Consider the pious boasting in these naive words of Deuteronomy:

> Observe them [the statutes and decrees] carefully, for thus will you give evidence of your wisdom and intelligence to the nations, who will hear all of these statutes and say, "This great nation is truly a wise and intelligent people." For what great nation is there that has gods so close to it as the Lord, our God, is to us whenever we call upon him? Or what great nation has statutes and decrees that are as just as this whole law which I am setting before you today? (Deut. 4:6-8).[67]

Evidently Deuteronomy's view of the law is firmly optimistic. But we may in fact quite rightly ask what this great originality is, this specific wisdom that Deuteronomy attributes to the Decalogue. After all, the set of commandments, apart from the command concerning the sabbath, was part of an ancient wisdom common throughout the East. There are many points of contact between the Decalogue and the "negative confession" used in Egypt[68] and in Babylon.[69] Thus in an "examination of conscience" engraved on a Babylonian magical tablet, we find a list of questions to be asked of the pilgrim who consults the priest about an illness or worry:

> Has he separated son from father?
> Has he separated father from son?
> Has he separated friend from friend?
> Has he separated companion from companion?
> Has he failed to free the prisoner?
> Has he failed to release someone in chains?
> Has he offended a god or scorned a goddess?
> Has he showed contempt for father or mother?
> Has he mistreated an older sister?
> Has he said yes when he should have said no?
> Has he said no when he should have said yes?
> Has he used false scales?

> Has he taken money that did not belong to him?
> Has he moved boundary markers from their proper place?
> Has he set up false boundary markers?
> Has he gone in to his neighbor's wife?
> Has he shed his neighbor's blood?[70]

Would this list not provide an excellent basis for a moral system based on the Decalogue? Such questions are admittedly as old as mankind itself, and we need not go to Egypt or Mesopotamia to discover a prohibition of theft, murder, or adultery, since such a prohibition is written in man's heart and is the foundation of all human society. But if this be so, can we still speak of the originality of the Decalogue?

We can, because the absolutely unique and special element of Israel's law is its vital relationship to the covenant; the bond is as unbreakable as the pact that unites Israel to Yahweh. The originality of the Decalogue is that of the covenant. "The Decalogue is the deed of the Sinaitic covenant, inscribed on large stones entrusted by God to Moses . . . which are the tables of the covenant."[71] It introduces and prefaces the covenant; it prolongs it and gives it actuality at each moment. When Israel contemplates the "ten words," paradise itself is reflected in its eyes. "Here, then, I have today set before you life and prosperity" (Deut. 30:15). Israel's existence as a nation is unintelligible without the Decalogue, just as it is without the Exodus from Egypt.

This is why the promulgation of the "ten words" is presented *in the biblical tradition* in a formula used for establishing covenants between nations of the Middle East in the second millennium.[72] In other words, the Decalogue is seen as part of the covenant treaty between Yahweh and his people, and the treaty resembles those which the Hittite kings concluded with their vassals. The literary structure of these contracts often included the following elements: (1) preamble; name and titles of the "Great King"; (2) historical prologue, listing the benefactions of the "Great King" to his vassal; (3) stipulations imposed on the vassal; (4) clauses on the written redaction of the document, its preservation, and its public rereading; (5) summoning of witnesses; (6) blessings and curses.[73]

This pattern may be easily discerned in the biblical tradition concerning the Decalogue, and a parallel can be readily established between the Decalogue and a Hittite treaty:

BIBLICAL TRADITION	HITTITE TREATIES

Preamble

"I, the Lord, am your God" (Exod. 20:2a)	"These are the words of the Sun, Suppiluliumas, the great king. The king of the Hatti land, the valiant, the favorite of the storm-god." [74]

Historical Prologue

I "brought you out of the land of Egypt, that place of slavery" (Exod. 20:2b)	"I, the Sun, [made you, Aziras, my vassal]," etc. [75]

Stipulations for the vassal

"I will be an enemy to your enemies and a foe to your foes" (Exod. 23:22) "You shall not have other gods besides me" (Exod. 20:3)	"He who [lives in peace] with the Sun shall live in peace also with you. But he who is an enemy of the Sun, shall also be an enemy [with you]." [76] "You, Hukkanas, shall acknowledge no power but the Sun." [77]

Written record of the treaty

Moses "wrote on the tablets the words of the covenant, the ten commandments" (Exod. 34:28)	"I, the Great King [Mursil II], have written a tablet of the treaty with Rimisarma, sealed it with my seal, and given it to him. Let no one ever change what is written on this tablet." [78]

Preservation of the tablets

Moses "gave the Levites who carry the ark of the covenant of the Lord this order: 'Take this scroll of the law and place it beside the ark of the covenant of the Lord, your God' " (Deut. 31:26)	"A duplicate of this tablet has been deposited before the Sun-goddess of Arinna, because the Sun-goddess of Arinna regulates kingship and queenship. In the Mitanni land [a duplicate] has been deposited before Tissub, the lord of the *kurinnu* of Kahat." [79]

Ritual rereading

(Cf. the ritual reading of the law every seven years according to Deut. 31:10-13).	"At regular intervals shall they read it in the presence of the king of the Mitanni land and in the presence of the sons of the Hurri country." [80]

Summoning of witnesses

(Called as witnesses are heaven and earth [cf. Ps. 50:4-5], the book of the covenant [cf. Deut. 31:26], the stone at Shechem [cf. Josh. 24:27].)

"At the conclusion of this treaty we have called the gods to be assembled and the gods of the contracting parties to be present, to listen and to serve as witnesses."[81]

Blessings and curses

"If you continue to heed the voice of the Lord, your God, and are careful to observe all his commandments . . . . all these blessings will come upon you. . . .

"But if you do not hearken to the voice of the Lord, your God, and are not careful to observe all his commandments . . . all these curses shall come upon you" (Deut. 28:1-2, 15)

"If you, Mattiwaza, the prince, and (you), the Hurrians, fulfill this treaty and (this) oath, may these gods protect you, Mattiwaza, together with your wife, the daughter of the Hatti land, her children, and her children's children.

If you, Mattiwaza, the prince, and (you) the sons of the Hurri country do not fulfill the words of this treaty, may the gods, the lords of the oath, blot you out."[82]

The points of comparison must not be forced; the various biblical texts, like the various Hittite texts, have different sources and dates. Covenant treaties, moreover, did not all necessarily have the same literary structure. Finally, given the corrupt state of some of the biblical sources that were inserted into the Pentateuch, it is impossible to get back to the Exodus and Mount Sinai as they actually took place historically.[83] I do not think that the resemblance between the covenant formularies and the Hittite treaties dates back to the Sinai event: How could a group of semi-nomads have been interested in formularies used at the Hittite courts of the fourteenth century? On the other hand, we may readily believe that during the period of the kingdom the scribes liked to recast the ancient texts in this form. "At a time when Israel in both kingdoms sought to secure guarantees abroad by concluding treaties on every side, there was no better way of condemning such a policy and teaching the people to rely on God alone than by presenting the covenant itself as a treaty."[84] But the basis for such an interpretation lies in the first Yahwist commandment itself: "I, the Lord, am your God. . . . You shall not have other gods besides me" (Exod. 20:2-3), and the post-Sinaitic tradition was justified in thinking of God's relation to Israel as a covenant treaty. In any event, "to reduce the Decalogue to a set of moral precepts after the fashion of a catechism"[85] would be a serious exegetical mistake, as well as an injustice to the chosen people.

The covenant situation gave rise to quite new conditions of life. It involved a morality based not on law but on covenant; it meant that the whole vast sphere of human activity was subject to judgment according to the covenant. The Decalogue called men to account for their private life within the Jewish family and their daily round of activity within the clan. But because the Decalogue is part of the covenant, the whole of private life and the whole of daily existence were responsible to the covenant. We might even say, from this point of view, that the believer who had encountered the God of Sinai no longer had a private life, since he was always confronted by the God of the covenant; he would never be alone again, since he would always be with brothers who belonged to the same covenant.

b) Significance of the motivations

Because the laws are God's words, they have no need of being supported and explained by glosses or motivations that would justify them. These laws bind man's conscience not chiefly because they are reasonable and intelligible in themselves, but because they are promulgated by God. They rest on the transcendent authority of God, not on the human mind. Thus the statement "I am the Lord, your God" runs like a refrain through the ancient list of precepts in Lev. 19:13-18. This affirmation by itself is worth more than any number of justifications; it authenticates all the laws.

The extraordinary thing, given these conditions, is that these divine laws are in fact accompanied at times by "human" explanations.

The reference is not to prohibitions that are self-evident within the framework of Yahwism. A man did not have to be a scholar in Israel to know that he must not cook a goat in its mother's milk, for as everyone knew at that time, this was a Canaanite fertility rite;[86] that he must not weave a cloth with two different threads (Lev. 19:19), since this was a magical practice; and that he must not allow sorceresses in the country (Exod. 22:17), since they would endanger the purity of faith.

Our concern is rather with motivations meant to show that a prohibition is well founded and thus to elicit from the believer an obedience that is not mechanical but fully human, not reluctant but willing and joyous. Here are some examples. Judges are not to accept bribes, "for a bribe blinds even the most clear-sighted and

twists the words even of the just" (Exod. 23:8).[87] One must not treat
a foreigner roughly nor oppress him, because Israel had once been a
foreigner in the land of Egypt.[88] A hand mill or even its upper stone
is not to be accepted as a pledge, "for he [the creditor] would be
taking the debtor's sustenance as a pledge" (Deut. 24:6). If a judge
sentences a man to a whipping, no more than forty stripes are to be
given him, "lest . . . your kinsman should be looked upon as dis-
graced" (Deut. 25:1-3). If a betrothed woman consents to illicit
relations with a third party, both she and her accomplice are to be
stoned, he because he has had relations with his neighbor's wife,
and she because she did not call for help.[89] The wages of a day-
laborer are to be paid before the day is over, "before sundown on
the day itself, since he is poor and looks forward to them" (Deut.
24:15).

Especially interesting are the explanations that spring from
theological reflection and a deeper insight of faith. Thus the prohibition of murder is based on the fact that man is created in God's
image and the land in which God dwells must not be profaned by
crime.[90] The precept of sabbath rest is based either on the fact that
God himself "rested" on the seventh day according to the account of
creation or is to be seen as a festive celebration of the liberation from
Egypt.[91] The prohibition of perjury and false witness is motivated
by the fact that "the Lord will not leave unpunished him who takes
his name in vain" (Exod. 20:7). The prohibition against falsifying
weights and measures is based on the fact that those who commit
this crime are an abomination to the Lord, whereas he gives a long
life to those who avoid it (Deut. 25:13-16).

Sometimes the motivations offered relate directly to the message
that is at the heart of revelation — the message of God's nature and
of his love and mercy that extend to countless generations. The
concrete instance given in Exod. 22:25-26 (cf. Deut. 24:10-13),
though but one of many, is sublime from this point of view: a poor
man falls into debt and the creditor takes his cloak as a pledge; the
creditor must, however, give it back to the man before sunset, and
the reason: "This cloak of his is the only covering he has for his body.
What else has he to sleep in? If he cries out to me, I will hear him,
for I am compassionate." For the sake of a cloak taken as a pledge,
for the sake of a cry of distress in the cold night, Yahweh turns aside
for a moment from the government of the universe and the company
of the bright stars to listen to a poor man's lament.

What is the ultimate significance of these motivations? By helping a believer to a better understanding of the laws, they bring him to an intelligent and not simply material obedience. "Jahweh wants obedience, admittedly; but he also wants men who understand his commandments and ordinances, that is, men who assent inwardly as well. The obedience which Jahweh wants is the obedience of men who have come of age." [92] God has no liking for a "blind" submission, the homage of minds that are either anesthetized or in fear of death. He prefers the submission of a vigorous, healthy mind, for this is the only kind of submission worthy of him. He made men to be free and intelligent, not dolls or robots, and he has an infinite respect for this work of his hands. Sublime though his word and his laws are, they are not intended to crush man by their transcendence, but rather to be the basis of a dialogue with him as an intellectual being; they are to take root in his mind. Thus, by obeying, man does not deny his own intelligence but ennobles it.

c) Minimal requirements and the fullness of the Law

A final remark is called for. The precepts in Deuteronomy have a negative form; [93] they are chiefly prohibitions. They tell man what he is to avoid rather than what he is to do positively. If we look at these precepts in the context of the covenant, we see that they define more narrowly the conditions for belonging to Yahweh and the chosen people. We may think here of the ancient rituals which explain the conditions required for admission to the pilgrimage sanctuaries. When the believer asks: "O Lord, who shall sojourn in your tent? Who shall dwell on your holy mountain?" Yahweh replies: "He who walks blamelessly and does justice; who thinks the truth in his heart and slanders not with his tongue; who harms not his fellow man, nor takes up a reproach against his neighbor; etc." (Ps. 15:1-6). [94]

These are minimal requirements. They specify conditions for admission into the sanctuary but say nothing of the interior devotion of the believer who stands before "the face of the Lord" (Ps. 42:3) and gazes on his loveliness (Ps. 27:4). They establish a boundary line between sin and the realm of Yahweh.

In a similar way the Decalogue draws a circle, as it were, around the domain of Yahwist faith and the community of the covenant. At the edge of the circle are the powers hostile to Yahweh, all the forces of evil along with the nations subject to them and the sinners who travel the path of sin. At the center the faithful live their lives, walking "the way of the just" (Ps. 1:6) and protected by their fidelity

to the "ten words." Within the framework established by the covenant, no limits are set to their love and no restrictions placed on
their intimacy with the Lord: "You shall love the Lord, your God,
with all your heart, and with all your soul, and with all your
strength. Take to heart these words which I enjoin on you today"
(Deut. 6:5-6).

Deuteronomy wants the faithful not only to have these words
written in their own hearts but also to repeat them to their children,
to keep them in mind day and night, whether at home or abroad,
whether busy or at rest (Deut. 6:7). In short, life as a whole and the
little things of each day are to be illuminated by the great law of
love. Israel did not have to be avoiding murder, adultery, or idolatry
every hour of every day, but it did have to love God with its whole
heart every hour of every day.

III. GOD ENTERS INTO A COVENANT WITH HIS PEOPLE

*"This is the blood of the covenant which
the Lord has made with you"* (Exod. 24:8).

After having called and gathered his people and given them his
law in the "ten words," God entered into a covenant with them.
This rite of covenant is presented to us in three different sources.

1. Exodus 24:1a and 9-11

The first source consists of Exod. 24:1a and 9–11. It is undoubtedly the oldest. Moses, Aaron, Nadab, Abihu, and seventy elders
of Israel at Yahweh's command ascended the mountain and "beheld
the God of Israel" (v. 10). The text adds that they ate and drank (v.
12). This mention of a meal is very important. "The meal marks the
climactic moment in the account and must be taken as referring to a
covenant meal, analogous to the meals that sealed pacts between
human beings."[95] In the persons of its delegates, the whole of the
Sinai community was invited to share the Lord's table. The point
was not, of course, that God took part in men's meals or drew
nourishment from the sacrifices offered to him. He corrects such
ideas with a kind of amused irony in Psalm 50, which is a psalm for
the "covenant ritual":

> If I were hungry, I should not tell you,
>   for mine are the world and its fullness.

> Do I eat the flesh of strong bulls,
> or is the blood of goats my drink? (Ps. 50:12-13).[96]

Yet he does invite men to his table, and those invited enter the table-fellowship of God and the family created by the covenant.[97]

2. Exodus 24:3-8

The second source is represented by Exod. 24:3-8, which has been inserted within the text we have just discussed. But the compiler has not tried to harmonize the data by integrating the two accounts. According to Exod. 24:2, Moses alone is to approach God, whereas further on the elders accompany him. In any case, the rite is quite different. Moses reports to the people all the words (*debarim*) of Yahweh, and the people shout their agreement with them: "We will do everything that the Lord has told us" (v. 3). Moses puts Yahweh's words in writing. The next day he builds an altar and sets up twelve pillars to represent the twelve tribes. He has young men offer holocausts and communion sacrifices. Then he takes the "book of the covenant" (*seper habberit*) and reads it to the people. Half of the blood from the victims he splashes on the altar, half on the people, while saying: "This is the blood of the covenant which the Lord has made with you in accordance with all these words of his" (v. 8).

The "book of the covenant" is undoubtedly identical with the Decalogue.[98] We may suppose that the Covenant Code (Exod. 20:22–23:33) was interpolated between the promulgation of the Decalogue (Exod. 20:1-18) and the concluding of the covenant (Exod. 24:3-8). "All these words" in Exod. 20:1 evidently corresponds to "all these words" in Exod. 24:3-8.

The sacrificial role of the young men and especially the blood rite are archaic elements. The twofold sprinkling of altar and assembly, found nowhere else in the Bible, creates a communion "of blood" between God and the people. On the other hand, the erection of twelve pillars to symbolize the twelve tribes seems to be borrowed from the liturgy at Shechem, where the grouping of the twelve tribes first took place.

The second manner of concluding the covenant thus shows some primitive elements, the most important of which are the proclamation of Yahweh's "words" and the blood rite. The latter has the same function and significance as the communion meal in the first source. As we know, Moses' words, "This is the blood of the covenant," were to be repeated by Christ at the Last Supper.

3. *Exodus 34:1-28*

The third source is to be found in Exod. 34:1-28, a section called the "Yahwist code" of the covenant or the cultic Decalogue (in contrast to the ethical Decalogue in Exod. 20). It is introduced by a theophany in which Yahweh reveals himself as "a merciful and gracious God . . . rich in kindness and fidelity" (vv. 6-7), and by his statement that "here . . . is the covenant I will make" (v. 10). A series of laws is then listed; the list is not really a Decalogue (the laws cannot be reduced to ten without doing violence to the list) but a religious calendar for a community that has already adopted a settled way of life. Only the commandment to adore Yahweh alone and the prohibition of images (vv. 14 and 17) can be traced back to Sinai and Moses.

In addition to laws, this "Decalogue" also contains promises.[99] This suggests an important problem: Did the Sinai covenant comprise only laws or only promises or both? The problem is that of the relation between election and commandment, grace and law (to use New Testament language; cf. John 1:17), divine liberality and human obedience. We must say that the Sinai covenant is both grace and law. It certainly has its basis in the absolutely free gift which the "merciful and gracious God" makes to Israel of liberation from Egypt and entry into the Promised Land, but it also supposes that man in return obeys the law of Sinai. This is why the Decalogue, which communicates God's will, is prefaced by the reminder of his goodness, as if the gift freely given by God entailed the law which his people accepts: "I, the Lord, am your God, who brought you out of the land of Egypt, that place of slavery. You shall not have other gods besides me" (Exod. 20:2-3).

The covenant (*berît*) here shows its special nature over against merely human contracts. It is not like a bilateral pact between equal partners, since on God's side everything is a matter of initiative, liberty, and unmerited generosity. Only God can say: "I shall be your God, and you shall be my people." The people could never turn these creative words around and say: "You shall be our God, and we shall be your people." In the rabbinical tradition God is the "Lord of the covenant" (*Baal berît*), while the Israelites are but its "sons" (*benê berît*). The covenant rests on God's fidelity to his word, not on man's fidelity. There is, therefore, no common measure between grace and law, God's gift and man's observance, "the glory to be revealed in us" (Rom. 8:18) and man's insignificant response.

If, then, we understand covenant (*berît*) to be a bilateral contract regulating relations between equal partners, the contract of Mount Sinai is not a covenant; note that when God makes a covenant with Abraham, the latter is asleep in a kind of trance (Gen. 15:12)! But if we understand covenant to be a contract in which each gives what he has, that is, in which God gives everything and man gives nothing but his outstretched hands and his obedience, we can indeed speak of a covenant between God and his people. In commenting on God's words to Abraham, "My covenant with you is this . . ." (Gen. 17:4), Philo of Alexandria puts these words into God's mouth: "There are many kinds of covenant that bring grace and gifts to those who are worthy of them, but the most perfect kind of covenant is my very self." [100]

CONCLUSION

The celebration of the covenant began at the Exodus. It will continue throughout the history of the chosen people until the day when the promise given by the God of Sinai, "I will take you as my own people, and you shall have me as your God" (Exod. 6:7), is replaced by the reality as time passes over into eternity "so that God [the Father] may be all in all" (1 Cor. 15:28).

Before pursuing our inquiry further, we offer three remarks by way of conclusions from what we have thus far seen.

1. A structural pattern

In its essential lines the assembly of Sinai shows the following developmental pattern: God calls his people together; he addresses his word to them; he enters into a covenant with them.

We shall find the same pattern followed in connection with the assemblies of Shechem, of Josiah, and of Ezra. The pattern is, then, the manifestation of a basic rhythm in God's dealings with the assemblies of his people. The pattern is even so essential that it still provides the structure for our Masses. Across the centuries, in an unbroken tradition, our contemporary liturgy is connected with the ancient celebration of Sinai. The Mass contains the liturgy of the word (God gathers his people and speaks to them) and the Eucharistic liturgy (God renews his covenant in the body and blood of his Son). The two celebrations, of word and Eucharist, form a single liturgical act, according to the Second Vatican Council. [101] The structural unity of the Mass is thus derived from the great liturgy which the Church of the Exodus celebrated long ago in the desert of Sinai.

2. Qahal — *Church*

The Hebrew text uses the noun *qahal* as a name for the assembly of Sinai.[102] This term generally signifies either an assembly actually gathered or a community (with a personality of its own) that can be gathered.[103] The "*qahal* of the children of Israel" is therefore made up either of the whole community gathered at the foot of Mount Sinai around Moses, or of all the children of Israel whom Moses can call together when he wishes. In its first meaning of community actually gathered, *qahal* is ordinarily used in a liturgical or cultic context. In 72 instances out of the 111 in which *qahal* bears this meaning, there is question of a gathering for a religious purpose, usually in the presence of Yahweh, his ark, or his temple, with a reminder of the covenant and the law, and to the accompaniment of prayers and sacrifices.[104] One of the most splendid definitions of the Sinai *qahal*, "that desert assembly," as St. Luke calls it (Acts 7:38), is to be found in the Book of Numbers, when Korah, Dathan, and Abiram protest to Moses and Aaron: "The whole community, all of them, are holy; the Lord is in their midst. Why then should you set yourselves over the Lord's congregation?" (Num. 16:3).

The Greek translation of the Old Testament uses *ekklēsia* for the Hebrew *qahal* two-thirds of the time. The noun *ekklēsia* is derived from the verb *ek-kalein* which means "to call apart," "to convoke," and, in the middle voice, "to call to oneself." In secular Greek literature *ekklēsia* was the assembly of the people at Athens or any Greek city; the assembly was convoked by a herald, and those who were its members were "the called" (*ek-klētoi*). In the religious vocabulary of the Septuagint, *ekklēsia* retained its basic meaning of assembly but acquired a new connotation. It was the regular translation of the Hebrew *qahal* with its cultic and sacral meaning: the *ekklēsia*, according to the Septuagint, is the religious assembly of the children of Israel who have been called together by God himself.[105]

It is very interesting in this connection to observe that the first three occurrences of *ekklēsia* in the Greek Bible are in the Deuteronomic expression "the day of the assembly" (Deut. 4:10; 9:10; 18:16). The assembly in question is the assembly of Sinai, the one which God called out of Egypt and which received the ten words from him. Thus, in his second discourse in Deuteronomy, Moses says: "I ascended the mountain to receive the stone tablets, the tablets of the covenant which the Lord God concluded with you. . . . The Lord gave me the two stone tablets written with

God's own finger, on which were incised all the words which the Lord spoke to you on the mountain, on the day of the assembly" (Deut. 9:9-10, according to the Septuagint).

Fortunately, then, the Greek word *ekklēsia* used in the Septuagint connotes God's word which *calls* and gathers the assembly, or, in short, creates the Church. "The day of the Church," in the theology of Deuteronomy, is the day when God called the children of Israel together in a holy assembly and gave them the ten words of the covenant. This meaning of *ekklēsia* is important for an understanding of the mystery of the Church and also of the mystery of God's word. How unfortunate, then, that it has at times been forgotten or even played down or distorted! To many people the word "church" means first of all the building in which the faithful customarily gather to praise God (in this sense, people speak of building the Church, but they mean putting up a material building); secondarily, the word "church" means, to these same people, the assembly of clerics and the hierarchy (they speak of "ecclesiastical" customs or garb, or even "churchmen" as though the laity were not part of the Church).

In the vocabulary of the Bible, "church," on the contrary, refers first, and essentially, to the community which God *calls* together by his word and invites to celebrate the covenant. To build a church, in the language of Deuteronomy, does not mean to erect walls or establish a hierarchy, but to form the community of God's children, to make the word the focus of their lives, and to bring them into the covenant. All the faithful thus called to form a holy assembly are "ecclesiastics" in the sense that they form the *ekklēsia* of God.[106] Even if the multitude of members is dispersed throughout the Sinai desert, God's word is powerful enough to gather it together and form a "desert assembly." This assembly is not limited by walls and knows no boundaries; it already possesses, in germ, the same universality as God's word that has called it together and brought it into being.

Today we see the crumbling and even the collapse of institutional structures that once seemed to give the Church a stability which time could not destroy. At such a juncture the Sinai assembly is an opportune reminder that we can, and must, build an infinitely more solid Church by basing it essentially on the word of God. It is true enough that ever since Vatican II emphatically redefined the Church as the people of God,[107] no one may any longer identify the Church with the hierarchy or with "ecclesiastics." But there remains the strong temptation to regard our present uneasy situation as due simply to temporary upheavals and to look for other, supposedly more solid, human foundations to replace those which time has undermined. In short, there is the temptation to rebuild on better human words, whereas what is needed is to be constantly rebuilding on the rock of God's word. The Church of today has the opportunity to become once again "that desert assembly."[108] It is the Church's joy, not its punishment, that it must be ceaselessly born anew from the word of God,[109] and that it cannot exist as God's creation unless it finds its unwavering ground in his word.

3. *Place of the Sinai covenant in the history of Israel*

What place may be assigned to the Sinai covenant and the "desert assembly" in the history of Israel?

The assembly of the Exodus is not only the archetypal assembly of the people of God; it also is a very important stage in the irreversible movement of the Old Testament toward the light that shines in Christ. The successive stages of this sacred history may be sketched as follows:

"In the beginning," God by his word created the universe of heaven and earth, along with man, the bit of dust into which he breathed his "spirit" and which in consequence became living clay. When mankind fell into a universal state of corruption, God destroyed it in the waters of the deluge, but he saved Noah, the just man, from the destroying flood. Noah, the just man, replaced Adam, the sinner, and became the partner in a covenant that joined God to all of the human race. The rainbow was designated the sign of this covenant (Gen. 9:11-17).

This covenant acquires a personal character, as it were, when God later addresses Abraham, whom he called from Ur of the Chaldees and blessed greatly. He promised the patriarch a posterity as countless as the sands on the seashore or the stars in heaven and the possession of Canaan. This double promise forms the framework into which the many materials that enter into the history of the patriarchs are inserted; it gives these materials unity and cohesion.

The first promise is fulfilled when Abraham's clan multiplies in Egypt. Gathered at Sinai by the creative word and united to God by the covenant rite and the communion meal, the family of Abraham becomes the people of God. God's statement: "I am the Lord who brought you from Ur of the Chaldeans" (Gen. 15:7) is supplemented by his later statement: "I, the Lord, am your God, who brought you out of the land of Egypt" (Exod. 20:2). As long as the story concerned only the tribe of Abraham, it was, as it were, a domestic story; but with Moses the tribe becomes the "desert assembly."

The second of God's two promises to Abraham is fulfilled when the people of the Exodus enter the Promised Land and celebrate the assembly of Shechem.

---

[1] Cf. J. Guillet, *Themes of the Bible*, translated by A. J. LaMothe, Jr., (Notre Dame, Ind., 1960), p. 1. Cf. also H. Haag, "Pâque," *DBS* 6:1120–49, and *Vom alten zum neuen Pascha: Geschichte und Theologie des Osterfestes* (Stuttgarter Bibelstudien 49; Stuttgart, 1971). G. Fohrer, *Überlieferung und Geschichte des Exodus* (Berlin, 1964), analyzes chapters 1–15 of the Book of Exodus. On the spiritual significance of the Exodus, see Guillet, *op. cit.*, pp. 1–19; R. le Déaut, *La nuit pascale* (Analecta Biblica 22; Rome, 1963), especially pp. 149–63; Jacob, *op. cit.*, pp. 183–201; G. von Rad, *Old Testament Theology* 1, translated by D. M. G. Stalker (New York, 1962), pp. 175–279; J. Daniélou, *From Shadows to Reality: Studies in the Biblical Theology of the Fathers*, translated by W. Hibberd (Westminster, Md., 1960), pp. 153–226.

[2] Deut. 26:8. Cf. also Num. 23:22 and 24:8. There is an especially beautiful formulation in 2 Sam. 7:23: "What other nation on earth is there like your people Israel, which God has led, redeeming it as his people; so that you have made yourself renowned by doing this magnificent deed, and by doing awe-inspiring things as you cleared nations and their gods out of the way of your people, which you redeemed for yourself from Egypt?"

[3] For example, Dan. 9:15.

[4] Cf., for example, the "liturgy" that accompanies the taking of Jericho (Josh. 6:1-24). This text contains various additions (cf. A. Gelin, *Josué*, in *La Sainte Bible* 3 [Paris, 1935], pp. 42–43). The mention of the presence of the Ark doubtless comes from priestly circles which wanted the conquest of the city attributed to the Ark (cf. M. Fourmond, *Josué* [Paris, 1959], p. 45).

[5] Ps. 23:5. This Psalm, often called the "Good Shepherd Psalm," seems to link the theme of the Exodus with that of Yahweh as shepherd of his people. J. Guillet writes in this connection: "Most of the time, the march in the desert is described as the wandering of a flock led by its shepherd. Reflection upon the Exodus is one of the sources of the theme of the Shepherd" (*op. cit.*, p. 7); Guillet refers in this context to Hos. 11:1-4; Is. 63:11-14; Ps. 78:52. — On the cultic aspect of Psalm 23, cf. A. Szörenyi, *Psalmen und Kult im Alten Testament* (Budapest, 1961).

[6] 1 Cor. 10:4. The Apostle is here echoing a legend found in the Targumic tradition; cf. E. Ellis, "A Note on 1 Cor. X. 4," in *Journal of Biblical Literature* 76 (1957) pp. 53–56.

[7] Calendar in Exod. 23:14-17.

[8] Cf. Exod. 12:15-20; 13:3-16; 23:15; Lev. 23:5-8; Deut. 16:1-8; Num. 28:16-25. — On Passover, cf. P. van Imschoot, *Théologie de l'Ancien Testament* 2 (Tournai, 1956), pp. 176–82; J. Jeremias, "Pascha," *TDNT* 5:896–903; R. de Vaux, *Ancient Israel: Its Life and Institutions*, translated by J. McHugh (New York, 1961), pp. 484–93; De Vaux, *Studies in Old Testament Sacrifice* (Cardiff, 1964), pp. 1–26; H.-J. Kraus, *Worship in Israel: A Cultic History of the Old Testament*, translated by G. Buswell (Oxford, 1966), pp. 45–55.

[9] In Exod. 34:18-25, the two feasts are still distinguished from one another.

[10] Exod. 23:16; 34:22. On the Harvest festival, which was also called the Feast of Weeks or Pentecost, cf. Van Imschoot, *Théologie de l'Ancien Testament* 2:184–89; De Vaux, *Ancient Israel*, pp. 493–95; Kraus, *op. cit.*, pp. 55–61; E. Lohse, "Pentēkostē," *TDNT* 6:44–53.

[11] Cf. Deut. 16:10-11; Num. 28:26.

[12] "Pentecost" is the English equivalent of the Greek "pentēkostē," which means "fiftieth" (i.e., day). The term is used in the Septuagint in Tob. 2:1; 2 Macc. 12:32; cf. also Acts 2:1.

[13] Cf. J. van Goudoever, *Fêtes et calendriers bibliques* (Théologie historique 7; Paris, 1967), pp. 199–206.

[14] Deut. 16:13-16; 31:10. This is the name that later became generally accepted: Lev. 23:33-36; 2 Chron. 8:13; Ezra 3:4; Zech. 14:16; 2 Macc. 1:18; 10:6; John 7:2. — On the Feast of Tents, cf. De Vaux, *Ancient Israel*, pp. 495–502; Kraus, *op. cit.*, pp. 61–66, with bibliography on p. 61, note 94. On the relation of this feast to that of the New Year, cf. H. Cazelles, "Nouvel An," *DBS* 6:620–45.

[15] Cf. De Vaux, *op. cit.*, pp. 500–501. Eichrodt, *op. cit.*, 1:122–23, thinks, however, that this feast was not originally an agricultural festival, but an ancient custom of nomads, and that it had the Exodus as its central theme: "The heart of the Law . . . is the commemoration of the Wilderness wanderings, with their climax in the conclusion of the Sinai covenant" (p. 123).

[16] The Hexateuch includes, in addition to the Pentateuch, or first five books of the Bible, the Book of Joshua. On the sources which contributed to the Hexateuch, cf. G. von Rad, *Das formgeschichtliche Problem des Hexateuchs* (Stuttgart, 1938); M. Noth, *Überlieferungsgeschichtliche Studien* (Stuttgart, 1948); H. Cazelles, "Pentateuque," *DBS* 7:768–858.

[17] Von Rad, *Old Testament Theology* 1:106–7. Cf. also M. Noth, *The History of Israel*, revised translation by P.R. Ackroyd (New York, 1960²), pp. 110–21. Speaking of the crossing of the Red Sea, Noth writes: "Hitherto they [the people involved in the crossing] have been described as 'Israelites' in accordance with the tradition which was transmitted in the confederacy of the twelve tribes. But the 'Israel' of the twelve tribes only evolved on the soil of Palestine and even the name 'Israel' is not certainly attested before the entry into Palestine. The traditions concerning prehistoric events were shaped from the point of view of the situation as it was in Palestine and these traditions referred to 'Israel' as if 'Israel' had already existed for a long time. Historically speaking, the 'bringing forth out of Egypt' cannot have referred to the later Israel whose ancestors had not all shared a common pre-history. The departure from Egypt and the deliverance which took place 'by the sea' do not suggest a great number of tribes but a numerically fairly small group which was in a position, because of its size, to 'flee' from Egypt. It is usual to think, therefore, of individual components of what later became Israel, which had been in Egypt and may be considered the real transmitters of the tradition of the 'bringing forth out of Egypt' " (p. 117). On the activity of Moses, cf. H. Cazelles, "Moïse devant l'histoire," in *Moïse, l'homme de l'Alliance* (Tournai, 1959), pp. 11–27.

[18] Noth, *The History of Israel*, p. 117.

[19] A literal account should *strive* for the greatest possible objectivity, but it may not *claim* to achieve any objectivity save that which is possible for human perception (always marked by an element of subjectivity). In an essay on the historical character of the Synoptic Gospels, Cardinal Bea wrote: "The existence of definite modes of speaking, narrating, and of teaching which are proper to Sacred Scripture has always been recognized by all who have had any familiarity with the Bible. The meaning of such modes of speaking and expressing oneself is not always easy to determine. But it becomes progressively more intelligible as the literature of the ancient Near East comes gradually to light — a process that is as yet far from being finished" (Augustin Cardinal Bea, *The Study of the Synoptic Gospels: New Approaches and Outlooks*, edited by J.A. Fitzmyer, S.J. [New York, 1965], pp. 30–31). The Cardinal quotes the

encyclical *Divino afflante Spiritu* of Pius XII: "It is absolutely necessary for the interpreter to go back in spirit to those remote centuries of the East, and with the aid of history, archaeology, ethnology, and other sciences, determine what literary forms the writers of that ancient period intended to use and did in fact employ" (p. 31; cf. *Enchiridion Biblicum*, no. 558).

[20] In fact, poetry is a superior form both of expression and of understanding. We should note that the most essential elements of divine revelation in the Bible are given in poetic dress; cf. von Rad, *Old Testament Theology* 1:109.

[21] "The most ancient confession of faith," according to E. Jacob, *op. cit.*, p. 184; for another view, cf. P. Buis and J. Leclercq, *Le Deutéronome* (Paris, 1963), p. 167. On this history-centered creed, cf. R. P. Merendino, *Das deuteronomische Gesetz: Eine literarkritische, gattungs- und überlieferungsgeschichtliche Untersuchung zu Dt 12–26* (Bonner Biblische Beiträge 31; Bonn, 1969), pp. 351–63. There are other professions of faith in Deut. 6:20-24; Josh. 24:2-13; Pss. 77, 78, 105, 136; Neh. 9:7-25.

[22] On the importance of Shechem, cf. below, Chapter 2.

[23] According to the Yahwist and Elohist traditions: Gen. 28:10-22; 35:1-9, 14-15.

[24] According to the traditions in Gen. 21:22-31. According to Gen. 46:1-4 (the Yahwist and Elohist traditions), Jacob offered sacrifice there to the God of his father Isaac.

[25] According to Josh. 4:19-24 and 5:2-12.

[26] Cf. 1 Sam. 1:7, 24; 3:3, 15.

[27] According to Judg. 21:19-21.

[28] According to the tradition in 1 Kings 3:4.

[29] On the ancient sanctuaries, cf. De Vaux, *Ancient Israel*, pp. 289–94 and 302–11.

[30] Cf. Is. 50:2.

[31] On the traditions which make up the Pentateuch, cf. M. Noth, *Überlieferungsgeschichte des Pentateuch* (Stuttgart, 1948); H. Cazelles, "Pentateuque," *DBS* 7:770–858.

[32] The traditions are mingled as the writer chooses. The following verses in chapter 14 are attributed to the Yahwist tradition: 5b, 6, 9ax, 10b, 13-14, 19b-21ax, 24-25b, 27aB, 30-31. The following are assigned to the Priestly tradition: 1-4, 8-9aB, 10a, 15-18, 21aB, 22-23, 26-27ax, 28-29, Cf. M. Noth, *Überlieferungsgeschichte des Pentateuch*, pp. 18, 32. On Exod. 14, cf. also G. Fohrer, *Überlieferung und Geschichte des Exodus* (Beihefte zur Zeitschrift für die alttestamentliche Wissenschaft 91; Berlin, 1964), pp. 97–110.

[33] On the opposition between God and the sea, cf. O. Eissfeldt in his *Kleine Schriften* 3 (Tübingen, 1966), pp. 257–64; the article appeared first in *Studia Orientalia Ioanni Pedersen septuagenario* (Copenhagen, 1953), pp. 76–84.

[34] Other descriptions of the crossing of the Sea of Reeds are to be found in Pss. 78:13-14; 107:43; 136:13-15; all these borrow their imagery and themes from Exod. 14. It is well known that some traditions, such as that in Deut. 11:3-4, distinguish between the departure from Egypt and the crossing of the sea (cf. P. Buis, *Le Deutéronome* [Verbum salutis 4; Paris, 1969], pp. 183–84). In contrast, there is still another tradition, evidently very old, which seems to have no knowledge of the departure from Egypt and the crossing of the sea, or at least does not speak of them; according to this tradition, Israel "found favor in the desert" (Jer. 31:2; cf. Hos. 9:10; Deut. 32:10); cf. H.W. Wolff, *Dodekapropheton Hosea* (Biblischer Kommentar 16; Neukirchen, 1961), pp. 212–13. This last tradition was probably repressed and obscured by the more lively, structured tradition that is represented by Exod. 14 and acquired a kind of monopoly in the writing of the history.

[35] Cf. Deut. 7:6: "You are a people sacred to the Lord, your God; he has chosen you . . . to be a people peculiarly his own." These stereotyped formulas are also found, with insignificant variations, in Deut. 14:2, 21; 26:19; 28:9.

[36] Cf. Hos. 2:1-2; Jer. 31:9, 20; Is. 49:14-16. R. le Déaut, *La nuit pascale*, p. 230,

note 44, refers to a Targumic image according to which "the afflicted state of Israel in Egypt is compared to the situation of a child still in its mother's womb; the Exodus and the entry into the Promised Land correspond to the child's coming forth into the world."

[37] Hos. 2:16-17, 21-22; 3:1. Cf. also Jer. 2:2; 31:2-4, 21-22; Ezek. 16 and 23; Is. 54:4-6; 62:4-5. This nuptial theme will culminate in the New Testament in Eph. 5:27; 2 Cor. 11:2; and Apoc. 21:2, where the Church is a spotless virgin espoused to Christ. On this theme, cf. W. Eichrodt, *op. cit.*, 1, pp. 250–58; P. Grelot, *Man and Wife in Scripture*, translated by R. Brennan (New York, 1964), pp. 57–68; E. Stauffer, "Gameo," *TDNT* 1:648–57; J. Jeremias, "Nymphē," *TDNT* 4:1099–1106; P. Claudel, "Le thème biblique: Dieu époux de son peuple, l'Eglise épouse du Christ," *Assemblées du Seigneur*, no. 16 (1962), pp. 54–77; A. Neher, *L'essence du prophétisme* (Paris, 1955), pp. 247–55. Cf. also the bibliography in *L'Eglise dans la Bible* (Studia 13; Montreal, 1962), p. 188. On the exegesis of the Canticle of Canticles, cf. A. Robert, R. Tournay, and A. Feuillet, *Le Cantique des Cantiques* (Paris, 1963).

[38] On this subject, cf. R. le Déaut, *La nuit pascale*, pp. 88–100 and 218–37.

[39] Cf. the great Hallel, Psalm 136. The same movement of thought is to be found in Jer. 32:17-21, in the psalm of Neh. 9:6-37, and in Ps. 95.

[40] On the Decalogue, cf. A. Eberharter, "Décalogue," *DBS* 2:341-51; W. Eichrodt, *op. cit.*, 1:70–97 especially; P. van Imschoot, *Théologie de l'Ancien Testament* 2:83–90; G. Auzou, *De la servitude au service: Etude de Livre de l'Exode* (Connaissance de la Bible 3; Paris, 1961), pp. 279–316; E. Nielsen, *Die zehn Gebote* (Acta Theologica Danica 8; Copenhagen, 1965). Cf. the bibliography given in the *Dictionnaire Encyclopédique de la Bible*, col. 427. And cf. J. J. Stamm and M. E. Andrew, *The Ten Commandments in Recent Research* (Studies in Biblical Theology, 2nd series, 2; Naperville, Ill., 1967).

[41] G. von Rad, *Old Testament Theology* 1:187. In Exod. 19:1, the Hebrews, having left Kadesh, reach Sinai; in Num. 10:10 they leave Sinai and come to Kadesh. On the stay at Kadesh, cf. *Dictionnaire Encyclopédique de la Bible*, cols. 1872–74 (with bibliography, col. 1879).

[42] Cf. Strack-Billerbeck, *Kommentar zum Neuen Testament aus Talmud und Midrasch* 1:970.

[43] Cf. Mark 10:3, 4; 12:19; John 8:5; etc.

[44] On the Covenant Code, cf. H. Cazelles, *Etudes sur le Code de l'Alliance* (Paris, 1946), and "Pentateuque," *DBS* 7:810–13; A. Alt, "The Origins of Israelite Law," in his *Essays on Old Testament History and Religion*, translated by R.A. Wilson (New York, 1967), pp. 103–71; O. Eissfeldt, *The Old Testament: An Introduction*, translated by P. R. Ackroyd (New York, 1965), pp. 212–19. The date of the redaction of the Code is controverted. H. Cazelles, "Pentateuque," *DBS* 7:810, writes: the Covenant Code "continues to be regarded as the oldest collection of juridical principles"; the Mosaic sources, written or oral, which the Code contains, were put to use in the period of the prophets, not before the ninth century but before the fall of Samaria in 722. The *Dictionnaire Encyclopédique de la Bible* says: "Most modern critics think that the Code in its present form dates from the ninth or eighth century, or even from the seventh century B.C.; they agree, however, that it contains much older elements that date from the period of the Judges" (col. 325). The Code shows similarities to the Code of Hammurabi (first half of nineteenth century), the Egyptian Edict of Horembeb (1340–1320), and the Hittite Laws (one version of which dates from the first half of the fourteenth century); this seems to indicate the existence of an ancient customary law among the Semites which may have been the source of various legislations (cf. H. Cazelles, *Etudes sur le Code de l'Alliance*, pp. 147–68). Biblical criticism attributes the redaction of the Covenant Code to the Elohist tradition; cf. below, Chapter 2, section 2, subsection 3.

[45] It belongs to the Yahwist tradition and may be called the "Yahwist Covenant Code."

[46] The ideal is thus formulated from God's viewpoint: "Be holy, for I, the Lord, your God, am holy" (Lev. 19:2; 20:7-8, 26; 21:6, 8, 15, 23). The final redaction of Leviticus occurred only after the Exile, but many precepts in the Holiness Code are evidently older. Summing up the views of the exegetes, A. Clamer writes: "For some, the definitive redaction of Leviticus 17–26 took place around 570 in circles influenced by the prophet Ezekiel (Steuernagel); for others, it took place toward the end of the Exile (Wellhausen, Kuenen, Smend, Holzinger)" (*Le Lévitique*, in L. Pirot and A. Clamer, *La Sainte Bible* 2 [Paris, 1946], p. 10). Cf. also H. Cazelles, "Pentateuque," *DBS* 7:823–27, who writes: "It is very probable that the Holiness Code is a centralizing code that collected the usages of the southern sanctuaries" (col. 824).

We should also note the Ordinance for Festivals in Num. 28–29, which prescribes for the feasts of the year (cf. Lev. 23). Though placed in Numbers, this Ordinance cannot be connected with Mount Sinai. It belongs to the Priestly source, is largely postexilic, and represents "priestly regulations that must have been observed after the return and the restoration of the Temple and its worship" (Cazelles, "Pentateuque," *DBS* 7:851).

[47] On the Deuteronomic Code, cf. R. M. Merendino, *Das deuteronomische Gesetz*. In its present literary form, the Code may date from the seventh century; cf. J. L'Hour, *La morale de l'Alliance* (Cahiers de la Revue Biblique 5; Paris, 1966), p. 79. Merendino, *op. cit.*, p. 402, thinks the redaction of Deuteronomy is not earlier than the reform of Josiah in 622, and even believes there was a post-Deuteronomic edition (p. 407).

[48] R. de Vaux, *Histoire ancienne d'Israël* 1: *Des origines à l'installation en Canaan* (Paris, 1971), p. 424. On "Mosaic religion," cf. pp. 424–40.

[49] The point is disputed. W. F. Albright, *From the Stone Age to Christianity: Monotheism and the Historical Process* (Baltimore, 1946), writes: "The founder of Yahwism was certainly a monotheist" (p. 207). Perhaps. But the texts do not prove it.

[50] Cf. R. de Vaux, *Ancient Israel*, pp. 475–83.

[51] Cf. De Vaux, *op. cit.*, pp. 415–56, and *Studies in Old Testament Sacrifice*; H.-J. Kraus, *Worship in Israel*, pp. 112–24.

[52] Cf. Von Rad, *Old Testament Theology* 1:212–19; Kraus, *op. cit.*, pp. 125–34.

[53] Cf. R. de Vaux, "Arche d'Alliance et Tente de Réunion," in *A la rencontre de Dieu (Mémorial Albert Gelin)* (Le Puy, 1961), pp. 55–70.

[54] Cf. O. Eissfeldt, "Lade und Stierbild," *Kleine Schriften* 2 (Tübingen, 1963), pp. 282–305.

[55] W. Eichrodt, *op. cit.*, 1:291.

[56] *Ibid.*

[57] On the Decalogue, cf. H. Cazelles, "Pentateuque," *DBS* 7:809–10, and cf. *DBS* 2:341–51; J.-J. Stamm and M. E. Andrews, *The Ten Commandments in Recent Research*; W. Beyerlin, *Herkunft und Geschichte der ältesten Sinaïtraditionen* (Tübingen, 1961), pp. 59–78; E. Nielsen, *Die zehn Gebote*.

[58] According to G. von Rad, *Old Testament Theology* 1:189, the cosmic setting probably reflects "the 'festival legend' belonging to a major cultic celebration, the old festival of the renewal of the covenant."

[59] The redactor has evidently not been concerned to integrate the text of the Decalogue into the narrative: "So Moses went down to the people and told them this. Then God delivered all these commandments" (Exod. 19:25–20:1). Then the text of the Decalogue is given.

[60] Cf. P. Buis and L. Leclercq, *Le Deutéronome*, pp. 63–73.

[61] Cf. W. Beyerlin, *op. cit.*, p. 59 (in opposition to E. Nielsen, *op. cit.*, p. 102).

[62] According to E. Nielsen, *op. cit.*, p. 68. Cf. also A. Gelin, "Moïse dans l'Ancien Testament" in *Moïse, l'homme de l'Alliance*, p. 41.

[63] In Exod. 20:8-11, for example, the fact that after his work of creation God rested on the seventh day is offered as a motive for observing the sabbath; in Deut. 5:12-15,

on the contrary, the motive given is that the sabbath day is sacred to Yahweh as a day of commemoration of the Exodus.

⁶⁴ A. T. Patrick, "Origine et formation du Décalogue," *Ephemerides Theologicae Lovanienses* 40 (1964), p. 250.

⁶⁵ Exod. 20:1; 24:3, 7; 34:1, 27; Deut. 4:10, 13, 36; 5:5; 9:10; 10:2, 4. The term "Decalogue" *(dekalogos)* is patristic, not biblical, in origin. It occurs first in Clement of Alexandria, *Paedagogus* III, 89 (cf. *Sources chrétiennes* 158, p. 170) and in Irenaeus of Lyons, *Adversus haereses* IV, 15, 1: *PG* 7:1012 (cf. *Sources chrétiennes* 100, p. 546).

⁶⁶ Exod. 34:28.

⁶⁷ Same ideas in Ps. 147:19-20: "He has proclaimed his word to Jacob, his statutes and his ordinances to Israel. He has not done thus for any other nation; his ordinances he has not made known to them."

⁶⁸ Cf. H. Cazelles, "Loi Israélite," *DBS* 5:515–16. Cf. also L. Desroches-Noblecourt, "La religion égyptienne," in *Histoire générale des religions* 1 (Paris, 1960), pp. 219–23.

⁶⁹ Cf. P. Dhorme, *La religion assyro-babylonienne* (Paris, 1910), pp. 211–41. Irenaeus puts the Decalogue on the level of "natural precepts" *(naturalia praecepta)* in *Adversus haereses* IV, 15, 1 (cf. *Sources chrétiennes* 100, p. 548).

⁷⁰ P. Dhorme, *op. cit.*, pp. 226–28.

⁷¹ R. de Vaux, *Ancient Israel*, p. 147; the author cites Exod. 24:12; 31:18; Deut. 9:9.

⁷² The similarity was first pointed out by G. E. Mendenhall, *Law and Covenant in Israel and in the Ancient Near East* (Pittsburgh, 1955). On this subject cf. D. J. McCarthy, *Old Testament Covenant: A Survey of Recent Opinion* (Richmond, 1972), which presents the state of the question up to 1966; a long postscript to this English-language edition treats of significant later material.

⁷³ Cf. W. Beyerlin, *op. cit.*, pp. 62ff.; N. Lohfink, *Das Hauptgebot: Eine Untersuchung literarischer Einleitungsfragen zu Dtn 5–11* (Analecta Biblica 20; Rome, 1963), pp. 108–12; J. L'Hour, *La morale de l'Alliance*, pp. 9–10; P. Buis, "Les formulaires d'alliance," *Vetus Testamentum* 16 (1966) pp. 396–411.

⁷⁴ Treaty of Suppiluliumas with Aziras of Amirru; text in *ANET*, p. 529. Cf. W. Beyerlin, *op. cit.*, p. 62, citing E. F. Weidner, *Politische Dokumente aus Kleinasien: Die Staatsverträge in akkadischer Sprache aus dem Archiv von Boghazkoi* (Leipzig, 1923), p. 58. On Suppiluliumas, king of the Hittites (ca. 1380–1345), cf. *Les religions du Proche-Orient: Textes babyloniens, ougaritiques, hittites* (Paris, 1970), pp. 479ff.; R. de Vaux, *Histoire ancienne d'Israël* 1:100–102.

⁷⁵ Same treaty, *ANET*, p. 528.

⁷⁶ Same treaty, *ANET*, p. 529.

⁷⁷ Treaty of Suppiluliumas with Hukkanas; cf. W. Beyerlin, *op. cit.*, p. 63.

⁷⁸ Cf. W. Beyerlin, *op. cit.*, p. 65, citing E. F. Weidner, *op. cit.*, p. 80. On Mursil II (ca. 1335–1300), cf. *Les religions du Proche-Orient*, pp. 482ff., 513ff.

⁷⁹ Treaty of Suppiluliumas with Mattiwaza, king of Mitanni (Upper Mesopotamia); cf. *ANET*, p. 205.

⁸⁰ Same treaty, *ANET*, p. 205.

⁸¹ *Ibid.*

⁸² Same treaty, *ANET*, p. 206. The treaty has the curse first, the blessing second. Cf. also J. L'Hour, *op. cit.*, pp. 83–103.

⁸³ Cf. R. de Vaux, *Histoire ancienne d'Israël* 1:413, and D. J. McCarthy, *op. cit.*, who observes that "much work remains to be done in tracing the history and milieu of the [covenant] form within the Hebrew people" (p. 57). In this matter we may distinguish (1) what really happened in history; (2) what the sources enable us to see; (3) the interpretation given by the post-Sinaitic tradition.

⁸⁵ E. Nielsen, *op. cit.*, p. 103.

[86] Exod. 23:19; 34:26; Deut. 14:21. In the Ugaritic poem *Birth of the Gods* (52:14), we find the recommendation: "Cook a goat in milk, a lamb in cream." The reference is to a sacrificial meal in honor of a fertility goddess (A. G. Barrois, *Manuel d'archéologie biblique* 2 [Paris, 1953], p. 334.

[87] On this subject, cf. R. de Vaux, *Ancient Israel*, p. 149, and G. von Rad, *Old Testament Theology* 1:197.

[88] Exod. 23:9.

[89] Deut. 22:23-24. In Old Testament law, betrothal conferred the same rights and obligations as marriage itself; cf. Strack-Billerbeck, *Kommentar zum Neuen Testament* 2 (Munich, 1961³), pp. 393–94.

[90] Gen. 9:6 (Priestly tradition) and Num. 35:33-34.

[91] Exod. 20:8-11 (Elohist tradition) and Deut. 5:12-15

[92] G. von Rad, *Old Testament Theology* 1:198.

[93] The positive formulation of the precept concerning honor due to parents (Exod. 20:12; Deut. 5:16) seems to be more recent; we find a negative and apparently older formulation in Exod. 21:17 and Deut. 27:16.

[94] Cf. Ps. 24:3-6; Is. 33:15-16. On these rituals, cf. H. Gunkel, *Einleitung in die Psalmen* (Göttingen, 1933), pp. 408–9; R. Kittel, *Die Psalmen* (Kommentar zum Alten Testament 13; Leipzig, 1929), pp. 44–45; H.-J. Kraus, *Psalmen* (Biblischer Kommentar 15/1; Neukirchen, 1960), pp. 111–12.

[95] R. de Vaux, *Histoire ancienne d'Israël* 1:414. Covenant meals are mentioned in Gen. 26:30; 31:54; Josh. 9:14; 2 Sam. 3:20. On the covenant, cf. D. J. McCarthy, *op. cit.*

[96] Cf. M. Mannati, *Les Psaumes* 2 (Paris, 1967), p. 145.

[97] St. Paul expresses this idea by saying that "those who eat the sacrifices . . . share in the altar" (1 Cor. 10:18) and, through the altar, in God (v. 20).

[98] Cf. O. Eissfeldt, *The Old Testament: An Introduction*, pp. 212–13, and R. de Vaux, *Histoire ancienne d'Israël* 1:415. For M. Noth, in his *Exodus: A Commentary* (translated by J. S. Bowden; Philadelphia, 1962), pp. 174–75, the "book of the covenant" is, on the contrary, to be identified with the Covenant Code. On Exod. 24:3-8, he writes elsewhere: "It seems doubtful to me that this passage can be attributed to any source; it may rather be an addition to the book of the covenant" (*Überlieferungsgeschichte des Pentateuchs*, p. 33, note 115).

[99] Cf. vv. 10b and 11b. According to M. Noth, *Exodus*, these verses are additions "in deuteronomistic language" (p. 215). For O. Eissfeldt, on the contrary, they are part of the earliest source: *Kleine Schriften* 4:12–20. R. de Vaux, *Histoire ancienne d'Israël* 1:417, regards both promises and laws as parts of the original covenant.

[100] *De mutatione nominum* 58, in *Les oeuvres de Philon d'Alexandrie* 18 (Paris, 1964) p. 59.

[101] *Constitution on the Sacred Liturgy*, no. 56. Cf. below, Chapter 12.

[102] On *Qahal* cf. M.-C. Matura, "Le qahal et son contexte cultuel," in *L'Eglise dans la Bible* (Studia 13; Paris, 1962), pp. 9–18. On *ekklēsia*, cf. P. Garriga, *La palabra ekklēsia: Estudio teológico* (Barcelona, 1958), and *idem*, "Ecclesia dans l'Ecriture et les communautés primitives," *Dictionnaire de spiritualité* 4:370–84. Cf. also K. L. Schmidt, "ekklēsia," *TDNT* 3:501–36; A. Medebeielle, "Eglise," *DBS* 2:487–91; V. Warnach, "Church," *SV* 1:101–13, with bibliography pp. 113–16. Note that Matura, *art. cit.*, pp. 10–11, challenges the first meaning assigned to qahal by F. Zorell in his *Lexicon Hebraicum et Aramaicum Veteris Testamenti*, p. 714, scil. "actus conveniendi," i.e., the act of assembling the community.

[103] *Qahal*, used 128 times, has the first meaning (assembly actually gathered) 111 times, the second only 17 times.

[104] Cf. M.-C. Matura, *art. cit.*, p. 11.

[105] The word *ekklēsia* occurs 81 times and, with only four exceptions, as the translation of *qahal* (the exceptions: 1 Sam. 19:20; Neh. 5:7; Pss. 26:12; 68:27); cf.

Matura, *art. cit.*, p. 12. Other words used to translate *qahal* are: *synagōgē* (gathering), *ochlos* (crowd), *plēthos* (multitude), and *systasis* (assembly).

[106] This is Paul's viewpoint when he speaks of his readers as "called to holiness" (Rom. 1:7) or "called to be a holy people" (1 Cor. 1:2). L. Cerfaux comments: "Christians . . . have been *called*. They are saints because they have been called and chosen" (*The Church in the Theology of St. Paul*, translated by G. Webb and A. Walker [New York, 1959], p. 119).

[107] *Dogmatic Constitution on the Church*, nos. 9–17.

[108] "Every local Church is a reincarnation of the desert assembly and as such is called the Church of God," says L. Cerfaux, *op. cit.*, p. 114, note 39.

[109] The *Decree on the Church's Missionary Activity*, no. 6, says: "All over the world indigenous particular churches ought to grow from the seed of the word of God . . ." (*Vatican Council II: The Conciliar and Post Conciliar Documents*, edited by Austin Flannery, O.P. [Collegeville, Minn., 1975], p. 819; henceforth cited as "Flannery," with page reference).

Chapter 2

THE ASSEMBLY OF SHECHEM
(ca. 1200)

INTRODUCTION

After the entry into Canaan, the people of God were once again gathered as a "church" at the holy place of Shechem.[1] The choice of venue was a splendid one, for longstanding traditions had made this ancient Canaanite place of pilgrimage the focus of countless memories.[2] It was near the old sacred oak of the oracles[3] that Abraham had pitched his tents after leaving Ur; there he had been granted a vision and God had renewed his covenant with him.[4] There, too, Jacob, before setting out for Bethel, had buried the foreign gods and fetish rings of Leah and Rachel.[5] The bones of Joseph were buried there, brought back from Egypt, a pagan land, so that they might be interred in holy ground.[6] (There, too, in the messianic era, at the well of Jacob, "near the plot of land which Jacob had given to his son Joseph" [John 4:5], Jesus would promise the Samaritan woman the water that becomes a fountain of eternal life and would speak to her of worship in spirit and truth.)

The sources for our picture of the assembly at Shechem are the following:

Josh. 24:1-28, which is the principal source. The passage is the conclusion of the Book of Joshua and, for practical purposes, of the whole story of the Exodus. Thus it makes a literary unity of the covenant at Sinai and the covenant at Shechem. The section has evidently been inserted at a later date into the narrative proper to the Book of Joshua. In the preceding chapter Joshua issues his final plea to the people ("I am old and advanced in years": 23:2) and makes known his last wishes. But then, instead of dying, he takes vigorous charge of the assembly at Shechem and looks forward to

39

the future with great optimism ("As for me and my household, we
will serve the Lord": 24:15). He dies at last in 24:29-31. We are
justified, therefore, in thinking that 24:29-31 originally followed directly on chapter 23.

Deut. 27:1-26. The redactor presents the celebration at Shechem
as being the execution of an order from Moses, thus putting it under
the patronage of the great prophet and connecting it with the events
of the Exodus. He also gives a collection of very ancient laws, which
have been called the Dodecalogue of Shechem.[7]

We need simply mention Deut. 11:29-31 and Josh. 8:30-35. The
latter depends almost entirely on Deut. 27 and 11:29-31; both texts
confirm the importance of the Shechem covenant.[8]

We may also mention the Covenant Code of Exod. 21–23, which
we have already discussed and which has some connection with the
celebration at Shechem.

These texts, especially the older ones among them, have reached
us in a disorganized literary state. They have undergone numerous
alterations and extensive redactional correction. They have often
been inserted into a new literary framework, somewhat as a
goldsmith might highlight the beauty of an ancient jewel by putting
it into a new setting. Some passages are like medieval fortresses
which have crumbled with time but are constantly being rebuilt.
Yet, despite the successive restorations, it is still possible to determine amid the ancient ruins what the original plan of the citadel
must have been.

The celebration of the assembly at Shechem unfolds according to
the pattern initiated at Sinai: God calls and gathers his people; he
gives them his law; he enters into a covenant with them.

I. GOD CALLS AND GATHERS HIS PEOPLE

In the Lord's name, Joshua called all the tribes of Israel together
in a holy assembly: "Joshua gathered together all the tribes of Israel
at Shechem, summoning their elders, their leaders, their judges
and their officers. When they stood in ranks before God, Joshua
addressed all the people: 'Thus says the Lord, the God of Israel
. . .' " (Josh. 24:1-2).[9] At Shechem, Joshua thus took over the role
Moses had played at Sinai. Like Moses, he led the people into "the
presence of God," and, like Moses, passed on God's words to the
assembly.

It may be possible to determine somewhat more precisely the

historical event and situation to which the account in Josh. 24 refers. We know that the gathering at Shechem was not a kind of national legislative assembly that met only once in the history of Israel. For, in fact, the people were accustomed to meeting every seven years "to appear before the Lord, your God" and to hear his word (Deut. 31:10-12).[10] Shechem played an especially important role in these gatherings. It was not only a place where fairs were held at which people bought and sold, arranged marraiges and proclaimed divorces, passed laws and harmonized tribal customs; it was also a religious center where Israel attained a deeper awareness of its own unity, listened to the proclamation of the Law (the religious charter that bound the twelve tribes together), and celebrated the renewal of the covenant. The account in Josh. 24 highlights the importance of this ancient custom. During the two centuries separating the entry into Canaan from the establishment of the Davidic monarchy (ca. 1000), with its political and religious centralization, Shechem was the heart of the Promised Land.

The text of Josh. 24 also shows Israel preserving the memory of an extraordinary assembly that had to deal with an especially serious situation that arose after entry into Canaan. The tribes that had stayed behind in Palestine and preserved the traditions of Jacob had not experienced the wonderful events of the Exodus or shared in the Sinai covenant. Now they met their sister tribes that had come up from Egypt with Moses and Joshua and were proponents of a fervent Yahwism. A crisis was inevitable, a crisis in which nomadic tribes which championed a pure and integral faith confronted tribes which were no longer mobile and were attached, moreover, to pagan practices and customs. Joshua demanded that those who had come up with him should make a choice:

> Now, therefore, fear the Lord and serve him completely and sincerely. Cast out the gods your fathers served beyond the River and in Egypt, and serve the Lord. If it does not please you to serve the Lord, decide today whom you will serve, the gods your fathers served beyond the River or the gods of the Amorites in whose country you are dwelling. As for me and my household, we will serve the Lord (Josh. 24:14-15).[11]

In his analysis of this text, G. von Rad writes:

> The account of the "assembly at Shechem" (Josh. xxiv) suggests that, in an hour fraught with drama, the house of Joseph, through its spokesman Joshua, simply forced upon the rest of the clans the decision for or against Jahweh. For, as was noticed long ago, this story is perfectly incomprehensible from the standpoint of the later idea ac-

cording to which all of the clans were at Sinai. What sense would
Joshua's summons to put away the foreign gods and decide for Jahweh
have had then? The story therefore preserves a very ancient memory
of a cultic antagonism which developed among the clans because of
the entry of the worshippers of Jahweh, and over and above that of an
event of far-reaching significance for the history of the cult, namely
the founding of the old Israelite Amphictyony.[12]

The story of Shechem is thus the story of a renunciation, a choice,
and the strengthening of community: just as Jacob had renounced
the foreign gods he buried at Shechem, so the tribes descended
from the patriarch must once again bury there the Amorite gods
whose country they had occupied and choose Yahweh in their stead.
By doing so, they become a more integral part of the community of
the chosen people and share the faith of the Sinai assembly. The
tribal family descended from Abraham becomes a more tightly knit
unity, not simply because it is descended from a common forebear
but especially because all the members agree to answer the same
call of God.

II. GOD GIVES HIS LAW TO HIS PEOPLE

After calling together his people, God once again addresses his
word and his law to them. The sources for Shechem are especially
rich in this area.

1. In the *account in Josh. 24*, God, through the mouth of his
spokesman Joshua, recalls in broad outline the main stages in the
history of salvation. The story begins with the recall of Terah, at Ur
of the Chaldees, father of Abraham; it moves on to the patriarchs,
Abraham, Isaac, and Jacob, the stay in Egypt, the Exodus under the
leadership of Moses and Aaron, the passage of the Sea of Reeds, the
crossing of the Jordan, the capture of Jericho, and the occupation of
Canaan.[13] The conclusion, which is an addition in the best
Deuteronomic style, is an admirable summary of this wide-ranging
historical poem in which every event sings of God's freely given
love: "I gave you a land which you had not tilled and cities which
you had not built, to dwell in; you have eaten of vineyards and olive
groves which you did not plant" (Josh. 24:13).[14]

This proclamation of the history of salvation was supremely important for the Shechem assembly. Because of it the gathering of the
twelve tribes was not simply a joyful family reunion at which
brothers conversed with one another, but a holy meeting where
men conversed with God and celebrated the memory of his wonder-

ful deeds of long ago. Yahweh's intervention in the past was the guarantee of his effective presence in the today of his people. Because those past events were proclaimed in the ancient sanctuaries, the present moment of history, burdensome, threatening, or commonplace as it might be, was linked with the wonderful events of the earlier time. By accepting integration with the tribes that had experienced the Exodus, the Palestinian tribes which had not known the God of Sinai made a spiritual pilgrimage to the sources of faith and entered into the great movement of history, that broad river that would carry them to endless shores known only to God.

God did not intend to conduct a monologue at Shechem any more than he had at Sinai. His word was not a snaffle to muzzle his people but an invitation to a dialogue with him. In the account in Joshua, the people's response is especially keen and fervent. When called to choose between Yahweh and the gods of the Amorites, the assembly answers repeatedly in words that almost form a refrain: "Far be it from us to forsake the Lord for the service of other gods" (Josh. 24:16); "Therefore we also will serve the Lord, for he is our God" (24:18); "We will still serve the Lord" (24:21); "We are indeed [our own witnesses that we have chosen to serve the Lord]!" (24:22); "We will serve the Lord, our God, and obey his voice" (24:23).[15]

These protestations of fidelity on the part of the people are very valuable. They signify that God's word has attained its purpose when man offers the Lord his free acceptance of it.

2. The *account in Deut. 27* presents us with the most grandiose of all liturgies of the word.[16] The two mountains, Ebal (940 meters high) and Gerizim (881 meters high), between which the ancient sanctuary of Shechem was situated, provided an ideal backdrop for this great celebration. The tribes of Simeon, Levi, Judah, Issachar, Joseph, and Benjamin stood on Mount Gerizim; the tribes of Reuben, Gad, Asher, Zebulun, Dan, and Naphthali stood opposite them on Mount Ebal.[17] The law, the "Dodecalogue of Shechem,"[18] was then proclaimed, and the people ratified each curse with its "Amen." The "Amen" here is more than a simple expression of agreement; it is a kind of self-cursing and an especially solemn form of commitment.

> "Cursed be the man who makes a carved or molten idol . . . and sets it up in secret!" And all the people shall answer, "Amen!"
> "Cursed be he who dishonors his father or his mother." And all the people shall answer, "Amen!"
> "Cursed be he who moves his neighbor's landmarks." And all the people shall answer, "Amen!"

> "Cursed be he who misleads a blind man on his way!" And all the
> people shall answer, "Amen!"
> "Cursed be he who violates the rights of the alien, the orphan or
> the widow!" And all the people shall answer, "Amen!"

Next come four prohibitions of sexual relations between close
relatives and of bestiality. Then the Dodecalogue continues with:

> "Cursed be he who slays his neighbor in secret!" And all the people
> shall answer, "Amen!"
> "Cursed be he who accepts payment for slaying an innocent man!"
> And all the people shall answer, "Amen!"
> "Cursed be he who fails to fulfill any of the provisions of this law!"
> And all the people shall answer, "Amen!" (Deut. 27:15-26).[19]

The encounter with God entails an irreversible choice — a decision that means life or death. It requires the acceptance of the
divine order of things and the renunciation of evil.

The formulation of the prohibitions, as well as the grouping of
them into a code, is very ancient, probably as ancient as the Sinai
code.[20] Each curse must have been chosen after long experience.
Yet the choice is far from perfect. As Israel listened to God's word,
its ear was not fully attuned to his voice; its conscience was still that
of the groping adolescent, and a great deal of time would be required for it to discern with lucidity and formulate with preciseness
the clear will of God.[21] God himself must accept the fact that he
must spend a long time teaching his people how to love him!

The ritual for the proclamation of the Dodecalogue seems somewhat idealized. How could the voice of a single man have been
heard by twelve tribes spread out over two mountains?[22] It is likely
that a ritual used with smaller groups (perhaps at Shechem itself)
was projected back and read into the procedure at the original
Shechem assembly. But what the rite signified was validly applied
to that original event: The voice of God alone could unite the twelve
tribes into a living "church" and lead them to commit themselves
through their "Amen."

3. In reporting the end of the Shechem meeting, the narrator
tells us: "So Joshua made a covenant with the people that day and
made statutes and ordinances for them at Shechem, which he
recorded in the book of the law of God" (Josh. 24:25-26). Exegetes
have hunted for this collection of Shechemite laws that were
recorded in "the book of the law of God." They inevitably turn their
attention to the Covenant Code in Exod. 20:22–23:10.

It is true, of course, that the tradition in Exod. 24:3 connects the Covenant Code with the Sinai covenant and thus claims the highest biblical patronage for it.[23] It is clear, however, that only with difficulty can the text of the Code itself be harmonized with the statement in Exod. 24:3.[24] Deuteronomy seems even to have no knowledge of the Code.[25]

On the other hand, the Covenant Code is very appropriate to the legislative assembly at Shechem. It is made up, as we know, of religious and cultic laws, on the one hand, and popular customs that have acquired the status of laws, on the other. Now, as we pointed out above, the Shechem assembly represents the encounter, before Yahweh, of the house of Joseph that has returned from Egypt and the tribes that stayed behind in Palestine. In a similar fashion, the Covenant Code brings together cultic laws which the people of the Exodus brought with them and customs in force in Canaan. Both the cultic laws and the popular customs would be needed in order to regulate the religious and social life of the twelve tribes, since the latter would now share the same Yahwist faith and the same agricultural way of life. The Covenant Code is really "the law of the tribal federation."[26]

What is the spiritual significance of the Covenant Code? This code is the charter for the grouping of the twelve tribes under a single legislation. It is thus the bond that unites them despite their diversity and particularisms. More than that, the Code is God's word. Consequently, it gathers the tribes around Yahweh and his covenant; it is the bond that separates them from the other nations and links them to the Lord. The union of the tribes has God for its focus, and a like adherence to his word as its means.

We must add that the word of God, which links the sister tribes to one another, is also the center in which the whole legislation of Israel comes together and is unified: the legislation of the Decalogue, that of the cultic laws which regulated the offering of firstlings and first fruits as well as the ancient agrarian festivals, and that of the customs which regulated social life. In this connection the following comparison may be made: Just as "at Shechem the Lord Yahweh, who had revealed himself at Sinai, became the God of all the tribes of Israel,"[27] which met there "before God" (Josh. 24:1), so too at Shechem all the religious, cultic, and social laws of the twelve tibes met "before God" and became part of the "book of the law of God" (Josh. 24:6). This fact is extremely important for the customs recorded in the Covenant Code (whatever be the hypotheses enter-tained about their Mosaic or Shechemite origin, and whatever be their similarities with Canaanite laws [28]).

In Israel, "every establishment of regulations between men is first and foremost an agreement reached with God." [29] Through these regulations God spells out his universal lordship over the many areas, however humble, of man's life. The transcendent God of Sinai, whom man may not look upon and continue to live (Exod. 20:19), looks with tender love upon men and their daily affairs, their troubles and their petty concerns. The Covenant Code shows that he is interested even in the fate of animals and the fallow land; he speaks of the ass's foal that has broken its paw, the sheep that browse in a field or a vineyard, the ill-tempered bull that may gore someone, the ox that has gone astray and must be led back to its owner, the donkey that sinks under its load and must be helped, the olive grove and the vine that must be allowed to rest every seventh year. He speaks also of love and marriage, and is concerned with the fate of the young girl who has been seduced, the widow, the orphan, the foreigner, and the poor man's cloak that has been taken as a pledge. He anticipates cases of uncovered cisterns, thefts of cattle, loans of money. [30]

Never was any baal concerned to such an extent with those who worshiped him. Yahweh, the transcendent God, is also the God closest to his people: "What great nation is there that has gods so close to it as the Lord, our God, is to us?" (Deut. 4:7).

III. GOD RENEWS THE COVENANT WITH HIS PEOPLE

The climax of the Shechem celebration was the renewal of the covenant. Unfortunately, the sources at our disposal are not as accurate as we would like; scholars suspect that they project back onto the Shechem event usages proper to the time when the accounts were edited.

The account in Josh. 24:25 is the most succinct, simply relating the fact: "So Joshua made a covenant with the people that day." There is no mention of a communion meal; in all likelihood such a meal was so obviously part of such a renewal that there seemed no need to mention it. In fact, the very omission shifts the emphasis to the importance of the word as proclaimed and accepted by the people. The word alone was the necessary basis of the covenant.

Deut. 27:4-7 is detailed. The rites for the sacrifices, according to this account, had been prescribed by Moses himself: "When, moreover, you have crossed the Jordan, besides setting up on Mount Ebal these stones . . . you shall also build to the Lord, your God, an altar made of stones that no iron tool has touched. You shall make this altar of the Lord, your God, with undressed stones, and shall offer on it holocausts to the Lord, your God. You shall also sacrifice peace offerings and eat them there, making merry before the Lord, your God" (Deut. 27:4-7). In putting this command in the mouth of Moses, the Deuteronomic redactor means to say that the celebration at Shechem was fully in the tradition begun by the first legislator. He also stresses the importance of the meal, a feast of joy celebrated "before the Lord, your God."

Josh. 8:30-31 is in the same vein. The redactor evidently wishes to insist that the rite ordained by Moses was carried out in the smallest detail, with religious exactness. The redactor is a rubricist at heart and writes with evident satisfaction: "Later Joshua built an altar to the Lord, the God of Israel, on Mount Ebal, of unhewn stones on which no iron had been used, in keeping with the command to the Israelites of Moses, the servant of the Lord, as recorded in the book of the law. On this altar they offered holocausts and peace offerings to the Lord."

As at Sinai, Israel here offered both holocausts and communion sacrifices.[31] "The holocaust is above all an act of homage, expressed by a gift. Thus it becomes the perfect type of sacrifice, of homage rendered to God by the total and unreserved making over of a gift."[32] The communion sacrifice or peace offering is an offering in which part of the victim is eaten in a joyous fraternal feast held in the presence of the Lord.[33] In the holocaust Israel acknowledges that it is God's servant; in the peace offering the servant enters into communion with his Master who invites him to his own table. The covenant is sealed when the servant thus enters into a loving communion with his Master.

As a memorial of these events, Joshua set up a commemorative stone (*massebah*): "Then he took a large stone and set it up there under the oak that was in the sanctuary of the Lord. And Joshua said to all the people, 'This stone shall be our witness, for it has heard all the words which the Lord spoke to us'" (Josh. 24:26-27).[34]

As time passed, this stone was often to hear the words of the Lord to his people, and Ebal was often to echo the shout of the assembly: "The Lord [is] our God!" (Josh. 24:17, 24). For, the gathering at Shechem was especially important precisely because it was not just a solemn assembly that would never meet again; rather it initiated a tradition, that of the festival of covenant renewal.

But "renewal" must be properly understood. God renews nothing, because he has never retracted anything, but the people renews the ardor of its commitment to fidelity. Every seven years Israel would make a pilgrimage to Shechem or some other ancient sanctuary "to see the face of the Lord," hear the law proclaimed again, and renew the covenant. It may even be that the assembly described in Josh. 24 was "one of these periodic renewals, to which the presence of the aged leader lent a special significance which the redactor has tried to bring out."[35] The text of Josh. 24 may be regarded as "the 'foundation charter' of the ancient Israelite Yahweh amphictyony."[36] In any case, the Deuteronomist bears witness to this especially solemn festival of the covenant when he writes:

> On the feast of Booths, at the prescribed time in the year of relaxation which comes at the end of every seven-year period, when all Israel goes to appear before the Lord, your God, in the place which he chooses, you shall read this law aloud in the presence of all Israel. Assemble the people — men, women and children, as well as the aliens who live in your communities — that they may hear it and learn it, and so fear the Lord, your God, and carefully observe all the words of this law. Their children also, who do not know it yet, must hear it and learn it (Deut. 31:10-13).[37]

By means of this septennial celebration of the covenant, each generation was spiritually called to the assembly at Shechem, made the pilgrimage to Sinai with Joshua, made the covenant a living present reality for itself, and encountered its God anew. Whatever the misdeeds of Israel and whatever the sins that burdened it on its journey, its history unfolded solemnly "before the Lord." The Deuteronomist sums up in admirable fashion this universal presence of the covenant God to each new generation when he says: "The Lord, our God, made a covenant with us at Horeb; not with our fathers [alone] did he make this covenant, but with us, *all of us* who are alive here *this day*" (Deut. 5:3).[38]

CONCLUSION

In what respect does Shechem represent an advance over Sinai? The assembly over which Joshua presided was not only the first that, according to the tradition, effectively brought the twelve tribes together (as we pointed out above); it was also the first to be celebrated in the Promised Land. Thus it equivalently says that the Church of the children of Israel now possesses the "land" as its inheritance. The word which had called Israel out of Egypt now gives it, as part of the covenant, the country of Canaan. In setting up the altar of sacrifice, Joshua accomplishes for the whole people what Jacob had prophetically anticipated in buying a field at Shechem and building an altar there to "El, the God of Israel" (Gen. 33:19-20). Joshua is saying that the whole community now possesses this holy land over which the Lord rules.

The chosen people must still discover, on its long journey toward the New Testament, that this holy land in its fullest and most transcendent form is the heaven of Jesus Christ and that this paradise of God will not be conquered by the armies of Joshua but by the Church of the poor and the meek, of whom the Lord will say: "Blest are the lowly: they shall inherit the land" (Matthew 5:5).

[1] On the assembly of Shechem, cf. M. Noth, *Das System der Zwölf Stämme Israels* (Stuttgart, 1930); A. Alt, "Die Wallfahrt von Sichem nach Bethel," in his *Kleine Schriften zur Geschichte des Volkes Israel* 1 (Munich, 1953), pp. 79–88; G. Mendenhall, *Law and Covenant in Israel and the Ancient Near East* (Pittsburgh, 1955), pp. 41–44; J. L'Hour "L'Alliance de Sichem," *Revue Biblique* 69 (1962) pp. 5–36, 161–84, 360–68; D. J. McCarthy, *Treaty and Covenant: A Study in Form in the Ancient Oriental Documents and in the Old Testament* (Analecta Biblica 21; Rome, 1963), pp. 145–49; H.-J. Kraus, *Worship in Israel*, pp. 134–46; R. de Vaux, *Histoire ancienne d'Israël* 1:610–14.

[2] Gen. 12:6 observes that "the Canaanites were then in the land [i.e., in the time of Abraham]." On Shechem, cf. R. de Vaux, *Ancient Israel*, pp. 289–91.

[3] Cf. Judg. 9:37: "Diviners' Oak" (Elon Meonenim).

[4] Gen. 12:6-7 (Yahwist tradition; cf. M. Noth, *Überlieferungsgeschichte des Pentateuch*, p. 29).

[5] Cf. Gen. 35:2–4.

[6] Cf. Josh. 24:32 (Elohist tradition; cf. M. Noth, *op. cit.*, p. 38).

[7] Deut. 27:1–26. On this passage, cf. J. L'Hour, *art. cit.*, pp. 161–78; P. Buis and J. Leclercq, *Le Deutéronome*, pp. 171–75.

[8] On Deut. 11:29–31, cf. J. L'Hour, *art. cit.*, pp. 166–68; P. Buis and J. Leclercq, *op. cit.*, pp. 97–98. On Josh. 8:30–35, cf. J. L'Hour, *art. cit.*, pp. 178–82.

[9] Verse 1b of chapter 24 is a borrowing from Josh. 23:2: "He [Joshua] summoned all Israel (including their elders, leaders, judges and officers)."

[10] Cf. A. Alt, "Die Wallfahrt von Sichem nach Bethel," *Kleine Schriften* 1:191–92.

[11] On Josh. 24:14, cf. L. Desrousseaux, *La crainte de Dieu dans l'Ancien Testament* (Lectio divina 63; Paris, 1970), pp. 182–92.

[12] G. von Rad, *Old Testatament Theology* 1:16. Cf. A. Gelin: "an amphictyony is a religious grouping of people around a common sanctuary" (*Josué*, in Pirot-Clamer, *La Sainte Bible* 3 [Paris, 1935], p. 57). Cf. also R. de Vaux, *Ancient Israel*, pp. 92–93: "At Shechem the twelve . . . took counsel together."

[13] Josh. 24:2–13. The underlying material for this historical conspectus seems to be

very old, but the literary reworking is evident (cf. J. L'Hour, *art. cit.*, pp. 24–25): verse 5b is clumsily connected with verse 6 ("So I brought you out of it. I brought your ancestors out of Egypt": JB), betraying a redactional addition; in verse 7 the redactor seems to forget that in the text before him God is speaking, and makes him say: "They [the Israelites] cried out to the Lord"; verse 10 depends on Deut. 23:5-6; verse 11a reflects Josh. 3:10, and verse 12a, Exod. 23:27ff.; verse 12b is a gloss.

[14] The text summarizes Deut. 6:10-13.

[15] For source criticism, cf. J. L'Hour, *art. cit.*, pp. 27–28.

[16] The text of Deut. 27 in its present state shows no redactional unity. Cf. J. L'Hour, *art. cit.*, pp. 161ff. A. Clamer writes: "Attempts to reconstruct an original text are purely conjectural; what may be suggested as probable is that ancient elements which are authentic echoes of the events leading up to the renewal of the covenant were supplemented by newer elements, undoubtedly of liturgical origin, with little concern for adapting them satisfactorily to their context" (*Le Deutéronome*, in Pirot-Clamer, *La Sainte Bible* 2 [Paris, 1946], p. 685). For the localization of the celebration, cf. P. Antoine, "Gerizim," *DBS* 3:537–41.

[17] Cf. Deut. 27:12-13.

[18] On the Shechem Dodecalogue, cf. A. Alt, "The Origins of Israelite Law," in *Essays on Old Testament History and Religion*, pp. 147–49. In discussing non-biblical covenant treaties, J. L'Hour observes: "There is a striking preponderance of curses over blessings; this characteristic will be found in the Bible as well" (*art. cit.*, p. 9).

[19] The final curse, in Deuteronomic style, is an addition at a more recent redactional stage.

[20] "We may at least surmise that it [this list] is as old as the Decalogue" (P. Buis and J. Leclercq, *Le Deutéronome*, p. 173).

[21] The law of God is changeless and eternal, but man's knowledge of it may be partial and progressive. Cf. R. Maritain, *Histoire d'Abraham* (Paris, 1947).

[22] It is true that Deut. 27:14 attributes the proclamation to the Levites: "The Levites shall proclaim aloud to all the men of Israel." But this verse is a late addition to the original text: "The redactor in recording the curses of Deut. 27:15-26 put them in the mouth of those who would most likely exercise such a role in his own day" (J. L'Hour, *art. cit.*, p. 169).

[23] Cf. Exod. 24:3: "Moses came to the people and related all the words and ordinances of the Lord." These last terms refer to both the "ten words," i.e., the Decalogue, and the Covenant Code.

[24] The Code contains a number of laws that apply to a nomadic society (note the importance given to flocks, which are the chief resource of nomads, and the serious penalties for the stealing of animals; see, for example, Exod. 21:37, which requires a thief to make four- or fivefold restitution). But the Code also contains legislation that presupposes some settled communities; it speaks, for example, of a "house" (not a tent) with walls that can be broken through, of doorposts and shutters (cf. Exod. 21:6; 22:1); it also speaks of cisterns and wells, fields and vineyards. All this supposes a degree of settling down that is incompatible with nomad life in the desert and steppe of Sinai.

[25] The only condition Deut. 4:12-13 and 5:2-22 give for the Covenant is the observance of the Decalogue, not of all the laws contained in the "Covenant Code."

[26] R. de Vaux, *Ancient Israel*, p. 143, writes: "We cannot be certain that the Code of the Covenant, in the form in which it has come down to us, is the actual law promulgated by Josue at Shechem, but we can say that internal evidence and the witness of tradition agree in dating this Code from the early days of the settlement in Canaan, before the organization of the State. It is the law of the tribal federation." We may add that the exegetes have found literary contacts between the Covenant Code and the Shechemite texts. In concluding his study of these contacts (*Revue Biblique* 69 [1962] pp. 350–61), J. L'Hour says: "All these elements in Deut. 27 and Exod. 24:3-8 have their origin in the covenant reported in Josh. 24. Since, moreover,

Exod. 24:3-8 is inseparable from the Covenant Code, we may say that the whole of Exod. 20:24-23:9 is to be identified with the 'law' of Josh. 24:25" (p. 361).

[27] G. Auzou, *La don d'une conquête: Etude du Livre de Josué* (Paris, 1964), p. 184.

[28] Cf., e.g., F. Michaeli, *Textes de la Bible et de l'Ancien Orient* (Cahiers d'Archéologie 13; Neuchâtel, 1961), pp. 91–96.

[29] J. L'Hour, *art. cit.*, p. 364.

[30] All these examples are taken from Exod. 21–23.

[31] Cf. Exod. 24:5.

[32] R. de Vaux, *Studies in Old Testament Sacrifice*, p. 37.

[33] Cf. Deut. 12:7 JB: "You will eat in the presence of Yahweh your God and be thankful for all that your hands have presented."

[34] The clause "that was in the sanctuary of the Lord" was added to the original account at a later date.

[35] A. Gelin, *Josué*, in Pirot-Clamer, *La Sainte Bible* 3, p. 132. T. Robinson justly observes that the conquest of Shechem could have been undertaken only after other areas of Canaan had been occupied; this indicates that the liturgy in Josh. 24 did not take place immediately after the entry into Palestine (*A History of Israel* 1 [Oxford, 1932], p. 125).

[36] H.-J. Kraus, *Worship in Israel*, p. 137. But see the restrictions suggested by W.H. Lerwin, "Le sanctuaire central avant l'éstablissement de la monarchie," *Revue Biblique* 72 (1965) pp. 161–84, against the theory of an amphictyony and against Shechem as a central sanctuary. In this connection we note that at Shechem there was a sanctuary of Baal Berit, i.e., Baal of the Covenant (cf. Judg. 9:4, 46). Israel's tradition seems, therefore, here as elsewhere, to have taken over a Canaanite tradition and purified it in the light of the Yahwist faith.

[37] Deuteronomy attributes this law to Moses himself, who is supposed here to give it to Joshua (attribution to Moses was a way of emphasizing the importance of the law). On the festival of the covenant, cf. G. von Rad, *Old Testament Theology* 1:193; A. Alt, *Kleine Schriften* 1:70–71; H.-J. Kraus, *op. cit.*, pp. 140–41.

[38] A. Arens, *Die Psalmen im Gottesdienst des Alten Bundes* (Trier, 1961), speaks in this connection of "the actualization of the original assembly."

[39] Cf. M. Noth, *History of Israel*, pp. 92–93.

Chapter 3

THE ASSEMBLY OF JOSIAH
(622 B.C.)

INTRODUCTION

The establishment of the monarchy and its religious significance

In holy convocation after holy convocation the "Church" of the children of Israel deepened and strengthened its unity.

Six centuries separated the assembly at Shechem, with Joshua at its head, from the assembly at Jerusalem, over which King Josiah presided. The decisive event which brought magnificence and great joy to the people of God on their long journey, but which often also marred that journey with bloodshed and tears, was the establishment of the monarchy in behalf of the Davidic dynasty at the beginning of the first millennium.

After the period of the Judges (ca. 1200–1025) and within the framework provided by the Israelite amphictyony, a kingship not in the service of the covenant was inconceivable. It was really the covenant that bound the tribes together; it was the covenant that gave a face and a soul to the amorphous confederation of tribes; it was also the covenant that made possible the more or less peaceful annexation of the indigenous peoples, the exorcising of their sanctuaries and pilgrimages, and the subjection of their baals to Yahweh; it was the covenant, finally, that transformed the human kingship of David's house into a stage in a messianic, divine history.

It is with this in mind that one scholar speaks of "identifying covenant with kingship; that is, the monarchy became responsible for the covenant and was judged in the light of it."[1] Before being made king, David was, depending on the circumstances of the moment, simply the leader of a troop in Saul's pay, an outlaw whose followers were rebels or insolvent debtors, or a sheikh who raided the Negeb in the service of the Philistines who had set him up as "king" in Ziklag.[2] But once he had been anointed king of Israel, the Lord entrusted the covenant and its blessings to him. The former trooper became "son" of God according to the royal charter contained in Nathan's prophecy: "I will be a father to him, and he shall be a son to me" (2 Sam. 7:14).[3] God spoke over him the following enthronement formula: "I myself have set up my king on Zion, my holy mountain. . . . You are my son; this day I have begotten you" (Ps. 2:6-7).[4]

The throne of David thus became "the Lord's royal throne over Israel" (1 Chron. 28:5), and the king himself was covered to a degree with the mantle of God's own glory. According to the Psalms,[5] he is fairest in beauty of the sons of men; grace is poured out on his lips, and the fragrance of myrrh and aloes permeates his garments. He terrifies his enemies; his sharp arrows pierce his enemies, who bite the dust, and his club crushes their skulls. But to the weak and poor he is a "savior," a man of tender compassion; he ransoms the humble man who calls out to him, and the lowly Israelite who is helpless. Throughout his life justice will flourish; the mountains and hills shall yield peace for his people. His name will be held in veneration through the ages, as long as the sun shines in the heavens. His coming marks the beginning of an era of everlasting prosperity and plenty — even on the mountaintops men shall harvest grain!

In such panegyrics as these, there is undoubtedly a strong element of Oriental hyperbole and court rhetoric.[6] Yet someday the texts would be applied with total truth, when the kingship first held by David reached its divine climax in Jesus Christ. As J. Steinmann has observed with good reason: "The divine sonship of the king, his priesthood, his role as supreme judge, his universal victory over the world, and his unending life were all a preparation for the major statements of messianic theology. The hyperbolic descriptions of the royal Psalms will serve as framework for the formulations of Christ-ology."[7]

The monarchy meant the establishment of a new capital that would replace the old sanctuaries and put an end to activities there. David chose Jerusalem.[8] At the time, the city was only a Jebusite citadel of modest size. A daring surprise attack carried out by a handful of crafty mercenaries gave the king control of the place. The important village had no biblical past and therefore no claims;

moreover, it had ever remained untouched by Yahwist traditions, and its Canaanite past made it, on the contrary, a rather suspect place. But precisely because it had been "neutral"[9] in the disputes that had formerly pitted the old sanctuaries against each other, Jerusalem could now become the center for them all. In addition, its geographical location was admirable for this purpose, since it could serve as point of juncture between the northern and southern tribes. David turned the modest citadel into a proud fortress. From this point on, Jerusalem became part of religious history and would be the spiritual capital of mankind to the end ot time.[10]

In order to give the royal city an aura of sacredness, David had the ark of the covenant brought there.[11] The move was a clever one, and further evidence of David's shrewdness. In addition to being the political capital of the realm, the city thus became the religious center of Yahwism, since the ark, which was the object of such intense veneration, was the common possession of the twelve tribes. To it were attached the most splendid memories of the past; the thought of it filled the heart of all Israel with tender love, as it had the heart of the aged Eli.[12] During the Exodus it had accompanied the people during their desert journeyings;[13] it had come to their aid during the period of the Judges, it had been venerated in the old sanctuaries,[14] and it had been the visible sign of God's presence among his followers.[15] In olden times, when the ark came to a halt the people sang: "Return, O Lord, you who ride upon the clouds, to the troops of Israel" (Num. 10:36). Now the multitudes beyond counting came to visit it and found in Jerusalem the center of their faith. It would be left for Solomon to build the Temple, the holiest part of which would house the ark of God (1 Kings 6:19).

All these events brought into existence a new order of things in Israel. After the austere years of the Exodus and after the bitter period when Canaan was conquered, Israel's ideal in the "good old days" of the Judges had been for men to enjoy this land flowing with milk and honey, in the peaceful surroundings of family and clan. Yahweh's blessing was that each individual should live in peace beneath his own fig tree, possess his own vineyard and olive grove, love his wife, who would be beautiful as a doe and fruitful as a vine,[16] and find happiness in children that were like olive plants around his table.[17] With a smile of delight the Deuteronomist redactor sums up the ideal thus:

> As your reward for heeding these decrees and observing them care-
> fully, the Lord, your God, will keep with you the merciful covenant

which he promised on oath to your fathers. He will love and bless and multiply you; he will bless the fruit of your womb and the produce of your soil, your grain and wine and oil, the issue of your herds and the young of your flocks, in the land which he swore to your fathers he would give you. You will be blessed above all peoples; no man or woman among you shall be childless nor shall your livestock be barren (Deut. 7:12-14).

Could piety and well-being be more pleasurably united?

With the coming of the monarchy, this dream of simple peace and happiness became a thing of the past. The "modern age" began and Israel became like the other nations.[18] The kingdom seemed already powerful, and the ideal now accepted was to make it even more powerful. It had conquered its enemies; the ideal now was to look for new enemies and to take their territory from them. The Davidic dynasty ruled the people completely, and the people were bound to their king in their inmost thoughts and in even the most spontaneous expressions of their piety. In return, the royal family opened its own history to the knowledge and participation of the people. Even the most insignificant or intimate matters, including bickerings in the harem and rivalries between courtesans, became state business. Never had the covenant seemed more closely linked with the history of Israel; never had God seemed so close to his people.

If kingship had been exercised in fidelity to the covenant, it could have meant the progress of the people as a whole toward peace and happiness; the doors of history would have opened before them. Unfortunately, the experience of kingship meant blood and sorrow for the people.

The accession of Solomon to David's throne seemed for a moment to give the lie to pessimistic forecasts. The Chronicler is enthusiastic:

Thereafter Solomon sat on the throne of the Lord as king in place of his father David; he prospered, and all Israel obeyed him. All the leaders and warriors, and also all the other sons of King David, swore allegiance to King Solomon. And the Lord exalted Solomon greatly in the eyes of all Israel, giving him a glorious reign such as had not been enjoyed by any king over Israel before him (1 Chron. 29:23-25).

But the hopes or dreams of the royal archivists were one thing; the harsh realities of history were something quite different. The indecent ostentation at the court could not hide the inner weakness of the kingdom. The many taxes and hours of forced labor, as well as the idolatry imported by the countless foreign women in the royal harem and installed on "the mountain of scandal," made the gov-

ernment a disappointment to the people and hateful in God's eyes.
No one could with impunity play pharaoh in a realm consecrated to
Yahweh.

Immediately after Solomon's death the kingdom fell apart. The
northern kingdom made Samaria its capital,[19] while the southern
kingdom retained Jerusalem. In 721 the Assyrians took Samaria and
deported its inhabitants; in 587 it was Jerusalem's turn. The reform
of Josiah took place in the interval, around 622.

I. GOD CALLS AND GATHERS HIS PEOPLE

1. The reform of Josiah

Under Tiglath-Pileser III (745–727), Assyria reached the pinnacle
of its power. It was to remain there for more than half a century,
especially under Salmanasar V (726–722), Sargon II (721–705),
Sennacherib (704–681), Esarhaddon (680–669), and Ashurbanipal
(668–621). The "lion of Ashur" held in its claws an immense realm
extending from the Persian Gulf to the Mediterranean, and its slash-
ing blows left a trail of blood as far as Thebes. But this colossal
empire, held together as it was only by bloodshed, contained the
seeds of its own downfall and tended irreversibly toward destruction. By about the middle of the seventh century, Egypt had at the
practical level regained its independence. In 652, Shamash Shuru-
kin, king of Babylon, rebelled against Ashur and involved the Elamites and Arameans in his revolt; it took the Assyrian armies four
years and countless atrocities to put down the rebellion, but the
victory exhuasted their strength. The Medes and Persians were
threatening the eastern frontier, and the Scythians the northern.
The death of Ashurbanipal (around 626) began the rush for spoils
and revenge. The conquered peoples turned and attacked the lair of
the lion who formerly had "snatched enough for his cubs, and
strangled for his lionesses; . . . filled his dens with prey and his
caves with plunder" (Nahum 2:13).

Nineveh, the royal city, which had been so proud of the incomparable library of Ashurbanipal, fell in 612, and the prophet Nahum
painted a grim picture of the destruction of this city "fair and charming, a mistress of witchcraft, who enslaved nations with her harlot-
ries, and peoples by her witchcraft" (Nahum 3:4).

All these conflicts between the great powers must have seemed
"providential" to the tiny Jewish people, and the fall of tyrants
elicited from them only cries of gladness. The collapse of the "pa-

gan" kingdoms seemed to herald the hour when the kingdom of Yahweh would be restored in the holy land. To this restoration Josiah (640–609) devoted all his spiritual energies and all his political skill. It was due to him, "the most important king to rule over Israel after David, that the kingdom once again attained a unity and position of power such as it had not experienced since the days of his royal ancestor."[20] The old kingdom was thus to be re-established, and Yahweh would gather in it all the dispersed children of Israel. To Josiah God entrusted the task of making the Deuteronomic ideal a reality: one people, one faith, one land.

Josiah began with the most urgent task, that of interior conversion. He had the splendid idea, surely a divine inspiration, of beginning with himself. His encounter with Yahweh was the great event of his life. "In the eighth year of his reign, while he was still a youth, he began to seek after the God of his forefather David" (2 Chron. 34:3).[21]

It was a passionate quest, and one that had immediate repercussions at the political level. From 627 on, Josiah took the bold resolution of refusing further tribute to Nineveh. By doing so, he rejected allegiance not only to Ashurbanipal but also to the Assyrian gods who were thought to protect the king of Ashur as their "son" and to rule over the territories he had conquered. Josiah's action was at the same time a claim that Yahweh was sovereign Lord even over the rascals of the Assyrian pantheon. Ashurbanipal was forced to react to such a sacrilegious insult, but he did not stir. Was it strength that he lacked, or time? Josiah defied the Assyrian garrisons, which seemed unable to shake off their lethargy, and began to win back for Yahweh the northern cities in the land of Samaria.[22] Each city retaken was a victory for national unity.

The Assyrian occupation had badly tarnished the purity of the Yahwist faith. The countryside was alive with idols; in fact, according to Jeremiah, there were as many gods as there were cities in Judah and as many baals as there were alleyways in Jerusalem.[23] Popular piety had established a kind of peaceful coexistence between the true God and the idols of a family or locality. Yahweh was acknowledged as supreme in principle and was invoked on great occasions as the national God. But for the small affairs of life and for shadier bits of business, people counted on the complacent help of the mongrel gods. Impious Ahaz voiced the thoughts of many when he said: "Since it was the gods of the kings of Aram who helped them, I will sacrifice to them that they may help me also" (2 Chron.

28:23). We need hardly add that priests of every kind swarmed in these numerous sanctuaries and gained a profitable living by exploiting the piety of the people.

Josiah had his hands full in trying to purify the land that belonged to Yahweh, but he took the right steps:

> He began to purge Judah and Jerusalem of the high places, the sacred poles[24] and the carved and molten images. In his presence, the altars of the Baals were destroyed; the incense stands erected above them were torn down; the sacred poles and the carved and molten images were shattered and beaten into dust, which was strewn over the tombs of those who had sacrificed to them (2 Chron. 34:3-4).[25]

The reform, begun at Jerusalem, soon spread like an oil slick to "the cities of Manasseh, Ephraim, Simeon, and in the ruined villages of the surrounding country as far as Naphtali" (2 Chron. 34:6).[26] To condemn the places of idolatrous worship and prevent (in theory at least) a return to the forbidden practices, the king had the bones of the pagan priests burned on the altars (2 Chron. 34:5).

There remained the task of cleansing and renewing the very heart of Jerusalem, namely, the Temple. It was greatly in need of such a cleansing, for the wave of paganism that had swept over Judah had turned the Temple into an Assyrian emporium and a place where prostitutes swarmed. The king ordered the sanctuary cleared of the all the objects "that had been made for Baal, Asherah, and the whole host of heaven" which vied for the idolatrous service of the people (2 Kings 23:5).

> He also put an end to the pseudo-priests whom the kings of Judah had appointed to burn incense on the high places in the cities of Judah and in the vicinity of Jerusalem, as well as those who burned incense to Baal, to the sun, moon, and signs of the zodiac, and to the whole host of heaven. . . . He tore down the apartments of the cult prostitutes which were in the temple of the Lord, and in which the women wove garments for the Asherah. . . . He did away with the horses which the kings of Judah had dedicated to the sun; these were at the entrance of the temple of the Lord, near the chamber of Nathanmelech the eunuch, which was in the large building. The chariots of the sun he destroyed by fire. He also demolished the altars made by the kings of Judah on the roof (the roof terrace of Ahaz), and the altars made by Manasseh in the two courts of the temple of the Lord. He pulverized them and threw the dust into the Kidron Valley. The king defiled the high places east of Jerusalem, south of the Mount of Misconduct, which Solomon, king of Israel, had built in honor of Astarte, the Sidonian horror, of Chemosh, the Moabite horror, and of Milcom, the idol of the Ammonites (2 Kings 23:5-13).[27]

All the cult objects spoken of here were imported from abroad. Consequently, in expelling the pagan gods from the national sanctuary, Josiah was proclaiming in a violent way that the period of Assyrian overlordship was definitively past and that Yahweh was reclaiming his rights in his Dwelling and eliminating foreigners from his realm.

2. *The discovery of the "Book of the Law"*

As a fitting climax to his work of national healing, the king undertook the restoration of the Temple. It was the spring of 622, and the work of restoration had begun. There then occurred an event of such importance that it would be the basis of all future reforms and would have a decisive influence on Israelite and even on Christian piety: the discovery of the "Book of the Law of the Lord," that is, of Deuteronomy.[28] Josiah had sent his secretary, Shaphan, to Hilkiah the high priest with instructions. When Shaphan reached the Temple, Hilkiah told him: "'I have found the book of the law in the temple of the Lord.' Hilkiah gave the book to Shaphan, who read it. Then the scribe Shaphan went to the king and . . . informed the king that the priest Hilkiah had given him a book, and then read it aloud to the king" (2 Kings 22:8-10).

How could the "book of the law of the Lord" have gotten lost in the garrets or cellars of the Temple? We do not know. One hypothesis is that since "a number of legislative dispositions in the Book of Deuteronomy as we now have it could have been conceived and formulated only in the northern kingdom,"[29] the real place of origin of Deuteronomy — at least in its primitive form — is to be looked for, not at Jerusalem or in Judah, but among the scribes of the northern kingdom. Now, as a matter of fact, Hezekiah, king of Judah (d. 687), made it a point to collect the early traditions[30] among which the literary heritage of the northern kingdom had a special place. This work of assemblage was all the more urgent, since Samaria had just fallen into the hands of the invaders (721) and its population had been deported. It may be, then, that a Levite from Ephraim, perhaps a disciple of Hosea, fled the enemy, took refuge in Jerusalem, and stored in the Temple the religious charter of the Samaritan sanctuary to which he had belonged. On the basis of these Levitical documents from the north, a scribe may then have composed the "book of the law of the Lord."

What was Josiah's reaction when he heard what Shaphan read to him? He was overwhelmed: "When the king heard the words of the

law, he tore his garments" (2 Chron. 34:19). For, in order to stimulate the people to obedience, the author of the book not only gave an
attractive picture of great blessings but also brandished the weapon
of curses.[31] These included plague, fever, malaria, boils, tumors,
madness, blindness, drought, blight, weeds, locusts, wars, defeats,
deportations, and the destruction of the kingdom.[32] No scourge was
too severe should Israel prove unfaithful. And now it had deserved
all these punishments many times over! The nation seemed
doomed, the throne on the verge of collapse. The only question to
be answered was why punishment had been deferred. Perhaps the
threats were conditional? Or perhaps the "book of the law" was a
forgery? Had it been concealed in the Temple by a priest, even by
Hilkiah himself, in order to stimulate, or sustain the momentum of,
religious reform?[33] After all, only yesterday no one had known anything about the book!

To set things straight, therefore, the king ordered the high priest
and others: "Go, consult the Lord for me, for the people, for all
Judah, about the stipulations of this book that has been found, for
the anger of the Lord has been set furiously ablaze against us,
because our fathers did not obey the stipulations of this book, nor
fulfill our written obligations" (2 Kings 22:13).

To consult Yahweh meant to approach one of his prophets. Why
did they not go to Jeremiah? Was it perhaps that he had just begun
his ministry and that his background did not give him access to the
court at this time? Was it perhaps, too, that people were somewhat
leery of him? He could be a difficult man, and though he was mild
and tender-hearted, he also felt terrible rages against "rebel Israel"
and "traitorous Judah" (Jer. 3:11).[34] Moreover, at this period he
specialized in prophecies of catastrophe in which cities were put to
the torch and and corpses lay in heaps. In any event, the men sent
by the king preferred to approach a prophetess, thinking perhaps
that a woman would have pity on the king and on the women and
children. "So Hilkiah the priest, Ahikam, Achbor, Shaphan, and
Asaiah betook themselves to the Second Quarter in Jerusalem,
where the prophetess Huldah resided. She was the wife of Shallum,
son of Tikvah, son of Harhas, keeper of the wardrobe" (2 Kings
22:14).[35] Her answer sounded the knell of their hopes:

> The Lord says: I am prepared to bring evil upon this place and upon
> its inhabitants, all the curses written in the book that has been read
> before the king of Judah. Because they have abandoned me and have
> offered incense to other gods, provoking me by every deed that they

have performed, my anger is ablaze against this place and cannot be extinguished.

But to the king of Judah who sent you to consult the Lord, give this response: "Thus says the Lord, the God of Israel, concerning the threats you have heard. Because you were heartsick and have humbled yourself before God on hearing his words spoken against this place and its inhabitants, because you have humbled yourself before me, have torn your garments, and have wept before me, I in turn have listened — so declared the Lord. I will gather you to your ancestors and you shall be taken to your grave in peace. Your eyes shall not see all the evil I will bring upon this place and upon its inhabitants" (2 Chron. 34:24-28).[36]

God thus gave his definitive approval to the book that had been found in the junkrooms of the Temple, and he told them his word had been unconditional: his anger "cannot be extinguished." The only promise he would make concerned the king himself: Because of his personal piety, the king would live out his days in peace and have a fitting funeral. All in all, the reign of this most pious of the kings of Israel would in the last analysis be simply a short moment of peace in the midst of bloodshed and tears, a ship moving peacefully across the waters of despair.

What was to be done? Josiah tried to be artful with God. But was that possible? Yes — and even easy! Yahweh was, after all, a God of tender compassion, slow to anger and full of love. Had he not promised fidelity to uncounted generations of those who should love him and keep his commandments?[37] He was therefore to be taken at his word, and the conversion of the mass of the people would force his compassionate love to get the best of his anger. If he had spared the king, why should he not also have mercy on the people? Over a century before, the prophet Micah had foretold that the kingdom was on its way to destruction, that every house in Jerusalem would be razed, and that Zion would become a plowed field.[38] Yet thus far nothing of all this had happened; the prophecy seemed to have been negated by history, or at least its fulfillment had been deferred; perhaps it would be deferred for still another hundred years, perhaps even permanently.

In any event, the people had to be gathered together as quickly as possible to hear "the book of the law of the Lord," and the national conversion must be begun. "The king now convened all the elders of Judah and Jerusalem. He went up to the house of the Lord with all the men of Judah and the inhabitants of Jerusalem, the Levites, and all the people, great and small" (2 Chron. 34:29-30).[39]

Thus God used the king to gather his people once again; once again, as he had done at Sinai through Moses and at Shechem through Joshua, he established the "church" of the children of Israel. By mysterious paths which he had traced in the tangled underbrush of history, God brought his people to hear his word.

II. GOD GIVES HIS LAW TO HIS PEOPLE

Josiah embodied the ideals both of David and of Moses. As a new David he had made the royal throne the center of a restored national unity, after this unity had been undermined by the infidelity of the people and the armies of Assyria. Now it was his turn to be the new Moses and proclaim the law of God: "He had read aloud to them [all the people] the entire text of the book of the covenant that had been found in the house of the Lord" (2 Chron. 34:30).[40]

Almost all scholars accept that this "book of the covenant" is Deuteronomy, or at least a very old form of the latter.[41] The Book of Deuteronomy, according to its own testimony, is "torah," or law, or "book of the torah."[42] How did Josiah and those who listened to the reading understand this "law"?

Deuteronomy takes the form of a series of addresses which Moses delivered just before his death, while the people were living in the plains of Moab.[43] When he conversed face to face with the Lord on Mount Sinai (which Deuteronomy prefers to call Mount Horeb), the lawgiver of the covenant received from God not only the Decalogue but "all the commandments, the statutes and decrees" (Deut. 5:31). It is this wide-ranging expression of the divine will that Moses transmits to the people as they make ready to enter the Promised Land.

In the discourses of Deuteronomy we find an echo of the sermons given to the people by the Levites in the old sanctuaries of the north at the festival of covenant renewal.[44] The epic story that began with the Exodus did not come to an end with the entry into Canaan, an event now vanished in the mists of time the way a watercourse vanishes in the desert. Far from it, for the covenant which Moses entered into was "eternal," in the sense that the love of Yahweh for his people would persist through the coming centuries and the future generations. Each new generation was invited to take part in the dialogue at Mount Sinai and to become "today" God's people.[45] When the covenant was renewed every seventh year[46] in a liturgical celebration which recalled the procedure at Mount Sinai, the Levites proclaimed the ever-present word of God. They commented on it, adapted it to the new circumstances of a new time, and made it topical for the benefit of new hearers — in short, they preached a homily on it.

Since the traditions concerning the Exodus had for practical purposes not evolved at all between the tenth and the seventh centuries, yet had retained a certain malleability, the Deuteronomistic preachers could easily adapt them to the patterned discourses they wished to give. Around the central theme of the covenant at Horeb these preachers grouped very old and very divergent sacral and juridical traditions. The Book of Deuteronomy ends up as a mosiac of sermons in which all lines converge on the central fact of the covenant. The book may also be compared to an immense stained-glass cathedral window in which the colors are filled with joyous life when the rays of the sun — the covenant — pass through them.

In this window, with its flamboyant colors, Josiah and his people saw their own history set out before them. The essential lines of that history were very simple. Although Israel was "really the smallest of all nations" (Deut. 7:7), it had as its own the greatest of all the gods, the God who rose infinitely above all the others and ruled them all with his eternal power. He was Yahweh, "the God of gods, the Lord of lords, the great God, mighty and awesome" (Deut. 10:17). He chose Israel from among the nations, saved her with powerful hand and outstretched arm, snatched her from the grasp of Pharaoh, and brought her out of the slave camps of Egypt.[47]

Because of the promise given to the ancestors and the covenant concluded with them and renewed first at Horeb and then in the plains of Moab, Israel became the sacred possession of God: "You are a people sacred to the Lord, your God; he has chosen you from all the nations on the face of the earth to be a people peculiarly his own" (Deut. 7:6).[48] As a result, the phrases "the Lord, your [singular] God" and "the Lord, your [plural] God" recur like a tireless refrain throughout this lengthy hymn in praise of the God who loves and saves his people ("the Lord, your God, . . . loves you": Deut. 23:6; cf. 7:8).[49]

Deuteronomy insists that the covenant was made with the whole people, not with a ruling oligarchy or even with the tribes, still less with the king. In making this point, Deuteronomy simplifies the evidence of history, passes over the differences that once set the tribes apart from each other, and minimizes the importance and role of the monarchy.[50]

Now that Israel has become God's people, she must listen to his voice. But this listening to the word is not a heavy burden, a crushing weight; it is rather a delightful food for the soul,[51] a radiant light for the eyes. It is a blessed duty which Israel must fulfill at each stage of its history, in the "today" of God: "This day you have become the people of the Lord, your God. You shall therefore hearken to the voice of the Lord, your God" (Deut. 27:9-10).

The essential thing that the Lord utters is his summons to loving obedience: "And now, Israel, what does the Lord, your God, ask of you but to fear the Lord, your God, and follow his ways exactly, to love and serve the Lord, your God, with all your heart and all your soul, to keep the commandments and statutes of the Lord which I enjoin on you today for your own good?" (Deut. 10:12-13).

Nowhere had the law of love been so movingly formulated, nowhere had the law of the old covenant come so close to that of the new covenant. In fact, in the statement of Deuteronomy which both Josiah and Jesus proclaim, the two covenants become one: "You shall love the Lord, your God, with all your heart, and with all your soul, and with all your strength" (Deut. 6:5; cf. Matthew 22:37; Mark 12:30; Luke 10:27).

All the other precepts are intended simply as paraphrases of this first, supreme commandment. All the activities of the believer are to be motivated by this law, and the whole life of Israel is to be inspired by this "You shall love." Even trials are to be only a testing of love: "Remember how for forty years now the Lord, your God, has directed all your journeying in the desert, so as to test you by affliction and find out whether or not it was your intention to keep his commandments" (Deut. 8:2).

Never had God's word taken on such a tone of human tenderness or appeared to be so close to men:

> This command which I enjoin on you today is not too mysterious and remote for you. It is not up in the sky, that you should say, "Who will go up in the sky to get it for us and tell us of it, that we may carry it out?" Nor is it across the sea, that you should say, "Who will cross the sea to get it for us and tell us of it, that we may carry it out?" No, it is something very near to you, already in your mouths and in your hearts; you have only to carry it out (Deut. 30:11-14).

But this message that dwells with such tender love in the heart of each believer also has its rough, even violent side; it is also intransigent in its demands. This aspect becomes evident in the struggle with the Canaanite gods. The cult of the latter was a constant threat to the purity of the Yahwist faith, and a confrontation between these gods and Yahweh, the God of the desert, was inevitable, once the passage from a nomadic to a sedentary life had been made. Was it so evident, people asked, that the God of nomads in the Sinai desert should also be the God of the land of Canaan, the God who made the earth fertile and the flocks fruitful? The Canaanite cults, with their sensuality and their focus on nature, were fully adapted to the rhythms of agricultural life; in the temples of these local gods the atmosphere was that of a rural fair. Consequently, these cults were a continual temptation, while the worship of Yahweh, the God without a human face, required spiritual discipline and sacrifice. It was a struggle to the death between the all-powerful but invisible and distant God and the gods, so close to men, of life and love whose cult could be celebrated in drunkenness and unbridled sexuality.

Deuteronomy's answer to the agressive and seductive baals took two forms. One was the holy war, which Deuteronomy raises almost to the status of an institution. The military camp becomes not only "the cradle of the nation"[52] but also its school of faith. The battles and victories of the people were first and foremost the battles of Yahweh with Baal and Yahweh's victories over him. Even when the enemy was more numerous, better organized, and stronger, Israel was not to hesitate to enter battle and risk her life, for God was with her. The holy war was thus more an act of faith than a simple military operation. An important function of the priests was to preach homilies before battle:

> When you go to war against your enemies and you see horses and chariots and an army greater than your own, do not be afraid of them, for the Lord, your God, who brought you up from the land of Egypt, will be with you.
>
> When you are about to go into battle, the priest shall come forward and say to soldiers: "Hear, O Israel! Today you are going into battle against your enemies. Be not weakhearted or afraid, be neither alarmed nor frightened by them. For it is the Lord, your God, who goes with you to fight for you against your enemies and give you victory" (Deut. 20:1-3).[53]

The second part of Deuteronomy's answer is theological: Yahweh is the only God Israel is to honor; no peaceful coexistence with other cults is possible. At the very heart of Yahwism there was a basic intolerance of other divinities; in this respect it was probably a unique thing in the history of religions. Yahweh was "a consuming fire, a jealous God" (Deut. 4:24).[54] Such a total rejection of syncretism entailed the rejection also of other places of worship; the faith was one, therefore there could be but one worship in one temple.[55] The baals had many, mutually exclusive faces; they called their worshipers to countless different places of devotion; each was connected with a specific sanctuary and was its prisoner. Yahweh, on the contrary, summoned all his worshipers to a single place of worship.[56] But though he had decided on this spot as "the dwelling place for his name" (Deut. 12:11), he was not limited to a single place as the baals were. It was rather that, although the immense universe was his throne,[57] he chose that those who loved him should pay him homage at Jerusalem.

The body of Deuteronomic teaching was presented in a direct, penetrating, and easily grasped manner. As eulogists sometimes simplify the history of their hero or the legends surrounding him so that they may more easily make it the basis of edifying discourse and practical moral applications, so the Deuteronomic preachers simplified the history and theology of Israel. According to them, there were no more problems. Live according to the covenant and observe the law, and you will guarantee yourself life and happiness; disobey and you certainly condemn yourself.

> Here, then, I have today set before you life and prosperity, death and doom. If you obey the commandments of the Lord, your God, which I enjoin on you today, loving him, and walking in his ways, and keeping his commandments, statutes, and decrees, you will live and grow numerous, and the Lord, your God, will bless you in the land you are entering to occupy. If, however, you turn away your hearts and will not listen . . . you will certainly perish (Deut. 30:15-18).

All that is needed, then, is to listen to Moses and obey the laws he promulgated in the Book of Deuteronomy. Had that great prophet not been the incomparable "servant of the Lord" (Deut. 34:5) — not chiefly a violent man who could kill in a rage or smash the tablets of the Law, but first and foremost "by far the meekest man on the face of the earth" (Num. 12:3)?[58] Moreover, Israel will always be served by prophets who are the successors of Moses. If ever a prophet comes along who does not accept and proclaim everything in the book of the law, that is, in Deuteronomy, this will simply mean that he is a false prophet, and he is to be killed without hesitation.[59]

Such, in its essentials, is the tenor of the "book of the law" that was discovered in the Temple and promulgated by Josiah. By taking the form of addresses by Moses, the book was an invitation to the people to make a spiritual pilgrimage to Mount Sinai and to hear the law of God once again. Thus it connected the age of Josiah with the

Exodus period; it threw a bridge across the centuries; it stopped the clock, or, rather, it brought all times into the presence of the God of the desert. Ever since the Exodus, six centuries before, the people had become foolishly stiff-necked; they had slipped into a spirit of stubborn rebellion and allowed their uncircumcised hearts to become hardened. Deuteronomy wiped away six centuries of disobedience and introduced the people to the "today" of Sinai.

"You are all *now* standing before the Lord, your God . . . that you may enter into the covenant of the Lord, your God, which he concluded with you *today* . . . so that he may *now* establish you as his people" (Deut. 29:9, 11-12). "Be silent, O Israel, and listen! *This day* you have become the people of the Lord, your God" (27:9). "*This day* the Lord, your God, commands you to observe these statutes and decrees. Be careful, then, to observe them with all your heart and with all your soul. *Today* you are making this agreement with the Lord: he is to be your God. . . . And *today* the Lord is making this agreement with you: you are to be a people peculiarly his own" (26:16-18). ". . . this whole law which I am setting before you *today*" (4:8; cf. 4:39; 9:3; 11:32; 30:18). "I set before you here, *this day*, a blessing and a curse" (11:26).[60]

This "today" runs through Deuteronomy like an obsessive refrain and a repeated prayer, as the author seeks tirelessly to bring his message home to listening Israel. The today in which Josiah's people live is thus fused with the today of the Exodus, and both are identified with the today of God in whose presence the word is actualized in ever new circumstances. Deuteronomy challenges the ordinary view of history, according to which time passes in an irreversible stream. The book is a hymn of adoration addressed to the eternal present of God in which the word constantly addresses men each day of their lives. Once again, that is, "today," the Lord offers life and death to his beloved people and begs them to choose life.

> I call heaven and earth today to witness against you: I have set before you life and death, the blessing and the curse. Choose life, then, that you and your descendants may live, by loving the Lord, your God, heeding his voice, and holding fast to him. For that will mean life for you (Deut. 30:19).

By accepting the covenant with God, Josiah and his people chose life.

III. GOD RENEWS HIS COVENANT WITH HIS PEOPLE

Using the ancient liturgy first celebrated at Mount Sinai, Josiah renewed the covenant after the word of God had been proclaimed.

"Standing by the column, the king made a covenant before the Lord that they would follow him and observe his ordinances, statutes and decrees with their whole hearts and souls, thus reviving the terms of the covenant which were written in this book. And all the people stood as participants in the covenant" (2 Kings 23:3).[61]

The Passover of Josiah

In order to bring these events to a fitting conclusion, Josiah conducted a very solemn celebration of Passover sometime later.[62] He saw personally to the organization of the festivities, for he wanted them to be quite special, and issued directives to the priests, Levites, singers, and gatekeepers.[63] "When the service had been arranged, the priests took their places, as did the Levites in their classes according to the king's command" (2 Chron. 35:10; cf. v. 16). The Passover ritual was scrupulously observed, "as . . . prescribed in the book of Moses" (2 Chron. 35:12).[64]

The king himself had provided the victims. The writers tell us with an air of satisfaction that the ceremony required thirty thousand lambs and kids, plus three thousand oxen for the laity, two thousand six hundred lambs and kids and three hundred oxen for the priests of the Temple, and five thousand cattle and five hundred oxen for the Levites.[65] It was an immense slaughter for a colossal festival at which songs were sung amid the thick smoke from the burning fat of animals. The influx of pilgrims was enormous. The pilgrimage to Jerusalem for the Passover was obligatory according to the book of the law (Deut. 16:16); there could be no question of religious indifference toward this obligation at the very moment when a reform was in full swing, nor could anyone ignore the king's summons and celebrate the feast at a local sanctuary.[66] If religious conviction or patriotism did not prove strong enough motives, the royal police could effectively help the undecided to prove their piety.

This Passover was, then, a great national celebration; its atmosphere was that of a great fair in which family joy, religious enthusiasm, and political pride all played their part. In the Judean countryside, around the village well in the evenings, the Passover of Josiah would long be remembered. "No such Passover had been observed in Israel since the time of the prophet Samuel, nor had any king of Israel kept a Passover like that of Josiah, the priests and Levites, all of Judah and Israel that were present, and the inhabitants of Jerusalem" (2 Chron. 35:18).

This celebration by Josiah represents a memorable stage in the history of the spiritual meaning of Passover. Before Josiah, it had been a family feast at which people offered God the first fruits of the barley harvest. Each family was an autonomous, self-sufficient community of worship; it prepared its own sacred meal and then celebrated the feast, thus consecrating, as it were, the intimate domestic life of the family. Now, as celebrated by Josiah and as prescribed in Deuteronomy, Passover became a *national* festival and a memorial of the Exodus. The celebration involved more than individual families; it had national significance, and its purpose was to help mold all the families into a single people of God. The worshiping community was no longer the individual family but the nation.

By thus celebrating the anniversary of its entrance upon the stage of history, Israel reaffirmed its existence as the holy people of God. No longer was Israel made up simply of families living side by side in the same land and forming in this fashion the people of God; Israel was not a single people that included all families within a single country, under a single law, and professing a single faith, in accordance with the ideal of Deuteronomy. Passover had become the supreme festival of the *ekklēsia* of God.

CONCLUSION

History likes to remove the wrinkles from the face of the past, and it has therefore left us a picture of Josiah as an ideal king. The Book of Kings has words of unique praise for him: "Before him, there has been no king who turned to the Lord as he did, with his whole heart, his whole soul, and his whole strength, in accord with the entire law of Moses; nor could any after him compare with him" (2 Kings 23:25). In the eyes of the historian, Josiah turns into the second David promised by God: "He pleased the Lord and conducted himself unswervingly just as his ancestor David had done" (2 Kings 22:2).

Josiah's reform had two sides to it — a political and a religious one. In the political sphere Josiah sought to re-establish the kingdom of David in defiance of the Assyrian superpower; in the religious sphere he tried, with the help of "the book of the law of Moses," to restore the pure Yahwist faith that was being corrupted by the influx of Canaanite divinities. In his own thoughts and intentions the two tasks were undoubtedly linked very closely to each other, perhaps even completely identified. We can sum up both tasks at once by saying that Josiah tried to turn his political state into a holy church. What was to be the fate of a work undertaken with so much optimism and hope?

1. The political sphere

Later history was to make a stern and uncompromising distinction between the political and the religious. Its judgment, as pronounced in events which were under Yahweh's direction, was a pitiless condemnation of both throne and nation. The political state which Josiah had rebuilt with such great effort was to fall apart, while the holy church which Deutoronomy shaped was to last forever.

In 609, Pharaoh Neco (609–593) came to the aid of the king of Assyria. His expedition was, of course, not purely altruistic in character, and Neco may have used the excuse of helping a brother in order to take over part of the now crumbling Assyrian empire. Josiah, for his part, had good reason to think that Neco's ambitions extended to the Israelite kingdom.[67] Neco entered Palestine and asked Josiah's permission to use the pass over Carmel at Megiddo, along the road from Egypt to Syria, which Egyptian military convoys had been using for centuries. Josiah refused. Because he wanted to save his strength and time as well, Neco sent an ambassador to negotiate: "What quarrel is between us, king of Judah? I have not come against you this day, for my war is with another kingdom, and God has told me to hasten. Do not interfere with God who is with me, as otherwise he will destroy you" (2 Chron. 35:21).

This was too much, for the insult was an insult to Yahweh himself. Sure of himself, Josiah accepted conflict and sent his chariots into battle. The Egyptian archers aimed for the royal chariot, and the king's armor was not strong enough to resist their arrows. Josiah was shot and he collapsed with the words: "Take me away, for I am seriously wounded" (2 Chron. 35:23). They took him back to Jerusalem along the rough mountain roads but he died as they reached the royal palace at nightfall.

The tragic end of Josiah was a scandal to religious-minded Israelites. Here at last there was a faithful king according to the heart of God. Why, then, did death sweep him away at the height of his success? His death seemed as mysterious and devastating as that of the one "thrust through" in the prophecies of Deutero-Zechariah.[68]

On August 10, 587, twenty-two years after the disastrous battle of

Megiddo and thirty-five years after the discovery of the Book of Deuteronomy, the Chaldean battering rams breached the walls of Jerusalem, and the city went down in fire and blood. Under cover of night Zedekiah, last heir to the Davidic line, tried to escape the massacre with his retinue and to flee eastward into the desert of Judah. The Chaldeans spotted him as he crossed the Jordan valley near Jericho, captured him, slew his sons before his eyes, then blinded him, put him in chains, and led him off to Babylon. The blood-spattered corpses of his sons was the last thing this most unfortunate of Josiah's descendants saw, and that was the vision he took with him into the night of captivity.

The earthly kingdom of the Davidic dynasty was destroyed; the political order established by Josiah vanished forever. Deuteronomy had been God's final effort to "soften" the hardened hearts of his people and to save them from deportation. The effort failed. Israel destroyed itself. True enough, God will save his people even in the midst of exile, and the tears of the deported and their muffled sobs "by the streams of Babylon" (Ps. 137:1) will find favor with him where Josiah's army and its iron-clad chariots had not. God will even stir his people to sing their most beautiful love songs "by the waters of Babylon," but these will no longer be political songs.

2. *The religious sphere*

In the religious sphere, more accurately in the sphere of God's word, Josiah's work will have an incomparably great effect. The discovery of the law was one of the key moments in the religious history of Israel and in the establishment of the canon of Scripture. Before its discovery, Deuteronomy was not yet regarded as "God's writing." As noted earlier, it was simply a collection of laws, originating in a northern sanctuary and inserted into a collection of sermons. After its discovery, Deuteronomy was regarded as a book of the law.[69] R. Kittel writes: "Up to this point, law was either an oral response given by priests or written customary law that was observed and protected by the weight of habit. Now there was an officially acknowledged code of law, a 'canonical' book. Here we have the first evidence of a holy book, 'Sacred Scripture' in the strict sense of the term."[70] When Josiah held the Book of Deuteronomy in his hands and proclaimed it to his people, he was holding God's explicit will in book form; he was holding the first Bible.

From the assembly of Josiah down to that of Ezra, Deuteronomy will be "the only law in force for almost two centuries."[71]

[1] A. Gelin, "Messianisme," *DBS* 5:1175.

[2] Cf. 1 Sam. 18:5; 22:2; 27:5-7. On the accession of David to the throne, cf. J. H. Gronbaek, *Die Geschichte vom Aufstieg Davids* (Copenhagen, 1971), especially pp. 186ff. on David in Ziklag and his coronation as king of Judah.

[3] The prophecy of 2 Sam. 7:5-16 is the charter of the Davidic dynasty. On this charter and its reinterpretation in other biblical texts, cf. J. Coppens, *Le messianisme royal: Ses origines, son développement, son accomplissement* (Lectio divina 54; Paris, 1968), pp. 39–63.

[4] Cf. E. Podechard, *Le Psautier* 1 (Lyons, 1949), pp. 16–17; H.-J. Kraus, *Die Psalmen* (Biblischer Kommentar, Altes Testament 15; Neukirchen, 1961[2]), pp. 17–20.

[5] The following statements are based on Pss. 45, 72, and 110.

[6] This style is usual in the literature of the Ancient East. A letter of Adad-shum-usur describes as follows the benefits deriving from the accession of a new king (probably Ashurbanipal): "A prosperous regime, lasting days, years of justice, abundant rain, considerable floodwaters, flourishing trade! The gods are well disposed, reverence for the gods is widespread, the temples are wealthy. . . . Old men are agile, children sing, maidens are joyous; matrons conceive, bear children, rear boys and girls; childbirth is uncomplicated. In their joy mothers tell their children: 'The king, our lord, has brought life!' You deliver those long held in prison! Those long ill you restore to health! The hungry are filled, the emaciated grow fat, the naked are clothed!" (P. Dhorme, *La religion assyrobabylonienne* [Paris, 1910], pp. 172–73). On the religious significance of kingship in Israel, cf. J. de Fraine, *L'aspect religieux de la royauté israélite: L'institution monarchique dans l'Ancien Testament et dans les textes mésopotamiens* (Rome, 1954) and R. de Vaux, *Ancient Israel*, pp. 100–114.

[7] J. Steinmann, *Les Psaumes* (Paris, 1951), p. 63.

[8] Cf. 2 Sam. 5:6-10 and 1 Chron. 11:4-8. Cf. L.-H. Vincent, "Jérusalem," *DBS* 4:914-19.

[9] The word is that of A. Alt, "Jerusalems Aufstieg," in his *Kleine Schriften* 3:254. He adds: "We should think of the beginnings of Jerusalem as quite modest. To associate the idea of the future capital with the beginnings of Jerusalem is to make a realistic grasp of the situation impossible."

[10] Cf. Is. 2:2-4; Micah 4:1-3; Ps. 87. On the traditions which later attached themselves to the Holy City, cf. G. von Rad, *Old Testament Theology* 1:39–48.

[11] Cf. 2 Sam. 6:12-23.

[12] Cf. 1 Sam. 4:13.

[13] Cf. Num. 10:33-36.

[14] The ark was in the camp at Gilgal (according to Josh. 7:6), and in the sanctuaries of Shechem (according to the Deuteronomist text of Josh. 8:33), Bethel (according to Judg. 20:27), and Shiloh (according to 1 Sam. 3:3).

[15] Cf. 1 Sam. 4–6; 2 Sam. 6; 1 Kings 8.

[16] Cf. Prov. 5:18-19; Ps. 128:3.

[17] Cf. Ps. 128.

[18] The anti-monarchical text in 1 Sam. 8 preserves the nostalgic memory of the distant age of the Judges. On the anti-monarchic currents, cf. S.W. Baron, *A Social and Religious History of the Jews* 1 (2nd. rev. and enlarged ed.; New York, 1952), pp. 91–93.

[19] Samaria was founded by King Omri (885–874); cf. 1 Kings 16:23-24. On Samaria, cf. A. Parrot, *Samaria, the Capital of the Kingdom of Israel*, translated by S.H. Hooke (Studies in Biblical Archaeology 7; London, 1958).

[20] O. Procksch, *Theologie des Alten Testaments*, p. 219.

[21] Josiah was only sixteen at the time. On the reform of Josiah, cf. J. Steinmann, *Le prophète Jérémie* (Lectio divina 9, Paris, 1952), ch. 6: "The Discovery of Deuteronomy and the Josian Reform" (pp. 85–102); P. Buis, *Josias* (Témoins de Dieu

16; Paris, 1958), pp. 31–59; O. Procksch, *Theologie des Alten Testaments*, pp. 219–23; T. Robinson, *A History of Israel* 1:411–26; M. Noth, *History of Israel*, pp. 272–80; R. Kittel, *Geschichte des Volkes Israel* 2 (Stuttgart, 1925⁶), pp. 402–13.

²² After 622 Josiah will intervene directly as ruler in the sanctuary at Shiloh and in those of Samaria, according to 2 Kings 23:15-19.

²³ Jer. 2:28. Jeremiah was a contemporary of Josiah; he received his call as a prophet in about 627.

²⁴ The "sacred pole," or asherah, was dedicated to the goddess Asherah. According to the Ugaritic texts, she was the Phoenician goddess of vegetation; in the Bible she is the consort of Baal.

²⁵ The Chronicler describes the reform in terms that recall the earlier reforms of Asa (2 Chron. 14:1-4) and Hezekiah (2 Chron. 31:1).

²⁶ According to the Second Book of Kings (23:15-20) the reform was specifically concerned with Bethel and Samaria, but the Chronicler looks at the larger picture and attributes considerable scope to the reform.

²⁷ The Book of Kings places this reform after 622 so as to make it a consequence of the discovery of the book of the law.

²⁸ The discovery is related in 2 Chron. 34:14-21 and 2 Kings 22:3-10. On the identification of the "book of the law" with Deuteronomy, see the next section of this chapter.

²⁹ H. Cazelles, *Le Deutéronome* (Paris, 1950), p. 13.

³⁰ This included the proverbs attributed to Solomon: cf. Prov. 25:1: "These also are proverbs of Solomon. The men of Hezekiah, king of Judah, transmitted them." On this point, A. Barucq, *Les Proverbes* (Paris, 1964), observes: "The fall of Samaria and the threat to Judah may have stimulated the fixing of traditions otherwise in danger of being dispersed" (p. 193).

³¹ Deut. 28:16-19. In the curses of Deut. 28:15-68, verses 47-68 seem to have been added to the original text at a later date; cf. P. Buis and J. Leclercq, *Le Deutéronome*, pp. 179–81.

³² Cf. Deut. 28:20-45.

³³ Cf. R. Kittel, *Geschichte des Volkes Israel* 2:408–9.

³⁴ The oracles in Jer. 2–6 date from the time of Josiah.

³⁵ "Keeper of the wardrobe," i.e., the wardrobe of the king.

³⁶ Cf. also 2 Kings 22:11-20.

³⁷ Cf. Ps. 103:8; Deut. 5:10.

³⁸ Micah 3:12. This oracle is dated by Jer. 26:18-19 as belonging to the reign of Hezekiah.

³⁹ Cf. 2 Kings 23:1-2a.

⁴⁰ Cf. 2 Kings 23:2b.

⁴¹ Deut. 31:9, 11, 12. On the meaning of "torah," see below, Chapter 5, section 1/1. — As a matter of fact, neither the code nor the discourses of Deuteronomy originated all at the same time. But we may maintain with M. Noth (cf. *Gesammelte Studien zum Alten Testament* [Munich, 1966], p. 59) that the "original form" of Deuteronomy is to be found in the Book of Josiah. O. Eissfeldt, *The Old Testament: An Introduction*, says: "We may regard as assured the identification of the original Deuteronomy with the law book discovered in 621 and made the foundation of Josiah's reform or at any rate playing a decisive part in it" (p. 232). Cf. T. Robinson, *A History of Israel* 1:425–26; R. Kittel, *Geschichte des Volkes Israel* 2:405–11.

⁴² Cf. Deut. 28:61; 29:20; 30:10. On Deuteronomy, cf. especially H. Cazelles, *Le Deutéronome*, pp. 7–19; *idem*, "Pentateuque," *DBS* 6:813–22; H. Junker, *Deuteronomium* (Würzburg, 1952); G. von Rad, *Old Testament Theology* 1:69–77 and 219–31; O. Eissfeldt, *The Old Testament: An Introduction*, pp. 219–33; P. Buis, *Le Deutéronome* (Paris, 1969); N. Lohfink, *Das Hauptgebot* (Rome, 1963); G. von Rad, *Deuteronomy*, translated by D. Barton (Philadelphia, 1966), Introduction; G. Seitz,

Redaktionsgeschichtliche Studien zum Deuteronomium (Stuttgart, 1971); M. Weinfeld, *Deuteronomy and the Deuteronomic School* (Oxford, 1972). On the Deuteronomic Code, cf. R. Merendino, *Das Deuteronomische Gesetz.*

[43] Cf. Deut. 1:1-5. Deuteronomy ends with the death of Moses on Mount Nebo and his burial in "the ravine opposite Beth-peor in the land of Moab" (Deut. 34:1-12).

[44] Cf. A. Alt, "Die Heimat des Deuteronomiums," in *Kleine Schriften* 2:250–75; H. Cazelles, "Pentateuque," *DBS* 7:813.

[45] Cf. Deut. 27:9: "This day you have become the people of the Lord, your God."

[46] Cf. Deut. 31:10-11.

[47] Deut. 7:7-15 summarizes the theme of Yahweh's choice of the Israelite people, "really the smallest of all nations" (7:7); cf. also Deut. 10:14-17.

[48] Cf. also Deut. 32:8-9: God established separate peoples throughout the world according to the number of their deities, "while the Lord's own portion was Jacob, his hereditary share was Israel."

[49] The words "the Lord, your [singular or plural] God" occur over three hundred times in Deuteronomy; cf. P. Buis and J. Leclercq, *Le Deutéronome*, p. 20.

[50] What Deut. 17:14-20 says of the king is very much understated in comparison with the emphatic pronouncements of the royal Psalms. In Deuteronomy the kingship seems to be a reluctantly given concession to a new generation. The Deuteronomic preachers were insistent that the king must cut back on his horses, harem, and treasury, and meditate daily on Deuteronomy, lest he "become estranged from his countrymen through pride" (17:20).

[51] Cf. Deut. 8:3: "Not by bread alone does man live, but by every word that comes forth from the mouth of the Lord."

[52] G. von Rad, *Der Heilige Krieg im Alten Israel* (Zürich, 1951), p. 14.

[53] Cf. also Deut. 7:17-24.

[54] Cf. Deut. 6:15. J. Touzard, "Juif (Peuple)," *Dictionnaire apologétique de la foi catholique* 2, cols. 1577–80, describes monotheism as understood by Deuteronomy.

[55] Deut. 12:2-12. The prohibition against following other gods (cf. Deut. 6:14: "You shall not follow other gods, such as those of the surrounding nations") will lead Israel finally to the denial that other gods exist and the assertion that one God alone truly exists; in other words, monolatry will lead to monotheism. Deuteronomy represents a stage in this development (cf. Is. 44:6: "I am the first and I am the last; there is no God but me").

[56] As we may readily imagine, this centralization of cult greatly aided Josiah in his efforts at political centralization. He used fire and sword to eliminate the ancient sanctuaries (cf. 2 Kings 23:15-20), though all the people venerated these because of the patriarchal traditions connected with them. It was unfortunate that he thus solved his problem by massacring his opponents instead of trying to win their allegiance. A hundred years earlier Hezekiah had shown himself more conciliatory in his efforts at reform; he was a man who would pray to "the good Lord" for the sinful people (cf. 2 Chron. 30:18-19). On the law that there must be only one place of worship, cf. below, Chapter 10, section 2/2.

[57] Cf. 1 Kings 8:27; Is. 66:1.

[58] Compare Num. 12:3 with Num. 25:4 and Deut. 9:17! On the picture of Moses given in Deuteronomy, cf. G. von Rad, *Old Testament Theology* 1:294–95.

[59] Cf. Deut. 18:14-21; 13:2-6. The importance Deuteronomy gives to prophetism, as well as its rejection of a dynastic kingship by divine right, shows how groundless is the hypothesis that Josiah or the high priest hid the Book of Deuteronomy in the Temple in order at a later date to play a pious charade of discovering it and using it as the basis of a reform. Cf. R. Kittel, *Geschichte des Volkes Israel* 2:408–9.

[60] The "today" of Deuteronomy bears witness to the fact that each celebrating community makes the Sinai assembly a present reality. A. Arens, *Die Psalmen im Gottesdienst des Alten Bundes*, speaks of an "actualization of the original assembly" (pp. 25–28).

[61] Cf. 2 Chron. 34:31. In point of fact, the king did not make a covenant, as 2 Kings and 2 Chronicles put it, but simply renewed the promise of fidelity. God alone can make the covenant, since men cannot constrain God but only promise fidelity and then renew the promise. This is what Josiah did.

[62] The discovery of the law and the celebration of the Passover took place in the same year, the eighteenth of Josiah's reign, according to 2 Kings 22:3 (= 2 Chron. 34:8) and 2 Kings 23:23 (= 2 Chron. 35:9). The celebration of this Passover is described in 2 Kings 23:21-23 and at much greater length in 2 Chron. 35:1-19.

[63] Cf. 2 Chron. 35:2-3, 15.

[64] The ritual for the Passover celebration is given in the "book of the law," that is, in Deuteronomy (16:1-8). It would be more accurate to say that Josiah celebrated the feast of Unleavened Bread. It was only after his time that the two feasts of Passover and Unleavened Bread were joined into one (cf. P. Buis, *Le Deutéronome*, p. 264).

[65] Cf. 2 Chron. 35:7-9.

[66] The Temple was the royal sanctuary, and its priests were servants of the king; it was the king's privilege and duty to see to the upkeep of the Temple. Thus a pilgrimage to the Jerusalem Temple was not only an act of piety directed to the Lord but also a manifestation of allegiance to the king.

[67] Cf. C. Schedl, *History of the Old Testament* 4 (Staten Island, N.Y., 1972), pp. 338–40. On the death of Josiah, cf. 2 Kings 23:29-30 and the more detailed account in 2 Chron. 35:19-25.

[68] Zech. 12:10 and John 19:37. On Zech. 12:10, cf. P. Lamarche, *Zacharie, IX–XIV: Structure littéraire et Messianisme* (Paris, 1961), pp. 80–85.

[69] Cf. Deut. 17:18; 28:58; 29:19; 31:9; 26; cf. also 2 Kings 23:8-11.

[70] R. Kittel, *Geschichte des Volkes Israel* 2:412. Of course, Israel did not wait for the Josian reform to put the prophetic oracles in writing. Hos. 8:12 refers to many written ordinances of Yahweh, thus indicating the existence of a "sacred scripture" as early as the middle of the eighth century. Cf. J. Steinmann, *Le prophétisme biblique des origines à Osée* (Lectio divina 23; Paris, 1959), p. 200; H. W. Wolff, *Dodeka-propheton Hosea* (Neukirchen, 1961), p. 185. But this "scripture" did not enjoy official status as law of the realm as Deuteronomy did.

[71] P. Buis and J. Leclercq, *Le Deutéronome*, pp. 26–27.

Chapter 4

THE ASSEMBLY OF EZRA
(ca. 398?)

The fall of Jerusalem had meant, it seemed, the definitive failure of God's effort to build up the community through his word. Yet, in the very depths of Israel's catastrophe, Ezekiel foretold the gathering of all the sheep of the house of Israel, scattered though they now were over the hills and in foreign lands.[1] Like the new creation of which Second Isaiah sings, the pitiful caravan of the ransomed, the "little remnant" of the survivors, set out on a new exodus. Once again they crossed the lonely desert filled with blinding light. Once again they encountered God in Jerusalem, a Jerusalem now burnt to the ground indeed, yet ringing with joy at the return of her children. And once again the pilgrims gathered to hear anew the word of God that had scattered them and was now drawing them together again. "Those whom the Lord has ransomed will return and enter Zion singing, crowned with everlasting joy; they will meet with joy and gladness, sorrow and mourning will flee" (Is. 35:10).

The assembly of Ezra thus takes place at the moment when God dries his people's tears. The Book of Nehemiah describes the assembly in some of the Bible's most beautiful pages.

I. GOD CALLS AND GATHERS HIS PEOPLE

1. The mission of Ezra

The Chronicler paints a flattering portrait of Ezra: "He was a scribe, well-versed in the law of Moses which was given by the Lord, the God of Israel. . . . the hand of the Lord, his God, was upon him. . . . Ezra had set his heart on the study and practice of the law of the Lord and on teaching statutes and ordinances in Israel" (Ezra 7:6, 10).[2]

In the seventh year of the reign of Artaxerxes (398?), Ezra left Babylon for Jerusalem.[3] A number of Zionists went with him, among them priests, Levites, and other officers of the Temple. The king had issued a very generous rescript permitting all the inhabitants of Judah who wished to do so to return to Palestine, authorizing Ezra to use funds collected, or received from the king, for the restoration of the Temple worship at Jerusalem, stipulating that the royal treasury would advance the credit needed for the same purpose, and establishing "the law of your God" as the law of the restored state. This last proviso was, of course, the decisive one. During the centuries separating Ezra from Jesus, the Israelite community will be rebuilt on the basis of God's word, officially acknowledged and promulgated as such. According to the express will of the king of Persia, it was Ezra's task to make this law known to a people that might have forgotten it and to take steps against anyone who might violate it.[4]

In the fifth month after leaving Babylon, Ezra reached Jerusalem and made himself known to the populace. As early as the seventh month he organized the assembly of the whole people, with the word of God as its focus. "Now when the seventh month came, the whole people gathered as one man in the open space before the Water Gate, and they called upon Ezra the scribe to bring forth the book of the law of Moses which the Lord prescribed for Israel" (Neh. 7:72–8:1).

As a matter of fact, there had been a long preparation for this plenary assembly of the people. In 538 — therefore about a hundred forty years earlier — an edict of Cyrus had authorized the Jews to return to Jerusalem and rebuild the Temple.[5] The work was enthusiastically begun, but then lagged and was almost abandoned, so great was the desolation and poverty of the country. In addition, the individual was seriously tempted to "hurry to his own house," clear away the ruins, and build himself a "paneled house" (Haggai 1:9 and 4); at the same time, however, the foundations of the Temple were left untouched, and people whispered to each other throughout the land: "Not now has the time come to rebuild the house of the Lord" (Haggai 1:2).[6] It took all the energy and persuasiveness of the prophets Haggai and Zechariah to encourage the downhearted Zionists to turn back to the great work and overcome both their worry about their neighbors and their own feeling of wretchedness.[7]

At last, in the spring of 515, the dedication of the Temple was cele-brated.[8] Undoubtedly the new structure recalled but little of the splendor of the former royal sanctuary. The elders of Jerusalem who had seen Solomon's Temple had good reason to weep as they looked at the new Temple, even if, according to the official chronicle, the people were overjoyed at it.[9] Especially missed during this festival of renewal was the presence of the ark of the covenant, which had disappeared during the disaster of 587. The ark had formerly been the visible pledge of God's presence among his people. To console the Israelites, the prophets would be constantly insisting that God was no less present in the new Temple than he had been in the old.[10]

In rebuilding the Temple, the newly returned Jews were also rebuilding the heart and center of their religious life. Yesterday they had been scattered among the nations; today they were reassembled around Yahweh's house and formed once again the great worshiping community attached to the sanctuary.

The coming of Nehemiah to Jerusalem (around 410?) gave new impetus to Zionism. Three days after his arrival Nehemiah in-spected the city walls, making his visit by night so as not to arouse speculation about his intention.[11] He summed up the results of his inquiry by telling those concerned: "You see the evil plight in which we stand: how Jerusalem lies in ruins and its gates have been gutted by fire. Come, let us rebuild the walls of Jerusalem, so that we may no longer be an object of derision!" (Neh. 2:17). Against ill-natured opposition, the people eagerly set to work. The Chronicler reports, with a touch of patriotic sentimentality: "Every builder, while he worked, had his sword girt at his side" (Neh. 4:12). It is difficult to picture the masons on their scaffolds wielding both the trowel and the sword, but the image catches the reader's attention and high-lights both the difficulty of the work and the courage of those who set about it. Fifty-two days later the wall was finished (Neh. 8:17) and its dedication was celebrated (12:27-43).

Since the community had been scattered by sin, it could be gathered together again only by grace. Yet, according to what the prophet Malachi tells us,[12] the religious practice of the first re-turnees left much to be desired. The priests were blatant in their contempt for the sacrificial ritual and thus profaned God's holy name among the nations.[13] The sabbath rest, which was a sign of the covenant and a symbol of the freedom of the children of Israel, was hardly observed at all,[14] while the tithes and other taxes owed the

Temple were no longer paid. People were trying, as it were, to trick God.[15] Finally, the frequent marriages with foreign women were a constant threat to the purity of the Yahwist faith.[16] After all, wasn't marriage to a woman who in the prophet's judgment was "the daughter of an alien God" the equivalent of an attack on the unity of God's people?[17] Yet such improper unions were to be found even in priestly families.[18]

Religious reform was thus a pressing need. It would not have served the cause of Yahweh's rule simply to gather the people again while leaving them in their sins, or to rebuild the walls while letting faith decay, or to leave Babylon, the place of captivity, behind while returning to Jerusalem with the bonds of exile still unloosed. It was Ezra's merit that he set forcefully to work on the task of religious renewal. The question of mixed marriages, though it offends our modern sensibilities, was certainly the most important. Ezra drew up a list of the people involved in such marriages and required them to dismiss their foreign wives and the children born to them.[19] In this way the methods by which the community increased in numbers also helped in purifying the community's faith.

II. GOD GIVES HIS LAW TO HIS PEOPLE

The Chronicler has left us a splendid description of the solemn reading of the law to the "Church" which had returned from exile:

> Now when the seventh month came, the whole people gathered as one man in the open space before the Water Gate, and they called upon Ezra the scribe to bring forth the book of the law of Moses which the Lord prescribed for Israel. On the first day of the seventh month, therefore, Ezra the priest brought the law before the assembly, which consisted of men, women, and those children old enough to understand. Standing at one end of the open space that was before the Water Gate he read out of the book from daybreak till midday, in the presence of the men, the women, and those children old enough to understand; and all the people listened attentively to the book of the law. Ezra the scribe stood on a wooden platform that had been made for the occasion; at his right side stood Mattithiah, Shema, Anaiah, Uriah, Hilkiah, and Maaseiah, and on his left Pedaiah, Mishael, Malchijah, Hashum, Hashbaddanah, Zechariah, Meshullam. Ezra opened the scroll so that all the people might see it (for he was standing higher up than any of the people); and, as he opened it, all the people rose. Ezra blessed the Lord, the great God, and all the people, their hands raised high, answered, "Amen, amen!" Then they bowed down and prostrated themselves before the Lord, their faces to the ground. The Levites Jeshua, Bani, Sherebiah, Jamin,

Akkub, Shabbethai, Hodiah, Maaseiah, Kelita, Azariah, Jozabad, Hanan, and Pelaiah explained the law to the people, who remained in their places. Ezra read plainly from the book of the law of God, interpreting it so that all could understand what was read. Then [Nehemiah, that is, His Excellency, and] Ezra the priest-scribe [and the Levites who were instructing the people] said to all the people: "Today is holy to the Lord your God. Do not be sad, and do not weep" — for all the people were weeping as they heard the words of the law (Neh. 7:72–8:9).[20]

The proclamation of the law took place in the seventh month, that is, at the Feast of Tents.[21] This was the most popular of the Feasts, the most crowded and joyous of the annual pilgrimages. It was called simply "the feast of Yahweh" (Lev. 23:39 JB), that is, the greatest of feasts. It was on this occasion that Solomon had dedicated the Temple, the ark of the covenant had been installed in it, and "the Lord's glory" had taken possession of the Temple, thus giving a sensible sign of God's presence among his people (cf. 1 Kings 8).

Such was the festive context for Ezra's reading of the law. The hearing of the word was part of the great festival celebrated in recognition of the return to Jerusalem; indeed, the reading was itself a festival. It recalled the ark and "the two stone tablets which Moses had put there at Horeb, when the Lord made a covenant with the Israelites at their departure from the land of Egypt" (1 Kings 8:9). The reading also was a reminder of the Lord's glory which had taken possession of the Temple on the day of its dedication. Now it was God's word that dwelt among his people and kept alive the memory of the Sinai covenant.

The Chronicler insists on the "universality" of the assembly: it is made up of "men, women, and those children old enough to understand" (Neh. 8:2 and 3). He also notes the presence of the twelve assessors who stood with Ezra, half on his right, half on his left. Tradition has preserved the memory of these faithful followers who have become historical personages recalling the twelve tribes of Israel. Thus the whole community of the children of Israel was gathered with the word of God as its center and focus.

In relating the event, the redactor seems conscious that he is recording an important historical moment. He describes the reading of the law according to a rite that will be traditional for centuries in the readings in the synagogue. Ezra reads the original Hebrew text, using thus a language which had become archaic, especially since the deportation (although it remained a living language in some

Jewish circles down to the second century, as the Qumran manuscripts prove). The Levites then translated the text into Aramaic, the chief language of Assyro-Babylonia, which had also become the ordinary language of the repatriated Jews. In other words, the reading of the law was immediately followed by a translation or paraphrase; here we have the beginnings of the targum,[22] as well as of what would later be the liturgical homily.

The Chronicler is so convinced of the importance of this translation into a "living" language that he twice calls attention to it in additions that are evidently from his pen: "The Levites . . . explained the law to the people . . . The Levites . . . were instructing the people" (Neh. 8:7 and 9). The first of these additions is so awkwardly inserted into the original text that it disturbs the narrative sequence: the Levites seem to explain the text even before Ezra has read it.

III. GOD RENEWS HIS COVENANT WITH HIS PEOPLE

The hearing of God's word is followed by the renewal of the covenant. God, of course, does not have to renew his promise, since he has never broken it, but the people does have to reassert its fidelity. The people take a solemn oath "to follow the law of God which was given through Moses, the servant of God, and to observe carefully all the commandments of the Lord, our Lord, his ordinances and his statutes" (Neh. 10:30; cf. 10:1).[23]

According to the ancient custom that began at Mount Sinai, a festive meal expresses the joy proper to the covenant:

> He [Ezra] said further: "Go, eat rich foods and drink sweet drinks, and allot portions to those who had nothing prepared; for today is holy to our Lord. Do not be saddened this day, for rejoicing in the Lord must be your strength!" And the Levites quieted all the people, saying, "Hush, for today is holy, and you must not be saddened." Then all the people went to eat and drink, to distribute portions, and to celebrate with great joy, for they understood the words that had been expounded to them (Neh. 8:10-12).

The word of God creates a festive people and fills them with joy and exultation. The walls just built are less effective in protecting Israel than is the joy of the Lord that surrounds her like a strong rampart: "Rejoicing in the Lord must be your strength!"

No one is forgotten in the feast of fellowship. The poor man who has nothing prepared receives his share of the rich foods and sweet drinks. For the covenant, which is a communion with the Lord, also means communion between brothers. The family of God's children is a family of brothers and sisters.

CONCLUSION

1. A people formed by God's word

For an understanding of the history of Israel, and therefore of Christianity, which emerges out of that history, the assembly of Ezra is extremely important. It marks the beginning of a new and irreversible stage in Yahwist religion: the birth of Judaism.

When Israel was living according to the Deuteronomic ideal — a single people, gathered in a single country, governed by a single law, and grouped around a single king — political sovereignty and the permanence of the Davidic dynasty gave some guarantee to its existence as God's people. In other words, Israel existed as a people consecrated to God because it possessed a country, was enlightened by God's word, and was governed by David's house, which the Lord himself had chosen. But now, through the might of the Chaldeans, God had stripped Israel of its kingship; he had given the Promised Land, "my heritage, the beloved of my soul" (Jer. 12:7), over to the destroyer; he had allowed the collapse, one after another, of the ancient social structures of this people of kings and brothers. The extraordinary thing was that, despite all this, the Israel of Ezra still thought of itself as God's people. It was a people without a country and without a king; henceforth it would define its own existence in terms of adherence to the law. The movement of history has in a sense been halted, and despite the struggles of the Maccabean rebellion, the four centuries between Ezra and Jesus will be empty and silent.

Meanwhile, however, the religion of the Torah and the worship of the Book will arise on the ruins of the old structures and in the silence of the passing years. The God of Israel's holy history will become the God of Israel's holy law. The assembly of Ezra the scribe, whom the Chronicler respectfully calls "scribe of the law of the God of heaven" (Ezra 7:12, 21),[24] becomes an assembly whose center and focus is the word of God. The law acquires an absolute value; it judges and blesses or condemns the people. It becomes everything to Israel — truth, light, salvation, liberation, joy. "We have for our encouragement the sacred books that are in our possession," says the redactor of the Book of Maccabees (1 Macc. 12:9), and when one brother prays for another, he asks the Lord to open the other's heart to the law.[25] The Jews will meditate on the law, study it, and comment on it until the day when those "teachers of the law" who brood over it with great love will discover in it the face of Jesus Christ.

[1] Cf. Ezek. 34:11-16.

[2] On Ezra, cf. R. de Vaux, "Israël," *DBS* 4:763–69; H. Cazelles, "La mission d'Esdras," *Vetus Testamentum* 4 (1954) pp. 113–40; H.H. Schraeder, *Esra, der Schreiber* (Tübingen, 1930); G. von Rad, *Old Testament Theology* 1:85–92; W.O.E. Oesterley and T. Robinson, *A History of Israel*, pp. 111–41; C. Schedl, *History of the Old Testament* 5 (Staten Island, N.Y., 1973), pp. 187–205 (Renewal of Covenant and Law); F. Michaeli, *Les livres des Chroniques, d'Esdras et de Néhémie* (Commentaire de l'Ancien Testament 16; Neuchâtel. 1967).

[3] The mission of Ezra is recounted in Ezra 7, with the time pinpointed in 7:7. But the date of the mission is still disputed. If the reference is to the seventh year of the reign of Artaxerxes I (465–424), the year is 458; cf. O. Eissfeldt, *The Old Testament: An Introduction*, pp. 541–57. But if the reign in question is that of Artaxerxes II, the year is 398; cf. Oesterley and Robinson, *op. cit.*, p. 118. Finally, if the reading in Ezra 7:7 should be "thirty-seventh year" instead of "seventh year," the year must be 428, a date that has the advantage of bringing the activities of Ezra and Nehemiah into close temporal connection. M. Noth, *History of Israel*, p. 320, thinks that the date given in Ezra 7:7 is "a post-chronistic addition" and cannot provide a reliable point of chronological reference. Cf. also H. Cazelles, "Pentateuque," *DBS* 7:854, and Schedl, *op. cit.*, 5:202–5.

[4] Cf. Ezra 7:25-26. The action of the Persian kings in financing the return of the exiles and the rebuilding of the Temple was not due to a special favor which Israel alone enjoyed but was part of a general policy adopted toward subject peoples. Whereas the Babylonian and Assyrian emperors in practice cut these peoples off from their roots and deported them in order to crush resistance and give Babylon an amorphous cosmopolitan population, the Persians respected both sacral traditions and national languages. By this "wise policy they strove, certainly not without success, to strengthen their empire" (M. Noth, *History of Israel*, p. 304). See also M. Noth, *Gesammelte Studien zum Alten Testament* (Munich, 1966), p. 105.

[5] Cf. Ezra 1:1-4.

[6] The situation of the refugees was rendered even more difficult by agricultural disasters (drought and famine: Haggai 1:6 and 10-11), which the prophet Haggai interpreted as God's way of urging them to show greater zeal in rebuilding the Temple (Haggai 1:9).

[7] Ezra 6:14: "The elders of the Jews continued to make progress in the building, supported by the message of the prophets, Haggai and Zechariah, son of Iddo." On the attitude of the Samaritans, cf. A. Alt, "Die Rolle Samarias bei der Entstehung des Judentums," in his *Kleine Schriften* 2:316–37.

[8] Cf. Ezra 6:15. The texts on the rebuilding of the Temple are Ezra 2:1–4:5 and 4:24–6:22.

[9] Cf. Ezra 6:16.

[10] Cf. Haggai 2:4-9; Zech. 2:14-17.

[11] See Neh. 2:11-13. The texts on the rebuilding of the walls are Neh. 1–4; 6:1–7:72; 11:1-20, 25a; 12:27-32, 37-40, 43.

[12] Malachi exercised his ministry in the years 488–460. Cf. A. Deissler and M. Delcor, *Les Petits Prophètes*, in Pirot-Clamer, *La Sainte Bible* 8/1 (Paris, 1964), p. 624.

[13] Cf. Mal. 1:6–2:9.

[14] Cf. Mal. 3:1-5. The fact is confirmed by Neh. 15:22.

[15] Cf. Mal. 3:6-10.

[16] Cf. Mal. 2:10-12; Neh. 13:23-27. To cases of mixed marriage Malachi adds those of divorce, concerning which Yahweh says: "I hate divorce . . . and covering one's garment with injustice" (2:16).

[17] Cf. Mal. 2:11 JB: "Judah . . . has married the daughter of an alien god." Cf. Neh. 13:27: "Must it also be heard of you that you have done this very same great evil, betraying our God by marrying foreign women?"

[18] Cf. Neh. 13:28.

[19] Cf. Ezra 9:10. We may note that in ancient Israel such marriages were not prohibited (cf. Gen. 41:45; 48:5-6; Num. 12:1-10; Ruth 1:4; 2 Sam. 3:3), but they were later on, chiefly by Deuteronomy (cf. 7:1-4). History had shown that the prohibition was fully justified as a measure of self-defense; yet it would be necessary to be on guard lest self-defense lead to the establishment of a Jewish ghetto.

[20] The account is somewhat confused. Neh. 8:5-9 seems to be speaking of another reading of the law, and the final redactor, fearful of losing anything, inserted it into the basic text (cf. L.W. Batten, *The Books of Ezra and Nehemiah* [International Critical Commentary; Edinburgh, 1913], pp. 355–57). This explains how in Neh. 8:3 Ezra reads the law until midday, while in 8:5 he opens the book and begins the reading all over again. In Neh. 8:4, in the phrase "for the occasion," the noun is *dabar*; the phrase could thus also be translated as "for the word."

[21] Cf. Neh. 7:72; 8:13-14. The "feast of the seventh month" (8:14) is the Feast of Tents according to Lev. 23:34. Cf. R. de Vaux, *Ancient Israel*, pp. 496–98; also J. van Goudoever, *Fêtes et calendriers bibliques*, pp. 49–55 and p. 27, note 2. According to A. Arens, *Die Psalmen im Gottesdienst des Alten Bundes*, pp. 70–76, the proclamation of the law would have taken place on the Temple square.

[22] On the targum, cf. below, Chapter 7, section II/1.

[23] In the expression "we are entering into a firm pact" (Neh. 10:1), the verb used is "to cut," as in the traditional expression "to cut a covenant." Note that Nehemiah 9, inserted between 8:18 and 10:1, should properly follow on Ezra 10:44. The reading of the law, the feast (certainly a covenant meal), and the commitment of the community are elements in a single celebration.

[24] The title was the official one of "the secretary in the Persian Government who was responsible for the department dealing with Jewish religious matters" (G. von Rad, *Old Testament Theology* 1:88).

[25] Cf. 2 Macc. 1:1-4: "The Jews in Jerusalem and in the land of Judea send greetings to their brethren, the Jews in Egypt. . . . May he [God] open your heart to his law and his commandments and grant you peace."

Part Two

FROM THE RETURN FROM CAP-TIVITY TO THE NEW TESTA-MENT

The assemblies of Moses at the time of the Exodus, of Joshua at Shechem, and of Josiah and Ezra were but brief moments in the long historical life of Israel, but they were decisive moments. They are like great piles that tower over the river of time and the course of history, and they support the bridge that leads from the Exodus to the New Testament, from Moses to Jesus. The last arch of the bridge spans four centuries, linking the Church of Ezra with the first generations of Christians.[1]

The period of Israel's life during which (as we said earlier) there are no historical advances is nonetheless very rich in religious values. The everyday secular life of the people of God is largely hidden from our view, both in the Persian period[2] (538–333) and in the Hellenistic period (333–63). Yet during those hidden years of its history Israel continued to evolve in the religious sphere and to make real, even if slow and sometimes sluggish, progress toward the New Testament. Various indications — like islands revealing the existence of ancient continents now sunk beneath the sea — tell us that the word continued to do its work; it never ceased to gather the community together around the Lord, to create the Church of God, and to weld it into unity.

The two main elements to be noted in this period are the formation of the canon of Scripture and the celebration of the word in the synagogue liturgy. The Church of the New Testament was heir to both of these, and they continue to nourish its life even today.

85

[1] We remind the reader once again that the precise length of this period is uncertain, because the Synod of Jamnia, of which we shall speak further on, dates from about 90–95 A.D., and because it is difficult to say exactly when the New Testament period begins.

[2] Speaking of the Persian period, M. Noth says: "We know almost nothing about the history of Israel in this long period. And even what we do know is, generally speaking, limited to the narrow confines of the small province of Judah with Jerusalem as its centre" (*History of Israel*, p. 337).

Chapter 5

THE FORMATION OF THE CANON OF SCRIPTURE

INTRODUCTION

Once the community had become aware, especially during the period of its dispersal in exile, of the privileged place the word occupied in its life and destiny, it undertook to collect its ancient traditions and the testimonies of those who had spoken in God's name, and to reread and meditate on the texts thus assembled. Everyone was aware that the word does not "fall" but remains standing through the centuries: "Every promise has been fulfilled for you, with not one single exception" (Josh. 23:14; cf. 21:45). All the traditions which had marked Israel's path through the ages had therefore to be gathered up, and the messages of the great inspired men of other days had to be collected, for if Israel wished to continue the dialogue with the God of its fathers, it must hear the voice of the past. How else could men interpret the present and predict the future, since the whole of sacred history was contained, as in a palimpsest, in the promises uttered by the prophets?

The word of God creates the ecclesial community; but it could also be said that the ecclesial community "creates" the word of God. For the community submits the books of the past to the test of its own faith; it determines who the men are in whom it hears the authentic voice of the Lord; it gathers up into a "canon"[1] the books scattered along its historical path; it watches jealously over this sacred trust; it actualizes the ancient prophecies for the sake of the current generation at a time when the prophets have fallen silent. The community does not invent the word (for a revealed religion such a statement would be meaningless), but it does inventory it, drawing up a balance sheet, as it were, and calling attention to the riches contained in it. Such a process is something like what the Church does when gathered in a Council: The Church does not invent new truths but simply gives voice to the wealth contained in the revealed faith. The novelty is not in the statement of the faith but only in the perception the community now has of it.

How did the work of fashioning the canon proceed? The Palestinian canon came into existence gradually and almost without men being aware of it. It did not make its appearance suddenly, like a complete entity fallen from heaven, but was formed through the series of additions within the communities. The formation followed the rhythm established by the life of the communities and by their understanding of the word. As a result, the Bible was a kind of library for which the Holy Spirit drew up the official catalogue, with the help of the communities.

Nehemiah had, we are told by the Chronicler, already put together a library containing "the books about the kings, the writings of the prophets and of David, and the royal letters about sacred offerings" (2 Macc. 2:13).[2] But this was simply an unofficial collection, and besides, the Spirit's choice in setting up his library did not necessarily match the choice made by men. The Spirit always acts with supreme independence: "The wind blows where it will" (John 3:8). The human mind may not clearly grasp the criteria the Spirit follows in his choice, and thus the choice of any particular book as part of the canon will remain as mysterious as God's choices in calling men.

What makes a book worthy of being part of the canon is not its degree of religious spirit nor any "odor of sanctity" clinging to it nor its power to edify. We are indeed justified in hoping for great results when we open a "sacred book," but the Bible is not necessarily a collection of holy or edifying stories (a glance into it proves that!). It tells rather the sacred history that is made up of the histories of sinful men. The essential criterion guiding the formation of the Palestinian canon was simply the fact that the community, under the guidance of the Spirit, heard the authentic voice of the Lord in this or that book and consequently venerated the book for that very reason.[3]

We must add that tradition did not lead the different communities to the same conclusions.[4] Or to put it more clearly, the various communities did not regard the same traditional books as inspired. There were notable differences between the Samaritans, who attributed inspiration only to the Pentateuch; the communities of Alexandria and the Diaspora, which had a considerably longer list of canonical books; the Qumran community, which regarded as inspired certain writings of the movement to which it belonged; and the Palestinian communities, which followed the Pharisaic tradition.

I. THE PALESTINIAN CANON

The Jewish tradition divided the Bible into three parts: the Torah, or Law; the Nebiim, or Prophets; and the Ketubim, or Writings.[5]

1. The Torah, or Law

The Torah, or Law, consists chiefly of the Yahwist, Elohist, Deuteronomic, and Priestly traditions as gathered into the five books of the Pentateuch: Genesis, Exodus, Leviticus, Numbers, and Deuteronomy. The formation of this group of writings went on for almost nine centuries. The earliest writings date from the period of Moses, while the latest, consisting of Priestly traditions emanating from the Babylonian schools which were under the influence of Ezekiel, belong to the period of the return from exile. The work of redaction and compilation which produced the Pentateuch was finished by the fourth century.[6] Here we have the oldest part of the canon and the heart of the Bible. It formed the center around which the other books took their places and in function of which they were judged; thus even the greatest prophecies will often take the form simply of a projection into the future of the events recorded in the Pentateuch.

2. The Nebiim, or Prophets

The second part of the Bible contains the Nebiim, or Prophets. This part is itself divided into two: the former prophets, which included the Books of Joshua, Judges, Samuel, and Kings,[7] and the latter prophets, which included Jeremiah, Ezekiel, Isaiah, and the twelve minor prophets (these last gathered in a single collection, the Dodekapropheton). We may regard this second part of the canon as having reached its definitive form during the third century, B.C. Jesus ben Sirach knew it and used it in his "Praise of Israel's Great Ancestors,"[8] which he wrote probably in the decade ending in 180. We may note that Daniel (who knew the Book of Jeremiah[9]) was not regarded as one of the prophets; his book was written before 165.

3. The Ketubim, or Writings

The third part of the Bible consists of the Ketubim, that is, the (other) Scriptures, or, as they are also called, the Hagiographa. This part contains (1) the Psalms, Proverbs, and Job — books listed as major hagiographa; (2) the Song of Songs, read on the eighth day of Passover; the Book of Ruth, read on the second day of Pentecost; Lamentations, read on the ninth day of the month; the Book of Qoheleth, or Ecclesiastes, read on the second day of the Feast of Tents; and the Book of Esther, read on the Feast of Purim; and finally (3) the Books of Daniel, of Ezra–Nehemiah, and of Chronicles, or Paralipomena.

When Jesus speaks in Luke 24:44 of the Law, the Prophets, and the Psalms, he refers to the Ketubim by naming the most important book in this section of the canon, the book that took pride of place in the synagogue liturgy. The redaction of the Ketubim took place over a period of more than a thousand years, since some fragments of the Book of Psalms [10] may date from the time of David or even from the eleventh and twelfth centuries. On the other hand, it was only slowly that the Ketubim, as a collection distinct from the Law and the Prophets, became part of the Palestinian canon.

When the Jewish Community was dispersed after the fall of Jerusalem in 70 A.D., it felt the need of a normative canon as a help in conserving the heritage of the past and preserving what remained of its unity. A synod was held at Jamnia (in Hebrew, Jabneh), thirteen miles south of Jaffa. The meetings of the Sanhedrin had been transferred there shortly before 70, and an important rabbinic school grew up there. At this synod the various books thus far mentioned were officially accepted as making up the Law, the Prophets, and the Writings. These are the Scriptures now called "proto-canonical."

The Jamnia decision did not, however, cover the whole of the Jewish tradition. It reflected, rather, the Pharisaic position and the Palestinian canon.[11] At Alexandria, Jews had accepted into the Greek Bible the Books of Tobit, Judith, Wisdom, Sirach, Baruch, and First and Second Maccabees, as well as parts of Esther (10:4–16:24) and Daniel (3:24-90 and 13–14). Although the Synod of Jamnia had excluded these books, now called deutero-canonical, Christian tradition opted to accept them as divinely inspired.[12]

Finally, certain other books, such as the Psalms of Solomon, the Third and Fourth Books of Maccabees, and the Prayer of Manasses, although contained in the Septuagint, are considered apocryphal by both the Jewish and the Christian traditions.

II. GREATNESS AND LIMITATION OF THE WRITTEN WORD

The writing down of God's word and the establishment of the canon of Scripture created a situation that was new in Israel's history. The essential element in the new situation was that God's word now shared in what might be termed the greatness and the limitation of codified writings.

As long as the word was proclaimed orally, it passed from mouth to ear within the ecclesial community. In these circumstances the word was very rich and fluid; it was as spontaneous as the life out of which it emerged and was highly adapted to the particular situations within which it was spoken; finally, it was spoken within the warm intimacy that characterized the great family of Israel. At the same time, however, the influence of the word thus spoken tended to be limited to the Israelite family and to the particular circumstances that elicited it. Now that the word was written down, it could easily be broadcast throughout the world and fully manifest its universality. No longer was it necessary to go to Palestine in order to hear the prophets; one needed only to unroll a scroll, whether one was in Babylon or Alexandria. There was no longer any need to wait for oracles to be spoken; God seemed to speak whenever man wished, since the scroll was always there.

The spread of God's word was considerably accelerated when the Seventy made the Greek translation of the Hebrew Bible. This work of translation began fairly early, probably around the middle of the third century B.C., and was completed around 150. Thanks to the Septuagint, God no longer spoke exclusively in Hebrew but began to use the everyday language of the Mediterranean peoples. Now the old Bible of the Jews could spread throughout the entire world and influence it.

The result was what might be called a democratization of the proclamation of God's word. The schools of the Law made the Torah known to the people. The more this nation of priests and kings (almost wholly lacking now any political existence) was dispersed throughout the world, the more necessary it became to study and know the Law. Through being committed to writing the word drew near to men and became their intimate. Wisdom had formerly been thought of as a royal princess enthroned beside God since before the mountains were piled up on the earth and before the springs of water were dug. Now she abandoned the eternal ages and descended into time, coming democratically and lovingly down among the children of men. Now she taught in the streets, raised her voice at the crossroads, and called out in the public squares: "My children, come and listen to me!" [13] The natural habitat or *Sitz im Leben* of her act of proclamation, the place at which she entered into and took root in the lives of the faithful, was no longer limited either to the solemn assemblies of former times or to the synagogue meetings. Now she took up her residence in the hearts of men: "How fortunate is the man who . . . delights in the law of Yahweh and meditates on it day and night" (Ps. 1:1-2).

But the writing down of the word also entailed certain dangers. The transition from living word to mute Bible is perilous, for it is a transition from the spirit to the letter. The Spirit of God, who inspires the spirit of man, is life, and while the letter too can be the bearer of life if it is filled with the Spirit, it is also able to kill.

Thus what the word gained in universality and influence, it was in danger of losing in intensity and vitality. The Law had in olden times left its impress on the whole life of Israel and had been the basis for the recurring renewals of the covenant; now it ran the risk of becoming a collection that was of interest only to the antiquarian. The Psalms, with their heartrending laments and their shouts of triumph, might become simply an anthology of poetry. The prophets had uttered oracles more penetrating than any sword, more burning than hot coals, as did Amos, who crossed the hills of Samaria with the message: "Prepare to meet your God, O Israel" (4:12); or Jeremiah, who sobbed in his distress: "You duped me, O Lord, and I let myself be duped" (20:7); or Ezekiel, who spoke so violently in branding the infidelity of the two sisters Oholah and Oholibah, that is, Samaria and Jerusalem (Ch. 23). These and all the great speakers of inspired words were in danger of becoming simply writers of books, and their oracles of being read as poems.

The transition from word to writing was indeed a perilous one. The written text might well become a *corpus mortuum* for grammarians, philologists, and etymologists. Instead of transmitting the word with all its power and ardor, men sometimes vivisected it. Once set down on the dead page, the prophecies were defenseless against the quibbling of the scribes, and the Torah would be besieged by the legalists. Is it not significant that the growing importance of the scribes and legislators as a class coincided with the decline of prophetism? This is not to deny that scribes and jurists did what they could to prepare the way for the coming of Jesus. Some of them did it with great humility, devoting a wealth of love and intelligence to the service of the word, so that their commentaries remind us of the Gospel. A mysterious dawn, prelude to the light that shines in the New Testament, seems to have begun to gleam in their hearts. Yet the danger was there of replacing the religion of the God of the Scriptures with a religion of the Scriptures of God. The message was in danger of hardening into a rigid book. Nor was the danger purely imaginary, for though Jesus succeeded in making the Old Testament flower into the universalism of the Gospel, others imprisoned it in the ghetto of their particularism.

III. GREATNESS AND LIMITATION OF THE CANON

The establishment of the canon of Scripture [14] likewise had elements of greatness and limitation.

On the positive side, the canon of Scriptures gave the ecclesial community a unique kind of certainty, since the canon embodied an official judgment as to the books that captured the authentic words of God. It thus marked off the boundaries of the field of Scripture, within which the faithful could now walk with full assurance, since they were no longer forced to move over the quicksands of the apocrypha. It marked out clearly the foundations on which the faith of the community could build.

Israel felt a deep pride as it made the canon its point of reference. What other nation on earth was in a similar happy situation? The Jewish historian Josephus writes: "We do not have vast numbers of books, discordant and conflicting, but only twenty-two, containing the record of all time and with reason believed to be divine. . . . It is evident from our actions what is our attitude to our own scriptures; for though so many centuries have gone by, no one has presumed to add, take away, or alter anything in them, but it is innate in every Jew from the day of his birth to regard them as the ordinances of God, to abide in them, and if needed be to die for them gladly." [15]

The canon also afforded the community a powerful shield against the apocrypha, closing the gates against the purely human writings whose stammerings threatened to obscure the clear voice of God's word. And in fact, between the second century B.C. and the first century A.D., that is, precisely in the period when the canon was being fully established, the muttering of the apocrypha became a loud uproar. Writings claiming to be inspired proliferated. In the narrative genre there were the Book of Jubilees, the three Books of Ezra and Maccabees, the Testament of Adam, the Life of Adam and Eve, the Apocalypse of Moses, the Ascension of Isaiah, and the Testaments of Job and of Solomon, to mention only the main items. In the didactic genre there were the Book of Enoch, the Assumption of Moses, the Fourth Book of Ezra, the Apocalypses of Abraham, Elijah, Baruch, Zephaniah, Ezekiel, etc. Against this outpouring of apocrypha that vied for the attention of readers, the canon of Scripture proved a providential safeguard for the faith of the community.

Alongside that we may call the greatness or merit of the canon, there are also aspects that are in a sense limitations or weaknesses of the canon. An official list of sacred books could give the impression that men wanted to imprison God's message within the covers of a collection of books. Out of respect for the words spoken of old, it was said that God spoke no longer; in fact, men even asked him not to speak any more.[16]

But God's freedom cannot be limited by any canon. All the books contained in the canon indeed contain the authentic word of God; but all of God's words are not necessarily contained in these books! God can speak outside the official framework which men accept. And the Psalmist tells us (Ps. 95:7-8) that if we hear God's voice today, we should not harden our hearts against it. From this point of view the relation between the word and the canon resembles the relation between grace and the sacraments. All the sacraments indeed communicate the grace of Jesus Christ, but not all graces come to us through the sacraments. The Lord can bestow his grace apart from the traditional sacramental order, as he wishes and to whomever he wishes. He can also speak apart from the Bible, as he wishes and to whomever he wishes. Even if, at the ecclesial level, these latter words do not have the same importance and significance as the word contained in the canon, that is, if they are meant essentially only for the person to whom they are addressed, they are nonetheless fully authentic.

We must add that in making known his will and his promises, God speaks not only through the Torah and the Prophets but also through the events of history.[17] During the period after Ezra, Israel became deeply familiar with the Scriptures and sought eagerly after the God of the Sacred Scriptures, but it was in danger of losing sight, to some extent, of the God who acted in its sacred history. Its heart became somewhat hardened and no longer had the spiritual flexibility which had enabled it of old to dialogue readily with Yahweh on all the paths on which history led it.

There would come a time when the scribes, their eyes fastened on the sacred books, would eagerly search out the word of God, even though the living word, the Word of God, Jesus the Messiah, was there before them, speaking to them face to face. Their eyes, now wearied by reading without the messianic light and without an eschatological awareness, had become myopic. "Search the Scriptures," Jesus told them; "they also testify on my behalf" (John 5:39). But the scribes had become moribund librarians, their eyes lovingly fastened on their ancient catalogues and unable to perceive and accept the messianic newness. They preferred to find their delight in reading the story of Moses according to the canon of the Old Testament. God, however, wanted to tell them the wonderful story of Jesus according to the New Testament.

---

[1] "The canon of Scripture is the list or collection, determined by tradition and the authority of the Church, of the books which, because they have a divine origin and an infallible authority, contain or themselves establish the norm of such truth as has been inspired by God" (E. Mangenot, "Canon," *DTC* 2:1554). This definition may be applied, with the necessary modifications, to the Palestinian canon followed by Ezra. — On the subject of the Palestinian canon, cf. Strack-Billerbeck, *Kommentar zum Neuen Testament aus Talmud und Midrasch* 4, Excursus 16: "Der Kanon des Alten Testaments und seine Inspiration" (pp. 415–51); F. Vigouroux, "Canon des Ecritures," *DB* 2:134–84; H.W. Beyer, "Kanōn," *TDNT* 3:596–602; R. Meyer, "Kryptō: Supplement on the Canon and the Apocrypha," *TDNT* 3:978–87; O. Eissfeldt, *The Old Testament: An Introduction*, section 75: "The Formation of the Canon" (pp. 562–71); M.–J. Lagrange, *Le judaïsme avant Jésus-Christ* (Paris, 1931), pp. 279–84; M.A. Beek, "Altes Testament," *Biblisch-Historisches Handwörterbuch* 1 (Göttingen, 1962), cols. 66–71; H. Haag, "La formation du Canon," *Mysterium salutis* 2 (Paris, 1969), pp. 167–75; P.R. Ackroyd, "The Old Testament in the Making," *The Cambridge History of the Bible* 1 (1970), pp. 105–59.

[2] Cf. F.-M. Abel, *Les livres des Maccabées* (Paris, 1949), pp. 307–9.

[3] The same principle holds in the dispensation of the new covenant. When all is said and done, the canonical books are those which the Catholic Church has considered to be canonical. Canon 12 of the First Council of Toledo (400?) says: "If anyone maintains that any scriptures save those the Catholic Church acknowledges are to be accepted as authoritative or given veneration, let him be anathema" (*DS* 202; *Enchiridion Biblicum*, no. 29). — On the New Testament canon, cf. H. von Campenhausen, *The Formation of the Christian Bible*, translated by J. A. Baker (Philadelphia, 1972).

[4] Cf. P.R. Ackroyd, *art cit.*, pp. 142–55: "The Canon in the Different Jewish Communities."

[5] This threefold division is found in the Bible itself, e.g., in 1 Macc. 12:9; in the Prologue to the Book of Sirach 1:1, 8-10, 24-25; and in the Gospel of Luke 24:44 ("The law of Moses and the prophets and psalms"). — The Jewish tradition likes to think of Ezra as the source of the Palestinian canon; cf. O. Eissfeldt, *op. cit.*, pp. 562–64.

[6] Cf. P. Grelot, "The Formation of the Old Testament," in Robert-Feuillet, *Introduction to the Old Testament*, p. 598: "In the Persian period it [the Torah] is fixed in its definitive form." Cf. O. Eissfeldt, *op. cit.*, p. 565; R. Meyer, "Kryptō," *TDNT* 3:978 ("The Torah was closed by c. 300 B.C.").

[7] These historical books were classified as prophetic because according to tradition they had been written by prophets: the Book of Joshua supposedly by the Joshua on whom, according to Num. 27:18, the Spirit rested; the Books of Judges and Samuel by the prophet Samuel; and the Books of Kings by the prophet Jeremiah. — The distinction between the former and the latter prophets is fairly recent; it is not found in the early rabbinic literature (cf. Strack-Billerbeck, *op. cit.*, 4:222).

[8] Cf. Sir. 44:1–50:24. On the date of composition of the Book of Sirach, cf. C. Spicq, *L'Ecclésiastique*, in Pirot-Clamer, *La Sainte Bible* 6 (Paris, 1946), p. 539; O. Eissfeldt, *op. cit.*, p. 597.

[9] Cf. Dan. 9:2. On the date of composition of the Book of Daniel, cf. M. Delcor, *Le livre de Daniel* (Paris, 1971), pp. 13–19.

[10] Such as, for example, Psalms 18 and 68; cf. H.-J. Kraus, *Die Psalmen* 1, p. lviii.

[11] The Sadducees regarded only the Pentateuch as canonical. At the other extreme, the Qumran community tended to regard some of the sect's own writings as inspired.

[12] The canonical character of the deutero-canonical books was called into question again in the Protestant Reformation of the sixteenth century. The problem of the proto-canonical and deutero-canonical books arose from the position taken by the rabbis at Jamnia. Concerning the Christian tradition, H. Haag writes: "The Christian Septuagint differed from the Jewish. The Christian Septuagint was established by the early Church. The fact is that the Fathers of the Church did not find in the Septuagint what they already considered canonical, but rather that they considered canonical what reached them in the Septuagint" (*art. cit.*, p. 172).

[13] See, e.g., the hymns to Wisdom in Prov. 1:20-33 and 8:22-26.

[14] As Y. Congar remarks in his *Tradition and Traditions: An Historical and a Theological Essay* (translated by M. Nasby and T. Rainborough; New York, 1966), we should speak at this point less of the fixing of a canon than of the acceptance of "the principle of a canon." The author notes that "an official and definitive list of inspired writings did not exist in the Catholic Church until the Council of Trent" (p. 38). In the time of Christ the tradition was still hesitant with regard to some of the sacred books, since the Canon followed at Alexandria included more books than were to be found in the Palestinian canon (cf. F. Vigouroux, "Canon," *DB* 2:137–43).

[15] Josephus, *Against Apion*, quoted by Eusebius in his *History of the Church* III, 10, 1–5 (here translated by G. A. Williamson [Harmondsworth, England, 1965], pp. 119–20). The testimony embodied in *Against Apion* dates from about 93 A.D. The "twenty-two books" refer to the Palestinian canon.

[16] This is what happened in Judaism after the coming of Jesus Christ; the Jews were unwilling to admit that the word of Jesus could be the word of God.

[17] Cf. below, Chapter 14.

Chapter 6

THE READING OF THE WORD OF GOD IN THE SYNAGOGUE SERVICE

INTRODUCTION

The second institution that is highly characteristic of the four centuries between Ezra and Jesus is the liturgical service of the synagogue, or, more precisely, the reading of the word of God in the synagogue service. After observing that "the law of the God of heaven," as promulgated by Ezra, was the starting point for the other writings that make up the Old Testament, M. Noth goes on to say:

> The reading and knowledge of this holy book which, characteristic- ally, was later called simply "the law," in spite of its basic narrative, thereby became an essential task of the pious community and the pious individual; and this provided the impulse for a particular form of divine service alongside the central sacrificial rite in Jerusalem, a form which it was possible to cultivate outside Jerusalem as well, above all in the Diaspora, and which consisted in the reading aloud and interpretation of sections of "the law." . . . The canonising of the Pentateuch as sacred scripture was the first step that was bound to lead to the synagogue and to scribal exegesis.[1]

The worship proper to the synagogue was simply the giving of institutional form, for the good of all, to the beatitude with which the Psalter begins: "Happy the man who . . . delights in the law of the Lord and meditates on his law day and night" (Ps. 1:1-2).[2] It also was the fulfillment of the commitment each Jewish community made to meditate, with a love that was proof against time, on the "Law" that had called it into existence and continued to be the ground of its life.

From the viewpoint of the Christian liturgy, the institution of the synagogue service was extremely important, for the readings in our liturgical celebrations are a direct inheritance from the worship in the synagogue. Historical study, however, has not yet succeeded in informing us adequately of the origins of the synagogue service, or for that matter of the origins of the synagogue itself. This venerable institution was for many centuries the center of Israel's life and determined the rhythm of its prayer, yet there still lies over it the veil of poetry that lends ancient things their aura of mystery. The documents we have are sometimes difficult to date and are in any case fairly late; thus the Mishnah, our chief source of information, is from the second century A.D.[3] Its interpretation of history is often marked by the partiality that love begets. Gradually, however, the past is yielding up its secret; some conclusions are still doubtful, but the information of which we are assured is quite rich enough.

1. Date

Jewish tradition chose to make Moses himself the origin of the service of readings. Philo of Alexandria, born twenty years before the Christian era began and thus a contemporary of Jesus, showed how widespread this belief was when he wrote that Moses "made note of the beauty [of the seventh day, that is, the Sabbath] on the holy tables of the Law; he impressed it on the minds of all when he commanded that after every six days men should celebrate the seventh . . . by devoting themselves solely to the love of wisdom [literally: philosophy] and thereby scrutinizing their consciences and improving their ways."[4] (Philo speaks here of "philosophy" in order to make himself understood by his non-Jewish readers; in his view, the study of the law springs from love of wisdom.)

In thus putting the reading service under the patronage of the great lawgiver, the intention was to bestow on it the dignity that stems from long duration. The point also being made was that the practice was based on the Deuteronomic prescription which Moses was thought to have issued: "On the feast of Booths . . . at the end of every seven-year period, when all Israel goes to appear before the Lord, your God, in the place which he chooses, you shall read this law aloud in the presence of all Israel" (Deut. 31:10-11).

James, the brother of the Lord, who presided over the Jerusalem community in apostolic times, sums up the popular belief when he says, in the discourse reported in Acts: "After all, for generations now Moses has been proclaimed in every town and has been read aloud in the synagogues on every sabbath" (Acts 15:21).

The modern historian has certainly reduced the number of these "generations." It is clear, nonetheless, that Israel had a very old tradition with regard to the reading of the sacred books. The custom of the synagogue service grew up only gradually and developed slowly, following the rhythm of the community's life. The service was in fact the fruit of the ancient tender love God's people had for the word that had brought it into existence. There was a continuity between the solemn reading of Deuteronomy by Ezra during the eight days of the Feast of Tents and the reading of Isaiah by Jesus in the synagogue of Nazareth (Luke 4:16-21).

As the two extreme possible dates for the establishment of the synagogue service of readings, we may take the period of Ezra, or the beginning of the fifth century, as the earliest, and the middle of the third century as the latest. The institution can hardly antedate the time of Ezra, for there is nothing to support the hypothesis that the synagogue service existed even before the Exile. On the other hand, it is easy to understand how the conditions of exile could play a decisive role in the establishment of the synagogue. "Isolation from Jerusalem and the temple undoubtedly favoured the development of gatherings and buildings for worship in the exile, so that the exiles might well have brought the synagogue back with them from Babylon to Palestine."[5]

At the other extreme, we may not date the beginning of the synagogue service later than the middle of the third century, since there is historical evidence for the existence of synagogues in the Diaspora at this period (as, for example, the inscription at Schedia in Egypt that dates from the time of Ptolemy III Euergetes (247–221).[6] Synagogues, however, were built essentially as places for the reading of the law.[7] This was the same period during which the canon of Scripture was established for the Nebiim, or Prophets.[8] It was this canon that provided the community with a list of the prophetic books which might be read in the synagogal service after the proclamation of the Torah. It was also around 250 that the Greek translation or Septuagint version of the Pentateuch was completed, a translation that nicely met the needs of worshipers in the Diaspora.

2. Temple and synagogue

It has been said that

> Worship in the synagogue, where Jews gathered to read the law and to pray, was simply an extension of worship in the Tem-

ple. . . . Anyone who betook himself to the synagogue morning and
evening of sabbaths and feast days could legitimately think of himself
as part of the assembly of the children of Israel at Jerusalem; he
shared in their offerings, songs, and prayers.[9]

We may observe, in this connection, that for the festival celebrated by Ezra (really the birthday of Judaism) the reading of the
law is described as done according to the ritual in use later on in the
synagogue. Thus the writer turns that reading into the first
synagogal service, as it were. The reading is introduced by a blessing, as in the later tradition; the reader stands on a platform which
evidently recalls the ambo or bema of the synagogues; the law is
translated, which suggests the manner in which the targums came
into being; finally, the reporter of the assembly of Ezra mentions the
communion meal but avoids speaking of sacrifices, an omission
which underlines the parallel between the assembly held by Ezra
and the assemblies in the synagogue.

We may also recall here the institution of the groups of laymen
known as *ma'amadot*:[10] when the sacrifices in the Temple were
offered in the presence of one of these groups, they were regarded
as offered by all of the people. Since it was evidently impossible for
everyone to be constantly present in Jerusalem, the laity were divided into twenty-four classes (corresponding to the twenty-four
classes of priests); each class in turn, as delegate of the entire
people, took part in the Temple worship. A group from one class
would go to Jerusalem, while the rest of the group would remain
back in their village and gather each day in the local synagogue to
celebrate the same hours of prayer and read the same passages from
the Torah as were being celebrated and read at Jerusalem. In this
way worship in the synagogue was linked with worship in the Temple.

I. THE READING OF THE LAW, OR TORAH

A. THE EVIDENCE OF TRADITION

1. *Opening blessing*

The heart of the celebration in the synagogue was the reading of
the Law, or Torah, that is, the Pentateuch.[11] This reading was
usually introduced by a blessing which the reader pronounced. This
custom could undoubtedly claim to originate with Ezra, for the
Chronicler tells us that Ezra began his solemn reading of the law on
the Feast of Tents with a blessing which the people accepted with

upraised hands and a double "Amen!" (Neh. 8:6).[12] When this blessing is mentioned in the Mishnah[13] (in the second century,
therefore), it is further to be explained by the fact that the readings
occurred within a prayer service and were fittingly to be framed
within praise of God, the Master of all life through his word.

Tradition has preserved the memory of the formulas used in such
blessings, and some of them are very beautiful. The reader begins
by exhorting the assembly: "Bless Yahweh, who is supremely
blessed!" The assembly answers with an acclamation: "Blessed be
you, Yahweh, who are supremely blessed forever and ever!" Then
the reader pronounces a ritual blessing: "Blessed be you, Yahweh,
our God, king of the world! You have chosen us out of the midst of
the nations and given us your law. Blessed be you, Yahweh, who
give us the law."[14]

2. Readings for feasts and sequential readings

On the feast days it was natural to read those passages from the
Pentateuch which related to the event being commemorated. But
on the sabbaths (unless a feast day occurred on one or other of them)
there was to be a sequential reading (*lectio continua*) of the whole
Pentateuch. Each of these two ways of reading the Bible had a
theological signification. In practicing a sequential reading of the
Pentateuch, the Church of the old covenant, guardian of the Scriptures, was saying that the whole of Scripture, even such pages as
seemed barren and were harsh in style, possessed in fact the incomparable dignity of being the word of God on which the community
must base its faith. On the other hand, in choosing certain passages
to be read on feast days, the Church was saying that it knew how to
adapt the word to the needs of its children and the requirements of
its liturgy.

This concern for the community would lead the tradition to omit
the translation of some passages judged disedifying, lest they cast a
shadow over the memory of the ancestors. Thus, according to the
Mishnah[15] the following were to be read but not translated into the
vernacular: the stories of Reuben's incest (Gen. 35:22), the golden
calf (Exod. 32), David's adultery with Bathsheba and the murder of
Uriah (2 Sam. 11:2-17), Amnon's incest with his sister Tamar (2
Sam. 13:1-22). The good of the community — whether the ancient
community of which the Bible speaks or the present community
which reads it — is more important than the mere material understanding of the text.

3. *Triennial cycle and annual cycle*

There were two forms of sequential reading: the Palestinian cycle and the Babylonian cycle.

The Palestinian cycle divided the reading of the Pentateuch to cover three years.[16] Each reading covered a section, or seder, the limits of which had been determined by tradition. The five books of the Pentateuch had been divided into 154 sections, to fit the greatest possible number of sabbaths that could occur in a three-year period. This did not mean that all the traditions, springing up as they did in the fertile soil of popular piety, were fully in harmony: some sources speak of 161 or 167 or even 175 readings (which spread the reading of the Law over a period of three and a half years). The figure 175 was venerated on the grounds that it corresponded to the length of Abraham's life according to Gen. 25:7. Commenting on the text of Ps. 68:19, "You have ascended the height, you have taken captivity captive, you have received the gift because of the man," Rabbi Joshua ben Levi (ca. 250) explains: "The 175 sections . . . correspond to the years our father Abraham lived. For it is written: You (that is, Moses) have ascended the height (of Sinai), you have taken captivity captive, you have received the gift (of the law) because of the man (Abraham). . . . That is why Moses established 175 sections for the reading of the Torah; such was the sacrifice of praise to be offered perpetually each sabbath."[17]

The cycle in the Babylonian tradition, on the other hand, had only 54 sedarim and extended over only a single year. This tradition was probably of more recent origin than the Palestinian[18] but ended by supplanting the latter in most Jewish communities.[19]

4. *The organization of the cycles*

The historical fact of the readings has been solidly established, but the cyclic organization of the sections read has not yet yielded the secret of its origins to the historian's probing.[20] The documents we have are relatively recent, although they certainly bear witness to a practice that is very old. In the present state of the research the following facts are taken as certain:

—For the major feasts the readings were fixed from the second century, which was the period of definitive redaction of the Mishnah.[21] We may assume that this ordinance for *feast day readings* was in fact much older. When the Mishnah says: "The law commands the reading on each feast of what concerns it,"[22] it enunciates a simple rule of common sense which the liturgical communities must have long been following.

—Outside the feast days there must surely have been a *sequential reading* at this period, for the Mishnah sees the feast day readings as interrupting the usual order; the latter is to be taken up again after the feast.[23]

—The Mishnah does not know of the *sequential reading* of set passages that recur according to a *fixed cycle*. We may suppose that such an organization of the synagogue service arose after the redaction of the Mishnah and became mandatory only in the third century.[24]

5. *Days of celebration*

The starting point for this whole development was to be found in the prescription of Deut. 31:10 that the law was to be read every seven years at the Feast of Tents. We may assume that a similar reading was quite naturally included in the celebration of the covenant festival, then on the other feasts, and finally on sabbaths and on the fast days, which became numerous in the period preceding New Testament times. It finally refused to stop even with the sabbaths and took place within the week, on Mondays and Thursdays.[25] These two days were market days, when the rural population, which did not always have synagogues at its disposal, gathered in the towns and villages and could take advantage of the opportunity to hear the word of God.

The significance of these readings was brought out very well by the Jewish tradition. The text of Exod. 15:22 provided the basis for an allegory: ". . . traveling for three days through the desert without finding water," and the teachers of the law lovingly explained it:

> "Water" here means simply the Torah itself, in accordance with Isaiah 55:1, "All you who are thirsty, come to the water!" When they had been three days without the teaching of the Torah, they were exhausted. The prophets rose up among them and ordered that the Torah be read on the sabbath; then they were to skip the first day of the week [Sunday] and read again: Then skip the third and fourth days, and read on the fifth [Thursday]; and finally, skip the day of preparation for the sabbath [Friday]. Thus they would not pass three days without a reading of the Torah.[26]

Thus the law, whose observance (it has been said) gave body to the sabbath sacrifice of praise, became throughout the week the people's food; it allayed their hunger and restored their strength, so that they might not collapse on the journey which was taking them across the desert of the weekdays to the oasis of the sabbath.

6. *The readers*

Who was permitted to serve as a reader? In principle, this ministry was not restricted to a special class (priests, lawyers, or teachers of the law) but could be exercised by any Israelite: "Originally, all without exception could be invited to read the Torah to the congregation, including women and minors and even slaves."[27] The act of reading was made quite easy by the fact that the same passages recurred at regular intervals; thus the community had the opportunity to become familiar with the texts and to learn them by heart. The historian Josephus would claim, not without a touch of boasting, that children could recite the law more readily than tell you their own name.[28]

The person chosen by the leader of the synagogue rose and came to the pulpit for the reading. "He stood up to do the reading," says St. Luke (4:17), as he tells how Jesus performed the office of reader in the synagogue of Nazareth. The community probably decided in advance who was to proclaim the word, for the person was expected to exercise this function with the greatest possible dignity and therefore to prepare the text out of respect for the word (even if he happened to be familiar with the text already).

Rabbi Aqiba ben Joseph, whose learning and piety were the bright jewel of the Jewish community after the debacle of 70 A.D., gave a splendid example in this regard. "One day the leader of the synagogue called on Rabbi Aqiba for the public reading of the Torah to the community. But he was unwilling to go up [on the platform where the lectern was]. His disciples said to him: 'Master, have you not taught us that the Torah means life and length of days to you? Why, then, do you refuse to do the reading?' He answered: 'By heaven! I have refused only because I have not been able to go through the text two or three times in advance. A man has no right to proclaim the words of the Torah to the community unless he has repeated them to himself two or three times in advance. That is how even God himself acts . . . even though to his eyes the Torah is as luminously clear as starlight. For when he was about to give the Torah to the Israelites, then, according to Job 28:27, 'he saw . . . and appraised it' and 'gave it its setting.' Only then, as the following verse tells us, did he communicate it to man."[29]

Not one but several readers discharged the office.[30] There were

three readers for ordinary weekday services, seven or even more for
the sabbaths and the great feasts.[31] This arrangement was rich in
spiritual meaning: In the synagogal service it was not the individual
who was the bearer of the word but the entire community, represented by its various readers. The reading thus became impersonal
in a sense; it was not limited to a privileged appointed few but was
enriched with the personality of the community as a whole. The
whole people listened to the word, but the whole people also proclaimed the word. God spoke to the community through the community.

7. Translation and translators

The text, after being read in Hebrew (the language of revelation,
which had become the language of student and scholar), was immediately translated into Aramaic.[32] The translator was called a
meturgeman, and the translation a *targum*. It is true enough that
Hebraizing circles sometimes showed a certain distrust of Aramaic;
they said men were to avoid praying in Aramaic because the angels
commissioned with presenting our prayers before God's throne did
not understand this language.[33] But the pressures of history could
not be withstood, and it was necessary to use the Aramaic that had
replaced Hebrew as the vernacular.

There were detailed rules for the translator's activity; their aim
was chiefly to preserve the primacy of the Hebrew text over the
Aramaic paraphrase. The functions of reader and translator had to
be exercised by two different persons. The translator was to speak
after each verse so that the people might miss nothing of God's
word; he was not to speak more loudly than the reader. He was also,
and emphatically, forbidden to use, in the synagogue, a written
translation or even to let his gaze meet the Hebrew scroll; his whole
function was to provide an oral translation of the written word.

Everyone knows that in addition to having a thorough knowledge
of two languages, a translator must also be intellectually very humble, since, under the guise of explication, he may readily introduce
his own ideas into the text. R. le Déaut observes:

> It is likely that numerous ideas current in the world of the apocrypha
> (many of which were written in Aramaic), the apocalypses, and even
> of Hellenism entered the Jewish world by way of the translator-
> commentators in the synagogues. Their function gave them a wel-
> come opportunity for spreading their own ideas, and only a very
> broad kind of censorship existed that could keep them from yielding
> to the temptation.[34]

In principle, every competent person — even a minor, says the Mishnah[35] — could act as a translator; but it is understandable that in fact only the educated people of the community functioned in this way.

8. Final blessing

In order to round off the proclamation of the law, the final reader was to pronounce a blessing. Tradition justified this rite by comparing the reading of God's word to a meal: "If we are to recite blessings before and after eating the food that sustains our ephemeral lives, how much more should we do so for the law which represents eternal life!"[36] The formula handed down by the tradition reads: "Blessed be you, Yahweh, our God, King of the world! You have given us the Law of truth, you have sown in us the seed of eternal life. Blessed be you, Yahweh, who heap upon us the treasure of your Law."[37]

The formula itself may be relatively recent, but the occurrence of a blessing at this point is guaranteed for antiquity since the Mishnah speaks of it.[38]

B. Significance of the Reading of the Torah

When the people of the synagogue read the Torah, or five books of the Pentateuch, they were reading their own sacred history from its beginnings to the entry into the Promised Land. What was the spiritual significance of this reading? To begin with, what significance did Israel itself attribute to the reading?

1. A sacred history and a profession of faith

As the holy people of God, Israel had no profane or secular history. In its eyes, history existed at all only to the extent that it was sacred, that is, to the extent that God's marvelous interventions gave content to the passing years and centuries. God created the temporal duration of Israel, as he created everything else — for his beloved. Israel's "days," like those of the individual believer, were "in your hand" (Ps. 31:16 JB). God could truly be said to have "made" certain days, for he filled them with gladness and rejoicing and did wonderful things therein (Ps. 118:15–24). But there were also "days of the Lord" that were grief-starred and filled with darkness, when "the earth trembles, the heavens shake" at the coming judgment (Joel 2:1–10). Merely profane days, whatever their fullness from the human viewpoint, do not count, for they simply drift along the stream of time and are drowned in oblivion.

It is not simply the events marking the stages in the history of God's people that provide the measure of this history; rather, it is the spiritual fullness of the events that both creates the history and is the measure of its meaning. Israel seems to have had little interest in sheer facts as such; it had no sense of the importance of dates or of the precise value of a number, and its chronologies and genealogies were superficial or even the work of fantasy.[39] But its whole soul and all its powers of loving intuition were focused on the spiritual and theological significance of events.[40] Israel had put its hand with childlike trust into the hand of God; from that moment on, as it walked its historical road toward the great adventure, what mattered in its eyes was not the route or the stages of the journey but simply the fact of walking together with God.

This high degree of sensitivity to the religious aspect of reality had for its counterpart a lack of interest in the history of neighboring countries. Who were the contemporaries of Abraham? What was the name of the king of Ur? During what dynasties did the patriarchs live in Egypt? What was the name of Pharaoh's daughter who rescued Moses in his papyrus basket? Who was the Pharaoh of the Exodus? Israel did not know and showed no curiosity about these things, nor any concern to furnish points of reference so that its spiritual adventure might be located in relation to the stream of universal history. The great events were simply left floating on the ocean of the past wherever the narrators chose to put them, and the connecting links between the events were lost in the mist of time. But on each event shone the light of God.

In the Bible we find all sorts of materials, gathered and kept because a religious meaning was discerned in them; everything was heaped up and treasured, lest anything valuable be lost. But what disorder reigns! Sometimes two different traditions stand side by side or confront one another and complement one another. Which gives a more accurate picture of events? Which tradition concerning the Flood should we follow — the Yahwist or the Elohist? That is a question Israel never even asked. In its eyes, both traditions were good because each offered a theological truth. And what charming details we find, which some people would consider meaningless but which the Spirit of God nonetheless thought it worthwhile to keep! God himself closes the door of Noah's ark (Gen. 7:16); by so doing he gives his servant a final sign of his tender love before launching the house of tarred rushes on the tumultuous sea of the flood; God does not abandon this man who is the hope of a world renewed. When young Rebecca comes to the well of Nahor in the evening and gives water to Abraham's servant and his ten camels, it is God himself whose hand tilts the pitcher and thus signals the future wife of Isaac and heiress of Abraham (Gen. 24, especially vv. 42–44). It is by such details as these that God enlightens hearts. Through them the biblical story becomes a story of salvation and literally a "revealing"[41] of God.

This conception of history found expression in ways suited to it. Whether in the ancient narratives that circulated in the old Israelite sanctuaries or later in the writings which gave these narratives a fixed form, sacred history was expressed in a unique literary genre which had no equivalent in history as written by a Herodotus or a Thucydides. The Torah does not aim at giving an impersonal, objective account of the facts related; its intention is rather to present a *profession of faith*. Israel gives expression to its history in the form of an acclamation addressed to the God who works wonders. The historical data are not denied, but they are made subservient to faith. The narrative aims at a maximum theological content.

At times, in his love for the cause of Yahweh, the narrator may go beyond the historian, who is limited to and by the data of history. The narrator becomes a teacher and does not hesitate to schematize, simplify, and get straight to the real point. Consider, for example, the framework into which the accounts in the Book of Judges are fitted:

—The children of Israel do what is evil in the Lord's sight, and become servants of the Baals and the Astartes.
—The Lord delivers them into the hands of their enemies.
—In the midst of their distress they cry out to the Lord.
—He sends them a Judge-Savior.
—The land is now at peace for a number of years.
—Then the cycle begins all over again.

Here, then, we have a course in theology! How can we extract a chronology or put our finger on the objective historical events? Yet the essential thing, from the biblical viewpoint, has been said clearly and without any uncertainty: Yahweh's tender love for his people is inexhaustible; he repeatedly rescues them from their fears and distress; his good will toward Israel is greater than Israel's wickedness, his fidelity greater than Israel's infidelity.[42]

It is evident that a wide gulf separates our conception of history from that of Israel. We use ancient documents, the most objective we can find, to reconstruct the past. Israel does just the opposite: It starts with its own faith, and in the light of that it refashions and interprets the events of the past. "The characteristic of all Israel's contemplation of history is that it was a direct expression of her faith."[43]

Because it was a direct expression of faith, it was transmitted from generation to generation like a family possession and retold from age to age.

> What we have heard and know,
>   and what our fathers have declared to us,
> We will not hide from their sons;
>   we will declare to the generations to come
> The glorious deeds of the Lord and his strength
>   and the wonders that he wrought.
> He set it up as a decree in Jacob,
>   and established it as a law in Israel,
> That what he commanded our fathers
>   they should make known to their sons;
> So that the generation to come might know,
>   their sons yet to be born,
> That they too may rise and declare to their sons
>   that they should put their hope in God (Ps. 78:3–6).[44]

Given this perspective, we can better understand the significance of the reading of the Law. When the children of Israel gathered each sabbath, it was in order to join in proclaiming their faith, to recall the marvelous deeds of God, and to sing praise to the Lord in accordance with the "decree in Jacob" and the "law in Israel." When they listened to the Torah, they were not listening to a course in paleography or a dull lecture on ancient archives or an inventory of their annals or a recitation of the catechism. When they recalled the past in such a spirit of love, it was not in order to caress dead bones or embalm the corpses of their ancestors, but to celebrate the living God of Abraham and Moses.

Thus we can say that Israel, like the Church of our day, was never finished with reading the Torah, because it never stopped professing its faith. There is, however, something more.

2. A history actualized in the present

We Westerners represent time as linear. We like to think of history as unfolding in time along a line that is endless. At the center we put our own "today," with the past behind us and the future in front of us, and we situate ourselves by relation to a past that is now irreversible and a future that is not yet accessible. Israel's conception of time was different, for it situated itself basically by relation to God rather than to time. The important thing in its eyes was not its position within time, for time was an empty and unreliable thing that disappeared like a dream at waking and unraveled like a tattered robe.[45] The important thing was its relation to God, who stands over the everlasting ages and before whom all time is present in the single day of eternity: "A thousand years in your sight are as yesterday, now that it is past, or as a watch in the night" (Ps. 90:4; 2 Peter 3:8).

Israel looked at its own history with the eyes of God. It was as though Israel saw all events gathered into one place before it, with all their depth of religious meaning; it was as though events were no longer spread out through time and had lost their place and relative rank in the historical perspective. Or, to put it another way, it was as though all the different strata of the past were gathered up into the one present moment. Thus Psalm 114 treats as equally actual, and embraces in a single act of praise, both the crossing of the Red Sea and the crossing of the Jordan, even though the two events were forty years apart, according to the biblical tradition, and had taken place centuries ago. Deuteronomy summons to the foot of Mount Sinai not only the Church of the desert but all future generations as well, as though ever since the Exodus Israel had stood outside the stream of time: "The Lord, our God, made a covenant with us at Horeb; not with our fathers [only] did he make this covenant, but with us, all of us who are alive here this day. The Lord spoke with you face to face on the mountain from the midst of the fire" (Deut. 5:3-4).

Similarly, Psalm 95 says that the temptation which Yahweh allowed the people of the Exodus to undergo at Massah and Meribah still threatens each generation: "Oh, that today you would hear his voice: 'Harden not your hearts as at Meribah, as in the day of Massah in the desert' " (Ps. 95:7-8). The author of the Letter to the Hebrews will explain that this "today" embraces every day of our lives (Heb. 3:7-13).

It would be naive to think that because this biblical conception of history differs from ours, it is therefore less valid; no, it is simply different! Reflecting on the Israelite understanding of time, R. Aron writes:

> For a Jew, every fleeting moment has something of the savour of
> eternity. Present, past, and future run together, and in their meeting
> the present does not play a part of mere regret or expectation; it is, on
> the contrary, the link by which history is made to remain alive, by
> which the future is present before it has arrived and the past lives
> after it has gone by.[46]

Thus, the reading of the Torah was not only a profession of faith
but also an actualization of the ancient narratives for the benefit of
the community. As it read its ancient history, Israel was fully involved; it was living its own history. This community was the people
of whom the Torah was speaking. Together with the Church of the
Exodus, the Israel of a later day left Egypt, received the law at
Mount Sinai, wandered across the desert, and entered the Promised
Land. In every reading in the synagogue, the past lived in the
present.

In order to bring out more fully this actualization of the ancient
narratives of the Torah, the congregation mimed the texts. Thus on
the Feast of Passover the people ate the Passover lamb with loins
girt, sandals on their feet, staff in hand; they ate in haste as though
they must once again flee from an invisible Pharaoh.[47] On the Feast
of Tents, people lived for seven days in huts made of branches, in
memory of the encampments in the desert.[48] Instead of being a
useless exhumation of the past, the reading of the Torah thus became the liturgical celebration of the wonderful deeds by which the
Lord had redeemed his people.

II. THE READING OF THE PROPHETS, OR THE HAFTARAH

A. The Evidence of Tradition

After the proclamation of the Law came the Haftarah, or reading
of the Prophets.

1. Opening blessing

Like the first reading, this was introduced by a blessing. The
formula preserved by tradition reads as follows: "Blessed be you,
Yahweh, our God, King of the world! You have chosen the true
prophets and taken delight in their oracles, which were spoken in
truth. Blessed be you, Yahweh, who have chosen the Torah, your
servant Moses and your people Israel, and the prophets of truth and
justice!"[49]

2. A commentary on the Law

The reasons why a reading from the Prophets was introduced into the synagogal service are not clear. It is assumed that this second reading was regarded as a commentary on the Law, an explanation of it that showed the Law's continuing relevance. It is highly unlikely that in the early days of the synagogal institution this second reading had any autonomous existence; it must have derived its value entirely from its relation to the Torah and must have provided the basis for the homily. Only much later did this reading itself take on the significance attached to the proclamation of God's word.[50]

In order to assure that there would be such a commentary on the Torah, the readings were chosen precisely for the light they could shed on the ancient texts. Consequently there was not, in the beginning at least, a sequential reading of the Prophets,[51] as there was for the Law; instead a choice was made not only among passages but even among verses within a passage.[52] If the reading was to be from the twelve minor prophets, it was even possible to jump from book to book.[53]

The correspondence between the reading from the Law and the reading from the Prophets could not, of course, always be perfect. Without indulging in extremes of allegorization, it was not possible to find 165 passages from the Prophets that would perfectly illustrate the 165 sedarim from the Torah. In consequence, it was necessary to be satisfied with purely verbal connections. But this, it was thought, was enough, since the word of God had an inner unity in any event.

3. Date

At what period was this reading introduced into the synagogal service? Basing himself on the fact that a sequential reading did not determine the choice of passages, I. Elbogen maintains that "the reading from the Prophets is certainly less ancient than the reading from the Torah, but on the other hand it must antecede the establishment of the canon of the prophets."[54] Now the canon of the Prophets was established around 300 B.C.,[55] and consequently the reading from the Prophets may have been introduced in the third century. In New Testament times it is so traditional a part of the synagogal service on the sabbath that it is mentioned as self-evident.[56]

4. Final blessing

An important blessing terminated the reading service. It ran as follows: "Blessed be you, Yahweh, our God, King of the world, the rock on which all the ages rest, just toward all generations. Faithful God, you speak and things are, you command and they exist. Yes, all your words are justice and truth." Then the entire congregation, standing, replies: "You are faithful, Yahweh, our God, and all your words are faithful too. You are the Faithful One, the Living One, and you exist eternally! May your name and your memory rule over us always and through all the ages!" The reader then concludes: "You are faithful. Blessed be you, Yahweh, the God who is faithful in all his words!" [57]

B. Significance of the Reading of the Prophets

The reading of the Prophets did not have, in the Jewish tradition, the same high place as the reading of the Law. [58]

—The Law was read in its entirety and sequentially, in the form of passages chosen by tradition; the texts of the Prophets could be chosen freely by the reader.

—The reading of the Law was done by several readers; the reading of the Prophets, by one reader.

—The Law was translated verse by verse so that the community might hear the word of God in a strictly literal way; the prophets could be translated freely and in groups of three verses. [59]

—The reading of the Law was obligatory at all services, even the weekday ones; the reading of the Prophets was not universally prescribed (according to the Mishnah it could be omitted on Monday and Wednesday).

Despite the lesser esteem thus accorded the Prophets, this reading was to grow in importance, to the point of changing the meaning of the synagogal service.

1. Deeper understanding and spiritualization of the Law

Deuteronomy (18:15-18) had foretold that after Moses, God would raise up a new prophet who would continue to proclaim the word and make its demands known. From the Deuteronomic viewpoint, therefore, the prophetic movement was a prolongation of the revelation of the Torah at Mount Sinai and a renewed call to the ministry exercised by Moses. From the ninth to the fourth century (the period of classical prophetism), the prophets continued to rise like stars in the heaven of Israel and shed their light upon the Law: commenting on it, reminding men of its requirements, making it relevant and topical for their brothers. The prophets are

> the "disturbers of Israel" (Darmesteter), the spiritual guides of the theocracy, the defenders of the covenant, the founders of the new Israel. Inspired men with a message *(dabar)*, men of spirit *(ruaḥ)*, men ahead of their own time, they proclaim the religion of tomorrow and relate it to the religion of yesterday. They are the confidants and spokesmen of a God who reveals himself in history. They are attuned to all the interests of the living God and have a horror of any sort of politics or casuistry that might attenuate His word. The understanding of their message was favored by the historical disorders and the climate of catastrophe in which they preached. Their work is the heart of the Old Testament.[60]

Having become the intimate of God, the prophet grasps more fully and deeply the infinite virtualities and riches contained in the message of the Torah. Because he is both *rôeh*, or the "seer" who contemplates mysterious, hidden things, and *nabî*, or the herald who speaks in God's name (the "mouthpiece" of Yahweh: Jer. 15:19),[61] he enables Israel to become familiar with mystery, to contemplate the Invisible One, and to approach the Unapproachable One. He reveals the transcendence of God but also his nearness, his power but also his tender love, his stern demands but also his forgiveness. From Amos, Israel comes to know better the God of justice for the poor; from Hosea, the God of Love; from Isaiah, the holy God; from Jeremiah, the God of the new covenant; from Ezekiel, the God of personal religion; from Habakkuk, the God of faith; from Joel, the God of conversion and the outpoured Spirit; from Zephaniah, the God of the last Day and the rescue of the humble. Each prophet tells each generation of his discovery of the God who has broken into his life.

By contact with these great men of the spirit, Israel's religion is purified. It was in danger of becoming a social affair or even an affair of the royal court; now it is again suddenly a business of the heart: "You have been told, O man, what is good, and what the Lord requires of you: only to do the right and to love goodness, and to walk humbly with your God" (Micah 6:8). It was in danger of being overwhelmed by juridicism and legalism; now Israel learns that sin is not a failure to observe an external code but a failure of love, and that ritualism must make way for a religion that involves the soul: "It is love that I desire, not sacrifice" (Hos. 6:6; cf. Matthew 9:13 and 12:7).

It was well, then, that on every sabbath Israel should come into contact again with these words of fire that were to burn in her heart down the centuries. If the Old Testament period was a long catechumenate in preparation for the Christ, the prophets were the catechists. They did not have to invent their teaching (the Torah was sufficient), but they made men's heart intimately familiar with what was most divine in that teaching.

2. History in tension toward the future

Because he wants his dialogue with God to be uninterrupted, the prophet is a man very alert to perceive and interpret the messages he receives from on high. He is fully aware that Yahweh reveals himself to his people not only through the prophetic word but also through events, and therefore the prophet must examine ongoing history no less than the word. Both are manifestations of God. The prophet compares them and uses the one to interpret the other, placing history under the judgment of the word and shedding light on the word through events. "It is characteristic of biblical history that those who carry it forward are made aware of its *direction* through the teachings of the prophets. The prophet, the *nabi*, is someone who understands the 'sense' of history, what it means and whither it moves."[62] By knowing the past he gains a better understanding of the present and is able to interpret the major forces that give structure to the future. His interpretation depends not on mathematical deduction but on his deep sense of the flow of grace and the broken rhythms of sin. In short, he can interpret because his ear is attuned to his God. Thus the prophet's preaching becomes prediction.

The formula "Thus says the Lord" is complemented now by another: "Behold, the day is coming. . . ." The prophets thus shape a religion that is open to the future; as a result of their work, the past recorded in the Torah and actualized in the synagogue service acquires a new dimension. The Yahwist religion becomes a religion oriented to the "new age"; it becomes an eschatological religion.[63] The past turns into hope, the Law into prophecy.

The Law told, for example, of the creation of the first paradise, a splendid garden wherein God walked at the breezy time of day and, man, at peace with himself and the world, spoke familiarly to the animals and called each by its name (Gen. 2:19-20; 3:8). Sin, however, caused brambles and nettles to spring up everywhere. Then the prophets proclaimed a re-creation: *new heavens* and *a new earth*: "The hardships of the past shall be forgotten, and hidden from my eyes. Lo, I am about to create new heavens and a new earth . . . I create Jerusalem to be a joy and its people to be a delight" (Is. 65:16-18).[64]

The Law told of the departure from Egypt with a pillar of fire and a bright cloud leading the way. Now the prophet Hosea foresaw a *new exodus*, in which the virgin Israel, like a bride treading in the footprints of her husband, would follow Yahweh with all the tenderness of recaptured love: "I will lead her into the desert and speak to her heart. . . . She shall respond there as in the days of her youth, when she came up from the land of Egypt. . . . I will espouse you to me forever: I will espouse you in right and in justice, in love and in mercy; I will espouse you in fidelity" (Hos. 2:16-17, 21-22).

The Law told of the giving of the Decalogue on stone tablets, amid the lightning flashes of Mount Sinai. Now the prophet Jeremiah foretold a *new covenant*, under which God would imprint his law in men's hearts: "The days are coming, says the Lord, when I will make a new covenant with the house of Israel. . . . I will place my law within them, and write it upon their hearts" (Jer. 31:31, 33).

The prophets were constantly discovering the future to be a renewal of the past. They foretell a *new Jerusalem*, gleaming with gold and precious stones, over which the immense light of Yahweh's glory would rise and to which all the nations of the earth would stream;[65] a *new temple*, built with splendid proportions in an idealized Jerusalem;[66] a *new priesthood*, in which the sons of Levi, no longer bent upon collecting tithes and dues, would offer a pure oblation to the Lord;[67] a *new David*, whose birth would bring light to the peoples groping in darkness and the shadow of death, and upon whom the Spirit of God would rest in his fullness and who would inaugurate a paradisal age;[68] a *new gathering* of all the children of Israel, who would change from dry bones scattered on the desolate plains of captivity into a vast army;[69] and, above all, a *new heart* and a *new spirit*.[70]

Due to the reading of the Prophets, the synagogue service became a celebration of the God who continues to intervene constantly in the life of his people and who proclaims his "Day." The sacred reading of the ancient texts was thus not to be compared to a celebration of "the good old days," but was a moment of both trepidation and joy in which, through meditation on the past, men prepared themselves to welcome the God who comes.

This was the fundamental new element that the reading of the Prophets added to the reading of the Law in the synagogue service. It also represents the essential difference between the religion of Israel and the other religions of the ancient Near East. The latter were cyclical, that is, they were based on the rhythm of nature and repetitive succession of the seasons. They sacralized the cycle between one spring and another, one autumn and another. Once the cycle was completed, the whole thing began again from the beginning. The years came and piled up, each self-enclosed, each a prisoner; but history did not advance. There could be no history of salvation, but only a myth constantly repeated and never moving beyond itself. One such myth was that of the struggle between Marduk and the monster Tiamat, which marked the ritual of the Babylonian New Year, *akîtu*. It was repeated each New Year,[71] but it brought no hope, and time in Babylon remained undifferentiated, sterile, dead.

The religion of Israel was quite different, for it was historical and eschatological. Passover, a spring festival at which the first-born of the flocks were offered, became a memorial of the Exodus and a prophecy of the eternal feast. In the Babylonian religions, history is a cycle closed in on itself and the source only of despair; there will indeed be "another" spring, but there will be nothing "new" about it. For Israel, on the contrary, history breaks the cyclic pattern and opens toward God: there will be "another" spring, but it will bring the celebration of a new exodus in which the people will enter, along God's mysterious paths, into a new promised land. Babylon could set up a calendar for each day of its cyclic year and know that the same calendar would be good for endless years ahead. No such calendar could be established in Israel, since God was leading it by the hand. God makes Israel's ongoing history depend upon his "Days," transfiguring it by his "visitations," causing upheaval and ruin by his anger, protecting and consoling by his tender love. There is a constant process of maturation and constant transcendence of the past. When Abraham left Ur of the Chaldees or Israel left Egypt, they did so never to return but to commit themselves each day to a new spiritual journey.

Israel did, of course, experience certain cycles. The period of the Judges, for example, is filled with cycles of grace and sin, with alternations of safety and distress. But this very instability became a prayer: When would the Judge come who would bestow a lasting safety on God's people? Sometimes the same kind of cycle was to be seen in the life of a hero. Samson was such a one. His story begins with a great theophany, a sacrifice, and a vow (Judg. 13). Then it is darkened by his very unspiritual dealings with three women, one of them a harlot, who cause him great sorrow and undermine his divine charism. Possessor of the Spirit of Yahweh yet also a woman-chaser, Samson represents the instability of man, in whom dwell both gifts from God and human weaknesses. In this same context we cannot but think of David, beloved of God yet also an adulterer. In such men, then, we see a cycle, but it is a cycle that forces an eschatological question: When will he come who will save Israel, not for a brief time, but definitively and forever?

We must do justice to the people of God and recognize that among them were faithful Israelites who would receive the prophetic message with enthusiasm, wake Israel from too complacent a meditation on its own past and too sterile a delight in Abraham and David, and turn its gaze toward a future in which one greater than Abraham or David was coming. For there was undoubtedly a real danger that the proclamation of the prophetic message might be turned into a soporific reading of the literary annals of God's people instead of a listening to the living God: that men might respect the prophets as they would a library collection instead of celebrating the God of the prophets; that they might be lulled by a dream of the past instead of building the future by continuing the dialogue with the Lord of history.

---

[1] M. Noth, *History of Israel*, p. 342. On the synagogue, cf. M.-J. Lagrange, *Le judaïsme avant Jésus-Christ*, pp. 285–91; W. Bacher, "Synagogue," *Hasting's Dictionary of the Bible* 4 (New York, 1902), pp. 636–43; G.F. Moore, *Judaism in the First Centuries of the Christian Era* 1 (Cambridge, 1927), pp. 281–307; Strack-Billerbeck, *Kommentar zum Neuen Testament aus Talmud und Midrasch* 4:115–52 ("Das altjüdische Synagogeninstitut"); W. Schrage, "synagōgē," *TDNT* 7:798–828; K. Hruby, "La synagogue dans la littérature rabbinique," *Orient syrien* 9 (1964), pp. 473–514, and *Die Synagoge: Geschichtliche Entwicklung einer Institution* (Zürich, 1971).

[2] Cf. The encomium of the scribe in Sr. 39:1-11, and G. Vermes, "Bible and Midrash: Early Old Testament Exegesis," *Cambridge History of the Bible* 1 (Cambridge, 1970), pp. 199–203.

[3] The Mishnah is a collection of oral traditions and laws (as opposed to the written "law," or Scripture) and forms the nucleus of the Babylonian and Palestinian Talmuds. The definitive version of the Mishnah was edited by Rabbi Judah ha-Nasi I

(135–200 A D.), but it incorporates the results of the juridical activity of Jewish writers from the second century B.C. on, and the traditions it embodies may date from still much earlier.

⁴ *De opificio mundi* 128 (edited by R. Arnaldez, in *Les oeuvres de Philon d'Alexandrie* 1 [Paris, 1961], p. 226). Flavius Josephus (born c. 37–38 A D., died c. 95) writes that Moses "has given us the most beautiful and necessary of all teachings, and we must listen to it not just once or twice or even many times. He ordained that once each week we should set aside all other occupations and gather to hear the law and learn it by heart" (*Contra Apionem* II, 17). The belief in the Mosaic origin of the synagogue readings is perpetuated in the rabbinic literature; cf. *Megillah* 3:6, in *The Mishnah*, translated by H. Danby [Oxford, 1933], p. 205.

⁵ W. Schrage, *art. cit.*, pp. 810–11. H.-J. Kraus, *Worship in Israel*, remarks: "Important preparatory steps towards the establishment of this institution, which was later to be so important for Judaism, were taken during this sojourn abroad" (p. 230). Cf. also R. le Déaut, *Introduction à la littérature targumique* (Rome, 1966; *ad usum privatum*), p. 34, and K. Hruby, "La place des lectures bibliques et de la prédication dans la liturgie synagogale ancienne," in *La Parole dans la liturgie* (Lex orandi 48; Paris, 1958), pp. 26–27.

⁶ Cf. Schrage, *art. cit.*, p. 811.

⁷ A synagogue at Jerusalem bore the inscription (in Greek): "Place of assembly for the reading of the law"; cf. R. Bultmann, "anaginōskō," *TDNT* 1:344.

⁸ Cf. I. Elbogen, *Der jüdische Gottesdienst in seiner geschichtlichen Entwicklung* (Frankfurt, 1931³), p. 159. On the date of the canon for the Torah and the Prophets, see Chapter 5, above.

⁹ A. Arens, *Die Psalmen im Gottesdienst des Alten Bundes*, p. 74.

¹⁰ On this institution, cf. Elbogen, *op. cit.*, pp. 237–39; Moore, *op. cit.*, 2:12–15. [*ma'amad* is, literally, a "place of standing"; cf. J. Bowker, *op. cit.* (cf. Chapter 7, note 8, below), p. 9. — Tr.]

¹¹ Our information on the readings in the synagogues comes basically from the treatise *Megillah* in the Mishnah. *Megillah* (= scroll) deals with the reading of the scroll of Esther, but also gives details on the reading of other portions of Scripture (for *Megillah*, cf. Danby, *op. cit.*, pp. 201–7).

Secondary literature: A. Buchler, "The Reading of the Law in a Triennial Cycle," *Jewish Quarterly Review* 5 (1893), pp. 420–68, on the reading of the Torah, and 6 (1894), pp. 1–73, on the reading of the Prophets; Elbogen, *op. cit.*, pp. 155–94; Moore, *op. cit.* 1:296ff.; J. Mann, *The Bible as Read and Preached in the Old Synagogue* 1 (New York, 1971²) and 2 (by J. Mann and I. Sonne; Cincinnati, 1966), which treats of the Palestinian triennial cycle; A. Arens, *op. cit.*, pp. 160–210; C. Perrot, "La lecture synagogale d'Exode XXI, 1–XXII, 23 et son influence sur la littérature néotestamentaire," in *A la rencontre de Dieu: Mémorial Albert. Gelin* (Le Puy, 1961), pp. 223–39, and "Luc 4, 16-30 et la lecture biblique de l'ancienne synagogue," in J.E. Menard (ed.), *Exégèse biblique et Judaïsme* (Strasbourg, 1973), pp. 170–86 (this second article summarizes the results reached by the author in his *La lecture de la Bible dans la synagogue: Les anciennes lectures du sabbat et des fêtes* [Hildesheim, 1973]); K. Hruby, "La place des lectures bibliques et de la prédication dans la liturgie synagogale ancienne," in *La Parole dans la liturgie*, pp. 23–64, and "La synagogue dans la littérature rabbinique," *Orient syrien* 9 (1964), pp. 473–514; R. le Déaut, *Introduction à la littérature targumique*, pp. 38–51.

¹² The historian may well ask whether the redactor is not here projecting back into the text of Nehemiah the practice he knew in his own time.

¹³ *Megillah* 4:1 (Danby, *op. cit.*, p. 205).

¹⁴ Strack-Billerbeck, *op. cit.*, 4:159.

¹⁵ *Megillah* 4:10 (Danby, *op. cit.*, p. 207).

[16] The triennial cycle began in the month of Nisan in the first year; cf. R. le Déaut, *La nuit pascale*, pp. 218–21. A. Guilding, *The Fourth Gospel and Jewish Worship: A Study of the Relation of St. John's Gospel to the Ancient Jewish Lectionary System* (Oxford, 1960), presupposes two cycles, one beginning in Nisan, the other in Tishri. Cf. also J. Mann, *op. cit.*, 1:6–7.

[17] Strack-Billerbeck, *op. cit.*, 3:597; cf. Arens, *op. cit.*, p. 165.

[18] According to C. Perrot, "Luc 4, 16-30 et la lecture biblique de l'ancienne synagogue" (cf. note 11, above), pp. 174–75, this system of readings dates from perhaps the end of the second century.

[19] The development was a slow one. Thus, fragments of the Palestinian Targum from the Cairo Geniza, which bear witness to the Jewish tradition in the first third of the second century, and the manuscripts of which date from the seventh century and earlier, still carry rubrics for the ancient triennial cycle (cf. R. le Déaut, *Introduction à la littérature targumique*, pp. 109–12).

[20] "The origin, motive, and date of the grouping [of the readings] are still obscure" (Elbogen, *op. cit.*, p. 158).

[21] Cf. *Megillah* 3:4-6 (Danby, *op. cit.*, p. 205). The reference is to the four sabbaths preceding Passover and to the following feasts: Rosh Hashanah, Kippur, Passover, Pentecost, Hanukkah, Purim, the new moons, the days of fast, and the Feast of Tents.

[22] *Megillah* 3:6; cf. Danby, *ibid.* [But the interpretation here given to the *Megillah* differs from that of Danby; the author's interpretation has been followed. — Tr.]

[23] *Megillah* 3:4 (Danby, *ibid.*).

[24] A. Arens claims, with great assurance, that "all the probabilities show the Palestinian cycle for the Torah to date from the pre-Christian period" (*op. cit.*, p. 164), while A. Guilding speaks without hesitation of the "early evidence for the regular reading of the Law in the synagogues" (*op. cit.*, p. 6) and assigns the systems to 400 B.C. (p. 24). C. Perrot, "Luc 4, 16-30. . ." (pp. 174–75), thinks the organization of the reading cycles was certainly prior to the fourth century A.D. and may date from the end of the second.

[25] *Megillah* 3:6 and 4:1 (Danby, *op. cit.*, pp. 205–6).

[26] Strack-Billerbeck, *op. cit.*, 4:155.

[27] Elbogen, *op. cit.*, p. 170. Cf. Strack-Billerbeck, *op. cit.*, 4:155–57. *Megillah* 4:6 (Danby, *op. cit.*, pp. 206–7) requires only that the reader be suitably dressed (i.e., without ragged clothes).

[28] Cf. *Contra Apionem*, II, 18.

[29] Strack-Billerbeck, *op. cit.*, p. 158. On Rabbi Aqiba, cf. P. Benoit, "Rabbi Aqiba Ben Joseph, sage et héros du judaisme," *Exégèse et théologie* 2 (Paris, 1961), pp. 340–79.

[30] Except for cases of necessity, as when, for example, there was only one potential reader who knew Hebrew.

[31] *Megillah* 4:1-2 (Danby, *op. cit.*, p. 206).

[32] Cf. R. le Déaut, *Introduction à la littérature targumique*, pp. 40–45, for the essential data of the tradition on this point.

[33] Cf. K. Hruby, "La place des lectures bibliques. . .," p. 43.

[34] *Introduction à la littérature targumique*, p. 42.

[35] *Megillah* 4:6 (Danby, *op. cit.*, p. 206).

[36] Jerusalem Talmud: Treatise on the Blessings, VII, 7 (translated into French by M. Schwab, *Le Talmud de Jérusalem* 1 [Paris, 1960], p. 126).

[37] Strack-Billerbeck, *op. cit.*, 4:159.

[38] *Megillah* 4:1 (Danby, *op. cit.*, p. 205).

[39] Some of these characteristics are still discernible in the New Testament. Cf., for example, the genealogy of Jesus according to Matthew (1:2-17): it is perfect from a literary viewpoint (three times fourteen generations), but does not claim to be a completely objective representation of the historical data.

[40] Thus, for example, we are unable to trace the (real) path of the Hebrews in the desert of Sinai (despite the efforts of Num. 33), but we are given the theological explanation of the names of the oases of Marah (Exod. 15:23-25) and of Massah and Meribah (Exod. 17:1-7).

[41] R. Kittel, *Geschichte des Volkes Israel* 1:387.

[42] Need we say that Israel was not taken in by the didactic structure of these accounts, but instead placed the Books of Joshua, Judges, Samuel, and Kings among the "former prophets"?

[43] G. von Rad, *Old Testament Theology* 1:50.

[44] Cf. also Pss. 105:1-2; 44:2. Psalms 78 and 105 belonged to the "covenant ritual"; cf. M. Mannati, *Les Psaumes* 1 (Paris, 1966), pp. 41–46.

[45] Cf. Ps. 102:26-28; Is. 51:6-8.

[46] R. Aron, *Jesus of Nazareth: The Hidden Years*, translated by Frances Frenaye (London, 1962), pp. 43–44. See also the interesting remarks of P. Auvray on the temporal significance of the Hebrew verb, in his *L'hébreu biblique* (Paris, 1962), pp. 46–50. As is well known, the Hebrew perfect and imperfect can stand for the past, present, and future of our languages. Applying these observations to eschatology, Auvray writes: "The kingdom is coming, and the kingdom has already come. The end of time is in the distant future, but it has already begun. This is difficult for the modern Western reader to grasp and express, but it may have seemed quite simple to a contemporary of Jesus. The study of the Hebrew verb should be an indispensable introduction to the theology of the New Testament" (p. 50).

[47] Cf. Exod. 12:11.

[48] Cf. Lev. 23:42-43.

[49] Strack-Billerbeck, *op. cit.*, 4:168.

[50] Strack-Billerbeck, *op. cit.*, 4:165.

[51] Cf. Elbogen, *op. cit.*, pp. 178–79. Only around 300 A.D. do we find a set order of readings from the Prophets in the Palestinian tradition, and, toward the beginning of the fourth century, a lectionary for the Prophets in the Babylonian tradition; cf. Strack-Billerbeck, *op. cit.*, 4:170.

[52] *Megillah* 4:4 (Danby, *op. cit.*, p. 206).

[53] Strack-Billerbeck, *op. cit.*, 4:169.

[54] *Op. cit.*, p. 175.

[55] Cf. Chapter 5, above. The canon of the Prophets did not include the Book of Daniel, written around 165 B.C.

[56] Cf. Acts 13:14-15: "On the sabbath day they [Paul and his companions] entered the synagogue and sat down. *After the reading of the law and the prophets*, the leading men of the synagogue sent this message to them. . . ." Cf. also Acts 13:27.

[57] Strack-Billerbeck, *op. cit.*, 4:169. These particular formulas of blessing are from a relatively late ritual.

[58] Cf. Strack-Billerbeck, *op. cit.*, 4:162, 166–67; Elbogen, *op. cit.*, p. 179. On the prophets and prophetism, cf. A. Gelin, "The Prophets," in Robert-Feuillet, *Introduction to the Old Testament*, pp. 251–70; P. van Imschoot, *Theology of the Old Testament* 1:148–72; E. Jacob, *Theology of the Old Testament*, pp. 238–46; H. Krämer, R. Rendtorff, and R. Meyer, "prophētēs," *TDNT* 6:781–828; J. Chaine, *Introduction à la lecture des prophètes* (Paris, 1946²), pp. 11–41; A. Neher, *L'essence du prophétisme* (Paris, 1955); L. Monloubou, *Prophète, qui es-tu? Le prophétisme avant les prophètes* (Paris, 1968); J. Goldstain, *Les prophètes et leur lignée* (Paris, 1965). See the full bibliography given by T. Chary in his *Les prophètes et le culte à partir de l'exil* (Tournai, 1955). See also W.O.E. Oesterley and T. H. Robinson, *Hebrew Religion: Its Origin and Development* (London, 1957), pp. 222–32; R. Kittel, *Geschichte des Volkes Israel* 2:319–40.

[59] *Megillah* 4:4 (Danby, *op. cit.*, p. 206).

[60] A. Gelin, "The Prophets," in Robert-Feuillet, *op. cit.*, p. 256. E. Jacob, *op. cit.*, remarks that "the prophet is the man of God *par excellence*" and reminds us that the

title "man of God" was given only to Moses, Samuel, David, and the prophets (p. 239).

[61] Beginning with Amos, the terms "seer" and *nabî* are used as synonyms (Amos 7:12-14; Is. 29:10; 30:10). The etymology of *nabî* is disputed.

[62] C. Tresmontant, *A Study of Hebrew Thought*, translated by M. F. Gannon (New York, 1960), p. 27.

[63] G. von Rad, *Old Testament Theology*, speaks of "history related to eschatology" in the thought of the prophets (2:112–19). Cf. also O. Cullmann, *Christ and Time: The Primitive Christian Conception of Time and History*, translated by F. V. Filson (rev. ed.; London, 1962), pp. 94–106 ("The Connection between History and Prophecy [History and Myth]").

[64] Cf. also Is. 66:22; Apoc. 21:1.

[65] Cf. Is. 2:1-5 (Micah 4:1-5); 54:11-12; 60.

[66] Cf. Ezek. 40–48.

[67] Cf. Mal. 1:11-12; 3:6-10.

[68] Cf. Is. 9:16, 11:1-4. The whole message of Isaiah is focused on the Davidic dynasty and on Zion.

[69] Cf. Ezek. 37:1-14.

[70] Cf. Ezek. 36:26; 37:26-28.

[71] Cf. M. Eliade, *The Myth of the Eternal Return*, translated by W. R. Trask (New York, 1971): "During the course of the *akîtu* ceremony, which lasted twelve days, the so-called epic of the Creation, *Enûma eliš*, was solemnly recited several times in the temple of Marduk. Thus the combat between Marduk and the sea monster Tiamat was reactualized — the combat that had taken place *in illo tempore* and had put an end to chaos by the final victory of the god. . . . The combat between Tiamat and Marduk was mimed by a struggle between two groups of actors. . . . The struggle between the two groups of actors not only commemorated the primordial conflict between Marduk and Tiamat; it repeated, it actualized, the cosmogony, the passage from chaos to cosmos. The mythical event was present: 'May he continue to conquer Tiamat and shorten her days!' the celebrant exclaimed. The combat, the victory, and the Creation took place *at that very moment*" (pp. 55–56). On "cyclic time," cf. also M. Neher, *op. cit.*, pp. 58–81.

Chapter 7

THE HOMILY

I. THE HOMILY IN THE SYNAGOGUE SERVICE

The homily was inseparable from the reading of the Law and the Prophets. "Homily" here refers to the discourse explaining the word so as to make it more easily accessible to the community.[1] This was a discourse with its own special characteristics; as such, it was to be found in no other religion or cultic service. For if Israel was a people brought into existence by the word, its celebrations could not but be essentially liturgies of the word, while the discourses pronounced in these celebrations inevitably concerned the veneration and explanation of the word. "This is what the Scripture says," or "This is what is written" — these were the usual formulas the speaker used in linking his explanation to the readings.[2] They are marvelous formulas (formulas we would like to hear constantly on the lips of anyone today who wishes to speak of God!), for they imposed on the speaker the delightful obligation of constantly going back to the written text, drawing upon the word for what he had to say and making his human commentary a prolongation of the divine message.

The usual form the homily took was a straightforward explanation of the word of God. The best example of the homily from this point of view is to be found in the assembly of Ezra: "Ezra read plainly from the book of the law of God, interpreting it so that all could understand what was read" (Neh. 8:8). Ezra read the Hebrew text and then translated it into Aramaic, the customary language of the time.

At its best, the homily was an actualization of the word for the good of the community. The most striking example of it, from this new point of view, is Jesus' homily in the synagogue at Nazareth.

After reading from the Book of Isaiah, Jesus sat down for his homily; he began it with the words: "Today this Scripture passage is fulfilled in your hearing" (Luke 4:21).

Between these two homilies of Ezra and Jesus there is no essential difference, in the sense that the chief purpose of the homily was always to explain the word, show its topicality and relevance, and bring out the teaching it contained for the lives of those present at the synagogue service. God had formerly spoken to the ancestors through the events of history and the record of them in the sacred books. He was continuing to speak at the present time through the events of daily life. How were men to understand the mystery contained in words spoken today except by relating them to the word of God? How were they to comprehend today's history except by relating it to sacred history? How were they to interpret the laws of men except by relating them to the Law of God? During the four centuries separating Ezra and Jesus, the synagogue heard, as it were, a single long homily which, in its infinite variations and countless fresh ideas, sought always to help men understand their God and do his will.

In achieving his purpose, the speaker did not practice scientific exegesis as we understand it today. It was not, however, that he was ignorant or contemptuous of this intellectual approach. The whole history of Israel is a protest against such an assumption, for all study done by the chosen people was a study of Scripture. But in getting to the heart of God's thought, the preacher did not think it necessary to traverse the lengthy road of modern exegesis in order to grasp the mind of the inspired writer. Nor was he concerned with the question of authenticity; he simply accepted certain generalizations: The Law comes from Moses, the Psalms from David, and the Wisdom books from Solomon. He did not bother with the chronological position of the various oracles, for "the Rabbis . . . formulated a principle — 'There is no before and after in the Torah.' "[3]

The preacher took the sacred text outside its temporal and historical context, and pored over it endlessly, examining it with all his intellectual resources and with a stubbornness born of love. In order to nourish faith and influence life, he tried to make the word even more desirable and delightful. "If man explains the words of the Torah in public and does not make them more tasteful than milk and honey," says one midrash, "it would be better for him to say nothing."[4] It was also said that it should be as much a delight to listen to the words of the law as to gaze upon a newly married girl as she sits beneath the nuptial canopy.[5] Thus the reading service was considered a feast. For this reason no one was to begin or end the readings with a text of ill omen.[6]

While the homily took little account of history, it did make willing use of the edifying stories handed down by tradition. It had little use for scientific etymology, but it did like to dwell on the popular etymologies that made words alive and colorful. Above all, the preachers delighted in comparing sentences, in explaining the Bible through the Bible, in juxtaposing texts and bringing out the likenesses. The Bible was regarded as an enclosed universe in which every word looked to every other and all spoke of God. Especially admired was the linking of verses drawn from different sources. One day, as ben Azzaï was speaking in public, fire burst out all around him. "They asked him: 'Surely you are going to speak of the vision of the fiery chariots [in Ezek. 1]?' 'No,' he said. 'I am linking the words of the Torah with those of the prophets, and those of the prophets with those of the Writings. When I do this, the words of the Torah are as jubilant as on the day when they were given at Sinai. Now, when the Torah was given, it was given in the midst of fire. For, as Deuteronomy 4:11 tells us: the mountain blazed.' "[7]

II. THE SOURCES FOR THE HOMILY

Upon what sources did the speakers draw to deepen their piety and knowledge?[8] The most important traditional sources, for the later period, were the targum and the midrash.

1. The targum

A targum (a Hebrew word meaning "translation") was an Aramaic version of the Hebrew Bible and was used in the synagogal liturgy. The people, who now spoke Aramaic, were increasingly unable to understand Hebrew. Thus, at the beginning of the fifth century, Nehemiah was bemoaning the fact that children born of mixed marriages between Jews and Ashdodites, Ammonites, or Moabites did not know how to speak the Jewish language (Neh. 13:24).[9] But the popular movement from Hebrew to Aramaic was irreversible and had to be taken into account. The word that had been read in Hebrew had then to be translated into Aramaic; in other words, targums had to be made. We may say that the oral targum tradition goes back to the assembly of Ezra himself. The writing down of the targums for liturgical purpose was, however, a later phenomenon; it probably began before the second century B.C.[10]

Since the purpose of the targum was to provide a translation, that is, to make the Hebrew text intelligible, it was quite natural that the translators should add explanations or interpretations to their Aramaic versions. The targum thus resembled a proclamation of the word during which the reader added explanations in parentheses as he went. In the normal course of events, the explanations sought, as it were, to become part of the text proper, and they readily managed to do so. From the viewpoint of the community, there were two advantages to this amalgamation. First, the targum would retain the whole literal text of God's word that was being translated, and would thus preserve that text's status as inspired word. Second, it would at the same time make the text more accessible and familiar to the hearer.

Evidently it was easy to pass from targum to homily; at times the distinction completely vanished as the targum became a homily, or, if you prefer, the homily was transfigured into the word of God. In this matter everything depended on the quality of the translation, that is, its fidelity to the Bible. If the targum reproduced the word literally, as is ordinarily the case with the Onkelos Targum or the Babylonian Targum, it could be said to be a real proclamation of God's word. If, however, the targum paraphrased the text, as is the case with the Pseudo-Jonathan (i.e., the Palestinian or Jerushalmi I Targum, in which the Aramaic text is almost twice as long as the biblical text[11]), it came close to turning into a homily. We are speaking here of written targums, which show a certain amount of the restraint that characterizes writing. In an actual liturgy, where such controls were not operative, the translator could easily pass beyond translation into homily. Therefore, when we speak of the targums as sources for the homily, we must remember that in this case it may be hard to distinguish between the spring and the stream that flows from it.[12]

2. The midrash

The noun *midrash* comes from the verbal root *drsh*, which means "to examine, to seek out." A midrash represents the study of Scripture and the search for its meaning (in other words, the "exegesis" of Scripture). The Jewish soul devoted all its energies to this study — not only intelligence but a deep sensibility and the intuitions fed by unrestrained imagination.

Midrashic research aimed, rather than to discern the precise mean-ing, to draw from the text numerous and diverse ideas that resulted in maxims of justification and edification. The word of God in putting on the clothes of human language should not lose any of its universal meaning. It remains charged with a volume of knowledge and con-tains the universality of wisdom. It is to be approached with our own reason, but also it is to be treated with our imagination. Thus the authors of the midrashim proceeded.[13]

The midrash could take more than one form. Tradition distin-guishes between haggadah and halakah.

The verbal root of *halakah* means "to walk." Halakah had for its object the study of the legislative texts of the Torah and the explana-tion of the rules to be "followed" or the norms of "conduct." Such study was not a barren contemplation of archaic laws, but an effort to base on the past a legislation for the present. It sought to "discover the basic principles [of the Torah], so that one might make the text yield new rules for resolving new problems, and arguments for justifying customs that had become traditional."[14]

The haggadah represented the study especially of the narrative parts of the Bible, with a view to bringing out the spiritual content of the accounts and the events. It went in for amplifying the texts and their religious implications and for grafting onto them other narra-tives handed down by tradition. The end result was more stable than the halakah, because the latter, by definition, had constantly to adapt to the new situations which life created.[15]

III. PURPOSE OF THE HOMILY

1. *Actualization of the word of God*

The targum originated in the liturgy; the community, praying and listening to the word, was, as it were, the place where the targum was born and developed. The midrash, on the other hand, was more scholarly in style, and its natural place was the schools. Targum and midrash were like each other, however, and at times even indistin-guishable from each other, in that they applied the same methods in approaching and studying the sacred text.[16] The line of demarcation between them is therefore fluid and blurred. In addition, the hom-ily, which originates both in the targum and in the midrash, often mingles its own waters with those of its sources. Speaking of the Palestinian Targum, R. Bloch can say: "It is much more like a strict midrash than a translation. It is even likely that this targum was originally a homiletic midrash, or simply a series of homilies on Scripture that was read in the synagogue after the public reading of the Torah."[17]

This amounts to saying that a Jewish homily looked very much like a targum or midrash. They all belong to the same family, and in the homily we can discern the outlook peculiar to all those who pored over the Scriptures as members of the covenant community. They scrutinized the text in order to hear the word God was addressing to them there and then, for they knew that a study of the Bible unaccompanied by piety was as harmful as a piety without study of the Bible. For these men, to understand the Scriptures meant not only to grasp their meaning but also to accept them as referring to the present moment. The homily was successful, therefore, if the community celebrated the Passover of the Book of Exodus, listened to Moses' laws in Deuteronomy, entered the Promised Land with the Book of Joshua, praised David with the Books of Kings, acclaimed Emmanuel with Isaiah, shared Jeremiah's struggle, wept with Job, loved with the Song of Songs, and sang with the Psalms.

In every homily the community heard an echo of the words which sum up, as it were, all the homilies of the Jewish liturgy and provide the perfect model for the Christian homily: "Today this Scripture passage is fulfilled in your hearing" (Luke 4:21).

Was this kind of actualization simply a scholastic method inherited from the targum and the midrash, or did it represent an authentic approach to Scripture? As a matter of fact, it can claim the highest of patrons, since the Bible itself practices midrash.

The word of God "remains forever." It is spoken in time, but it transcends time; it is spoken within the limitations imposed by a particular context, but it is not a prisoner of these limitations. Moreover, the people of God receives it as a living word addressed to them at every point in their lives. "As long as there is a people of God that accepts the Bible as his living word, there will be midrash; only the name changes."[18] It is quite to be expected, therefore, that the Bible should explain its own meaning and be regarded as relevant and topical to those who wish to live by it.

Such explanation and actualization evidently become all the more necessary and urgent as the stream of history carries the readers and hearers of the Bible away from the period when God had spoken. Abraham himself, of course, had no difficulty in actualizing the command given him to leave everything and follow the call (this does not mean the effort required of him was any the less; he still had to obey). Later on, however, the people descended from the patriarch had to understand that the story of Abraham was still relevant to them and that they must answer God's call through faith. In a similar fashion, the contemporaries of Jeremiah had no difficulty in seeing the actuality of his prophecies: they could see the fulfillment, the here-and-now topicality, of those prophecies in the caravans of exiles who were leaving their corpses beside the routes that led to Babylon, and in the debris of the burnt-out Temple. But as the period of Jeremiah receded into the past, it took an effort to "re-read" the prophet's oracles. Consequently the interpretation of the Bible by the Bible became a re-interpretation in function of the particular community that was living at a given moment within the today of God.

There are plenty of examples of this procedure. Deuteronomy, for example, is ostensibly a collection of discourses Moses pronounced before his death. In fact, what the book does is to gather up pieces that vary greatly in literary style and in origin. In particular, we can hear in Deuteronomy an echo of the homilies which the Levites delivered to the people in the northern sanctuaries at the feasts of covenant renewal. One of the main literary techniques of Deuteronomy is to actualize, or make relevant and topical, the assembly at Sinai, for the good of the contemporaries of Josiah. The most striking evidence of this is the "today" that is constantly dinned into the ears of the hearers.[19] Deuteronomy is, as it were, eliminating six centuries of history and taking the assembly of Josiah back to the places of the Exodus in a kind of pilgrimage to the sources, where God will once again give them his law through the mouth of Moses.

Or take the Book of Chronicles. The author, a fourth-century Levite, undertakes to paint a great historical panorama of the Davidic dynasty, from its "beginnings" down to the start of the Exile. But what he gives us, in fact, is a theological meditation on the reign of Yahweh within the framework of the Davidic monarchy. His narratives depend upon some special sources, but they draw chiefly on the Books of Samuel and Kings. He rethinks these books, however, in relation to the needs of his meditation. He projects back into the Davidic age the cultic organization of his day, for this was the best way, in his view, of justifying such an organization. He reconstructs the past and mixes with it the hopes of the future; he re-creates an ideal kingdom — the kind he wanted to see his contemporaries build. David, who was really surrounded by hardened soldiers, becomes a type of the messianic king whom a community, sanctified by trials, was now awaiting. Such a meditation on history is a typical midrash.

We can see the same process at work in the "histories" of Judith and Esther, the encomium on the ancestors in Sirach (44:1–50:24), the historical Psalms 78, 105, and 106, or the fable of the prophet Jonah, with its great fish, straight out of folklore, and its Nineveh, built on such a colossal scale. In varying degrees all these texts make use of midrash and use a narrative concerning the past in order to give instruction concerning the present.

The case of the Song of Songs is especially instructive. Everyone knows the endless discussions that regularly crop up between exegetes of the Song; they will probably recur until doomsday! Some exegetes read the book as a song of human love, others as a parable of God's nuptial love for his people. But the two interpretations are not mutually exclusive; they represent only two complementary readings of the same text. In their original form the songs comprising the Song of Songs celebrated human love. The age-old expression of the mutual love of man and woman was sufficiently sacred and beautiful in itself to become part of the word of God. But these poems were destined to be more beautiful still when sung in the presence of God, who adds his own harmonics to it and intensifies nuptial love in the flames of his own love. When the synagogue read the Song, it delighted to relate it to God and to see in the human love represented there the love of Yahweh himself for his people. "All the ages are not worth the day on which the Song of Songs was given to Israel," said Rabbi Aqiba, "for all the Writings are holy, but the Song of Songs is the Holy of Holies."[20]

What other way was there of actualizing a nuptial song in the synagogal service except to interpret it as referring to God? The young shepherd who comes springing from hill to hill like a gazelle and leads his flock to feed upon the lilies[21] becomes Yahweh himself as he guides his people to the spiritual pastures of wisdom. The pretty dark-haired girl at his side, with her dove's eyes and pomegranate cheeks and her breasts like clusters from the vine,[22] has her charms interpreted allegorically and becomes the sacred spouse of Yahweh, the people God calls to love him. Did the Jews think God would blush at the beauty of the flesh and the intoxication of love, when he himself created these things? No! What the Jews were doing was to effect an actualization that enabled them to go beyond human love (with its limitations!) and read in the text the daily, yet everlasting story of God's love for Israel.

When a homilist proclaims: "Today this Scripture passage is fulfilled in your hearing" (Luke 4:21), he does so in perfect continuity with the biblical tradition. He is prolonging and amplifying, but not distorting, the movement of the text. His homily becomes a faithful echo of the eternal words, across the changing tides of time and history.

2. *The Jewish homily: A preparation for the New Testament*

We cannot, of course, claim that all the homilies preached from Ezra to Jesus were perfect and reflected only the authentic word of God. That would be as risky as claiming that all the homilies now preached by priests or pastors are necessarily a faithful echo of the Gospel. Defects today do not, admittedly, excuse defects in the past, but the present situation gives a point of reference for explaining the past. The Jewish homilists had their weaknesses; they said much that was useless and vain.[23] Such defects are to be expected, however, for they are manifestations of the human gravitational force, as it were, that pulls down the things of God, the human shadow on the divine light, the slag of history that conceals the gold of tradition. From this point of view we can indeed say that the slag hides the gold; from another point of view, however, we can say that it holds the gold in readiness. Once the gold has been discovered, we do not weigh it in the same scales with the slag.

The gold is priceless. For in its meditation on the living word and in the homilies which made that word relevant at each celebration, Israel was preparing itself to welcome the Gospel when it came; it was advancing toward the New Testament and the discovery of Christ. The best of this literature, especially the haggadah, formed what we might describe as the blank pages between the Old Testament and the New. The road leading to Christ passed through the modest homilies which obscure Jews preached in the countryside synagogues. It was there that a new people of God was evolving, there that its piety was being fed.

> The targums, which came into existence and were developed and transmitted in the synagogue liturgy, must have created a kind of average religious culture for all the Jews of the time. What were the wellsprings of piety for Mary and Joseph, for John the Baptist and his parents? Probably not only the text of the Old Testament. Surely not

the quibbling discussions of the doctors. Rather they lived in accordance with this tradition that was rooted in the Scripture, a tradition inherited from postexilic Judaism to which we owe what are perhaps the most profound of the biblical texts.[24]

3. *The Jewish homily: Anticipation of the Gospel*

God looked with favor on this tradition and blessed it by bestowing on it the highest honor appropriate to it: he took some of its elements into the New Testament and thus infused them with the dignity proper to the word itself. For the New Testament not only uses the methods of the targum and the midrash,[25] but even takes over some of the statements found in these. Such statements are among the best known in the Gospel. Thus the jubilant cry of the woman in the crowd: "Blest is the womb that bore you and the breasts that nursed you" (Luke 11:27), and the urging of the Sermon on the Mount: "Be compassionate, as your Father is compassionate" (Luke 6:36), were part of the targumic tradition before being part of the Gospel.[26]

So too, it was through the haggadah that the New Testament knew that "Moses was educated in all the lore of Egypt" (Acts 7:22); that the magicians who vied with Moses were named Jannes and Jambres (2 Tim. 3:8); that a miraculous rock, always ready to become a spring, accompanied the Israelites in the desert (1 Cor. 10:4); that the people received the law through the ministry of angels (Acts 7:53; Gal. 3:19; Heb. 2:2); that Solomon took Rahab for his wife (according to the genealogy of Christ in Matthew 1:5); that the drought which caused the famine in Elijah's time lasted three and a half years (Luke 4:25; James 5:17); that the archangel Michael argued against the devil over Moses' body (Jude 9).

But the important thing here is not the number of texts that might be adduced, nor the quality of the teaching, which often stays at the level of popular anecdote. Even if there were but a single example to cite, its significance would be unchanged. What we see happening is something very beautiful: tradition, in some of its constitutive elements, being raised to the level of the inspired word and clad in the latter's incomparable dignity. The truly extraordinary thing is that a Jewish homily, which an unpretentious speaker offered to his community after learning it through tradition and reading it in a targum (and, doubtless, after piously adding something of his own to it), should one day become the authentic word of God, inspired by the Spirit and foretelling Christ!

The religion of the chosen people here shows us one of its most basic traits, namely, that it was not a religion of a book, however inspired, but a religion focused on a message as lived by the community — and then written down in a book. The message of faith — received by Abraham as he left Ur, proclaimed by Moses in the desert, gathered up and expanded by the Deuteronomist preachers, made constantly relevant by the synagogal communities, and finally proclaimed again by Jesus Christ in the agony of the Cross and the light of the resurrection — was first lived by the community before becoming "Scripture." This people had the law of God in its heart (Is. 51:7) before possessing it on paper. It lived the law before reading it and heard God before speaking. How true the words with which the tradition answered a speaker who asked what he was to say in his homily: "You will learn it from God"![27]

4. Dignity of the tradition

A final remark is called for. We can glimpse in all that has been said the importance of the community and its tradition for the understanding of the Bible. The word creates the community, but the community interprets the word. It does this interpreting in the particular form which is its own tradition, with all the wealth this contains.

The principle is evidently true, first of all, for the celebrations in the synagogues, when the homilist expounds the word in dependence on tradition. But it also holds when the synagogue makes way for the Gospel and the "Old" Testament becomes the new covenant. The Jewish tradition forms a rich and irreplaceable link between the Law and the Prophets, on the one hand, and Jesus Christ, on the other.

> However transforming was the Christian revelation, it was from Jewish tradition that it drew not only its formulas, its images, its orderings, but even the very marrow of its ideas. . . . To discredit this intermediary link [rabbinical exegesis] is to question the soundness of the whole chain.[28]

To say this is in no way to lessen the originality of the New Testament, but simply to show where the latter has its roots. Just as Jesus, "son of David, son of Abraham" (Matthew 1:1), is part of the Jewish people in body and soul, so the Gospel has its roots in the Old Testament and cannot be understood or explained without reference to the Jewish community and its traditions and homilies.

When Mary taught Jesus the Jewish prayers of the Shemoneh Esreh (Eighteen Benedictions) and the Kaddish, she was at the same time teaching him the elements that would make up the Our Father.[29]

There is something more to be said, however. What is true of the passage from the Old Testament to the New is also true today for our contemporary understanding of the Book. We hear the word with the ears of Israel, we contemplate it with Israel's eyes — but ears and eyes now transformed by the Spirit. We must therefore know the Jewish tradition, approach it with a friendly attitude, and study it with the sympathy which alone will enable us to penetrate beneath the surface of another's thought.[30]

We must also bear in mind that tradition did not stop with the coming of the New Testament. It lives on and develops constantly in the history of the Church. Each day, we may say, the Church creates and invents its tradition. It creates it through its biblical studies but also through its devout meditation. A scientific exegesis that sticks to "the text" of the Bible and to the *hebraica veritas* is absolutely necessary. But so is popular understanding that is shot through with the intuitions of love, the kind of understanding represented by the homilies in the synagogues of Israel.

---

[1] On the homily in the Christian liturgy, cf. Chapter 15, below. Strack-Billerbeck, *op. cit.*, 4:171–88, speaks of the "sermon" but in fact is dealing with the homily. Elbogen, *op. cit.*, pp. 194–98, speaks of the "explanation of Scripture," and Moore, *op. cit.*, 1:305, of the "homily." Cf. also K. Hruby, "La place des lectures bibliques. . .," pp. 58–64.

[2] Strack-Billerbeck, *op. cit.*, 4:173. The formulas come from a midrash and bring out the spirit of the true homily.

[3] D. Daube, *The New Tesament and Rabbinic Judaism* (London, 1956), p. 7, note 1.

[4] Strack-Billerbeck, *op. cit.*, 4:173.

[5] *Ibid.*

[6] *Jerusalem Megillah* 3:7 (in M. Schwab, *op. cit.*, 4:243). We may note here that Luke 4:19, speaking of Jesus' reading in the synagogue of Nazareth, stops the quotation from Isaiah at 61:2a, thus omitting the words "and a day of vindication by our God" (61:2b).

[7] Strack-Billerbeck, *op. cit.*, 4:176.

[8] Cf. G. Vermes, "Bible and Midrash in Early Old Testament Exegesis," in *Cambridge History of the Bible* 1 (Cambridge, 1970), pp. 199–231; J. Mann, *op. cit.*, 1:11–15.

[9] On the targums, cf. R. le Déaut, *La nuit pascale*, pp. 19–63; *idem*, *Liturgie juive et Nouveau Testament: Le témoignage des versions araméennes* (Rome, 1965); *idem*, *Introduction à la littérature targumique*; *idem*, "Les études targumiques: Etat de la recherche et perspectives pour l'exégèse de l'Ancien Testament," *Ephemerides*

theologicae lovanienses 44 (1968) pp. 5–34, with bibliography (p. 34). Cf. also J. Bowker, *The Targums and Rabbinic Literature: An Introduction to Jewish Interpretations of Scripture* (Cambridge, 1969). The principal targums are: (1) the Targum on the Pentateuch, also known as Targum Onkelos (rather literal); (2) the Targum on the Prophets, also known as the Targum of Jonathan ben Uzziah; (3) the Palestinian Targum on the Pentateuch, which exists in a complete version called the Targum of Pseudo-Jonathan, and a shorter version called the Fragmentary Targum; (4) the Targum on the Writings. — On the fragments discovered in the Geniza at Cairo, cf. P. Kahle, *The Cairo Geniza* (London, 1947).

[10] On the dating of the targums, cf. R. le Déaut, *La nuit pascale*, pp. 26–32. To give one example: the copy of the Targum on Job that was discovered in Cave 11 at Qumran dates from the fifties A.D., while the language used in it dates from the second half of the second century B.C. (cf. R. le Déaut, "Les études targumiques," pp. 14–15).

[11] Cf. R. le Déaut, *Introduction à la littérature targumique*, pp. 85–91; J. Bowker, *op. cit.*, pp. 23–27.

[12] This is especially true of the Targum on the Prophets. We should recall that the Hebrew text was read in groups of three verses, which meant that the reader could even abridge the text in order to leave more time for explanation (cf. K. Hruby, *art. cit.*, p. 46).

[13] H. Lusseau, "The Other Hagiographers," in Robert-Feuillet, *op. cit.*, p. 498 (*midrashim* is the plural of *midrash*). — On the midrash, cf. especially R. Bloch, "Midrash," *DBS* 5:1263–81. The reader may also consult A. Robert, "The Literary Genres," in A. Robert and A. Tricot (eds.), *Guide to the Bible* 1 (rev. ed.; New York, 1960), pp. 505–9; P. Grelot, "Les fondements de l'exégèse chrétienne. 1: L'exégèse biblique dans le judaïsme," in Robert-Feuillet, *Introduction à la Bible*. 1: *Introduction générale; Ancien Testament* (Tournai, 1959), pp. 173–78 [the "General Introduction" was not included in the English translation, *Introduction to the Old Testament*]; A. G. Wright, *The Literary Genre Midrash* (New York, 1967), with the review by R. le Déaut in *Biblica* 50 (1969), pp. 395–413.

[14] R. Bloch, *art. cit.*, cols. 1266–67.

[15] We may also mention the pesher, which is attested almost exclusively at Qumran (cf. *Les textes de Qumran* 2 [Paris, 1963], pp. 46–48, 135–36). It studied the texts of the prophets. By analyzing the fulfillment of the ancient oracles, the pesher proposed to draw lessons for the present. There may have been both a haggadic pesher and a halakic pesher.

[16] R. le Déaut, *Introduction à la littérature targumique*, writes: "There is a striking resemblance between the methods of the targumists and those of the writers of midrash" (p. 58).

[17] "Quelques aspects de la figure de Moïse dans la tradition rabbinique," in H. Cazelles *et al.*, *Moïse, l'homme de l'alliance* (Tournai, 1955), p. 96.

[18] R. Bloch, "Midrash," *DBS* 5:1266.

[19] Cf. Deut. 4:8, 39; 9:3; 11:26, 32; 26:16-18; 27:9; 29:9, 11-12; 30:18.

[20] *Yedaim* 3:5 (Danby, *op. cit.*, p. 782). Cf. A. Robert, in A. Robert, R. Tournay, and A. Feuillet, *Le Cantique des Cantiques* (Paris, 1963), p. 42.

[21] Cant. 2:8-9; 6:3; etc. J. Winandy, in *Le Cantique des Cantiques* (Tournai, 1960), thinks we have here a love poem that has been transformed into a piece of wisdom literature.

[22] Cant. 4:1-3; 7:9; etc.

[23] The halakah especially got lost at times in juridical refinements that were unworthy of the word of God. Jesus would rise up in strong opposition to the ancient traditions when they obscured the clear will of God; cf. Matthew 15:1-20 (Mark 7:1-23); 23:1-30.

[24] R. le Déaut, *Liturgie juive et Nouveau Testament*, pp. 68–69.

[25] Cf. R. le Déaut, *op. cit.*, pp. 43–69; R. Bloch, "Midrash," *DBS* 5:1279–80.

[26] On these two texts, cf. R. le Déaut, *La nuit pascale*, pp. 51–52.

[27] Strack-Billerbeck, *op. cit.*, 4:172.

[28] L. Bouyer, *The Meaning of Sacred Scripture*, translated by Mary Perkins Ryan (Notre Dame, 1958), p. 248.

[29] On these prayers, cf. Elbogen, *op. cit.*, pp. 16–26 and 92–98. — On the Our Father, cf. E. Lohmeyer, *The Lord's Prayer*, translated by J. Bowden (London, 1965), and H. Schürmann, *Praying with Christ: The "Our Father" for Today*, translated by W.M. Ducey and A. Simon (New York, 1964). We may not reduce the relation between the Our Father, on the one side, and the biblical formulas and Jewish prayers, on the other, to a simple material similarity of words and formulas, for this similarity betokens a like *spirit*. At the same time, however, we should remember that the newness of the Our Father is a matter not chiefly of formulas but of situations, that is, the fact that it is Jesus Christ who teaches the prayer. He himself is the infinitely "new" in the New Testament.

[30] R. le Déaut writes in his *Liturgie juive et Nouveau Testament*: "Experience of this vibrant popular literature should lead to a more sympathetic study of the Jewish writings. Why do people so often refer to these as 'a hotch-potch' or a 'tangled, impenetrable underbrush'? If one of the main routes to a better understanding of the Christian message passes along these difficult roads, then such language as that will hardly encourage students to venture upon them" (pp. 76–77).

Chapter 8

THE PSALM

I. THE RESPONSE OF THE COMMUNITY

A. In the History of Israel

The total initiative is in God's hands, and he exercises it through his word. But his intervention does not take the form of a monologue to which the world is forced to listen. On the contrary, his intention is to enter upon a dialogue between his own tender love and man's royal freedom. His word addresses man, slipping into his heart, soliciting his response, requiring a choice. Not to respond to it is to refuse it. The man who has encountered God will never again be calm and at peace; or, better, his peace and tranquility are such that they will never cause an interruption in the dialogue once begun.

In its simplest form, the response was expressed in the "Amen" with which the people ratified the word. Thus, when the law was proclaimed in the assembly at Shechem, the people ratified each statement with a mighty "Amen" that echoed back from Mount Ebal and Mount Gerizim. At the assembly of Ezra, the people with upraised hands again responded "Amen" to the blessing pronounced upon them, and prostrated themselves, face downward, before Yahweh.[1]

We know, of course, that man's response to God's will for him cannot take the form of mere words; what is required is an obedience that is coextensive with life itself. To respond to God means living in a certain way, not saying certain words. It is this obedience that the human verbal response must express.

In recording the "Amen," the Bible is recording the unreserved

"Yes" of man to God, the full and joyous acceptance of God's word, thanksgiving for God's goodness. When God enters a man's life, what can the man do but kneel before him, full of joy and gratitude? Everyone knows the delightful story in which the Yahwist tradition has gathered up the memories of the marriage of Isaac and Rebecca. At Abraham's bidding, his servant returns with ten camels to the land of his master's birth, there to seek a wife for Abraham's son. He reaches the village of Nahor and halts by the well at the hour when the women come to draw water. There he humbly asks Yahweh for a sign that will enable him to recognize the chosen young woman: It will be the one who gives him water for himself and his camels. After receiving the sign, that is, after God has spoken and pointed out the lovely Rebecca, the servant "bowed down in worship to the Lord, saying: 'Blessed be the Lord, the God of my master Abraham, who has not let his constant kindness toward my master fail' " (Gen. 24:27). The servant responds to God's word with thanksgiving and praise.

When God's intervention was especially marvelous and decisive, when a great rescue filled the hearts of the liberated with a deeper joy, when a brief shout of praise seemed too banal to express the intense feelings of the heart, then the gratitude of the believer took a lengthier form; he broke out into a long litany of joy that might even become canticle or psalm. Thus we have the canticles of Moses, Miriam, Deborah and Barak, of Hannah, who had been barren, of King Hezekiah, of Hananiah, Mishael, and Azariah, of Judith and Tobit. These compositions all have the same underlying pattern: They begin by blessing Yahweh, thanking him, and singing his praise; then they recall his wonderful deeds and celebrate what he has done.

Thus, after the crossing of the Sea of Reeds, Moses and the children of Israel sing of Yahweh, their strength and deliverance, their Savior and Father. It is he who struck down the enemy, hollowed out the depths of the sea, made the waters stand like walls, and led his children to his holy mountain. Miriam, with a tambourine in her hand, echoed their song as she praised God: "Sing to the Lord, for he is gloriously triumphant; horse and chariot he has cast into the sea" (Exod. 15:21).[2] Again, after the defeat of Sisera, general of Jabin's army, who had for twenty years been oppressing the children of Israel with his nine hundred iron chariots, Deborah and Barak praise Yahweh and sing of him as the hero of ancient struggles: In the earthquake and the shaking of the heavens, in the torrential waters of the Wadi Kishon, he swept the enemy away and crushed kings (Judg. 5:2–31).

Hannah, who was barren, prayed in bitterness of soul: "O Lord of hosts, if you look with pity on the misery of your handmaid, if you remember me and do not forget me, if you give your handmaid a male child . . ." (1 Sam. 1:11). Then, when she became the mother of little Samuel, she broke out into a song of joy to God, her Rock and her Savior: It is he who breaks the bow of the mighty, but raises the needy from the dust; it is he who makes poor and makes rich, gives life and death; it is he who makes the barren wife bear seven sons, while the proud mother of many children languishes (1 Sam. 2:1-10).

There are other canticles, too: the canticle of King Hezekiah, who had been ill and whose life had almost been taken from him as a shepherd's is struck down by a desert wind, but who had returned from the gates of death (Is. 38:10-20); the canticle of Jonah, who, while imprisoned in the fish's belly, down amid the weeds of the abyss, down at the roots of the mountains, composed a ringing hymn of distress and thanksgiving (Jonah 2:3-10); the canticle of Tobit, who had been exiled to the realm of darkness but regained his sight and saw an angel (Tob. 13:1-17); the marvelous canticle of the three young men, Hananiah, Mishael, and Azariah, whose souls were kept from the sin of idolatry and whose bodies were preserved unharmed amid the searing flames of the fiery furnace (Dan. 3:26-90); and the canticle of Judith, who rescued her people as she tore herself from the embrace of Holofernes (Judith 16:1-16).

We may note here that these canticles, for the most part, do not belong to the original redaction of the narratives which now contain them. In other words, the songs arose in other contexts; they have other sources and later on were put in the mouths of the inspired singers who were thought to have uttered them. This is surely the case with the canticles of Moses, Hannah, Hezekiah, and the three youths, Hananiah, Mishael, and Azariah. By putting them into their present context and using them as songs of praise and thanksgiving, the tradition was showing how natural it is for man to respond with song to God's saving action and to praise him for his mercy.

The whole history of Israel thus turns out to be a continuous word of God, which the community acclaims with the words: "Give thanks to the Lord, for he is good, for his kindness endures forever."

This jubilant refrain, which recurs so often in cultic texts and liturgical celebrations,[3] also begins Psalms 106 and 107. The latter are two historical Psalms reviewing the chief events that shaped the life of Israel. This whole history, in its most hidden recesses, with all the wonders God had done in it and all the infidelities with which the community had burdened it, is thus placed under the sign of God's everlasting love and, consequently, transfigured by that love. This perspective is splendidly illustrated in the litany which makes up the Great Hallel, Psalm 136, where each historical statement is punctuated by the refrain "for his mercy endures forever."

B. In the Liturgical Celebration

1. The Psalm, an inspired response to God's word

Just as Israel in centuries past had welcomed the word with shouts of praise, so Israel in the synagogues welcomed the actualization of the word with similar praise. There was no question, of course, of composing, each sabbath and in each synagogue, a new canticle of Moses or an equivalent for Deborah's song. Gratitude must well up constantly in any assembly that listens to God, but the formulas for expressing it do not have to be constantly composed anew. A community may, without failing in its devotion, use older prayers; it can channel its praise through psalms written long ago; and it can make a collection of such songs. That is precisely how the Psalter, "the hymnal and prayer book of the postexilic community,"[4] came into existence.

In a lovely text, the rabbinic tradition emphasizes the vital link between the Psalms and the proclamation of the law. Referring to Psalm 92:2-4 ("It is good to give thanks to the Lord, to sing praise to your name, Most High, to proclaim your kindness and at dawn and your faithfulness throughout the night, with ten-stringed instrument and lyre"), the text comments: "We must obey and carry out what is said here. It is written: *with ten-stringed instrument and lyre*; this means that we must fulfill the *Ten Words* [the law of the Decalogue]."[5] It is possible also to regard the *Hallelu-Yah* (i.e., "Praise Yah[weh]") of Psalm 150 as a response of praise to the proclamation of the word. This Psalm closes the entire Psalter with an all-embracing doxology; in it, the acclamation "Praise the Lord" occurs ten times, as though to offer each of the "[ten] words of the covenant" (Exod. 34:28) a sacrifice of praise.[6]

In this connection we must note something that is important and peculiar to the religion of Israel. Prayer may be thought of as a cry rising from man's heart to the God whose name he does not know and whose face he seeks. That is what the prayer of the pagan is. The papyri of antiquity contain many such authentic, sometimes deeply moving prayers, written in terms that are like hands extended in the darkness toward the Godhead. These prayers are fully human, shot through with tears or cries of joy; but they are only human.

The situation of the chosen people was quite different. Israel was the people which the word had brought into being. Its first prayer was always to listen to God and to trace a picture of his face by means of the word spoken to it. And its first response was always the response which that word had itself stimulated. Its most perfect prayer was the one that gave the word the most perfect answer possible. Prayer that is thus a response did not do violence to the personality of Israel. Far from it, for had not the word itself created that personality? Israel's prayer was always fully human, for it sprang from a human heart with its joys and sorrows, yet at the same time it was divine.

Both of these aspects are expressed most fully in the Psalms. The Psalms are the outcries of men, and in this respect they resemble the prayers of the pagans; in fact, a number of biblical Psalms are twin brothers to pagan "psalms."[7] Yet, by receiving them into the canon of the Scriptures, God guaranteed their "inspiration," or divine character. In praying the Psalms, therefore, the synagogue was answering God with the very words of God.

2. *Relation between the cycle of readings and the Psalter*

As everyone knows, the Psalter is divided into five "books," each terminating with a cultic doxology.

The first book includes Psalms 1–41. It ends with the following doxology: "Blessed be the Lord, the God of Israel, from all eternity and forever. Amen. Amen" (Ps. 41:14).

The second book contains Psalms 42–72 and ends with a splendid doxology: "Blessed be the Lord, the God of Israel, who alone does wondrous deeds. And blessed forever be his glorious name; may the whole earth be filled with his glory. Amen. Amen" (Ps. 72:18-19).

The third book is made up of Psalms 73–89. It ends with: "Blessed be the Lord forever. Amen, and amen!" (Ps. 89:53).

The fourth book consists of Psalms 90–106 and ends with a doxology and a rubric for the people: "Blessed be the Lord, the God of Israel, through all eternity! Let all the people say, Amen! Alleluia" (Ps. 106:48).

The fifth book contains Psalms 107–150, and the last Psalm is nothing but a comprehensive doxology.

This division of the Psalter into five "books" is rather arbitrary. The groups have no literary unity; within each, the Psalms follow without any order at all, switching from sapiential sentences to prayers in time of persecution, from cries of victory to national mourning, tears of sorrow and shouts of joy. There are other possible classifications which have the advantage that they create genuine unities.[8] Thus one might group the Psalms assigned to David (Psalms 3–41 and 51–72),[9] the psalter of Asaph (Psalms 50 and 73–83) and the sons of Korah (Psalms 42–49, 84, 85, 87, and 88), the Pilgrim Psalms (120–134), or the Psalms of the Hallel (Psalms 113–118). The fact of certain doublets has also been pointed out,[10] which implies that some collections of Psalms existed prior to the formation of the Psalter and its division into five "books."

As a matter of fact, the five books of the Psalter seem intended to correspond to the five books of the Torah. The division of the Pentateuch was the model for the division of the Psalter, or at least the model in the light of which tradition understood the division of the Psalter.[11]

Is it possible to specify the relationship more closely? The research that has been done, especially since the beginning of this century,[12] has not yet reached any clear and universally accepted conclusions. H.-J. Kraus sums up the common view (or common hesitation) when he says: "It has not always proved possible to determine clearly the extent to which the Psalter was used in connection with the readings in the celebrations of the Jewish community."[13]

3. The cultic Psalms

The name "cultic" is given to those Psalms which originated in, or at least were used in, the liturgy of the Temple or in other liturgical celebrations.[14] It is evident that before the Psalter as a whole came to be used in the synagogues, there were cultic Psalms which could be readily drafted for use in the liturgical prayer of the synagogue.

a) Liturgies

Among the literary genres of the Psalter,[15] we may list in first place the *liturgies*, that is, Psalms which present us with liturgical celebrations. Thus, Psalm 134 is a *lucernarium* ["ceremony by lamplight"], or night office. Psalm 24 consists of two parts: (1) the first, verses 1-6, is a "threshold liturgy," and enumerates the conditions for entry into the sanctuary (cf. also Ps. 15); (2) the second part, verses 7-10, is based on the accounts of the bringing of the ark from Shiloh to Jerusalem, and echoes celebrations connected with the David cycle (cf. also Psalm 132).

With these liturgies in the proper sense we may group Psalms whose titles indicate their use in public worship. Psalm 29 is intended for the Feast of Tents, according to the Septuagint.[16] Psalm 30 is "a song for the dedication of the Temple." Psalm 92 is "for the sabbath day," while (again according to the LXX) Psalms 24, 48, 94, and 93 are for the first, second, fourth, and sixth days, respectively, after the sabbath.

Then there are the Pilgrim Psalms, comprising Psalms 120–134, which were probably a pilgrim's songbook for the "ascent" to Jerusalem.

Finally, there is the Hallel (Psalms 113–118), which was recited at the Passover meal and during the immolation of the victims for it.[17]

b) Enthronement Psalms

The enthronement Psalms, also known as the Psalms of Yahweh's kingship, are chiefly Psalms 47, 93, 96, 97, 98, and 99. S. Mowinckel went beyond H. Gunkel and suggested as the "vital context" (*Sitz im Leben*) of these Psalms an annual feast of Yahweh's enthronement.[18] Not all the exegetes have accepted the hypothesis of such a feast;[19] the majority are in agreement that the royal Psalms were cultic poems for the Feast of Tents.

c) The Songs of Zion

There is a group of Psalms called "the Songs of Zion" (the name occurs in Psalm 137:3). These are songs of tender love, or nostalgia, or exalted joy. They were sung by the dancing pilgrims as they went up to Jerusalem, "mother" of the nations, or sung with sobbing voices "by the streams of Babylon" (Ps. 137:1) in order to intensify the exiles' longing or allay their pain. These songs include Psalms 46, 48, 76, 84, 87, 122, and 132, and all have a cultic origin.[20]

d) Royal Psalms

These celebrate the earthly monarchy of Israel and its spiritual significance as regards the Messiah and eschatology.[21] Psalms 20 and 89, and the liturgy of the royal feast in Psalm 144 are regarded as cultic. To them may be added Psalms 18 and 21 (which are also songs of thanksgiving) and Psalm 132 (classified among the Songs of Zion).

e) Psalms for the Covenant Ritual

M. Mannati suggests this title for Psalms "the details of which are fully intelligible only when the Psalms are seen as part of the celebration of covenant renewal."[22] He is referring to Psalms 50, 81, 111, 115, 135, and 145 (which present almost the whole of the ritual); Psalms 78, 105, 106, 114, and 136 (which reflect the commemorative discourse on the occasion); and Psalms 1, 137, and 112 (which contain the part of blessings and curses).

f) Hymns

Classified as cultic are Psalms 33, 92 (?), 100, 121, 135 (cf. vv. 19-20), 136 (the Great Hallel), 145, 147, 148, and 150, as well as Psalms 146 and 149, which are also listed among the enthronement Psalms.

g) Various other genres

Among the Psalms of *collective thanksgiving*, Psalms 65, 66, 67, 68, and 118 (end of the Hallel) are considered cultic. Among the Psalms of *individual thanksgiving*, Psalms 9/10, 21, 27, 40, 107, and 116 are taken as cultic.

Among the Psalms of *collective trust*: Psalms 115 and 125. Among the Psalms of *individual trust*: Psalms 27, 121, and perhaps 23.

Among the Psalms of *collective supplication*: the laments in Psalms 44 and 94, along with Psalms 80 (?), 85, 108, and 126. Among the Psalms of *individual supplication*: Psalms 7, 22, 25 (?), 26, 55, 56, 61, 102, and 109 (?).

Among the *wisdom Psalms*: Psalm 91.

Among the *prophetic exhortations*: Psalms 50, 75 (?), 81, 82, and 95.

Not all these categories, of course, are of the same importance, nor are they equally well defined from a literary viewpoint. One and the same Psalm may sometimes fall into two different classes. Points of detail are also open to discussion. Yet, when all is said and done, an inventory yields about seventy-seven Psalms that are cultic in character.[23] This is a striking figure, for it means that about half of the Psalter is connected, either in origin or in use, with the liturgy.

By making these songs its own, the synagogue was emphasizing its continuity with the liturgical celebrations in the Temple. The praise given God through the Psalms was replacing the bloody sacrifices of the Temple (cf. Ps. 50:23). But as time went on, this simple substitution was to create an entirely new situation. By introducing the cultic Psalms into the service of readings from the Law and the Prophets, by singing in the humblest rural synagogues the songs that accompanied the sacrifices of thanksgiving in the Temple, the joyous processions of the enthronement festivals, and the jubilant Feast of Tents, the synagogal liturgy was, as it were, making the worshiping community of Jerusalem worldwide in membership. A new ecclesial assembly was being created, consisting not simply of the community that celebrated the liturgy in the Jerusalem Temple, but of the worldwide community, from Babylon to Italy and from Macedonia to Egypt, that listened to God's word and responded to it with the Psalms. A new Temple was gradually being erected, in which each synagogue was a spiritual stone.

Soon the time would come when the Romans would raze the Temple at Jerusalem and suppress its liturgy, and yet they were not able to destroy the new community or interrupt the praying of the Psalms. When the Psalms passed from Temple to synagogue, they were rescued from Jerusalem's destruction in 70 A.D., and thus they created the situation in which Jesus would say: "An hour is coming when you will worship the Father neither on this mountain nor in Jerusalem. . . . An hour is coming, and is already here, when authentic worshipers will worship the Father in Spirit and truth" (John 4:21, 23).

II. PRAISE AND THANKSGIVING

The Psalms were a mirror held up to Israel. In these poems that had sprung from hearts both rebellious and faithful, from souls that had known death and rebirth, the people could see its own face as created by the word and moulded by dialogue with God. What was the characteristic expression on Israel's face as it accepted the word? In the symphony of the Psalms, with its countless joyous and sorrowful voices, what is the major theme?

We said earlier that the people responded to God's interventions in its history with an "Amen!" or "Yes!," that is, with a cry of praise and thanksgiving. The canticles of Moses, of Miriam, of Deborah and Barak, of Hannah the mother of Samuel, of Judith who triumphed over Holofernes, of the elder Tobit, and of the three young men Hananiah, Mishael, and Azariah are some examples of the response in praise of God. In the synagogue service the Psalms had the same function as these canticles — they were the community's response of praise and thanksgiving to the word that told them of God's great deeds. The synagogue called the Psalms *tehillim*,[24] which means "hymns" or "thanksgivings." Despite the range of literary genres the Psalter contains (from enthronement hymns to national lamentations), it was seen as being in its entirety an immense hymn of praise, a ceaseless act of thanksgiving.

The two basic and central subjects of this praise and thanksgiving are creation and the election of Israel. In other words, the Psalter focuses on God insofar as he fashions creation in all its beauty and majesty, and insofar as he leads Israel.

1. Creation

Creation reflects the transcendent beauty of God. From its heavenly temple his glory is poured out upon the earth,[25] and transforms it in turn into a vast temple in which the roaring wind, the leaping mountains of Lebanon, the quaking wilderness of Kadesh, the storm-twisted cedars, and the lightning all celebrate a cosmic liturgy in honor of the Lord of the universe: "The God of glory thunders . . . and in his temple all say, 'Glory!' " (Ps. 29:3, 9).

Creation is not lifeless or dumb. The heavens "tell" of God's glory, the mountains "cry out for joy" before him, the earth and all fruits are ecstatic with joy, and the trees of the forest dance for joy before the face of the Lord as he comes.[26] Every one of the Psalms which speaks of creation shows it jubilant before God and filled with the proclamation of his glory. The eyes of Israel as it gazes out upon the world in the Psalms are filled with admiration and awe. Israel looks upon the world as God did when he first looked upon his work and found it to be good.

The Psalms amplify this cosmic praise by summoning God's creatures to join in tribute to him:

> Praise him, all you his angels,
>   praise him, all you his hosts.
> Praise him, sun and moon;
>   praise him, all you shining stars.
> Praise him, you highest heavens,
>   and you waters above the heavens. . . .
> Praise the Lord from the earth,
>   you sea-monsters and all depths;
> Fire and hail, snow and mist,
>   storm winds that fulfill his word;

You mountains and all you hills,
    you fruit trees and all you cedars;
You wild beasts and all you tame animals,
    you creeping things and you winged fowl (Ps. 148:2-4, 7-10).[27]

But the stars and the angels did not wait for man's invitation before singing their Creator's praises. When God was laying the foundations of the world, "the morning stars sang in chorus and all the sons of God shouted for joy" (Job 38:7). In inviting the stars and the angels to join him, man shows simply that he is uniting his praise to that of the stars and the angels, as a brother joining his brothers.

Seeing the beauty of creation, the Psalmist naturally passes over to praise of the Creator: "O Lord, our Lord, how glorious is your name over all the earth!" (Ps. 8:2).

Such praise of God arises out of contemplation of the wonders of creation: the vault of heaven which God spread like a tent over the earth; the dazzling light that clothes the Lord like a glorious mantle; the winged wind on which he travels and the clouds that serve as his chariot; the mountains that tremble and smoke when he touches them, the depths of the earth that he holds in his hand, the dry land that he shapes like a potter shaping clay.[28] But the Psalmist also gazes with wonder on the humble things God has made, as though making them for his own relaxation: the bird that sings in the branches, the stork that nests in the cedars, the chamois and the marmots that find shelter among the rocks, the fabulous Leviathan which God formed "to make sport of it" (Ps. 104:26) and to "put him in leash for your maidens" (Job 40:29), and the incredible Behemoth who walks in the bogs and whose "bones are like tubes of bronze" (Job 40:18). All of these are wonderful, and all of them stir us to praise and bless God: "At the works of your hands I rejoice. How great are your works, O Lord!" (Ps. 92:5-6).

In taking these Psalms and making them part of its services, the people of the synagogue made the word their teacher. They learned from it the spirit of praise and gratitude, so that their response to the word was blessing, praise, and the glorification of God. Israel became, as it were, one with the stars, the sun, the sea, the fog and the wind, the snow and the frost, Leviathan and Behemoth, in a brotherhood of praise and thanksgiving. Creation praises God; Israel made that praise its own and crowned it adding its own blessing of the Lord.

The Israel of the Psalms experienced nothing of Paul's bitter sorrow as he looked at creation and saw it subjected to corruption, broken by its enslavement, and groaning in the pains of childbirth.[29] Instead of seeing the earth as covered with thorns and thistles, the symbol of the curse which Adam's sin had brought upon it, Israel preferred to contemplate the world as adorned with the rainbow, symbol of the covenant God had made with Noah.[30] Instead of thinking of the world as an enemy because of sin, Israel preferred to think of it as a brother through God's grace. Looking out upon the world, Israel's reaction was: "Bless the Lord, O my soul!" (Ps. 104:1, 35).[31]

2. The history of Israel

To the theme of creation Israel added that of Israel's history: "Bless the Lord, O my soul, and forget not all his benefits. He pardons all your iniquities . . . he crowns you with kindness and compassion" (Ps. 103:2-4).[32]

The Israelite passes easily from God who creates the world to God who shapes history and effects in it the salvation of his people. In one and the same movement of thanksgiving he praises the God who counts the stars and gives the little birds their food and the God who builds Jerusalem and brings the exiles back home (Psalm 147); the God who hangs the great lights in the vault of heaven and sets the earth firmly upon the waters and the God who rescues his people from the grasp of Pharaoh, Sihon, and Og, and gives them a land as their inheritance (Psalm 136); the God who creates the light of day and the God who lights the lamp of the Law (Psalm 19).

The Psalms delight in emphasizing the continuity between what we today call creation and redemption, nature and grace. It is not an accident that the five books of the Torah begin with the account of the creation of "the heavens and the earth and all their array" (Gen. 2:1).[33] The creation itself becomes a prelude to the formation of Israel. God made the world for the sake of his first-born son; therefore the election of the people of the promise is the glorious crown of creation and sets the seal of perfection upon his work.

This history, even in its most hidden recesses and obscure windings, is permeated by God's presence. It belongs to him, and he shapes it as a potter shapes the clay: "We are the clay and you the potter: we are all the work of your hands" (Is. 64:7).[34] So much is this history God's work that when one tribe fails to come to another's aid in battle, it is said to have failed to help Yahweh himself (Judg. 5:23). Why so? Because all the battles of Israel are the battles of

Yahweh, and in the victories of his people it is God himself who is victorious.

Everything in this history is matter for admiring praise. When Psalms 106 and 107 paint with broad strokes a picture of Israel's life and history, they preface it with an acclamation: "Give thanks to the Lord, for he is good, for his kindness endures forever!".

This acclamation represents the judgment which believing Israel passed on its own history: It saw that history as the work of God's love, and therefore it broke out into thankful praise. We find the Israelite proudly hymning the election of Abraham and the covenant (Ps. 105:6, 42); the story of Isaac, Jacob, and Joseph, the rescue from Egypt, and the settlement in Canaan (Psalm 105); the establishment of the monarchy and the election of David (Psalm 89); the choice of Zion as "the city of the great king," the sight of which frightens his enemies (Psalm 48); the Temple where God's glory dwells (one day here is worth a thousand happy days elsewhere! — Ps. 84:11); the victories won to the cry of "The Lord of hosts is with us; our stronghold is the God of Jacob" (Ps. 46:4); and, above all, the gift of the Law, on which the Israelite meditates in his heart day and night (Psalm 1). Israel can say with pride: "He has not done thus for any other nation"! (Ps. 147:20).

The history of the individual believer fits quite naturally into the larger picture of sacred history as a whole, and is filled with the same stream of praise. Men thank God for the favors he does for his friends (Psalm 4); for the rescue of the poor man "in the midst of lions" (Psalm 57); for the lonely man, whose tears God collects in his flask (Psalm 56); for the persecuted man, whom he surrounds with a rampart (Psalm 71); for the abandoned man, whose solitude he fills with his own tender love (Psalm 22); for the accused man whose burden he himself will bear (Psalm 55); for the pardoned sinner, whom he rings round with glad cries of freedom (Psalm 32). As it sang that "all the paths of the Lord are kindness and constancy" (Ps. 25:10), the synagogue was learning that everything is a fit subject for praise and thanksgiving.

But what of the lamentations? When the synagogue repeated these Psalms of distress,[35] can we say that it was receiving the word with praise and gratitude?

We may begin our answer by observing that many desolate laments end in joyous praise.[36] In order to show how great God's act of rescue was, the singer first shows the distress man was in; sobs of suffering serve as a prelude to thanksgiving. The most extensive example of this practice is Psalm 22, which opens with the cry of abandonment: "My God, my God, why have you forsaken me?" Here is an unfortunate man subject to every kind of earthly suffering: He is rejected by God, who is deaf to his pleas; he is scorned by men and despised by the people; he is surrounded by enemies, who attack him like lions or bulls or hounds; they tie his hands and feet and bring him down to the dust of death; and he is ill and emaciated to the point where all his bones can be counted. We might almost say that no man has ever been afflicted in all these ways at the same time. True enough. But the remarkable thing is that these depths of suffering are replaced by heights of joy and gratitude. The man who was crushed by suffering and trampled by his enemies is heard by God; he who was hopeless is saved. Then he sings the Lord's praises in the presence of all his brothers, "in the midst of the assembly." He associates all of Israel with him in his joy. The poor share in his sacrifice of thanksgiving and are filled at his communion meal. Moreover, "all the ends of the earth" and "all the families of the nations" shall acknowledge God's lordship as they see this act of deliverance and shall become his servants. Evidently, then, Psalm 22 is describing not so much the experience of a poor man as the course of prayer itself: "For he [the Lord] stood at the right hand of the poor man" (Ps. 109:31) and changed his tears into cries of joy. Thus, in using Psalm 22, the synagogue was not simply reciting a lament but also singing a song of thanksgiving.

Not all the Psalms of lamentation have as striking an ending as Psalm 22. But all without exception are directed toward prayer and supplication; that is, they seek a hearing which will then give rise to praise. Shall a man turn a tearful face to God if he does not hope that God will wipe those tears away? Would he sigh before God if he did not know that he was heard? The laments of the Bible are never turned in upon themselves in despair; they do not spring from a narcissistic contemplation of suffering. Instead, they are always a prayer to God, and in them, suffering is accompanied by the peace and joy of trust, hope, and praise. The Psalter contains not a single lament that is nothing but a lament.[37]

In the songs of the most profound suffering, prayer reaches its maximum intensity, and praise, even of a silent kind, is most full of love. Lamentation and the taste of tears are part of every human prayer. Israel, for its part, had long known that life, even if lived close to God, is full of unanswerable problems. Israel knew that good is rewarded and evil punished, but also that the account is not settled in our present life. Sinners are often happy, and just men despairing; the wicked grow fat and the faithful waste away. When this happened, the Israelite asked God: "What are you doing?" (Job 9:12). He asked God the question with which the laments so often begin: "My God, why . . . ?"[38]

Death was the greatest of the unsolved problems, especially if it came after a life filled with blessings from the Lord. What the Israelite feared about death was not so much its intrinsic suffering; death, after all, was inescapable; it was foreseen and allowed by God. "In your hands is my destiny" (Ps. 31:16); it is God who keeps our life "bound in the bundle of the living" (1 Sam. 25:29).[39] No, what struck fright into the Israelite soul was the possibility of separation from God and of being destined never more to praise him. The bitterness of death for the Israelite finds expression in questions like these:

> Will you work wonders for the dead?
>   Will the shades arise to give you thanks?
> Do they declare your kindness in the grave,
>   your faithfulness among those who have perished?
> Are your wonders made known in the darkness
>   or your justice in the land of oblivion? (Ps. 88:11-13).

The Israel of the Psalms never received a satisfactory answer to these questions. Yet the silence of God did not cause hope to lessen. For, to the uncertainty of Sheol the Psalmist could oppose the certainty of God's love:

> Therefore my heart is glad and my soul rejoices,
>   my body, too, abides in confidence;
> Because you will not abandon my soul to the nether world,
>   nor will you suffer your faithful one to undergo corruption (Ps. 16:9-10).[40]

This immense confidence with its challenge to death echoes the cry of Job: "Slay me though he might, I will wait for him" (Job 13:15). May we not say that the lament here turns into one of the highest forms of praise?

In all the Psalms, even in the tearful laments, the synagogue experienced at every liturgical celebration the truth of the words of Psalm 147, "It is fitting to praise him"! (v. 1).

¹ Cf. Deut. 27:15-26; Neh. 8:6. The "Amen" is also found as a conclusion to the doxologies which end the first four books of the Psalter: Pss. 41:14; 72:19; 89:52; 106:48 (=1 Chron. 16:36). Cf. H. Schlier, "amēn," TDNT 1:335–38.

² On the date of composition of this song, cf. R. Tournay, "Recherches sur la chronologie des Psaumes," *Revue biblique* 65 (1958), pp. 335–57 (the song may have been composed for the famous Passover of Josiah in 622 by a priest or Levite attached to the Jerusalem Temple).

³ With minor variations it is found in the canticle attributed to David in 1 Chron. 16:1-36 (= Pss. 105:1-5, + 96 + 106:1, 47-48; for the refrain, cf. 1 Chron. 16:34); the canticle at the transfer of the ark to the Temple, in 2 Chron. 5:13; the canticle at the dedication of the Temple by Solomon, in 2 Chron 7:3, 6; in Jehoshaphat's triumphant war hymn, in 2 Chron. 20:21; in the song accompanying a sacrifice in the Temple, in Jer. 33:11 and Ezra 3:11; and in Pss. 100:5; 106:1; 107:1; 118:1, 2, 3, 4, 29; 136:1-26.

⁴ H.-J. Kraus, *Psalmen* 1:xviii. Cf. H. Schmidt, *Die Psalmen* (Handbuch zum Alten Testament, Erste Reihe 15; Tübingen, 1934): "The Psalter is the hymnal of the postexilic community" (p. iii); and R. Kittel, *Die Psalmen* (Kommentar zum Alten Testament 13; Leipzig, 1929⁵⁻⁶), p. xv.

⁵ *Midrash Pesikt* (A. Wünsche, *Aus Israels Lehrhallen* V/2, p. 10, quoted in A. Arens, *op. cit.*, p. 198).

⁶ Cf. Arens, *op. cit.*, p. 177.

⁷ Cf., e.g., A. Barucq, *L'expression de la louange divine et de la prière dans la Bible et en Egypte* (Institut Francais d'Archéologie Orientale, Bibliothéque d'Etude 33; Cairo, 1962).

⁸ H.-J. Kraus, *op. cit.*, 1:xiii–xvii.

⁹ Psalms 3–41 and 51–72 are said to have been composed by David, except for the last, which is supposedly by Solomon (cf. 72:1), yet ends with the notation: "The prayers of David the son of Jesse are ended" (72:20). We must conclude that these indications are no longer where they originally belonged.

¹⁰ Thus Psalm 14 = Psalm 53; 70 = 14:14-18; 108 = 57:8-12 + 60:7-14.

¹¹ Cf. H. Schmidt, *op. cit.*, p. iv: "The Psalter, doubtless with the Pentateuch in mind, was divided into five books by introducing doxologies at the end of Psalms 41, 72, 89, and 106." Cf. O. Eissfeldt, *The Old Testament: An Introduction*, p. 152; H.-J. Kraus, *op. cit.*, 1:xiv–xv; D. G. Castellino, *Libro dei Salmi* (Turin, 1955), p. 7.

¹² In 1904, E. G. King offered the hypothesis that the grouping of the Psalms in the psalter itself reflects the triennial cycle of readings from the Torah; cf. "The Influence of the Triennial Cycle upon the Psalter," *Journal of Theological Studies* 5 (1904), pp. 202–13.

¹³ *Op. cit.*, p. xviii. A. Arens, *op. cit.*, has offered an attractive hypothesis: The beginnings of the five books of the Pentateuch correspond to the beginnings of the five books of the Psalter (pp. 169–77). He has repeated and summarized his views in "Hat die Psalter seinen 'Sitz im Leben' in der synagogalen Leseordnung des Pentateuch?" in R. de Langhe (ed.), *Le Psautier* (Orientalia et Biblica Lovaniensia 4; Louvain, 1962), pp. 107–31. Arens based his hypothesis on the triennial cycle as reconstructed by R. G. French, *The Synagogue Lectionary and the New Testament* (London, 1939), and on the study of N. Snaith, *Hymns of the Temple* (London, 1951), who drew on the rabbinic tradition to propose an average of four pericopes a month. French acknowledges honestly that his conclusion is of "dubious clarity" (according to Arens, *Die Psalmen im Gottesdienst des Alten Bundes*, p. 177). R. Tournay, in his review of Arens, *Revue biblique* 69 (1962), writes: "We are therefore not fully convinced of the author's thesis, despite the impressive amount of work it represents and the massive documentation he has used in its support" (p. 611).

¹⁴ In determining the cultic character of a Psalm, we have generally followed the criteria proposed by A. Szörenyi, *Psalmen und Kult im Alten Testament* (Budapest, 1961). These criteria are: (a) mention of the Temple as the place where the Psalmist is

praying; (b) mention of the feast being celebrated; (c) mention of another liturgical action which is regarded as having taken place (pp. 396–412).

For the chronology of some of the Psalms, cf. the essays of R. Tournay, "Recherches sur la chronologie des Psaumes," *Revue biblique* 65 (1958), pp. 321–57; 66 (1959), pp. 161–90; "Le Psaume LXVIII et le Livre des Juges," *Revue biblique* 66 (1959), pp. 358–68; "Le Psaume CXLI," *Vetus Testamentum* 9 (1959), pp. 58–64.

The Psalter as such probably dates from the end of the third century (Kraus, *op. cit.*, p. xvii) or, at the latest, from the middle of the second (Eissfeldt, *op. cit.*, p. 451).

[15] The decisive work on the literary genres has been done by H. Gunkel, *Einleitung in die Psalmen: Die Gattungen der religiösen Lyrik Israels* (Göttingen, 1966²), and carried further by S. Mowinckel, *The Psalms in Israel's Worship*, translated by D. R. Ap-Thomas (2 vols.; Oxford, 1962; the Norwegian original, *Offersang og sangoffer*, here updated, appeared in 1951). Cf. also H. Schmidt, *op. cit.*, pp. iii–ix; A. Weiser, *The Psalms: A Commentary*, translated by H. Hartwell (Philadelphia, 1962), pp. 52–91. An excellent presentation of current research on the Psalter, together with bibliography, is given by J. Coppens, "Les études récentes sur le Psautier" and A. Descamps, "Les genres littéraires du Psautier," both in R. de Langhe, *op. cit.*, pp. 1–71 and 73–88.

For questions of detail, cf. the commentaries of Castellino, Kraus, and Mannati.

For the classification of the Psalms according to their literary genre, cf. P. Drijvers, *The Psalms: Their Structure and Meaning* (New York, 1965); L. Sabourin, "Un classement littéraire des Psaumes," *Sciences ecclésiastiques* 16 (1964), pp. 23–58; M. Mannati, *Les Psaumes* 1:41–74. The literary genres as such may be clearly defined, but the Psalms themselves do not always fit neatly into the categories, and the classification may differ from author to author.

[16] The LXX (Septuagint) provides more numerous liturgical indications than the Hebrew text does. This does not necessarily mean a later tradition; it need only mean a different recension, which is perhaps as old as the Hebrew.

[17] *Pesahim* 5:7; 9:3 (Danby, *op. cit.*, pp. 142, 148).

[18] Cf. H. Gunkel, *op. cit.*, pp. 94–116, and S. Mowinckel, *op. cit.*, 1:106–92. On the present state of the research into the Psalms of Yahweh's kingship, cf. E. Lipinski, "Les Psaumes de la royauté de Yahvé dans l'exégèse moderne," in R. de Langhe, *op. cit.*, pp. 133–272.

[19] O. Eissfeldt writes: "There is no necessity to assign [these Psalms] to a celebration which in any case is not actually attested but only surmised" (*op. cit.*, p. 110). Cf. H. Cazelles, "Nouveau an," *DBS* 2:409–13; R. de Vaux, *Ancient Israel*, pp. 504–6. In his *Worship in Israel*, H.-J. Kraus analyzes the autumn festival, while H. Riesenfeld, *Jésus transfiguré* (Lund, 1947), pp. 15–28, shows the importance of this feast in the Hellenistic period as the New Testament period was about to begin.

[20] Gunkel, Mowinckel, and Schmidt consider Psalm 46 to be an enthronement Psalm. Kraus, *Psalmen*, p. 341, sees it as meant rather for a feast of Zion. — Psalm 76 may have been an enthronement Psalm (Kraus, *op. cit.*, p. 525), and Psalm 84 may have belonged to the Feast of Tents.

[21] As S. Mowinckel, *op. cit.*, 1:47 remarks, the royal Psalms are not really a special genre, since prayer for the king can use genres as varied as the lament, the hymn, and the prophetic oracle. — Other Psalms usually classified as royal are 2, 18 (?), 20, 21, 45, 72, 89, 101, 110, 132, and 134 (?).

[22] *Op. cit.*, 1:41.

[23] As an example of how the figure can be pushed much higher: Mowinckel's view is that some forty Psalms are to be connected with the feast of Yahweh's enthronement.

[24] The Psalter is the *sepher tehillim*, "book of hymns." The root of *tehillim* is *halal*, "to praise."

[25] Cf. Is. 6:3: "All the earth is filled with his glory."

26 Cf. Pss. 19:2; 96:11-12; 98:4-8.

27 Cf. also Ps. 103:20-22.

28 Cf. chiefly Pss. 104; 95:4-5.

29 Cf. Rom. 8:19-22.

30 Compare "Cursed be the ground because of you!" (Gen. 3:17) with "Never again will I doom the earth because of man" (Gen. 8:21).

31 Psalm 104, which sings of the splendor of creation, begins and ends with the acclamation quoted.

32 Cf. E. Beaucamp, *The Bible and the Universe: Israel and the Theology of History*, translated by D. Balhatchet (Westminster, Md., 1963), Chapter 3: "The Universe as a Witness to History" (pp. 87–114).

33 Cf. W. Eichrodt, *Theology of the Old Testament* 2: 100–101. To Psalms 19, 136, and 147, already mentioned, may be added the Canticle of Ezra (Neh. 9), which begins with thanksgiving (v. 5) and goes on to praise God as the Creator of the world and of Israel's history.

34 Cf. Jer. 18:6: "Like clay in the hand of the potter, so are you in my hand, house of Israel."

35 The exegetes distinguish between individual laments and collective laments. Among the former are Psalms 3, 5, 6, 7, 13, 17, 22, 25, 26, 27, 28, 35, 38, 39, 41, 42–43, 51, 54, 56, 57, 59, 61, 63, 64, 69, 71, 86, 88, 102, 109, 130, 140, 141, 143. Among the latter are Psalms 60, 74, 79, 80, 83, 90, 137. Cf. H.-J. Kraus, *op. cit.*, pp. xlv and li.

36 Among the individual laments, this is the case in Psalms 13 (cf. v. 6); 27 (vv. 1, 6); 28 (vv. 6-8); 35 (vv. 9-10, 18, 28); 41 (v. 14); 43 (v. 4); 51 (vv. 10, 14, 17, 21); 54 (v. 8); 56 (vv. 13-14); 64 (v. 11); 69 (vv. 30-36); 71 (vv. 22-24); 86 (vv. 7-10, 12-13); 102 (vv. 13-23); 109 (vv. 30-31); 130 (vv. 7-8); 140 (vv. 8, 13-14); 143 (v. 8). Among the collective laments, cf. Psalms 90 (vv. 14-17); 85 (vv. 9-14); 73 (v. 13). Thus more than half the laments (24 out of about 42) contain elements of joy and thanksgiving.

37 On the literary genre of lamentation in the Psalms, cf. S. Mowinckel, *op. cit.*, 1:193-246; 2:1-25. Cf. also H. Gunkel, *op. cit.*, pp. 117–39 ("The Laments of the People"); on pp. 400–402 the author discusses the mingling of literary genres in the laments. H.-J. Kraus, *op. cit.*, p. li, deals under one heading with the laments, the songs of thanksgiving, and the hymns of trust, since he maintains that all of these have the same "vital context" (*Sitz im Leben*). We might add that the mingling of many literary genres in one and the same lament is due to the unity of the human person, who is capable of simultaneously experiencing very diverse feelings.

38 Cf. Pss. 22:2; 42:10; 44:24-25; 74:1; etc.

39 On the mystery of the beyond in the Old Testament, cf. R. Martin-Achard, *From Death to Life: A Study of the Development of the Doctrine of the Resurrection in the Old Testament*, translated by J.P. Smith (Edinburgh, 1960), and the concise presentation by A. Gelin in *The Religion of Israel*, translated by J.R. Foster (New York, 1959), pp. 90–101.

40 The early Church in its catechesis applied this Psalm to the resurrection of Christ; cf. Acts 2:26-28; 13:35.

Part Three

THE MESSIANIC AGE

Chapter 9

GOD CALLS AND GATHERS
HIS PEOPLE

*"To gather into one all the dispersed children
of God"* (John 11:52)

Through the ministry of his Son, God once again calls and gathers his people and thus forms the Church of the messianic age. St. John describes the mission of Jesus in this fashion: "Jesus would die for the nation — not for this nation only, but to gather into one all the dispersed children of God" (11:52).[1]

In this chapter we shall consider: the messianic gathering of Israel; the gathering of the nations; and the relation between the gathering of Israel and the gathering of the nations.

I. THE GATHERING OF ISRAEL

Through the mouths of his prophets God had proclaimed that he would once again gather his people and reunite them under the leadership of a new shepherd who would be the successor of David:

> I will take the Israelites from among the nations to which they have come, and gather them from all sides to bring them back to their land. I will make them one nation upon the land, in the mountains of Israel, and there shall be one prince for them all. . . . My servant David shall be prince over them, and there shall be one shepherd for them all (Ezek. 37:21-22, 24).[2]

In its prayers Israel asks God — who "rebuilds Jerusalem; the dispersed of Israel he gathers" (Ps. 147:2) — to hasten the fulfillment of his prophecies:

> Save us, O God, our savior,
>   gather us and deliver us from the nations (1 Chron. 16:35).[3]

Israel is sure of being heard:

> He . . . will again have mercy on you all.
> He will gather you from all the Gentiles
>   among whom you have been scattered (Tob. 13:15).

Jesus, when he comes, fulfills the prophecy. It is true, of course, that his gracious call gathers all the nations of the earth; yet the grace is offered first to Israel as the first fruits of the nations. It is to the brothers and sisters of Jesus according to the flesh that "the adoption, the glory, the covenants, the law-giving, the worship, and the promises. . . . [and] the patriarchs" belong (Rom. 9:4-5). To them too, therefore, the first call is rightfully addressed. With a patience inspired by divine love, the Savior tries to create the primordial messianic community: "O Jerusalem, Jerusalem. . . . how often have I yearned to gather your children, as a mother bird gathers her young under her wings" (Matthew 23:37; cf. Luke 13:34). He will state emphatically that he has been sent "only to the lost sheep of the house of Israel" (Matthew 15:24) and that he means to break the messianic bread only for the children of the kingdom and not to throw it to the dogs.[4]

Not everyone would appreciate the kind of messianic bread Jesus offered. Nationalists enraged by the Roman occupation were looking for a Messiah whose first act would be to muster an army against the Romans rather than to gather a Church. Intriguing theologians and inspired zealots dreamt of the wild Messiah of the apocalypses and identified the kingdom of God with the land of Palestine. Scribes and Pharisees imprisoned in their own hypocrisy had made a god in their own likeness and laws for their own convenience, and refused to answer Christ's call, some through indifference, some out of malice. They were all hoping for an army or trade or honors; their aim was to "suck the milk of nations and be nursed at royal breasts" (Is. 60:16). Jesus instead offered them the kingdom of heaven, and their disappointment was so great that it deafened them to his call.

On the other hand, the Church of the lowly, the authentic "Israel of God" (Gal. 6:16), found in the Gospel the fulfillment of their hopes. They formed the Church of the beatitudes, which was recruited from the poor in spirit, the lowly, the afflicted, the hungry, the merciful, the pure of heart, the peacemakers, and the persecuted (cf. Matthew 5:3-13). The very people whom the old law had dismissed from the worshiping assembly ("The blind and the lame shall not enter the temple" — 2 Sam. 5:8 JB),[5] are the ones who throng the messianic banquet hall: "Go out quickly into the streets and alleys of the town and bring in the poor and the crippled, the blind and the lame. . . . I want my house to be full" (Luke 14:21, 23).[6]

In accents of special love, Jesus gathers sinners. Are they not the poorest of the poor? And is not their spiritual distress the worst form of destitution? Jesus prefers the humility of the sinner who recognizes his sad state to the pride of the Pharisee who is enamored of his own uprightness. He says openly: "I have come to call, not the self-righteous, but sinners" (Matthew 9:13; Mark 2:17).[7] When, in an attempt to sully his reputation, the Pharisees accuse him of being "a friend of tax collectors and sinners" (Luke 7:34; Matthew 11:19),[8] they bear witnesses to the extent of his mercy.

But we must not misinterpret all this. The Church which Jesus gathers is not an assembly of blind and lame people or of sinners, but simply of believers who admit their blindness, lameness, and sinfulness to God in order to be saved by him. The people really crippled and blinded are the Pharisees, who "strain out the gnat and swallow the camel" (Matthew 23:24), who think they see but are actually in darkness. The assembly of Jesus, on the contrary, is a holy assembly, but its holiness consists less in the absence of sin than in the confession of it and the desire for salvation. It is an assembly whose poverty is enriched by the poverty of Jesus.[9] At its head is the Virgin Mary, who humbly accepted God's word.[10]

We must not, of course, unduly force the opposition between rich and poor, scribes or Pharisees and the lowly, as if the former were all unfitted for the kingdom and the latter all elect. There may have been "bad" poor people, who were filled with a longing for wealth, and rich people open to the kingdom. Among the latter there were, for example, the members of the family at Bethany whose hospitality Jesus readily accepted.[11] Among the Lord's disciples were Pharisees like Nicodemus, a member of the Sanhedrin;[12] Joseph of Arimathea, "a wealthy man" (Matthew 27:57), who "looked expectantly for the reign of God" (Luke 23:51),[13] and who, together with Nicodemus, buried the Lord; or the scribe who came to argue with Jesus and received a great compliment from him: "You are not far from the reign of God" (Mark 12:34).[14]

Evidently, then, the dividing line that defines the disciple of Jesus does not run between rich and poor, between the scribes and

Pharisees on one side and the ordinary people on the other. Instead, it runs through the heart of every man. There, in the depths of each person, the summons to the messianic gathering is heard; there it is that God forms his new people. All are called: the "chosen" are those who answer "yes" by an interior conversion.

II. THE GATHERING OF THE NATIONS

The gathering of Israel did not mean the installation of the twelve tribes in a new Jewish ghetto. On the contrary, it was a first step toward a gathering of all the nations. The call issued by Jesus knocked down the barriers raised by Judaism; it broke through the iron bars (though these were, indeed, also bonds of tender love) within which Israel had at times imprisoned the Yahwist religion. Without ceasing to be the glory of his people Israel, Jesus showed himself to be also a "light to the Gentiles" (Luke 2:31).[15] The assembly he establishes is all-embracing, and brings together the faithful "from every nation and race, people and tongue" (Apoc. 7:9).[16]

Inversely, all nations, races, peoples, and tongues become a single people that is enriched by the diversity of each; they form a single family, made up of those who are God's children through faith.[17] The ideal of Josiah in the Deuteronomic reform — one people, one faith, one king — is finally made a reality in the New Testament: "There is one Lord, one faith, one baptism; one God and Father of all, who is over all, and works through all, and is in all" (Eph. 4:5).[18] In this assembly there is no longer "Jew or Greek, slave or freeman, male or female" (Gal. 3:28).

The assembly formed by Jesus Christ is universal not only in its members but in space and time as well. The gatherings for worship in times past had for their spatial context Mount Sinai in the time of Moses, the pilgrimage to Shechem in the time of Joshua, the Temple at Jerusalem for Josiah and Ezra, and the synagogues in the age of Judaism. The backdrop for Jesus' life, on the other hand, is the universe; the new assembly he convokes is "ecumenical" in the full sense of the word, that is, it extends to the whole of the "inhabited" earth (*oikoumenē*).[19] The frontiers of the new promised land are coextensive, not with Palestine, but with the world; they no longer separate Jew and pagan, but unite them all in Christ. The only possible line of demarcation now is between believers and unbelievers. Through faith any man at all can become a citizen of this new city and live in a new fatherland, the Church of God. The faithful followers of Christ, who are immersed in mankind as messengers of the kingdom that knows no frontiers, are "the soul of the world."[20]

The assembly is also universal in time. The word is no longer proclaimed only on a single day or during a single feast, for the feast of the new covenant during which Jesus proclaims his Gospel will last until the end of time. In this respect all men are contemporaries of Jesus, since he is present to them all: "Know that I am with you always, until the end of the world!" (Matthew 28:20). Those who hear his call at the beginning of the messianic age have no advantage over those who receive it at the end of time. The Church is not more blessed during the time of its infancy than during the time of its adolescence or maturity, since Jesus is present to all times, being "the same yesterday, today, and forever" (Heb. 13:8). In every age the Church can repeat with utter truthfulness the words of Deuteronomy: "This day you have become the people of the Lord, your God" (27:9).

III. THE GATHERING OF ISRAEL AND THE GATHERING OF THE NATIONS

What is the relation between these two gatherings? Are they simply two parallel, or successive, acts, with no vital relation between them? Or are they rather interrelated as parts of the same call from the Messiah?

1. The nations take Israel's place

A first answer might be phrased in this way: "First, Jesus calls Israel. But Israel refuses his message because its expectations concerning the Messiah do not match what Jesus shows himself to be. Jesus then calls the nations, which take the place of the chosen people."

This interpretation of the history of salvation can appeal for support to various statements in the Gospel, such as the saying about the first and the last. The pagans who were the "last" to be called will become in fact the "first" and "will come from the east and the west, from the north and the south, and will take their place at the feast in the kingdom of God" (Luke 13:28-30). The Jews, on the contrary, though the first to be loved, will then be last: "the natural heirs of the kingdom will be driven out into the dark. Wailing will be heard there, and the grinding of teeth" (Matthew 8:12).[21]

The same idea is to be found in the parable of the invited guests as recorded in Luke 14:15-24. When those formally invited have refused to come, the master of the house sends his servant out to look for substitute guests: "Go out quickly into the streets and alleys of the town and bring in the poor and the crippled, the blind and the lame. . . . I want my house to be full, but I tell you that not one of those invited shall taste a morsel of my dinner" (vv. 21, 23-24).[22]

More threatening still for Israel, but a source of even greater joy for the pagans, is the parable of the murderous vine-growers. The owner of the vineyard will destroy the workers who refuse to make it bear fruit for him and even go so far as to murder his son. Then he will "lease his vineyard out to others who will see to it that he has grapes at vintage time" (Matthew 21:41; cf. Mark 12:9 and Luke 20:16). In the catechetically oriented Gospel of Matthew Jesus directly addresses the Jews and tells them unambiguously: "For this reason, I tell you, the kingdom of God will be taken away from you and given to a nation that will yield a rich harvest" (21:43).[23]

We must correctly understand these various statements. All of them have polemical contexts; in such contexts, statements are not always accompanied by all necessary qualifications. Jesus did not at all mean that the loss of some Jews would necessarily lead to the salvation of all pagans; his point was rather that the fidelity of pagans to the Gospel and their participation in the messianic salvation should stir the Jews, waken them from their indifference, and make them also believe in the Good News of salvation.[24]

The real Gospel rule is not that the tax-collectors and prostitutes should precede the Jews (Matthew 21:31), but that both will enter if they are converted to the Gospel. So, too, the believers who have come from paganism do not replace the believers who have come from Israel; rather, by reason of their faith in the Gospel, both share an inheritance that properly belongs to Israel. It is not a matter, then, of replacing "the children of the kingdom" with the nations (who could replace the apostles or the Lord's Mother?), but of the pagans sharing in the call given to Israel. Matthew's words are worth noting in this respect: "Many will come from the east and the west and will find a place at the banquet in the kingdom of God *with* Abraham, Isaac, and Jacob" (8:11).[25]

The messianic banquet Jesus inaugurates is the Jewish feast at which Abraham, Isaac, and Jacob sit, but all men may feel perfectly at home there because it is first and foremost the banquet set by God himself, and he invites the nations to it as he has already invited

Israel. Or, to use an image of St. Paul (Rom. 11:16-24): Israel is the natural olive tree with its holy roots in the ancient promises; God prunes it, cutting off the branches that have withered (the Jews who reject the Gospel); he also grafts on to it branches of a wild olive tree (the nations that now believe) but does not uproot these.

We cannot simply say, therefore, that Jesus gathers the nations because his people have refused to answer his call. For there is always "a remnant chosen by the grace of God" (Rom. 11:5), a true Israel that can welcome the nations at the threshold of the New Testament. We must, then, look deeper for the link which, in God's plan, connects the gathering of Israel and the gathering of the nations; we must see how God calls the nations, not because he is vexed with the Jews, but because he freely saves both.

2. The nations join Israel

We are saying here that the messianic gathering of Israel leads to the universal gathering of the nations. There are not, however, two successive gatherings, as though, after calling Israel, Jesus then called the nations. There are indeed two acts, but they are related as cause and effect. Jesus devoted the whole of his messianic activity to evangelizing Israel so that the nations, seeing the marvels he wrought, might join Israel and form with it a single people.[26]

a) "My mission is only to the lost sheep of the house of Israel"

There are some negative facts of which we must take account. The first is this: Though he did proclaim a universal Church that would be open to all peoples, Jesus never preached the Good News to the nations. Why was this?

The refusal of Jesus to preach salvation to the nations is not a simple fact but a principle that guided the whole of his ministry: "My mission is only to the lost sheep of the house of Israel" (Matthew 15:24).[27] This saying is part of the material proper to Matthew. The passive cast of the sentence (literally: "I have been sent . . . ") avoids using the sacred name of God, but "I have been sent" means in fact "God has sent me." The messianic ministry of Jesus and, in particular, his mission exclusively to the people of the promise follow the Father's plan of salvation. In preserving this saying, which could not but cause intense surprise in the Church after the resurrection, when the Church was deeply involved in missionary expansion, Matthew not only guaranteed its authenticity as a saying of the Savior; he also raised the problem of the mission to the Gentiles.

Jesus showed himself faithful to the limits set him by the Father, and nothing in the Gospels suggests that he ever went to evangelize the pagans. Having become "the servant of the Jews because of God's faithfulness in fulfilling the promises to the patriarchs" (Rom. 15:8), Jesus exercised his messianic ministry solely among the Jewish population and, almost always, on Jewish territory.[28] When he entered the territory of Tyre and Sidon (Matthew 15:21; Mark 7:24, 31) and went as far as Paneas or Caesarea Philippi (Matthew 16:13; Mark 8:27), he did not do so in order to proclaim the Good News to the non-Jewish population. He did so in order to escape from the crowds in Galilee, who, as Mark tells (3:20), used to press upon him so that he could not even get time to eat.

While in these foreign places, Jesus met pagans — but how could he avoid doing so? He worked miracles there, such as the cure of the Canaanite woman's daughter, but in this case an unconquerable faith practically forced him to work the miracle. Such miracles were indeed scraps fallen from the royal table of the children of the house. The messianic bread was broken first in the "holy land." In fact, apart from the pilgrimages to Jerusalem, Galilee was the center from which he moved out to the apostolate; more accurately, the center was the northern shore of the Sea of Galilee. Capernaum was *his* city. We find it startling to find Matthew saying: "He . . . came back to his own town" (9:1), referring to Capernaum.[29] The Messiah's mission was to gather all of mankind into a single people; yet here he is, tying his ministry to an insignificant Jewish town and staying there!

Even in Galilee, Jesus turned so exclusively to his own people that he avoided the Greek cities, such as Scythopolis, Gabai, Sepphoris, and Tiberias. Yet Sepphoris was less than four miles from Nazareth and less than six from Cana, while Tiberias lay on the Sea of Galilee. Even if Jesus passed through these places, the evangelists did not think the fact important enough to warrant a mention.[30]

b) "Do not visit pagan territory"

During the time of his own messianic ministry, Jesus forbade his disciples to go on any mission outside Israel: "Do not visit pagan territory and do not enter a Samaritan town. Go instead after the lost sheep of the house of Israel" (Matthew 10:5-6).

This prohibition is directly contrary to the order the Lord will give after his resurrection: "Go, therefore, and make disciples of all the nations" (Matthew 28:19). Like the statement in Matthew 15:24, the one in 10:5-6 is very old[31] and, once again, could not but surprise the early Christian community and especially the converts from paganism. It is notable, on the other hand, that the prohibition is part of the missionary discourse (Matthew 10), in which Matthew gathers up the various missionary directives Jesus gave his disciples in connection with their mission in Galilee.[32]

Now, behind the mission in Galilee looms the universal mission, and, in fact, the recommendations given are valid for the missionaries of every age. Except for the saying in Matthew 10:5-6! Here Jesus sets limits to his disciples' activity. In the south, they are not to go over into Samaria; in the east, the Decapolis and Gaulanitis are forbidden territory; in the west, Phoenicia, pagan territory, is similarly out of bounds. Jesus is clearly placing upon the mission of his disciples the same limitations the Father had placed upon his. "Go instead after the lost sheep of the house of Israel" echoes Jesus' statement about himself: "My mission is only to the lost sheep of the house of Israel." The mission of the disciples is like that of the Master; during his public life, the same territorial limits applied to both.[33]

c) Jesus condemns Jewish proselytism

The attitude of Jesus in limiting his messianic preaching to Galilee and Judea is all the more surprising since Jews had begun an intense missionary activity beyond the Palestinian ghetto and throughout the Mediterranean basin. The Jews of the Diaspora were ardent supporters of this effort. The Greek Bible enabled them to spread God's word among the pagans, while the apocryphal writings furnished them with excellent propaganda material. According to the *Testament of Levi*, missionaries are like a heavenly radiance spreading across the world: "The heaven is purer than the earth, and ye, the lights of Israel, are as sun and moon. . . . The light of the law . . . was given to lighten every man."[34] In the *Book of Enoch*, God orders the just to gather all the people of the world and reveal wisdom to them, "for ye are their guides."[35] Paul sums up the missionary pride of Israel when he says: "You feel certain that you can guide the blind and enlighten those in darkness, that you can discipline the foolish and teach the simple" (Rom. 2:19-20).

The rabbis had words of affection for proselytes who accepted the yoke of the Jewish law. To abandon idols is to come forth from the tomb,[36] it is to enter upon a new life and become like little children,[37] to become part of a community whose members love one another as brothers. Rabbi Jose explained: "If a proselyte dwells among you, love him as you love yourself. For, as it is said of Israel, 'You shall love your neighbor as yourself,' so it is said of the proselyte, 'You shall love him as yourself,' for all of you were proselytes in the land of Israel. Understand the attitude of the proselyte, for you yourselves were proselytes in the land of Egypt."[38] Even in their daily prayer, the *Shemoneh Esreh*, the Jews were mindful of the proselytes and asked God to heap his mercies upon them.[39]

The missionary propaganda was a resounding success. "Godfearers"[40] were recruited from all over the Mediterranean world — at Jerusalem and Rome, in Greece and Egypt. Though unwilling (or unable) to accept certain practices that smacked too much of Jewry, these people came in crowds to experience the joy of a monotheistic faith and to lead worthy moral lives. On his missionary journeys Paul met them at Caesarea, Antioch in Pisidia, Philippi, Thessalonica, Athens, and Corinth.[41] Many of them were women; one of the best known of these is Lydia, a dealer in purple goods from the town of Thyatira, of whom Luke says, in a delightful turn of phrase, that "the Lord opened her heart to accept what Paul was saying" (Acts 16:11). There must have been many Lydias among the proselytes. In fact, if we may believe Josephus, almost all the women of Damascus had converted.[42]

The proselytes were those who had accepted the whole of Jewish law, including circumcision. In describing the first Pentecost, Luke tells us how these people, who had come from all parts of the Mediterranean world, joined in a great Christian Babel as each one in his own language celebrated the wonders God had wrought (Acts 2:9-11).

Jesus knew of Jewish proselytizing and spoke of it. But the only statement the Gospels have preserved for us is one of condemnation. It is one of the harshest things the Lord ever said: "Woe to you scribes and Pharisees, you frauds! You travel over sea and land to make a single convert, but once he is converted you make a devil of him twice as wicked as yourselves" (Matthew 23:15).[43]

The accusation could not be more serious. Instead of extending God's rule, Pharisaic proselytizing increased the devil's hold on men; those converted by the Pharisees became servants of Satan.

In interpreting this ancient saying, we must undoubtedly allow a good deal for Matthew's editorializing[44] and the polemics behind it. At the time when Matthew was composing his Gospel, the Christian

mission was meeting vicious opposition from the Pharisaic pro-
selytizers; the Acts of the Apostles make it clear that the confrontation was not simply a matter of competition in "mission territory"
but at times even involved murder. The evangelist might well regard it as fair tactics to represent the Pharisees as "sons of hell,"
since the condemnation of the proselytes could not but hit equally
hard those who had converted them.

Doubtless, too, Christians could suppose that Pharisaic proselytism was at times infected with a shameful nationalism, so that it
was concerned less with the extension of God's kingdom than with
the increase of Pharisaic power.[45] By identifying revealed religion
with the Jewish nation, and the Jewish nation with the sect of the
Pharisees, proselytism here linked the conversion of hearts with
racist requirements. But, even admitting the truth of all this, it is
nonetheless a fact that Jesus' view of the Pharisees' mission was a
negative one.

All in all, we find in the New Testament sufficient data to justify
the following negative conclusions: Jesus never preached the Good
News to the pagans; during the time of his own messianic ministry
he forbade his disciples to take their mission outside Jewish territory; he condemned Pharisaic proselytizing. What are we to think of
all this?

d) "The nations shall stream to Jerusalem"

The attitude of Jesus becomes luminously clear and completely
intelligible if we see it in relation to the plan of salvation which the
Scriptures reveal.

When we think of "mission" today, we almost inevitably think of
Jewish missionaries leaving Palestine and bringing the Yahwist faith
to distant nations. But when the Old Testament speaks of "mission"
and the conversion of the pagans, it postulates an opposite movement entirely. Jewish missionaries do not leave Jerusalem and go off
to the nations; instead, the nations stream to Jerusalem. In other
words, the conversion of the nations and their sharing in the promises do not result from a centrifugal movement, but themselves
constitute a centripetal movement.

This movement of the peoples has been wonderfully described in
an old hymn that is recorded both by Isaiah (2:2-4) and Micah
(4:1-4) and has been dubbed "the high song of Zion."[46] The hymn
foretells a vast celebration, involving all the peoples of the world,
who come in triumphal procession to Jerusalem; there they shall

find peace with Yahweh, for his word, which has become the law for all peoples, makes war unnecessary:

> In days to come
> The mountain of the Lord's house
>   shall be established as the highest mountain
>   and raised above the hills.
>
> All nations shall stream toward it;
>   many peoples shall come and say:
> "Come, let us climb the Lord's mountain,
>   to the house of the God of Jacob,
>
> That he may instruct us in his ways,
>   and we may walk in his paths."
> From Zion shall go forth instruction,
>   and the word of the Lord from Jerusalem.
>
> He shall judge between the nations,
>   and impose terms on many peoples.
> They shall beat their swords into plowshares
>   and their spears into pruning hooks;
>
> One nation shall not raise the sword against another,
>   nor shall they train for war again.
> O house of Jacob, come,
>   let us walk in the light of the Lord![47]

The theme of the gathering of the nations is especially prominent in the last part of the Book of Isaiah.[48] The time of which the prophet writes is the period of the lengthy return and the interminable restoration. Israel has been scattered over the somber plains of Babylon and is now trying to re-establish its own unity. Its journey to the Promised Land sets other peoples in motion, and the pagans join the Jewish caravans. Thus, in the hymn in Is. 60:1-2, the return to Jerusalem, haloed as it is in the light of Yahweh, rouses the people who had been sitting in darkness and causes them to set out on their own journey to the Lord. Jews and Gentiles alike will share in the work of restoring Jerusalem; indeed it is the "sons of the foreigner" who will rebuild the walls of the holy city (v. 10). There is no need to bring God's word to the nations, for the nations will come seeking it. In Is. 56:6-8 and 66:18-20, Yahweh himself plays the part of the "missionary": "I shall come to gather nations of every language" (66:18).

The most expressive description of this centripetal movement is to be found in Zechariah:

> The inhabitants of one city shall approach those of another, and say, "Come! let us go to implore the favor of the Lord"; and, "I too will go

to seek the Lord." Many peoples and strong nations shall come to seek the Lord of hosts in Jerusalem and to implore the favor of the Lord. Thus says the Lord of hosts: In those days ten men of every nationality, speaking different tongues, shall take hold, yes, shall take hold of every Jew by the edge of his garment and say, "Let us go with you, for we have heard that God is with you" (8:21-23).

Statements like these give us the core of what Israel was thinking when it spoke of "mission." It had nothing to do with going out and pressing men into service, as the Pharisees did. On the contrary, it was the pagans who would beg for admission to the chosen people. Even today the words of Zechariah should be written on the heart of every missionary.

e) "We have heard that God is with you"

What causes this centripetal movement? Why should the world hasten to the God of the Jews? What determines the nations to join Israel is the wonders God works in Israel's behalf. He intervenes with resplendent power in their cause, protects them, and bestows his salvation on them. The latest of these interventions — the liberation from captivity, and the restoration — was especially striking. Because they see these great deeds of the Lord, the pagans will lay hold of the Jew's robe and beg him: "Let us go with you, for we have heard that God is with you."

Psalm 117 is extremely brief, but its ecumenical claims are vast. It is almost ingenuous in stating our theme, while simplifying it to the utmost degree:

> Praise the Lord, all you nations;
>   glorify him, all you peoples!
> For steadfast is his kindness toward us,
>   and the fidelity of the Lord endures forever.

Here the Psalmist first bids all men praise God. But why should they all praise the God of the Jews? Because "steadfast is his kindness." But to whom? "To us," that is, the chosen people. The nations, says R. Martin-Achard, "witness the kindnesses of God to his people; they do not benefit directly from them. They ought to rejoice in the glorification of Israel. Yahweh's plan is primarily concerned with the Israelites; the astonished pagans contemplate the privileges of the latter. . . . The whole world has a stake in the destiny of Israel."[49]

Consequently, when the messianic age begins and Jesus devotes himself to the gathering of Israel, he is working directly for the gathering into a single family of all the peoples of the world. Today still — for the messianic age embraces our day too — the gathering of the Church around the word is the first missionary duty.

¹ In this text, as in John 10:15-16, the unification of God's people is a grace made available by the death of the Lord. Cf. W. Grundmann, *Zeugnis und Gestalt des Johannes-Evangeliums* (Stuttgart, 1960), p. 61, and C.H. Dodd, *Historical Tradition in the Fourth Gospel* (Cambridge, 1963), p. 415, note 1.

² The theme of gathering is especially prominent in the Book of Ezekiel; cf. 11:17; 20:34, 41; 28:25; 34:12-13 (on which John 11:52 seems to depend, according to C.H. Dodd, *The Interpretation of the Fourth Gospel* [Cambridge, 1953], p. 368, note 1); 37:21; 39:27-28. Cf. also Jer. 29:14 and 32:37.

³ 1 Chron. 16:35 = Ps. 106:47. Cf. also the prayer in Sir. 36:13, and the prayer in *Psalms of Solomon* 8:34: "Gather together the dispersed of Israel, with mercy and goodness," and 17:28 (in R.H. Charles [ed.], *The Apocrypha and Pseudepigrapha of the Old Testament in English* 2:641 and 649 respectively).

⁴ Cf. Matthew 15:21-28. Mark will repeat the saying of Matthew 15:26: "It is not right to take the food of the children and throw it to the dogs," but because he has in mind the missionary activity of the Church after the resurrection, he introduces it with the words, "Let the sons of the household satisfy themselves at table *first*" (7:27).

⁵ Lev. 21:18-20 excludes from the priesthood the blind, the lame, the hunchback, anyone suffering from eczema, the rachitic, and the eunuch.

⁶ Cf. Th. Maertens, *L'assemblée chrétienne: De la théologie biblique à la pastorale du XXᵉ siècle* (Bruges, 1964), chapter 2: "L'oeuvre de rassemblement du Christ" (pp. 39–59). The point of the parable is not the lowly status of those invited, but the replacement of those invited first (=Israel) by those invited in their stead (=the pagans); cf. J. Jeremias, *The Parables of Jesus*, translated by S.H. Hooke (rev. ed.; New York, 1963), p. 64. Cf. L. Deiss, *Synopse* 1:129–30.

⁷ To avoid any misunderstanding, Luke explicates the meaning of the saying: "I have not come to invite the self-righteous *to a change of heart*, but sinners" (5:32).

⁸ In addition to its usual meaning, the term "sinner" may refer to someone whom the official theology of the time considered a "sinner" (even though he may not have been a sinner in God's sight). The Mishnah contains several lists of occupations considered "sinful" and regarded with disfavor on the grounds that they exposed their practitioners to failures in observance of the Law and the Pharisaic tradition. Among such occupations were those of tax-collector, shepherd, camel-drover, fuller, and boatman. Cf. J. Jeremias, *Jerusalem in the Time of Jesus: An Investigation into Economic and Social Conditions during the New Testament Period*, translated by F.H. and C.H. Cave (Philadelphia, 1969), pp. 87–144.

⁹ Cf. 2 Cor. 8:9: "He [the Lord Jesus] made himself poor though he was rich, so that you might become rich by his poverty."

¹⁰ Luke 1:48: "He has looked upon his servant in her lowliness." Cf. L. Deiss, *Mary, Daughter of Sion* (Collegeville, Minn., 1972), pp. 112–26: "The Song of the Poor of Yahweh."

¹¹ Cf. Luke 10:38-41; John 11:5.

¹² Cf. John 3:1-21 (see. v. 1); 7:50; 19:39.

¹³ Cf. Mark 15:43.

¹⁴ The redaction of Mark 12:28-34, in which the scribe plays a positive role, is clearly older than that of Matthew 22:34-40 and Luke 10:25-28, where the scribe is shown in an unfavorable light. Matthew 22:34 and Luke 10:25 say the scribe ques-

tioned Jesus "in an attempt to trip him up." We discern here a reaction of the early community: In the beginning the community was the object of hostility from "the Jews" and was not anxious to allow the Jewish lawyer in the Gospel the laudable role which the original Markan tradition had given him. Cf. S. Legasse, "Scribes et disciples de Jésus," *Revue biblique* 68 (1961), pp. 321–45; 481–506.

[15] The text applies to Jesus the prophecy concerning the "Servant of Yahweh" in Is. 42:6 and 49:6. Cf. also Matthew 12:18-21, which likewise cites the prophecy concerning the Servant in Is. 42:1-4: "In his name, the Gentiles will find hope."

[16] Cf. also 1 Tim. 2:4-5.

[17] Cf. Gal. 3:26: "Each of you is a son of God because of your faith in Christ Jesus."

[18] Cf. 1 Cor. 8:6; Eph. 3:6.

[19] Matthew 24:14; cf. Mark 14:9. On *oikoumenē*, cf. O. Michel, *TDNT* 5:157–59.

[20] "While they [Christians] dwell in both Greek and non-Greek cities, as each one's lot was cast, and conform to the customs of the country in dress, food, and mode of life in general, the whole tenor of their way of living stamps it as worthy of admiration and admittedly extraordinary. They reside in their respective countries, but only as aliens. They take part in everything as citizens and put up with everything as foreigners. Every foreign land is their home, and every home a foreign land. . . . In a word: what the soul is in the body, that the Christians are in the world. The soul is spread through all the members of the body, and the Christians throughout the cities of the world. The soul dwells in the body, but is not part and parcel of the body; so Christians dwell in the world, but are not part and parcel of the world" (*Epistle to Diognetus* 5:4–5; 6:1–3, translated by James A. Kleist, in *Ancient Christian Writers* 6 [Westminster, Md., 1948], pp. 169–70). Cf. H.-I. Marrou, *A Diognète* (Sources chrétiennes 33; Paris, 1965), pp. 63–65; L. Deiss, *Printemps de la théologie* 1: *Apologistes grecs du II*^e *siècle; Irénée de Lyon* (Paris, 1965), pp. 11–12.

[21] The saying about the first and the last is a "floating" saying whose meaning varies according to context. It is applied first to the relation of Jews and pagans (Luke 13:30; Matthew 20:16), then to the faithful within the Christian community (Matthew 19:30; Mark 10:31). On the sayings with which the parables end, cf. J. Jeremias, *The Parables of Jesus*, pp. 110–13. — On Israel and the Church, cf. G. Baum, *The Jews and the Gospel: A Re-examination of the New Testament* (Westminster, Md., 1961); R. Hummel, *Die Auseinandersetzung zwischen Kirche und Judentum im Matthäusevangelium* (Munich, 1963); P. Benoit, "La valeur spécifique d'Israël dans l'histoire du salut" and "L'Eglise et Israël," in *Exégèse et théologie* 3 (Paris, 1968), pp. 400–441.

[22] The parallel parable in Matthew 22:1-14, while asserting the rejection of Israel, has a catechetical purpose and emphasizes the need of a nuptial garment for the new guests (22:11-14).

[23] This sentence is missing in the parallel passages in Matthew and Luke; its presence is probably due to Matthew's editing and to his catechetical aims.

[24] In Rom. 11:11-14, Paul says that through Israel's "stumbling," "salvation has come to the Gentiles." This is a simplistic statement; its extremism is explainable by the very passionate tone of the whole section on the destiny of Israel. In fact, Paul also says that he exercises his ministry among the Gentiles "trying to rouse my fellow Jews to envy and save some of them" (v. 14). On Romans 11, cf. R. Baulès, *L'Evangile, puissance de Dieu: Commentaire de l'épître aux Romains* (Lectio divina 53; Paris, 1971), pp. 243–54.

[25] J. Schmid, *Das Evangelium nach Matthäus* (Regensburg, 1956), explains: "The meaning of the statement is not that the pagans will be accepted in place of Israel, as though the salvation of the pagans depended on the loss of Israel. The words are rather a threat to the Jews" (p. 165).

[26] On the missionary idea in the Old Testament, cf. H.H. Rowley, *The Missionary Message of the Old Testament* (2nd ed.; London, 1955); A. Gelin, *The Mission of Israel*, pp. 78–89; E. Jacob, *Theology of the Old Testament*, pp. 217–23; G.F. Moore,

op. cit., 1:323-53; ("Conversion of the Gentiles"); R. Martin-Achard, *A Light to the Nations: A Study of the Old Testament Concept of Israel's Mission to the World*, translated by J.P. Smith (Edinburgh, 1962); J. Jeremias, *Jesus' Promise to the Nations*, translated by S.H. Hooke (Studies in Biblical Theology 24; Naperville, Ill., 1953).

[27] On this saying, and on Matthew 10:5, cf. D. Bosch, *Die Heidenmission in der Zukunftsschau Jesu* (Abhandlungen zur Theologie des Alten und Neuen Testaments 36; Zürich, 1959), pp. 84–86.

[28] Cf. A. Alt, "Die Stätten des Wirkens Jesu in Galiläa territorialgeschichtlich betrachtet," *Beiträge zur biblischen Landes- und Altertumskunde* 68 (1949), pp. 51–72, reprinted in *Kleine Schriften* 1:436–55.

[29] Theoretically, a man had to have lived in a city or town for twelve months in order to become its "son"; cf. Strack-Billerbeck, 1:493–94. We need not conclude, however, that a year passed between the events of Matthew 4:13 and those of 9:1; it was simply that Jesus had lived long enough in Capernaum for people to speak of it as "his" town.

[30] A. Alt, *art. cit.*, writes: "The evangelists do not speak of Jesus being at Magdala, any more than they do of his visiting Sepphoris or Tiberias. From their silence we may conclude at least that these localities were never the centers of his public activity in Galilee" (*Kleine Schriften*, p. 450).

[31] On the Aramaisms in this passage, cf. J. Jeremias, *Jesus' Promise to the Nations*, p. 19, notes 3 and 5.

[32] On the missionary discourse, cf. L. Deiss, *Synopse* 1:82–85; L. Cerfaux, "La mission de Galilée dans la tradition synoptique," *Ephemerides theologicae lovanienses* 27 (1951), pp. 369–89, reprinted in *Recueil Lucien Cerfaux* 1 (Gembloux, 1954), pp. 425–69.

[33] D. Bosch, *op. cit.*, writes: "It is evident from Matthew 10:5-6 and 15:24 that Jesus deliberately limited his own activity, and that of his disciples, to Israel, the people of the old covenant" (p. 86).

[34] *Testament of Levi*, XIV, 3–4, in R.H. Charles, *op. cit.*, 2:312.

[35] *Book of Enoch*, CV, 1, in Charles, *op. cit.*, 2:431.

[36] *Eduyoth* 5:2 (Danby, *op. cit.*, p. 431).

[37] Cf. J. Bonsirven, *Textes rabbiniques des deux premiers siècles* (Rome, 1955), no. 1145, p. 294.

[38] Bonsirven, *op. cit.*, no. 200, p. 44.

[39] *Shemoneh Esreh* 13: "Towards true proselytes . . . may thy tender mercies be stirred, O Lord our God" (*The Authorized Daily Prayer Book*, edited by Joseph H. Hertz [rev. ed.; New York, 1963], p. 145). On the *Shemoneh Esreh* (i.e., "Eighteen," scil. Blessings), cf. M.-J. Lagrange, *Le judaïsme avant Jésus-Christ* (Paris, 1931), pp. 466–70, where the text according to the Palestinian recension is given. Cf. also Strack-Billerbeck, *op. cit.*, 4:208–9, where the older Babylonian recension is also given; Elbogen, *op. cit.*, pp. 27–60.

[40] On the proselytes (*prosēlytos* literally means "he who has come to join") and the God-fearers (*sebomenoi* or *phoboumenoi ton Theon*), cf. K.G. Kuhn, "prosēlytos," *TDNT* 6:727–44. Cf. also Strack-Billerbeck, *op. cit.*, 2:715–45; G.F. Moore, *op. cit.*, 1:326–28. In submitting to circumcision, the proselyte became fully a Jew, whereas the God-fearer usually remained in a sort of a half-way position, which might vary from profound adherence to the Jewish law (except for circumcision) to a mere sympathy.

[41] Cf. Acts 10:2, 22; 13:16, 50; 16:14; 17:4, 17; 18:7.

[42] Flavius Josephus, *De Bello Judaico*, II, 160.

[43] As J. Jeremias, *Jesus' Promise to the Nations*, observes, the saying is from an early Aramaic tradition, for it shows a number of Semitisms which confirm its authenticity: for example, the paratactic construction (literally: "Woe to you . . . for you

travel . . . and you make . . ."; the Pharisees are blamed, of course, not for travel-ing the world but for making others wicked); the phrase "sea and land," which is from the Bible; the expression "sons of hell" (= "wicked"), which is typically Semitic (pp. 17–18, and note 4 on p. 17).

[44] Matthew 23:13-36 evidently bears the mark of the author of the First Gospel. The seven curses against the Pharisees are meant to match the seven blessings on the poor in the Sermon on the Mount (Matthew 5:3-10). Matthew has reshaped the sequence, as is clear from a comparison with the parallel passage in Luke 11:39-53. He has used special sources of his own (cf. 23:15-22, 31-33). He has given a characteristically Matthean turn to some sentences: thus the triple "The man who swears by . . ." in 23:20-22 is from his pen (cf. Deiss, *Synopse* 1:28); and the apostrophe "scribes and Pharisees, you frauds!" is part of his vocabulary.

[45] J. Schmid, *op. cit.*, writes: "We must take into account that the motive [for Pharisaic proselytizing] was not strictly missionary; the aim was not to bring men to salvation, but to increase the personal influence of the Pharisees and the esteem in which Israel was held by the world" (p. 324).

[46] C. Schedl, *History of the Old Testament* 4:271.

[47] The oracle may be part of the Book of Emmanuel (cf. Is. 11:10-12), but its authenticity is sharply contested (cf. D. Bosch, *op. cit.*, p. 23). The universalism it shows seems to point rather to postexilic circles. — In Micah, as in Isaiah, the hymn ends with a liturgical exhortation; some scholars have therefore thought of it as part of a collection of readings for cultic gatherings (Eissfeldt, *op. cit.*, p. 318). With G. Buchanan Gray, *The Book of Isaiah* (International Critical Commentary; Edinburgh, 1912), pp. 44–48, we have divided the hymn into five strophes.

[48] We are referring to Trito-Isaiah (Is. 56–66); the redaction of these chapters (except for 63:7–64:11, which seems to date from the Exile) occupied the century it took for the restoration to be accomplished.

[49] *Op. cit.*, p. 52.

Chapter 10

GOD GIVES THE GOSPEL
TO HIS PEOPLE

INTRODUCTION

"God sent his word . . . brought
by Jesus Christ" (Acts 10:36 JB)

The Law which God gives to his people in the messianic age is the
Gospel. This simple statement is as rich in significance as Jesus
Christ himself. When we say "Gospel," we think indeed, first and
foremost, of the little book that has changed the world because it
tells us of the life and teaching of Jesus Christ as preserved by the
four evangelists. But "Gospel" means far more than what can be
contained in a book.[1] To grasp the full, rich meaning of the word, we
have to go back to a period in history when the book of the Gospels
had not yet been written, but the whole of the Gospel did already
exist, because Christ had manifested himself. The proclamation, or
kerygma, of the early Church sums up this Gospel that existed
before the written Gospels:

> This is the message he [God] has sent to the sons of Israel, the good
> news proclaimed through Jesus Christ who is Lord of all. I take it you
> know what has been reported all over Judea about Jesus of Nazareth,
> beginning in Galilee with the baptism John preached; of the way God
> anointed him with the Holy Spirit and power. He went about doing
> good works and healing all who were in the grip of the devil, and God
> was with him. . . . They killed him, finally, hanging him on a tree,
> only to have God raise him up on the third day (Acts 10:36-40).

Thus, in sending Jesus Christ, God sent his own word. Jesus is
the Gospel in his own person: a Gospel not written on paper but

174

made real in his birth at Bethlehem, his life, miracles, death, and resurrection. "If we were to sum up the content of the Gospel in a single word, it would be Jesus the Christ." [2]

The Letter to the Hebrews pinpoints the uniqueness of this revelation of the Father by the Son: "In times past, God spoke in fragmentary and varied ways to our fathers through the prophets; in this, the final age, he has spoken to us through his Son, whom he has made heir of all things and through whom he first created the universe" (Heb. 1:1-2). [3]

The word which God addressed to the fathers "through the prophets" was fragmentary and varied. It thus revealed both the "manifold wisdom" of God (Eph. 3:10) and the manifold weakness of men. God spoke "untiringly" (Jer. 7:13) because men were tireless in evading him: "When I called, no one answered; when I spoke, no one listened" (Is. 66:4). And when men did listen, God then respected the inevitable delays that marked their advance. He wanted the human ear to become attuned and to get used to his voice. He revealed himself in a fragmentary way because he wanted to win men over, to take them by the hand and lead them step by step to full knowledge of himself.

But the coming of the messianic age brought mankind's childhood to an end, and God now recapitulated all he had ever said in the single word which is his Son. In giving us his Son, he gave us all else besides (Rom. 8:32); and when this Son died once for all men (1 Peter 3:18; Heb. 9:26, 28), his sacrifice drew to itself all the sacrifices that had marked the history of Israel and would in the future mark the history of the Church. So too, the new word spoken by Jesus contained in itself all the wealth that had been conveyed in God's past words. It was the perfect form of all those divine convocations of the past: Sinai, Shechem, Josiah, Ezra, and the synagogal worship.

This decisive word comes "in this, the final age" (Heb. 1:2). The people of the Old Testament had known that these "last days" would dawn at the limits of history. In the person of Jesus, these last days emerge from the mist of time; the messianic sun rises over the world, and the end of time begins. The New Testament hope continually finds expression in such statements as: "upon [us] the end of the ages has come" (1 Cor. 10:11); "This makes us certain that it is the final hour" (1 John 2:18); "The consummation of all is close at hand" (1 Peter 4:7).

The "last days" include, of course, the "final day." This does not, however, imply that the final day is close in time. The precise moment of the final day is hidden in the mysterious depths of the Father's mind: "No one knows, neither the angels in heaven nor even the Son" (Mark 13:32; Matthew 24:36). The passage of two thousand years has taught us that the closeness of the last day is spiritual and not necessarily chronological. The real point is that with the coming of Christ we have entered upon the final period of mankind's history, which means the period in which God has nothing to say to us that he has not already said in his Son. Public revelation is closed,[4] simply because in Jesus it is complete.

Having received the treasure of the Gospel, mankind must now confront the returning Christ. The years may continue to pile up on the threshing-floor of time and be stored away in the granaries of eternity. The calendar of the world may continue to lose its months and years before the winds of history, as a rose sheds its petals at summer's end. Our task meanwhile is to explore the riches of revelation. But revelation itself will not grow richer, for the wealth it already contains is that of the Father himself. Its name is the Father's Son, Jesus Christ.

1. The new Law

The question we must now ask is: What is the new Law brought by Jesus Christ? Or, to make the question more pointed: Has the Gospel not replaced the Law? What, then, in the light of Jesus' coming, is the status of what we call today the "Old Testament"?

It takes only a glance to show us that its status is ambiguous. All the texts of the Old Testament were once highly topical and relevant, not only at the time in Israel's history when they were written, but also during the centuries when the synagogue was continuously actualizing these texts in its services. But the coming of Christ upset everything. Where the fire of the Gospel burns, the ancient texts seem to lose all relevance. When God's radiant light rises over the world, do we still need the little lamps of the prophets? When God speaks to us directly through his Son, do we need still to repeat the dialogues he once carried on with the prophets? When the community of the promise meets her messianic bridegroom (Mark 2:19) and puts on her wedding dress, does she any longer have use for the schoolbooks she carried to the synagogue?

In short, some texts of the Old Testament seem to have no value now for the faithful of the new covenant. Such, for example, are the minute prescriptions of Leviticus, which had their point for the sacristans of the time, or the list of David's officers, which the retired military men of the day might have found pleasant reading. We could give any number of similar examples. Passages which were sweet on Israelite tongues are now but witnesses to a history that is past and, for us, completely outdated.

But even as we make these observations, we feel uneasy. They are too one-sided and fail to do justice to God's word. For alongside the now irrelevant parts of the Old Testament stand revelations so perfect that the New Testament will have nothing to add to them. They are as complete as human words about God can be; they lead us to heights that tower over the whole of revelation and can afflict the human mind with vertigo. If we want to say that God is love, can we do better than to repeat Exod. 34:6-7, which sounds like a refrain throughout the history of Israel: "The Lord, the Lord, a merciful and gracious God, slow to anger and rich in kindness and fidelity"? Do we not have definitive revelations of God's love in Hos. 2:21-22 or Is. 49:14-16 or some verses of Psalm 145 (vv. 8-9)? When the Lord was asked what the first commandment was, he simply repeated the ancient *Shema, Israel* from Deuteronomy: "Hear, O Israel! The Lord is our God, the Lord alone! Therefore, you shall love the Lord, your God, with all your heart, and with all your soul, and with all your strength" (6:4-5; cf. Mark 12:29-30). Even the new covenant was discovered by the Old Testament (Jer. 31:31-34).

2. The mystery of Christ Jesus

The difficulty of deciding on the status of the Old Testament is brought home to us by the actions of Jesus himself, for sometimes he submits to the Law, sometimes he rejects its authority. Here are some examples.

He is "born under the law" (Gal. 4:4), but later says that "the law and the prophets were in force until John" (Luke 16:16).

He accepts baptism in order to "fulfill all of God's demands" (Matthew 3:15), but establishes a new order in which John's baptism is to be replaced, once for all, by Christian baptism.

He requires the leper he has cured to go to the priest and "offer for your cure what Moses prescribed" (Mark 1:44), but he himself breaks many of the laws of legal purity by associating with tax-collectors and sinners (Mark 2:16).

Like the Pharisees (Matthew 23:5), he has tassels on his cloak (Mark 6:56; Matthew 9:20) as prescribed in Num. 15:38–41; but he openly neglects the ritual ablutions before meals (Luke 11:38; cf. Mark 7:2-4).[5]

He attends the synagogue on the sabbath (Mark 1:21), does the reading, and preaches the homily (Luke 4:16-21); but he also scandalizes people there by violating the law of sabbath rest with a "work" of healing (Luke 13:10-17).

He goes to the Temple (Mark 12:41) and likes to teach there (Luke 21:37), but he also proclaims the coming of the messianic age, when true worshipers of the Father will serve him in a spiritual temple and will worship in Spirit and truth (John 4:21-24).

He celebrates the Passover according to the prescribed ritual and sings the Psalms of the Hallel at it (Mark 14:26), but at that very meal he institutes the Eucharist, which will permanently replace the old paschal meal.

To sum up all the examples in a generalization: He comes, as he himself says, "not to abolish [the law and the prophets], but to fulfill them . . . not the smallest letter of the law, not the smallest part of a letter, shall be done away with" (Matthew 5:17-18). At the same time, however, he abrogates important provisions of the Law (Matthew 5:31-32).

Undoubtedly we must note the relative character of these texts and not make the contradictions more absolute than they are. The texts often come from polemical contexts and are valid within certain situations. Thus, it may have seemed good tactics, in dealing with Christians converted from Judaism, to stress the links between the Messiah and the old prophecies, and to show him as standing on the road traveled by the Mosaic Law itself. Conversely, in dealing with converts from paganism, who had little concern with the fulfillment of the Jewish prophecies, it may have seemed better to emphasize the newness of the Gospel. These tactics would be quite normal.

We may add, too, that Jesus came at the moment of transition between the two Testaments[6] and stood "at the center of time."[7] This explains how in some circumstances, when he favors the law of the old covenant, he can be said to fulfill it, while in other circumstances, when revealing the eschatological kingdom, he can be said to be inaugurating it. Thus, when he accepts John's baptism that was aimed at repentance, he told the Baptist: "Give in for now. We must do this if we would fulfill all of God's demands" (Matthew 3:15).[8] "For now" (arti) John's baptism was effective; later it would give way to the baptism in water and the Holy Spirit.

Whatever the validity of these qualifying remarks, they leave our initial statement basically untouched: The attitude of Christ toward the Law was ambiguous. But the ambiguity of his attitude really derives from the ambiguity of his person; more properly, it derives from the breadth and depth of his own mystery. If the activity of Jesus is marked by paradox, it is because paradox marks his very being. "Jesus belongs to this world. Yet in the midst of it he is of unmistakeable otherness."[9]

He is a Jew,[10] from Nazareth in Galilee, faithful to the annual pilgrimages; he speaks Aramaic with the special accent that the people of Judea immediately recognized (Matthew 26:73). In his comparisons or parables of the sowing, the fields, the springs, the birds, the field lilies, the fishing net, all the pleasure he found in the Galilean countryside around the Lake shone in his eyes. Yet this same Jew forms a new family that is as all-embracing as the world itself, a family in which relationship depends not on flesh and blood but on obedience to the Father: "Whoever does the will of my heavenly Father is brother and sister and mother to me" (Matthew 12:50).

He is a man like us, truly "a son of man." He experiences hunger (Mark 11:1) and thirst (John 19:28); he eats, drinks, spits (Mark 7:33; 8:23); he sits down as a weary man on the rim of the well of Shechem (John 4:5) and sleeps on the cushion in Peter's boat (Mark 4:38). He trembles with joy (Luke 10:21), marvels at the unbelief of the people at Nazareth (Mark 6:6), is angry at his apostles, and is surrounded by female friends (Luke 8:2; John 11:5). He is filled with pity when he meets the widow of Naim (Luke 7:13), clasps the little children in his arms (Mark 9:36; 10:16), and weeps at Lazarus' tomb (John 11:35). Yet this same Son of Man is penetrated by the divine glory that transfigures him (Matthew 17:2).

He is a rabbi after the fashion of the masters in Israel; like them, he acquires disciples and trains them. But when he comments on the word of God, he does not do it like the others, who repeat the traditional formulas; rather, he teaches "with authority and not like their scribes" (Matthew 7:29). He always stays close to the crowds, and is a brother to the lowly. At a time when a rabbi who had any concern for his reputation would not have spoken to his own wife in public,[11] Jesus does not fear contact with women, children, tax-collectors, sinners, and prostitutes. "No man ever spoke like that before," was the report of the guards who had been sent to take him but were forced to return empty-handed (John 7:46).

He is the great prophet[12] who arises from among his people
(Luke 7:16) after the manner of the prophets of old. Yet, when he
speaks in God's name, he does not do it as the ancients did, who
introduced their oracles with the words: "Thus says the Lord." He
speaks in his own name and reveals a mystery he knows by personal
experience (John 3:11). He even goes so far as to bear witness to
himself: "What if I bear witness to myself? My testimony is valid
nonetheless" (John 8:14).

He is an apocalyptic visionary,[13] and he sometimes uses Old Testament images in his discourses (cf. Matthew 24:15). Yet nowhere
do we hear him speak of his visions in the manner of other apocalyptic visionaries. When he removes the veil from the future, he does it
with the authority of one who is Lord of history and "created the
eons" (Heb. 1:2 literally). His words bear the mark of eternity: "The
heavens and the earth will pass away, but my words will not pass"
(Matthew 24:35).

He is a legislator, as Moses had been. But he never puts himself
under Moses' authority. On the contrary, he claims a transcendent
authority for himself: "You have heard the commandment imposed
on your forefathers. . . . What I say to you is . . ." (Matthew
5:21-22).

He preaches repentance, as Jonah did. "But you have a greater
than Jonah here" (Matthew 12:38-42; Luke 11:32).

He is a master of wisdom, like Solomon; anyone who accepts his
yoke will find rest (Matthew 11:28-30). "But you have a greater than
Solomon here" (Matthew 12:42; Luke 11:31).

He is a descendant of Abraham, born centuries later. Yet his
existence is an eternal one: "Before Abraham came to be, I am"
(John 8:53).

He inherits the role of Jacob; on him, as on the patriarch long ago
(Gen. 28:10-17), the angels of God ascend and descend, thus sig-
nifying that in him heaven meets earth (John 1:51). Yet he is greater
than Jacob (John 4:12).

He is a descendant of David. It is when they address him in this
way that the Canaanite woman (Matthew 15:22) and the blind (Matthew 9:27; 20:31) catch his attention and win miracles from him.
But, "if David calls him 'Lord,' how can he be his son?" (Matthew
22:45).[14]

He is a king (Matthew 27:11). The kingdoms of the world that
Satan, a liar, pretends to be able to give him (Matthew 4:8-9) will in
reality become his by present from the Father, not from Satan: "Full

authority has been given to me both in heaven and on earth" (Matthew 28:18). Yet his kingdom is not of this world, for it is founded solely on faith and love; the only crown he receives from men is a circlet of thorns.

He is a priest.[15] But his priesthood transcends the categories of the Levitical priesthood and even puts an end to the worship in the Temple, for "there is something greater than the temple here" (Matthew 12:6). "Jesus, because he remains forever, has a priesthood which does not pass away. Therefore he is always able to save those who approach God through him, since he forever lives to make intercession for them. . . . [He is] made perfect forever" (Heb. 7:24-25, 28).

He is a savior, as the judges of old had been who rescued the people from oppression by the Philistines.[16] When the aged Simeon holds the infant Jesus in his arms, he can say with entire truth that his eyes behold the salvation of Israel.[17] But the salvation he offers reaches beyond Israel to the ends of the world (John 4:42). Nor is he interested only in souls, as if it were mankind's destiny to travel to a kingdom of "saved souls." Jesus saves man in his entirety, body and soul; in other words, he leads the person to eternal life (John 6:40).

He is the Christ or Messiah (Luke 2:11), that is, the One anointed as the kings and prophets of old had been.[18] But the anointing he has received is not an anointing with holy oil but an anointing with the Holy Spirit, who sends him to bring the Good News to the poor (Luke 4:18-19). "God anointed him with the Holy Spirit and power. He went about doing good works and healing all who were in the grip of the devil, and God was with him" (Acts 10:38).

He is a Son of God. He belongs to a people which as a whole is called the first-born son of Yahweh (Exod. 3:22; Jer. 31:9). He is also a Son of God by special title, as the king or the persecuted just man used to be.[19] But his sonship is unique. It transcends all others, just as his resurrection from the dead elevates him beyond us mortals. Paul will say that he "was made Son of God in power according to the spirit of holiness, by his resurrection from the dead" (Rom. 1:4).

In short: He is a man and he is God. And his being God transforms everything else.

The mystery of his person as God-man, then, sheds light on the mystery of his word. The ambiguity in his attitude to the word of God is part of his mystery, which in turn helps us understand the attitude, for, as man he submits to the Law, but as God he is superior to it. Because he possesses full authority, he transcends the

word and can walk in the field of the Scriptures as a sovereign
master who sets aside what is withered and dead and brings to fuller
development whatever bears fruit. The authority in question does
not derive from his power, as though he were imposing his word
simply because he is the master; it derives from his truthfulness,
because he is the Truth.

On the one hand, his word is divine. Admittedly, the word once
proclaimed at the Exodus and at Shechem, by Josiah and Ezra, and
in the synagogue services was also divine, for the prophets received
it from God, in whose name they spoke. Jesus' word, however, is
divine simply because he speaks in his own name. In other words,
his word is divine because he is God in person. When we hear him,
we hear God speaking (Luke 5:1).

On the other hand, this divine word reveals God. Again, the word
proclaimed in the Old Testament celebrations also revealed God.
But here the divine word that Jesus speaks reveals the speaker —
Jesus himself. The Law as proclaimed in the assemblies of the
Exodus, Shechem, Josiah, Ezra, and the synagogues now yields to
the new Law of the Gospel. And this new Law, this Gospel, is Jesus
himself. As Origen put it in an unforgettable statement, Jesus is
"himself the kingdom" (*autobasileia*).[20] Scripture is no longer a dead
book, wrapped in the mothballs of tradition. It is a person; it is the
Son of God himself.

With the coming of Christ, the community that is founded on the
word reaches a goal and also crosses a threshold. The goal it reaches
is that of the Scriptures, for the purpose of the Scriptures is to reveal
Christ. Anyone who has met the Christ of Scripture and laid hold of
him with the hands of faith and love, no longer needs Scripture to
reveal Christ to him. There are moments when he must close his
Bible. The word in the Old Testament was a way to Christ; Christ,
our God, is the fatherland to which we journey. One who has ar-
rived home has no longer any need of walking the road to it or asking
directions from the Law and the prophets.

With the coming of Christ, the community also crosses a
threshold to which the word, even though it paved the way for his
coming, could not bring the community. The "threshold" is the fact
that Jesus the Jew, "the carpenter, the son of Mary, a brother of
James and Joses and Judas and Simon" (Mark 6:3), is also the Son of
God. We said above that the Old Testament revelation of God
insofar as he is "a merciful and gracious God, slow to anger and rich
in kindness and fidelity" (Exod. 34:6) could not be surpassed in the

New Testament; all one can do is repeat it for all eternity as one says "God is love!" But there is something totally new in the new dispensation, something that constitutes a threshold the Old Testament could not cross. It is the fact that the divine mercy and graciousness, the divine kindness and fidelity, are incarnated in Jesus Christ.[21]

We also said above that no Law of the New Testament could transcend the law of love as expressed in the "Hear, O Israel": "You shall love the Lord, your God, with all your heart, and with all your soul, and with all your strength" (Deut. 6:4-5). But there is something totally new in the new dispensation, something that constitutes a threshold the Old Testament could not cross. It is the fact that from now on we must model our love on that of Christ; we must love as he does, and his love reaches even to the acceptance of death.

Jesus comes at the end of the Scriptures, as the Son of David, the blossom that opens on the rough stem of Jesse, the fruit of long generations that link him with the beginnings and the first man. All these generations, each made possible by the love of man and woman, were preparing for his birth according to the flesh, even though none of them could bring about this unparalleled mystery: the Son of God in a woman's womb.

Here again, there was a threshold the Old Testament could not cross. All the centuries that unfolded with the advance of history could not of themselves terminate in the miraculous presence of the Eternal within our time, of the Immutable within the human process. Jesus is indeed the fruit of the promise, but the reality surpasses what was promised, the fruit is more than was latent in the flower. There has been a discontinuity; something new has been introduced, for God alone can tie the thread of generations so as to make them lead from Adam to Christ. He alone can take the Old Testament across the threshold that leads to Christ. But in this passage the Old Testament becomes the New, and the veil is torn away.

3. *The problem*

Our task now is to determine more precisely the place of Jesus in relation to the Old Testament and to inquire more deeply into the New Law that he gives us. If one who has encountered Christ no longer needs the Scriptures insofar as they reveal Christ, he continues, however, to need them in order to deepen his knowledge of the Lord. The mission of the Old Testament is not finished.[22]

And yet we might think that it is finished when we read Paul's speech in the Areopagus at Athens (Acts 17:22-32). This discourse can serve as a model for Christian preaching in a pagan context. In it Paul proposes to his hearers the mystery of Christ dead and risen. He makes use of Scripture — how could this disciple of Gamaliel (Acts 22:3) fail to do so? — but he also makes use of Stoic themes which Jewish contacts with the Hellenistic world provided.[23] Here, then, we have a situation in which Paul thought it useless to show that Jesus was the Messiah of Jewish prophecy. Or, if he did give such a demonstration, Luke at least thought there was no point to recording the fact in Acts.

Here is another example, but of the opposite procedure: the baptism of the court official of Candace, queen of Ethiopia, on the road to Gaza. Luke reports the episode in Acts 8:26-40. The official was reading the prophecy of the suffering of the Servant of Yahweh in Is. 53:7-8. He had difficulty understanding the text, and Philip came to his aid. "Philip launched out with this Scripture passage as his starting point, telling him the good news of Jesus" (Acts 8:35). In this case, the Old Testament prophecy was enough by itself to lead the man to faith in Christ.

These two examples illustrate the problem.[24] In order to reach a general solution that applies to more than the individual cases of Paul at Athens and Philip on the Gaza road, the simplest thing will be to inquire of Christ himself and to ask the Testament we call "New" what it thinks of the "Old."

We shall see how Christ fulfills the history of Israel, the prophets, and the Law. The distinction between history, prophecy, and Law brings out three aspects of the same problem. Concretely, of course, history can be a prophecy, and prophecy can communicate laws. The distinction merely makes it easier to tackle the problem and obtain a precise answer.

I. THE FULFILLMENT OF HISTORY

Jesus "fulfills" the history of Israel and, thereby, the history of mankind. He is the point of arrival, and stands at the end of the road that leads this people from Ur of the Chaldees to the threshold of the New Testament.

It is a characteristic of this history that it is radically incomplete. It is often marked by bordeom, sometimes by distress, but it is always filled with hope. God intervenes at each stage, but he never brings the process to a definitive completion. The people journey onward without ceasing, never reaching rest.

God had promised Abraham that he would be the father of a people as numberless as the sand on the seashore or the stars in the sky. Now, the patriarch's clan had indeed multiplied to the point of becoming a people of twelve tribes. But could the prophecy be said to have been fulfilled when Israel played no leading role on the world stage in the theater of history, when it had continued to be a minor people within the Fertile Crescent, nestled in the hills of Palestine, wedged between the gigantic powers around it (Egypt, Assyria, Persia), and buffeted by the winds of history that blew across the Near East? According to the promise, this people was to be countless, yet it was of little importance in the calculations of those around it. "We are reduced, O Lord, beyond any other nation, brought low everywhere in the world this day" (Dan. 3:37).[25]

God had promised his people the possession of a "land" which was to be truly their own and in which every man could sit under his fig tree and enjoy the fruits of peace. And, in fact, the conquest of the land did begin under the Judges. Yet, six centuries later it had still to be finished; indeed, we might more truly say it had to begin all over again. Deuteronomy could still rekindle a fervent faith by promising the people the land as a reward for fidelity.[26] Could the promise be said to have been fulfilled in the time of Christ, when, in order to survive in its own country, the people had to pay tribute to Caesar and accept a Roman occupation? According to the promise, Israel was to "suck the milk of nations" (Is. 60:16), but in fact the nations had long been accustomed to slaking their thirst in Israelite blood.

God had promised David a house that would endure forever (2 Sam. 7:5-17) and a throne like the sun (Ps. 89:37). But, in fact, the vicissitudes of history had turned the eternal house into a "fallen hut" (Amos 9:11). The Davidic dynasty drained the cup of bitterness and reached the depths of humiliation when Zedekiah was dragged off to rot in a Babylonian dungeon after seeing his sons slain before his eyes and then being blinded (2 Kings 25:7). God had indeed been mindful again of David, according to the prayer in Psalm 132. But could the prophecy really be said to have been fulfilled when King Evil-Merodach, son and successor of Nebuchadnezzar, allowed Jehoiachin to lay aside his prison garb and eat as a beggar at the table of the king of Babylon (2 Kings 25:27-29)?

With a handful of wily mercenaries, David had conquered

Jerusalem and made it "the city of the great king" (Ps. 48:3). God had promised to dwell there forever in his sanctuary (Ps. 78:69) and to make it his resting place forever (Ps. 132:14). But in 587 the Chaldean battering rams breached the walls of the Holy City, and the Temple was engulfed in blood and fire. The edict of Cyrus in 538 allowed the Zionists to return home so that they might weep over the scorched ruins of the Temple and rebuild its walls. But could the prophecy really be said to have been fulfilled when, in Christ's time, a Roman garrison, housed in the fortress Antonia, looked down on the Temple plaza and could at a moment's notice control what went on there?

The bitter taste of history and its radical incompleteness are felt even in the books which are not concerned with history. Thus Job, plunged into suffering, comes to terms with it as best he can, through a faith that is the equal of his perplexity. But is the problem Job faces really resolved when the old man regains his share of happiness in the form of 14,000 sheep, 6,000 camels, 1,000 yoke of oxen, 1,000 she-asses, 7 sons, and 3 daughters (Job 42:12-14)? How could anyone be content with such an answer, which is almost a tease, since Job must lose it all again when he dies, and must face the same problem all over again?

So too, when the shepherd in the Song of Songs embraces the pretty brunette, can such a momentary happy ending (even if the moment lasted a lifetime) be a fully satisfying crown to the love of a man and a woman? That love, after all, is as strong as death and as sharp as one of Yahweh's arrows (Cant. 8:6); it desires to abide and be eternal, but death lies in wait for it and makes it its prey; when the hour comes, death will gather it in, like the fruit that falls in autumn.

Can we say that a man's life, even if passed before the eyes of God, even if blessed (Prov. 18:22) with a wife as fruitful as a vine (Ps. 128:3-4) and as graceful as a doe (Prov. 5:18), even if continuing until the man can see his children's children and die full of years (according to Ps. 90:10, eighty is a full number) — can we say that even such a life is the full answer to the problem of happiness and the full satisfaction of the basic right every creature has that is called into being by God? Qoheleth strips all illusions away with his bitter words: "The lot of man and of beast is one lot; the one dies as well as the other. Both have the same life-breath, and man has no advantage over the beast; but all is vanity" (Eccles. 3:19).

To ask these questions is not to slander the history of Israel or revelation. After all, the real greatness of the people of the promise is that they were a people of hope who were constantly questioning their God, a people waiting for a salvation greater than anything their history had brought them. Their true wealth was a heart that yearned for God; their true treasure was their poverty, that is, their capacity to receive Christ. God filled Israel's history with distress and misfortune so that it might become a history in search of salvation. He brought them to despair so that their hope might become the stronger. He let them lose their way so that they might travel a road not of this world. Without Christ — as we can verify even in our own day — Israel's history leads to the Wailing Wall of Jerusalem. And the face it turns to its past (symbolized by the Wall) is a face ravaged by tears.

With the coming of Jesus, the history of Israel reaches a divine term. In him the clan of Abraham becomes the universal Church. In him the Promised Land turns out to be the heaven the Father offers, and the departure from Ur was in reality a journey to paradise. In him the Davidic dynasty reaches the shores of God's eternity, since a son of David becomes Son of God. In him the earthly Jerusalem is transformed into the new city that comes down from God in heaven. In his death and resurrection Job receives an answer to the problem of suffering and death. In him the love song of the Song of Songs becomes the love song of Christ and the Church which is his spouse. In him the eighteen centuries of Israel's history terminates in the new reality that gives it its full meaning: "This is the time of fulfillment. The reign of God is at hand!" (Mark 1:14). The reason why in the past God had not definitively fulfilled his promises was so that he might fulfill them in Jesus Christ, in a way far surpassing the wildest dreams of men.

The problem of expectation is, of course, not peculiarly biblical or restricted to Israel. We need not call upon Job in order to raise the problem of suffering, nor upon Qoheleth to see that all things human are empty. The problem concerns mankind as a whole:

> Man goes to his lasting home,
>   and mourners go about in the streets. . . .
> And the dust returns to the earth as it once was,
>   and the life breath returns to God who gave it.
> Vanity of vanities, says Qoheleth,
>   all things are vanity! (Eccles. 12:5-8).

Consequently, in giving Israel its answer, God answers every human being. In its own history Israel came to "experience the ways of God with men,"[27] and these ways concern all mankind, since Israel is the first fruits of the nations (Jer. 2:3) and stands at the crossroads of mankind. In Jesus Christ, God teaches men that the journey to the eternal house is not a journey into emptiness but a victorious journey to God: "You have drawn near to Mount Zion and the city of the living God, the heavenly Jerusalem, to myriads of angels in festive gathering, to the assembly of the first-born enrolled in heaven, to God the judge of all" (Heb. 12:22-23).

We must go a step further and note that just as the whole history of Israel was a long preparation for the coming of Jesus Christ, so the history of mankind was a preparation for Israel and, through Israel, for Christ. This is true even of the sequence of carnal generations that were preparing for the ineffable wonder of a woman giving birth to God. The genealogy of Jesus does not reach back through the history of the chosen people only to David and then to Abraham (Matthew 1:1-16); it reaches back still further to the first man (Luke 3:23-38). How long a preparation for the body and heart of a single man! Mankind which had slowly evolved under the providential care of God was in its entirety ordered to him who is "the first-born of all creatures" (Col. 1:15).

Rightly, then, does the Bible begin the history of salvation long before the election of Abraham. The first eleven chapters of Genesis have a universal significance, as universal as the significance of the last pages of the New Testament. For the whole history of mankind, and not merely that of Israel, centers on Christ. Everything was a preparation for him, and everything reached its fulfillment in him.

> Jesus was born of a woman and was a son of Adam through his genealogy. He accepted in its totality the heritage that made him one with all sinful men. This is why the long historical experience of men, accumulated over the centuries and marked by the opposing energies of the creative plan and of sin, had fashioned the human substructure of his self and, at the same time, the social milieu within which his special lot was cast. Consequently, without in any way being compromised as Son of God, he summed up in his person the existential experience of all mankind and was assimilated to men in everything except sin.[28]

II. THE FULFILLMENT OF THE PROPHECIES

We are familiar with Pascal's words: "The prophecies are the strongest proof of Jesus Christ. It is for them also that God has made most provision; for the event which has fulfilled them is a miracle

existing since the birth of the Church to the end."[29] This strongest
of "proofs" involves more, however, than a mechanical use of Scripture texts which force the mind in a certain direction and necessarily lead it to the conclusion that Jesus is the Messiah. An apologetic
intention is indeed not entirely absent from the New Testament,
but it is secondary to the interests of faith, which is chiefly concerned with penetrating more deeply the supernatural personality
of Christ.

The question, "Is Jesus the Messiah?" is therefore less important
than the question, "Who is Jesus the Messiah?" St. Jerome re-
marked that "to be ignorant of the Scriptures is to be ignorant of
Christ."[30] *That* is why the New Testament community pores over
the Scriptures — in order to know Christ better. The fulfillment of
prophecy according to its spiritual meaning is much richer than its
fulfillment according to the mere letter, and also leaves each reader
his royal freedom. "The important thing for Christians is not the
biblical text but the event."[31] The event, in this case, is Christ.

Just as faith alone allows us to grasp the full spiritual wealth of the
event, so faith alone enables us to read the prophecies and find the
face of Christ in them. Pascal observes: "The understanding of the
promised blessings depends on the heart, which calls 'good' that
which it loves."[32] Scripture is a window opening on to Christ. It
reveals him rather than "proves" him. Or better still, it proves him
by revealing him. Faith in Christ is the light that shines through the
window and enables us to see beyond the letter. It does not create
its object, any more than sunlight creates the objects it illumines.
But it does enable us to discover the object and discern what it is
like.

1. "According to the Scriptures"

Using a formulation that was already traditional, Paul writes in
the First Letter to the Corinthians: "I handed on to you first of all
what I myself received, that Christ died for our sins *in accordance
with the Scriptures*; that he was buried and, *in accordance with the
Scriptures*, rose on the third day; that he was seen by Cephas, then
by the Twelve" (1 Cor. 15:3-5).[33]

This formulation of the paschal mystery is one of the oldest in the
Christian tradition, dating back perhaps to as early as 35–40 A.D. It
states that the climactic events of the history of salvation — the
Lord's death and resurrection — took place *according to the Scriptures*.

The certainty that Christ fulfilled the Scriptures has roots deep in the Christian consciousness; it formed the faith of the first community and is at the center of its understanding of Scripture.[34] Apart from this fulfillment, Christianity would have been simply one of the many religious sects that blossomed in the East. Given this fulfillment, Christianity is, on the contrary, the goal of the path history followed under God's direction, and the definitive, eschatological result of his interventions in the world. Christ himself is at the center of the Scriptures; he is the bond of unity among them all, since he is "the one Moses spoke of in the law — the prophets too" (John 1:45).[35] To believe in the Scriptures is to believe in Christ: "If you believed Moses you would then believe me, for it was about me that he wrote" (John 5:46).

At every point in the Gospels the early Christian community has given voice to its certainty that Christ fulfilled the prophecies. One of the documents that best reveals this frame of mind is to be found in St. Luke's account of the final apparitions of the risen Christ to his disciples (24:13-49), and especially to the travelers at Emmaus.

The account is characterized by theological formulations current in the early community. From the historical viewpoint, there is some vagueness about the events as such, but this is due to the literary genre to which the account belongs.[36] For, though the resurrection of Christ is to be situated in relation to history, the event as such transcends history. At this point Christ is already in his glory (Luke 24:26), even though he still walks the roads or eats grilled fish (Luke 24:42-43). The story of the travelers to Emmaus is based on the account of two witnesses, one of whom is named Cleopas. But around this assured testimony, the community, with Luke as its authorized interpreter, has formulated a profoundly beautiful theology of the risen Christ.

The resurrection had, it seemed, opened an impassable chasm between Christ and his disciples. Yet the community was not left orphaned, for Jesus still lived among his own. His own, however, did not recognize him, and Luke seems to be telling us: "You walk with the risen Christ, yet you do not recognize him! You travel with him but are ignorant of his presence!" But how are we to recognize him? Luke offers two possible ways. One is the breaking of bread: "When he had seated himself with them to eat, he took bread, pronounced the blessing, then broke the bread and began to distribute it to them. With that their eyes were opened and they recognized him" (Luke 24:30-31). When we welcome the stranger to our table and break bread with him while also giving him of our love, we can recognize the risen Christ.

The other means of recognizing Christ is the Scriptures. Jesus reproaches his disciples for their slow hearts and dull minds that have prevented them from seeing in the messianic events the fulfillment of the Scriptures: "What little sense you have! How slow you are to believe all that the prophets have announced! Did not the Messiah have to undergo all this so as to enter into his glory?" (Luke 24:25-26). Then, says Luke, "beginning with Moses and all the prophets, he interpreted for them every passage of Scripture which referred to him" (v. 27).

The theme of Christ's presence in the Scriptures and their fulfillment is taken up again with a similar emphasis in the account of the apparition to the apostles in Jerusalem (Luke 24:36-49).[37] Jesus says on this occasion: "Everything written about me in the law of Moses and the prophets and the psalms had to be fulfilled" (v. 44). Here Luke lists the three parts of Scripture according to the Jewish canon: the Law, or the five books of the Pentateuch; the Prophets, that is, the books considered prophetic; and the Psalms, which stand by metonymy for the hagiographical writings. The three parts, and thus the whole of Scripture, speak "about me." This is to say that there is a history of Jesus in the Law, a history of Jesus in the Prophets, and a history of Jesus in the Psalms. To read that history requires the grace of the risen Christ: "He opened their minds to the understanding of the Scriptures" (v. 45).

We can, of course, read the letter of Scripture without discovering the Messiah in it, as we can know the Jesus of history as a mortal man without having faith and discovering the Lord in him. This was the way the travelers to Emmaus were acting (Luke 24:16). It was also the state of Mary Magdalene who, despite the clarity of vision love gave her, did not at first recognize her *Rabbouni* (John 20:11-15); she was looking for the Jesus whom she had followed on the roads of Galilee, and she encounters the risen Lord. Such, too, was the state of the disciples who did not recognize Christ in the figure of the unknown man who broiled fish for them over the fire at early morning beside the Sea of Galilee (John 21:9). Thus, it is Jesus himself who, after his resurrection, discloses the meaning of the Scriptures. And the disciples will regret the sluggishness of mind that had kept them from recognizing, in the deeds and actions of Christ, the fulfillment of the Scriptures (John 2:22; 12:16).

We may add that the events Luke narrates occur on Easter, the day which opens a new period in the history of salvation, and the day on which, it would seem from Luke's chronology, Christ ascended into heaven.[38] Now that he is returning into the silence of God, who will continue to preach his message? The Scriptures will! They had been silent, as it were, as long as Christ was speaking, since the word of the prophets must give way to the word of the Son. But now they begin again to speak, just as they had once spoken beforehand of his life and message. "Search the Scriptures in which you think you have eternal life — they also testify on my behalf" (John 5:39). The community was thus invited to search the Scriptures and discover in them the face of Christ. What we now call the Old Testament was the community's first Gospel book.

2. *The community's meditation on the prophets*

The composition of the Gospels was a gradual affair, geared to the requirements of preaching the kingdom of Jesus Christ. The workshop in which the Church wrought the texts was the community itself in its meditation on the Scriptures.

The gatherings for religious feasts, whether in the Temple or in the synagogues, gave the community of believers an opportunity for expounding its faith in Christ on the basis of the Scriptures. Thus Peter preached his first sermon on Pentecost, taking Joel 3:1-5, Psalm 16:8-11, and Psalm 110:1 as his text; the conclusion he reached was: "Therefore let the whole house of Israel know beyond any doubt that God has made both Lord and Messiah this Jesus whom you crucified" (Acts 2:36). Paul, for his part, regularly attended the synagogue:[39] "Every sabbath, in the synagogue, Paul led discussions in which he persuaded certain Jews and Greeks" (Acts 18:4). At Antioch in Pisidia, "after the reading of the law and the prophets" (Acts 13:15), he preached Christ crucified, taking as his texts Deut. 1:31 and 7:1, Psalm 89:21 and 2:7, Is. 55:3, Psalm 16:10, and Hab. 1:5.[40]

It can of course be said that the texts cited matter less than the faith of the first community that the whole of Scripture speaks of Christ. Any text taken in isolation can seem weak in a discussion of it. But the Scriptures as a whole, when seen within the entire movement of revelation, converge on Christ. Like a lover, he attracts scriptural passages to himself. Thus, in Stephen's discourse (Acts 7:1-53) Luke can, on the basis of a symphony of quotations, offer a global vision of the history of salvation, with Christ dominating the whole.[41] In the mind of the first Christians, what we call the

Old Testament now belonged not to the synagogue but to the
Church, for since the Church possessed Christ, she also possessed
the key to the Scriptures.

Here are two examples which will give us a vivid insight into the
way the community worked with the Scriptures.

We are familiar with the story of Jesus' entry into Jerusalem on
Palm Sunday; all four evangelists tell it (Matthew 21:1-9; Mark
11:1-10; Luke 19:28-40; John 12:12-19). Reaching Bethphage,
Jesus sends two of his disciples ahead to look for an ass's foal on
which he can ride. Always careful about precise detail, Mark notes
that they found it "tethered out on the street near a gate" (11:4).
They untie it, bring it back to Jesus, and throw their cloaks over its
back to serve as a saddle. Jesus mounts the animal, and in this
modest fashion makes his entry as Messiah into Jerusalem. The
early community, according to Matthew 21:5 and John 12:15, saw in
this episode the fulfillment of the prophecy of Zechariah (9:9), which
Matthew quotes in this form: "Tell the daughter of Zion, Your king
comes to you without display astride an ass, astride a colt, the foal of
a beast of burden."

But while Mark 11:2 and Luke 19:30, as well as John 12:14, speak
of a single ass, Matthew 21:2 and 7 speak of a she-ass and her colt.
He emphasizes this: "You will find an ass tethered and her colt with
her. . . . They brought the ass and the colt and laid their cloaks on
them, and he mounted." (He seems to mount them both, but how
could he?). The text of Zechariah does mention an ass and a foal
(offspring of a she-ass), but they are one and the same animal; it is
simply poetic redundancy and the liking for synonymic parallelism,
so favored in Hebrew poetry, that cause two mentions of one and
the same thing. In Matthew, however, the fulfillment is made to
match the strict letter of the prophecy.

What are we to conclude? Is Matthew writing history in the light
of the prophecy or in the light of the event itself? In the last analysis,
the question of one or two asses is almost completely without importance. Matthew, after all, is writing a Gospel, that is, he is spreading
the Good News, and the Good News which brings joy to the world is
this: Jesus is the humble, modest king of whom the prophecy speaks
and who now comes to his people.

Here is the second example; it has to do with events connected
with the Lord's crucifixion. The prophecy in this instance is found in
Psalm 22. We will recall that all four evangelists (Matthew 27:35;
Mark 15:24; Luke 23:34; John 19:24) tell us of the soldiers dividing

up Christ's garments by casting lots for them. The point of this detail is to show that Christ was being treated as a common criminal. In itself, there was no need to mention the detail, since everyone knew the executioners had the right to share among themselves the garments of the condemned person. Moreover, nothing is said of the same procedure being applied to the two criminals who were being crucified with Christ. The real point, then, is that this detail is found in Psalm 22: "They divide my garments among them, and for my vesture they cast lots" (v. 19).

The early community regarded this Psalm as an especially rich prophecy of the Lord's Passion. Christ himself had recited the first verse of it on the Cross when he prayed: *"Eli, Eli, lema sabachthani?* — My God, my God, why have you forsaken me?" (Matthew 27:46). But the whole Psalm was speaking of him and his sufferings, and therefore the evangelists made use of it in redacting their accounts of the Passion.[42]

It is difficult to interpret this Psalm as used by the community for its profession of faith in the Son of God. But, in any case, we should not imagine the early community inventing this prayer of distress and desolation and putting it on the lips of the crucified Jesus. Luke, who is always looking to show Christ as the embodiment of peace, joy, and supreme beauty,[43] does not repeat the bitter words of Psalm 22:2, and instead has Christ use the peaceful prayer of Psalm 31:6: "Father, into your hands I commend my spirit" (23:46).

Since the crucified Jesus had himself prayed the Psalm, the evangelists could presume that the Psalm would also shed light on other aspects of the Passion. For example, in Mark 9:13 it serves as a prediction of the Passion after the transfiguration (the evangelists like to use for the predictions of the Passion words later used in the Passion narrative itself). Again, in Matthew 27:39 and Mark 15:29 it serves to describe the behavior of the passersby who insult the crucified Christ. Again, in Matthew 27:43 it describes the derisive laughter of "the chief priests and elders." It is quite possible and even probable that these men did deride Christ, but it seems unlikely that they used the very words of the Psalm in doing so. If they had, they would have put themselves among the "dogs" and "evildoers" who persecute the just man, and would thereby have been admitting that Jesus was an innocent just man whom they were persecuting. On the other hand, it was quite fair for Matthew to rank the chief priests and elders with the hooligans. Again, the division of the garments is a further element in the fulfillment of

Psalm 22	Matthew	Mark	Luke
God, *my God,* *why have you* *forsaken me?* (v. 2)	My *God,* *my God* *why have you* *forsaken me?* (27:46)	My *God,* *my God,* *why have you* *forsaken me?* (15:34)	
I am *despised* by the people (v. 7)		He would suffer and be *despised* (9:12)	
All those who were *watching* me *jeered* at me (v. 8)			The people stood there *watching*, and the leaders kept *jeering* (23:35)
They *tossed* the *head* (v. 8)	*tossing* their heads (27:39)	*tossing* their heads (15:29)	
He hoped in the Lord. Let him save him, since *he loves* *him* (v. 9)	He trusted in God. Let him rescue him now, *if he loves* *him* (27:43)		
They divided my *garments* and for my robe *cast lots* (v. 19; = John 19:24)	*They divided* his *garments* *casting* lots (27:35)	*They divided* his *garments* *casting* lots (15:24)	*Dividing* his *garments* they *cast lots* (23:34)
I will tell *your name* *to my brothers,* *I will sing your* *praise in the* *midst of the* *assembly* (v. 23)			*I will announce* *your name* *to my brothers,* *I will sing your* *praise in the* *midst of the* *assembly* (Heb. 2:12).

Psalm 22. Finally, we may note Heb. 2:12, which quotes Psalm
22:23 in speaking of Jesus's glory and of his mission to his "brothers"
(2:10-12).

What are we to conclude from all this? We cannot deny the
historicity of the Passion on the pretext that it is offered as the
fulfillment of the prophecy in Psalm 22. But neither can we deny
that some features of the Passion are told in the words of Psalm 22.
Perhaps we must even go further and say that the story of the
anonymous poor man of Psalm 22 is a universal story in which both
man's wretchedness and his hope of salvation are described. By
identifying himself with this poor man, Jesus took all human
wretchedness upon himself; he is the Poor Man par excellence. In
his Passion he bears men's sufferings, and in his resurrection he
represents their hope of deliverance.

3. The "collections" of citations

The community's reflection on the Scriptures, with a view to
discovering in them everything "about Jesus" (Acts 18:25), gave rise
to "collections" of biblical citations. These collections were put together in the workroom of the early Church, which is to say they
were put together by the community itself as it formed the New
Testament with the help of texts from the Old. These collections of
texts were what we might call "The Bible of the Early Church."[44]

We use the word "collections," but we need not think of sheets of
parchment carefully bound together. It is more likely that what we
have initially is an interpretative method passed on orally, a way of
reading the Scriptures without the veil over one's eyes. The collection which a catechist had at his disposal as he proclaimed Christ
Jesus, or what we might call the library at the Church's disposal, was
the community's memory which the Holy Spirit kept alive and
vivid. It is likely, however, that these memories were later put
into writing to form "anthologies."

Here is an example from Matthew. The Gospel contains about
fifty prophecies; of these, some thirty-seven are accompanied by
introductory formulas, which were a literary device for calling attention. Ten easily identifiable prophecies, however, are introduced by
the formula: "In order to fulfill (or: Thus was fulfilled) the prophecy
(of the Lord) according to Isaiah (Jeremiah, etc.) the prophet, who
says."[45] This formula was in common use in Palestinian circles,[46]
especially in the rabbinic schools.[47] These ten prophecies, more

than the others, give a glimpse of the original Hebrew. Moreover, they are easily detached from their present context, so that they can be taken as personal reflections of the evangelist himself (what the Germans call *Reflexionszitate*). Finally, the scholars have not been able to discern any principle that would account for the bringing together of these ten in the Gospel of Matthew. Consequently, it has been hypothesized that there was a booklet of selected texts in current use in Palestine which presented Jesus' life as the fulfillment of the prophecies.[48] Matthew, it is assumed, used the booklet to enrich his Gospel.

Some of these citations, called *testimonia* (testimonies), belonged to material used by catechists generally. These we might call the fundamental texts. In order to determine which ones fell into this class, C. H. Dodd works from a hypothesis: "Where two separate writers cite the same passage from the Old Testament, unless there are definite reasons to the contrary, they represent to that extent a common tradition."[49] We are justified in saying that when one and the same Old Testament text is cited by different New Testament sources, the text was accepted by the whole community as messianic, revealing Christ, bearing witness to him, and thus deserving the name of *testimonium*.

Consider, for example, Psalm 118(117). The Psalm is meant for worship and was probably connected with the Feast of Tents. It begins with an invitation to the whole people to join in praising God (vv. 1-2). "People" is then narrowed down to the family of Aaron (v. 3), then to the just (v. 4), and then to a single just man. Doubtless, we may see at work here the concept of "corporate personality," with this one just man representing the whole people of God.[50] In verses 10-15 we see the just man isolated and surrounded by all the Gentile nations; in the name of the Lord he repels them all, and his victory is a source of universal joy. This Psalm was very suited to expressing the ecclesial dimension of the mystery of Christ, and in fact it is cited in the Synoptic tradition, and by John, Acts, the Letter to the Hebrews, and the First Letter of Peter.

The New Testament saw, then, in Psalm 118 features of its picture of Jesus Christ. The citations, coming as they do from different New Testament sources, show that the early community considered the Psalm to be of special importance for preaching the mystery of Jesus:

Psalm 118[51]	New Testament	
v. 6	Heb. 13:6	
The Lord is my help,	*The Lord is my help,*	
what can men do to me?	*what can men do to me?*	
v. 10	John 10:24	
All the nations *surround-ed* me	The Jews *surrounded* him (Jesus)	
v. 16	Acts 2:23	
The right hand of the Lord has exalted me	(Jesus was) *exalted* by God's *right hand*	

Psalm 118	Matthew 21:42; Mark 12:10; Luke 20:17; cf. 1 Peter 2:7	Acts 4:11
v. 22		
The rock	*The rock*	The rock scorned
which the builders rejected	*which the builders rejected*	by all the *builders,*
has become the cornerstone.	*has become the cornerstone.*	become *the cornerstone*
This is the doing of the Lord,	*This is the doing of the Lord,*	
and it is marvelous in his eyes	*and it is marvelous in his eyes.*	

Psalm 118	Matthew 21:9; Mark 11:10; John 12:13	Luke 19:38
v. 26		
Blessed be he	*Blessed be he*	*Blessed* he
who comes	*who comes*	*who comes,* the king,
in the name	*in the name*	*in the name*
of the Lord	*of the Lord*	*of the Lord*

Psalm 118	Matthew 23:39; Luke 13:35
v. 26	
Blessed he who comes	*Blessed he who comes*
in the name	*in the name*
of the Lord	*of the Lord*

4. Implicit citations

In his discourse in the Temple after healing the paralytic at the Beautiful Gate, Peter says: "All the prophets who have spoken, from Samuel onward, have announced the events of these days" (Acts 3:24). "All the prophets" — a term more universal and more vague could not have been found, and yet the statement expresses quite well the conviction of the early community. We need only think of the long line of anonymous sufferers who walk through the psalms and whose tears are a continuous sad prophecy of Christ's passion. They did not, of course, think that they were either prophesying or composing biblical poetry when they prayed: "My God, my God, why have you forsaken me?" or "Into your hands I commend my spirit." They spoke thus because the words expressed their desires and softened their sorrow. Nonetheless, their bitter sobs did prophetically anticipate the prayer of Christ.[52]

The reader may perhaps be tempted to say: Wouldn't the simplest approach be to make an exhaustive list of the prophecies? Then the range of the prophecies could be exactly determined, and we would have a panoramic view of the Old Testament in which the New Testament would be reflected as in a mirror. The task would be long and somewhat boring perhaps, but at least we would finally have a "complete edition" of the prophecies.

But this is a dream that cannot be made real. You might as well try to sink a bottomless well. The reason is that, along with the explicit citations, clearly set off and easily listed, there is the vast store of implicit citations. It is a treasury filled with life, but we cannot do an audit of it because it makes constant use of biblical allusions and reminiscences.

Here is a well-known example, the *Magnificat*. The text seems quite simple and easily grasped, and yet its scriptural density is extraordinary.

From the *psychological* viewpoint, the text raises a number of problems and can only with difficulty be brought into harmony with its context. Elizabeth has just greeted her cousin Mary and recognized in her "the Mother of the Lord." Instead of answering the greeting, which would have been the expected act of courtesy, Mary responds with a hymn of thanksgiving and does not even mention the favor which Elizabeth has received from the Lord. The hymn itself, moreover, bears no mark of literary originality; Mary's thanksgiving flows out quite naturally in formulas created by Old Testament piety, especially the piety of the "poor people" of Yahweh. Evidently Mary has no intention of showing poetic talent and imagination.

From the *scriptural* viewpoint, we have here one of the greatest texts in the Gospel of Christ's infancy, and perhaps even in the whole of Luke's Gospel. It is entirely made up of biblical citations and reminiscences. They are put together to form, as it were, a rose-window, with the scriptural allusions as the glass bits inserted in the stone frame, and the whole being then illumined by the light of Christ. Into the window go the song of barren Hannah (1 Sam. 2:1), the canticle of Habakkuk (3:18), the thanksgiving of the redeemed community in Is. 61:10, a symphony of nine different Psalms,[53] Deuteronomy, and the Books of Job (12:19), Isaiah (41:8), Malachi (3:12), and Micah (7:20). All of these are called upon to celebrate Mary's messianic joy, and all may claim in a sense to have inspired her prayer. In this rainbow of quotations, the whole Old Testament weaves a crown of praise and adoration for Christ and, with the Virgin, rejoices in God, its Savior, or — according to the neat word-play of the original text[54] — in the Jesus (= Savior) whom she carries in her womb. Luke would have us think that in the *Magnificat* the whole people of the Old Testament, and especially the poor who hoped in the Lord, were acknowledging the Messiah and singing with Mary of their joy at their deliverance.

It is certainly possible to recite the *Magnificat* in a meaningful way and to make it part of authentic prayer without knowing anything of the biblical background that makes it so rich a composition. But in that event we would not really be repeating Mary's prayer of thanksgiving, that is, the prayer which Luke was inspired by the Holy Spirit to pass on to us. The text would have lost the breath of life that the evangelist breathed into it; it would still live, but its present soul would be one created by the human imagination.

The difficulty or, more accurately, the impossibility of counting up the prophecies so as to make a "complete edition" of them should not discourage us. On the contrary! If the whole of the Old Testament speaks of Jesus and if the life-story of Christ has been written down beforehand "in the law of Moses and the prophets and the psalms" (Luke 24:44), then any knowledge the believer has of the Old Testament will increase his knowledge of Jesus Christ. It is undoubtedly worthwhile, of course, to make an accurate list of the prophecies that are explicitly cited in the New Testament, since the explicit prophecies enable us better to understand the implicit; they are the key to a "Christian" understanding of the Bible. But it is also inspiring to know that the whole of the Old Testament speaks of Jesus. It makes little difference in the last analysis how deeply we plunge into this bottomless well, since the very effort to do so makes the living water flow more abundantly for us. It makes little difference in the last analysis what path we take to enter the forest of the Scriptures, since on every path we meet Jesus Christ.

III. THE FULFILLMENT OF THE LAW

We must be careful here about the way we use the word "law," since it can have different meanings.

"Law" may mean, first of all, the whole of the Scriptures, as in 1 Cor. 14:21, 34; Rom. 3:10-19; and John 10:34. It may also mean, more particularly, the five books of the Pentateuch. Then it is possible to speak of the Law and the Prophets,[55] that is, of the first two parts of the canon. Taking the word in this narrower acceptation, we dealt earlier in this book with the reading of the Law (the Pentateuch) and the Prophets (the books which the Jewish canon classified as prophetic) in the synagogal liturgy. By extension, "the Law and the Prophets" can also mean the whole of the Bible.

Finally, "the Law" can mean the collection of laws that express God's will for man and provide a rule of life and a way to God. The laws, as we know, were many in number, though all were expressions of the one will of God.

When we speak of "the fulfillment of the law," we refer to the way in which the New Testament, in the person of Christ, brings the Old Testament laws to their definitive perfection and effectively makes them lead over into the law of the Gospel. The problem is: *How* is this "fulfillment" accomplished? *How* is the law of the Gospel born out of the Law which Israel proclaimed?

We must advert again to the difficulty in interpreting the pertinent texts, since we must constantly bear in mind their polemical context. At the time when St. Paul was writing his great letters and the Gospels were being composed, the Christian community had already for several decades been the object of great hostility on the part of the "Jews." The latter accused the Christians of infidelity to the ancient faith of their fathers, while the Christians accused the Jews of infidelity to the new reality promised in the Scriptures. As the Christians saw it, the Jews' understanding was veiled, as it were (cf. 2 Cor. 3:15).

The Christian community, convinced of Christ's Good News, had no choice but to drop the Mosaic observances and to seek its own proper path even amid external persecution and internal groping. At Antioch, Paul had to oppose Peter's inconsistent manner of acting differently than he had previously taught (Gal. 2:11).[56] The way in which Christians reacted against the Law may sometimes seem exaggerated to us today; an extreme example of this tendency may be the contrast set up between law and grace. Thus, "though the Law was given through Moses, grace and truth have come through

Jesus Christ" — and yet the Law had been a revelation and a gracious gift![57]

Consequently, when the Jews accused Stephen of "speaking blasphemies against Moses and God" and of claiming "that Jesus the Nazorean will destroy this place and change the customs which Moses handed down to us" (Acts 6:11, 14), their accusation may not have been accurately formulated, but it did have some foundation.

Jesus himself, in St. John's Gospel, seems to disown the Old Testament. In his arguments with the "Jews" he likes to tell them: "It is written in *your* law." He cites Deut. 17:6 (in John 8:17) and Psalm 82:6 (in John 10:34). But was not "your law" the word of God, of which Jesus says elsewhere: "Search the Scriptures . . . they also testify on my behalf" (John 5:39)?

We must keep in mind, then, the painful conflict which is the framework for the problem of the Law. The conflict arose because the Law, which God intended as a "monitor" (Gal. 3:23-25), did not want to see its role as monitor and pedagogue terminated.

1. Beyond "human tradition"

The first service Jesus renders to the Law is to restore it to its primitive purity. The loving meditation of the scribes and doctors on the word of God over many generations had created human traditions or even at times routines. Tradition, which is the wisdom of history, can turn into a burden if it does not serve the Spirit; usage consecrated by habit can come to look like the embodiment of reason, and routine can wear the mask of principle. In the process of working on the sacred tests, men had allowed them to become dusty and lose their brilliance. The desire to take every possible case into account caused the underbrush of minor precepts and short-lived practices to grow as high and become as important as the essential laws. Men ferreted around in the texts and became prisoners of the letter. The dust had to be swept away. In some instances a scouring was needed.

Jesus did the job with a master's touch. He was too intelligent, of course, as well as too humble (Matthew 11:29), not to recognize the value of tradition. He himself submitted to its demands, as we have seen, and bore the burden it necessarily places on man. Consequently, Jesus' objection is not to tradition as such,[58] but to its distortions which obscure God's will as clearly manifested in his word and which also lay a hateful burden, contrary to God's will, on the "poor," that is, those not clever at exegesis. Consequently, Jesus' real objection to the Pharisees is that "you nullify God's word in favor of the traditions you have handed on" (Mark 7:13). He makes a number of more specific criticisms:

It does no good to offer sacrifices if you do not practice mercy (Hos. 6:2 = Matthew 9:13 and 12:7).

It does no good to keep extra fasts if you thereby deafen yourself to the invitation of what is new in the Gospel (Mark 2:18-22; Matthew 9:14-17; Luke 5:33-38).

It does no good not to work on the sabbath if you refuse to love your brother. The sabbath is a day meant for doing good, not for idleness.[59]

It does no good to wash your hands before eating if your heart is unclean.[60]

It does no good to dedicate an offering to the Lord by declaring it *korban* if you do this in order to avoid your filial duty to your parents (Mark 7:11; Matthew 15:6).

It does no good to pay tithes on mint and herbs and seeds if you neglect the more important precepts of the Law: justice, mercy, and good faith (Matthew 23:23).

It does no good to clean the outside of the cup if the inside is filled with loot and lust, so that you are comparable to a whitewashed tomb (Matthew 23:26-27).

These are only examples, but they illustrate a general truth: that human hands risk tarnishing the splendor of the word when they touch it. There is need of constantly returning to the source, discovering again the clear will of God, establishing a right hierarchy within his laws, and understanding that to love our neighbor "is worth more than any burnt offering or sacrifice" (Mark 12:33). "The tradition of our ancestors" (Mark 7:5), which should been a jeweled setting to bring out the splendor of the word, has instead become a vice squeezing the life out of it. Jesus rejects "human tradition" (Mark 7:8) — "your traditions," he says to the Pharisees (Mark 7:9, 13) — because it nullifies the word of God (Mark 7:13).

The function of the prophets, as guardians of the word, had been to protect the purity of the message, to draw out its spiritual content, and to keep it from being mired in the shifting sands of human disputatiousness. Jesus continues this ministry. The tradition of the ancestors had been, as it were, the synagogue's memory as men examined the Scriptures. In the new order, the Spirit who scrutinizes the teaching of Jesus would act as the Church's memory.

2. "At the beginning"

More than a simple sweeping away of accumulated dust was needed; there had also to be a return to the sources. Not only did the "dust" stirred up by men have to be removed, but even the continued existence of certain laws, which had value only for a limited span of time, had to be challenged.

Divine revelation had been given in stages throughout the history of Israel; God had, as it were, adapted his revelation to that history. Laws had been given to fit in with the wanderings of God's people on their long journey in search in Christ. Some dispositions of the Law had been conceived as transitory, as simply smoothing the path that would lead to the "law of the Gospel." There was need, then, to prune the overgrown tree of Judaism, to lighten the yoke so as to make it easy to wear (Matthew 11:30), and to return to God's will as clearly revealed "at the beginning."

Take divorce, for example.[61] "At the beginning," that is, in God's intention, marriage was the loving union of two persons, each of whom was a complement to the other (Mark 10:6-9). If God, through his spokesman Moses, permitted divorce, this was only because of the "stubbornness" of men's hearts (Mark 10:5). Now that the messianic age is here, there must be a return to the original ideal: "The two shall become as one. . . . Therefore let no man separate what God has joined" (Mark 10:8-9). The permission to grant divorces had been meant only for a certain period within the history of salvation, and the evangelical law of monogamy expresses God's original intention.

Here is another example, taken this time from the laws governing the place where sacrifice might be offered. Originally, the whole earth is the domain where God exercises his universal lordship; there is no spot that cannot become a place of prayer and sacrifice. Thus Exod. 20:22-24 readily accepts a plurality of places for sacrifice: "In whatever place I choose for the remembrance of my name I will come to you and bless you" (Exod. 20:24).

The later legislation in Deut. 12:2-13 is more restrictive: "You shall resort to the place which the Lord, your God, chooses out of all your tribes and designates as his dwelling and there you shall bring your holocausts and sacrifices" (Deut. 12:5-6). Other places of worship are to be dismantled (Deut. 12:2-3). The point of these prescriptions is to foster Yahwism and to eliminate the particularist cults of the Canaanites; it is also to strengthen the political unity that is the object of the Josian reform.

Final stage: the legislation of Lev. 17, in the "Code of Legal Holiness," simply takes for granted and ratifies this law on offering all sacrifice at one place.

By this long process the Temple at Jerusalem has become the center where the entire world is to offer prayer and sacrifice.

The Gospel does away with the sacrificial system of the Old Testament. It does not deny that these sacrifices were valid in their time. They were quite valid to the extent that they gave outward expression to the soul's interior self-giving, for in the last analysis sacrifice did not consist of a victim offered or the immolation but of the victim's self-offering, that is, the interior sentiments of the person who presented himself to God. The principle concerning sacrifice applies to all men at all times.

The reason why the Gospel does away with the sacrifices of the Old Testament is that "by one offering he [Jesus] has forever perfected those who are being sanctified" (Heb. 10:14). The hour has come when neither on Mount Gerizim nor on Mount Zion will men worship the Father (cf. John 4:21). The heart of the believer is the only temple adequate to the demands of the new covenant, and it is precisely such worshipers "in Spirit and truth" that the Father wants (John 4:24).

The law about worshiping at Jerusalem had thus been useful in its day, but it was not intended as an eternal law. It was simply a bridge permitting men to pass from the law of Exod. 20:20-24 to the Gospel of John 4:21-24. Now that the messianic community has crossed and reached the New Testament side, it has no interest in turning back to the bridge and remaining on it. It respects the bridge simply as a memento of the past.

In turning in upon itself, and precisely because it had such a deep love for the word and for tradition, Judaism became entrenched in transitional positions and tried to stop the course of history. What rich memories the Jews had from two thousand years of history! They loved to repeat the words "our father Abraham" (John 8:39). They belonged to Abraham — but God belonged to Christ. Their tradition, the rich treasure of the past, had become barren and yielded no profit for the future. In Christ, on the other hand, tradition continues to be vitally alive in the present and is constantly going beyond itself. Is that not the purpose of every authentic tradition — to be the source of new life?

The removal of the dust and the return to the sources were indispensable, but by themselves they were not enough. Advancing to

the Gospel side of the bridge took more than a movement backward
to the beginnings. Even if the Old Testament had been cleared of
the debris left by men, and even if a spiritual interpretation and
obedience had replaced a literal interpretation and obedience, the
Old Testament could not, apart from Christ, have become the sole
rule of the messianic kingdom. Only in and with Christ could the
Law become the Gospel.

3. *"Not to abolish but to fulfill"*

To fulfill the Law means to make it achieve the perfection which
God wills. And what is this perfection? Love. "Love is the fulfillment of the law" (Rom. 13:10). That is to say, love sums up in itself
all the laws, makes them the instruments in which its own
dynamism finds its outlet, establishes a hierarchy among them, and
enables them all to reach the supreme goal. The essential purpose of
Christ's "legislation" was to assure love that kind of unqualified
primacy.

The basic, as well as the most richly meaningful, text is Matthew
5:17-48, a section of the Sermon on the Mount. In six antitheses
having to do with murder and anger (Matthew 5:21-26), adultery
and evil desire (5:27-30), divorce (5:31-32), oath-taking (5:33-37), the
law of talion (5:38-42), and love of enemies (5:43-48), Jesus (according to Matthew) "fulfills" the old Law and changes it into Gospel.

We may note that Matthew 5:17-48 does not have the internal
unity it seems to have at the literary level.[62] Evidently the "fulfill-
ments" are not all equally profound and important. Matthew has
here again given free rein to his enthusiasm for grouping things,
even for packing them in together. But even when allowances have
been made for this, the central message of the passage is that the
Jewish Law had to be transcended. The passage gives clear expression to a "radicalism" that attacks and finally overthrows the
Pharisaic tradition for the sake of the Gospel: "Unless your holiness
surpasses that of the scribes and Pharisees you shall not enter the
kingdom of God."[63]

The whole section begins with the statement: "Do not think that I
have come to abolish the law and the prophets. I have come, not to
abolish them, but to fulfill them" (Matthew 5:20).[64] This is one of
the "I have come" statements that describe the messianic coming of
Jesus, whom the Father sends.[65] Above all else, Jesus is "he who
comes." Thus, he is telling us that his actions in regard to the Law
and the Prophets are central to his messianic mission.

The verb *plēroun*, "fulfill," can have various senses. It can mean to "obey an order or commandment." Jesus "fulfills" the Law in this sense because he submits to it and thereby "fulfills all of God's demands" (Matthew 3:15). To "fulfill" can also mean to "carry out a promise or prophecy"; in this sense, too, Jesus "fulfills" the Law and the Prophets. Finally, "fulfill" can mean "bring to perfection," and this is the sense that concerns us here.[66]

These various senses are not mutually exclusive. Thus when Jesus says that he "fulfills" the Law, we can take him to mean that he brings it to its final perfection, but also that he perfectly observes it. A. Descamps rightly observes: "This is why *plēroun* (v. 17), which in itself means only 'to observe perfectly' (referring to fidelity to the Law), acquires a Christian sense and means an observance animated by a completely new spirit that is to be defined by the whole of the 'Gospel.' "[67]

Each of Jesus' six antitheses is introduced by this, or an equivalent, formula: "You have heard the commandment. . . . What I say to you is. . . . This is an absolutely extraordinary statement. The words "It was said" (the impersonal turn of phrase was used to avoid having to speak God's name) meant: "God said."[68] "You have heard" evokes memories of the solemn reading of the Law in the synagogal office and echoes the *Shema*,[69] which began with "Hear, O Israel" and in which the pious Israelite daily opened his heart in order to hear God's word. It is this holy and sacrosanct Law, haloed with the glory of Sinai and the miracles of the Exodus, that Jesus corrects with his own statements: "What I say to you is. . . ." This was the formula the rabbis used in making clear how their views differed from those of other rabbis; they would never have used it to contrast their own views with the Law, for that would have been sacrilegious. Nor would any prophet ever have dared to speak thus in his own name; the prophet's mission was simply to transmit God's word. What would have been sacrilege in others becomes for Jesus the proclamation of his messianic mission.

"Jesus' radicalism"[70] is directed, on the one hand, to the believer who is subject to the Law. The latter now sees that he will be judged, not by his outward act, but by his heart; man's heart is the center of moral action, and it is the first thing that must be converted to the Gospel. Jesus' radicalism is directed, on the other hand, to the Law itself. At the end of this section Jesus proposes as the supreme law the imitation of the loving Father: "You must be made perfect as your heavenly Father is perfect" (Matthew 5:48). In

Luke this becomes: "Be compassionate, as your Father is compassionate" (Luke 6:36). This is how the Gospel effects the "fulfillment of the Law" through love (Rom. 13:10).

Let us take an example. Everyone knew the "law" of vengeance as formulated in the ancient song of ferocious Lamech: "If Cain is avenged sevenfold, then Lamech seventy-sevenfold" (Gen. 4:24). The first impulse of one who is wronged is to seek "revenge," that is, to return the wrong with interest. Ill will lurks, like a savage beast, in man's heart. Now God intervenes by laying down a law that will impose restraints. The ancient law of talion limited revenge to repayment in kind: "Limb for limb, eye for eye, tooth for tooth!" (Lev. 24:20).[71] Thus, for a broken tooth, Leviticus allowed the injured party to break one tooth of the wrongdoer, but no more than this. The law of talion is a first, timid step toward the Gospel. The just man will even avoid taking vengeance and commit his case to God (cf. Jer. 11:20); it is up to the Lord to "avenge" him.

In the Gospel Jesus goes further. He rejects the law of talion, requires men not to resist the wicked (Matthew 5:38-42), and even asks them to love their enemies and pray for their persecutors. Forgiveness, moreover, must be granted without limit. When Peter asks how many times we must forgive, and generously suggests "seven times," Jesus answers: "No, not seven times; I say, seventy times seven times" (Matthew 18:22).

Here the old measure for revenge has become, in the new covenant, the measure for pardon. Or better, since the numbers here have no numerical value, the measure of forgiveness is to be without measure. Thus a great cycle has been completed that runs from Lamech to Jesus, from Genesis to the Gospel. We have reached the "fullness" of the Law.

It would be very unjust to say that the Old Testament did not know the law of love; that it thought in terms purely of external observance; that it was grounded solely in fear. Undoubtedly an obedience that is purely external and based on fear was always possible; but so is it possible in the new covenant! But "nowhere does the Old Testament define obedience simply as outward conformity."[72] When the scribe asks which is the first of the commandments, Jesus answers by reciting the beginning of the *Shema*: "This is the first: 'Hear, O Israel! The Lord our God is Lord alone! Therefore you shall love the Lord your God with all your heart, with all your soul, with all your mind, and with all your strength.' This is the second, 'You shall love your neighbor as yourself' " (Mark 12:29-30).

Upon this twofold commandment of love the whole Law is based, and the prophets as well (Matthew 22:40). This interpretation represents the attitude of Israel to the "Law." The scribe, who here embodies a Judaism after God's own heart and is "not far from the reign of God," offers his own comment: "Yes, 'to love him with all our heart, with all our thoughts and with all our strength, and to love our neighbor as ourself' is worth more than any burnt offering or sacrifice" (Mark 12:33-34)

But in what, then, does the newness consist which the Gospel contrasts with the "oldness" of the Israelite Law?

4. *The newness of the evangelical law*

The new element which transforms Law into Gospel is Jesus Christ himself. St. Irenaeus of Lyons writes: "What, then, did the Lord bring when he came? You must understand that he brought a total newness because he brought himself, the one who had been foretold."[73] The Incarnation creates a new, evangelical way of keeping the commandments. That way consists in living according to the grace of the Incarnation (in other words, living as a son of God), allowing the death and resurrection of the Lord to bear their fruit in us, letting ourselves be set on fire by that love of God which the Holy Spirit pours out in our hearts (cf. Rom. 5:5). Paul gives us a deep insight into this new way of life in which the whole of morality is based on Christ: "It was through the law that I died to the law, to live for God. I have been crucified with Christ, and the life I live now is not my own; Christ is living in me. I still live my human life, but it is a life of faith in the Son of God, who loved me and gave himself for me" (Gal. 2:19-20).[74]

We may take as an example the law of love for our neighbor. The prophetic[75] and sapiential[76] traditions always linked this love, especially when it was love for the poor, to love of God. And yet Jesus says: "I give you a *new* commandment: love one another; just as I have loved you, you also must love one another" (John 13:34 JB). In what sense is the commandment "new"? The answer is that the entire newness of Jesus' commandment is concentrated in the words "as I have loved you." How has Christ loved us? He "loved me and gave himself up for me" (Gal. 2:20). *That* is what is new — his giving himself up to death on the Cross for us in atonement for the sins of

men. The love expressed in this fashion now becomes the new norm
for our love of our neighbor. Between the faithful of the old covenant and the faithful of the new, God has set this wholly new thing
that transforms the moral activity of Christians — the death and
resurrection of his Son.

Let us take once again as an example the statement in the Sermon
on the Mount: "Be compassionate, as your Father is compassionate"
(Luke 6:36). The Old Testament knew, of course, that God is compassionate; in fact, the word is one God used in describing himself to
his people (Exod. 34:6). The Israelites also knew that God's compassion or mercy was that of a father for his children (cf. Ps. 103:13).
They knew, finally, the commandment concerning mercy, for the
very formula used in the Gospel comes directly from the Jewish
tradition.[77] The Gospel, therefore, cannot claim any originality as
far as the content of the Law is concerned, but the spirit is indeed
new. A new situation has been created by the Incarnation, because
in Jesus the Father's merciful love has taken human form. To be
merciful in the new covenant means to imitate the Father's giving of
himself in his Son (cf. John 3:16) and to allow the Son's life to change
one's own life into a life characterized by mercy. "Christ is living in
me" — *there* we have the newness of the Gospel.

The believer's life in Christ according to the Spirit means that a
threshold has been crossed and that the crossing was made possible
only by the grace of the Incarnation. The Old Testament, although it
prepared for Christ's coming, could not by its own inner dynamism
produce the miraculous presence of God's Son in a woman's womb.
Although it prepared for the outpouring of the Spirit in the messianic age, it could not by its own inner dynamism produce the
marvelous animation of mankind by the Spirit of Jesus. Nor could it,
despite all its innate power to bear fruits of holiness, transform the
Israelite Law into the evangelical law; only the grace of the Incarnation could do that. With Christ's coming, a threshold is crossed, a
renewal and transformation takes place. The preparation made by
the old covenant, with all its inner riches, with its source of joy and
its reasons for lament, could only lead men to the threshold of the
new covenant. The unity of Scripture, which is due in part to its
perpetual renewals at ever higher levels, derives in the last analysis
from its single movement toward Christ. But it could not produce
Christ. Only a new intervention of the Spirit could do that.

In the new covenant, then, the letter of the old Law may be

retained, but it is also transformed and made new by the Spirit. The text remains, but in Jesus it takes on a higher meaning. "Jesus Christ does not so much explain the Old Testament as he transforms it. Or, more accurately, he explains it only after having transformed it. Just as his death, followed by his resurrection, effects the passage to the new covenant, so it transfigures the book in which the old covenant had been taught to men."[78]

5. A new law?

Did Jesus, then, proclaim a new law, a *nova lex*?

By emphasizing the newness of the Gospel as expressed especially in polemical situations, but in poetic contexts as well, Christians have been able to maintain that the Gospel is indeed a "new" law promulgated in opposition to that of Judaism.[79] Both the Law of Moses and the law of the Gospel are daughters of God, and their role is to serve as guides for God's people on the journey to the kingdom. But the elder daughter's role as "monitor" ceased once the community met the Messiah: "Christ is the end of the law" (Rom. 10:4).

Others, however, insist on the vital continuity between the two covenants and strongly disagree with the idea that Jesus gave us a "new" law. "The law which holds in the Church is identical with the 'law and the prophets.' Hence the Moses typology can only be intended to confirm the teaching of Jesus as authentic teaching from Sinai."[80]

As a matter of fact, the question whether or not the law is "new" is an ambiguous one. Everything depends on the meaning given to the terms "new" and "law."

"New" implies a relation to something else. One and the same law can be new in relation to an earlier law and old in relation to a later law. Thus, speaking of the Lord's commandment, St. John can say: "Dearly beloved, it is no new commandment that I write to you, but an old one which you had from the start. . . . On second thought the commandment that I write you is new" (1 John 2:7-8). It is possible, then, to speak of a new law when a law has simply been reasserted; in speaking thus, one would say nothing about the degree or depth of the renewal involved.

The term "law," too, can have several meanings. It may mean the whole of Scripture, or simply the Pentateuch,[81] or the Decalogue (cf. Rom. 5:13), or a basic requirement of God's will (cf. Gal. 5:3), or, finally, "the human institution which the Jewish people created: a legalist religion, with the help of which the Jews thought they could win salvation."[82] We shall take "law" here to mean the expression of the divine will. God's will may be expressed either in "eternal" laws (for example, the basic requirement to do good and avoid evil) or in "pedagogical" (*paidagogos*, a Greek word, means "leading a child") laws (cf. Gal. 3:24), that is, the laws which, during the provisional period of the old covenant, were to lead mankind to Christ.[83]

There is a sense in which we can say that Christ brought no new law. He simply brought the "old" law, as an expression of God's will, to its ultimate fulfillment by a developmental process. We mean a process similar to that which leads from flower to fruit or from childhood to adult maturity. The fruit is "new," of course, by comparison with the flower, but it is also part of the same developmental process that first produced the flower. The adult is "new" in relation to the child, but both are one and the same human person.

The temporary character of certain Old Testament laws (among the "pedagogical" laws) is not due to any special weakness in them. It is not weakness that makes a flower don the splendid clothing of a flower or that makes a child have a child's bright smile. The temporary character is due rather to the transcendent perfection of Christ. We no longer celebrate the Old Testament sacrifices because the perfection of the one sacrifice of Christ throws all others into the shadow and eliminates them. We no longer practice the restraint urged in the law of talion because Christ requires us to go much further and love our enemies with a love like that which the Father bestows upon all men. We no longer observe the prescriptions set down in Leviticus for the sacristans of the time because worship in spirit and truth can do without such ceremonial. We do not rebuild the Temple of Jerusalem because the presence of the God who dwells in the heart of each believer and is to be found wherever two or three brothers are gathered in his name is not limited to a building of stone at Jerusalem or Rome or anyplace else. We do not have to restore the Davidic royal line or the Levitical priesthood because Christ, who is both King and Priest, calls all men to form a Church, a kingly and priestly people.

Without indulging in paradox, we may say that the ultimate purpose of every law is to eliminate all laws and replace them with love. "If you are guided by the Spirit," Paul writes, "you are not under the law" (Gal. 5:18). All law, and especially the new law, tends by its inner dynamism toward a world that is animated by the Spirit. "The so-called *new law* is *new* only when it is no longer a law but the play of love which does the right whenever it does as it will." [84]

IV. ACTUALIZATION OF THE GOSPELS

The Old Testament announces Jesus and describes beforehand his life and his message of salvation. The messianic community writes down the life and message, with its eyes on the ancient Scriptures and its mind attentive to the living Spirit who is its memory (cf. John 14:26). A "new" Scripture is thus obtained that actualizes the message of the Old Testament. The new Scriptures— the "Gospels"—were composed to meet missionary needs and are now in their turn actualized by the Christian community as it celebrates the life and message of the dead and risen Christ.

Actualization of the Scriptures is a vital part of the whole biblical tradition, and the coming of Christ has not put an end to it. For Christ is contemporary with all generations: "I am with you always, until the end of the world" (Matthew 28:20). He is present in all the Old Testament preparations for his coming: "The writings of Moses are words of Christ." [85] He is present in a properly historical way during the time of his earthly life, when he walked the dusty roads of Galilee with his disciples, was nailed to the Cross, and rose from the dead. He continues to be present in a mystical but very real way in the midst of the world through his Church.

The Gospel is not a diary of the past. Or, more accurately, on the ancient historical events which remain forever the historical basis of its faith, the Christian community bases its celebration of Christ for the sake of the today in which the community lives. It listens to his word as if Christ were speaking today; it is present at his miracles and plays a part in them through faith as if Christ were performing those miracles right now. "For the Christians of the first generations — and for us Christians of today — the proclamation of the Good News was not a simple recall of past events, but a memorial of the Lord's deeds and actions and a celebration of the Christ who is constantly present in the ecclesial community." [86]

We can distinguish, therefore, a historical dimension, in which Jesus says certain words and works certain miracles, and a suprahistorical dimension, in which Jesus speaks to the Christian communities of every generation.

1. The Lord's discourses

The actualization goes on in different areas. The most obvious is that of the discourses. Men realized that the Lord's words were heavy with infinity (cf. John 6:67) and that they were far more lasting than the heavens and the earth (cf. Matthew 24:35). The community therefore made it a special point to collect the sayings in which the Lord was addressing not just his immediate hearers but the men of every time.[87] Here are some examples.

Matthew is outstanding in this regard. His mastery of the sources enables him to put the message of the kingdom into five lengthy discourses.[88] These five discourses, which contain the new law, may in his mind have corresponded to the five books of the Pentateuch, in which the old Law was contained.

Mark, though he does not go in much for discourses, could not avoid recording the parables (4:1-34). This "discourse by the lake" evidently goes beyond the primitive elements corresponding to strict historical fact.[89] In his section on the Galilean ministry he groups together five controversies (2:1–3:6), to which correspond five controversies during the Judean period (11:27-33 and 12:13-37).

Luke has put together, in the "long interpolation" or "Perean section" of his Gospel (9:51–18:14), a number of booklets of a catechetical nature in which the words of Jesus on a given subject are grouped.[90] These little collections were undoubtedly part of the pre-synoptic Gospel and were carefully brought together by the evangelist (cf. Luke 1:3).

The purpose of these various groupings of Jesus' words is evident: they are a way of actualizing his preaching in terms of the community that will read a given Gospel.

2. The Lord's deeds and actions

The deeds and actions of the Lord are also meant to be actualized. "Christ is living in me" (Gal. 2:20): Paul's cry is witness to the certainty that the Christian's life is bound up with the life of Jesus. To express the mysterious presence of Jesus in the hearts of his followers, the Apostle strains words to make them express the inexpressible. He even invents the verbs he needs by prefixing to them the preposition *syn-* (= with): the Christian suffers *with* Christ (Rom. 8:17; 1 Cor. 12:26), is crucified *with* him (Rom 6:6; Gal. 2:19), dies *with* him (2 Tim. 2:11), is buried *with* him (Rom. 6:4; Col. 2:12), rises *with* him (Eph. 2:6; cf. Col. 2:12 and 3:1), lives *with* him

(Rom. 6:8; 2 Tim. 2:11), is given new life *with* him (Eph. 2:5; Col. 2:13), is transformed into his image (Phil. 3:10), is glorified *with* him (Rom. 8:17), and reigns *with* him (Eph. 2:6; 2 Tim. 2:12). It is quite natural, therefore, that when the Christian reads the story of Jesus in the Gospels, he should discover his own story there as well.

Such actualization, profound though it may be, depends more on theological reflection[91] than on an analysis of the straightforward data of the Gospels. Here, however, we are interested rather in a kind of actualization of the deeds and actions of Christ that is written into the very texture of the Gospel narratives.

How is such an actualization to be disclosed at the level of the texts themselves? As is well known, the pericopes of the Gospels may represent quite varied redactional stages. The diversity may be due to their origin (who wrote the text? what milieu influenced the writing?), or their addressee (for whom was it intended?), or the date of redaction (at what period was it written?), or many other factors that depended on the free human beings of whom God made use and for whose initiative he had unlimited respect. For example, a story in Mark, showing little theological development, may be an echo of Peter's catechesis and may have been written very close to the event, while a discourse of Jesus in John may be rather distant from the historical event it represents. For the sake of clarity, we say that Mark sticks closely to the events, while John, in writing down the discourses of Jesus, combines his memories with his own faith-inspired meditation and with the theology of the milieu in which he writes.[92]

When the evangelists narrate the same facts and events, the differences between them are valuable to us because they reflect, as in a mirror, the faith of the communities involved. They show how this or that community read the account, appropriated it for their own use, and actualized it to meet their own needs. Let us look at some examples.

a) Cure of Simon's mother-in-law: Matthew 8:14-15; Mark 1:29-31; Luke 4:38-39

Jesus goes to Simon's house. Simon, originally from nearby Bethsaida (John 1:44), had come to live in his mother-in-law's house at Capernaum. Jesus already knew the house, for Capernaum had now become "his own town" (Matthew 9:1), a phrase which, in the usage of the time, suggests that he had been living there for at least a year. Jesus and Peter are accompanied by Andrew, James, and

John. Add these to Peter's mother-in-law and probably his wife and children as well, and you have a lot of people in and around Simon's house. The mother-in-law has been confined to bed. Luke diagnoses a severe fever (an attack of malaria, we would call it today). Jesus cures her. She gets up and immediately sets about serving her guests.

These are the basic facts which Peter may have narrated in his memoirs and which Mark tells us in a short account: "Immediately upon leaving the synagogue, he entered the house of Simon and Andrew with James and John. Simon's mother-in-law lay ill with a fever, and the first thing they did was to tell him about her. He went over to her and grasped her hand and helped her up, and the fever left her. She immediately began to wait on them" (Mark 1:29-31).

Luke's account is the same, in its broad lines, as Mark's (Luke 4:38-39). He does not mention the presence of Andrew, James, and John, whose calling by Jesus he will recount only later on (5:1-10). The omission has the advantage of clearing the scene and focusing attention on the chief person in it — Jesus. Luke observes that Jesus "leaned over her" (4:39 JB), in a gesture of kindness and solicitude. Luke also notes that Jesus "rebuked" the fever (4:39 JB). "Rebuke" (*epitimān*: to rebuke, censure, warn, threaten) is part of Luke's vocabulary (twelve occurrences against six in Mark and nine in Matthew), and we may assume that he introduced the verb into the account as he received it.

On two occasions the Synoptics connect the verb "rebuke (threaten)" with an exorcism. When Jesus expels the unclean spirit in the synagogue at Capernaum, he "rebuked him sharply: 'Be quiet! Come out of the man!' At that the unclean spirit convulsed the man violently and with a loud shriek came out of him" (Mark 1:25-26; cf. Luke 4:35). In the same fashion, when Jesus cures an epileptic boy, he "reprimanded the unclean spirit by saying to him, 'Mute and deaf spirit, I command you: Get out of him and never enter him again!' " (Mark 9:25; cf. Luke 9:42; Matthew 17:18).

The overtones of this verb should not be forgotten when we find it used in the curing of Simon's mother-in-law. Sickness, as the Bible sees it, is associated with the powers hostile to God. Jesus "expelled the spirits by a simple command and cured all who were afflicted" (Matthew 8:16). Here, in Simon's house, he threatens the fever in the same way that he threatens evil spirits. In pushing back the frontiers of suffering and death, he is enlarging the boundaries of the kingdom. Thus, far from being simply a kind act of Jesus on behalf of the future pope's in-laws, this cure is a powerful statement that "the kingdom of God is here!"

Matthew's account is, theologically speaking, the most developed of the three (8:14-15). To begin with, Jesus enters "Peter's house," for just as Mark likes to give Jesus the title "Lord," Matthew likes to give Simon the name "Peter," the name which Jesus had given him and by which he was known in the early community. Like Luke, Matthew omits mention of Andrew, James, and John as negligible supernumeraries. But in Matthew the omission of the mention of secondary personages is almost systematically done: "Jesus alone: that seems to be the rule for Matthew's narratives."[93]

Secondly, we will recall that in Mark the apostles intervene on behalf of the mother-in-law. We can almost hear them saying: "Rabbi, the mother-in-law cannot receive you; she is in bed with a fever." In Matthew, Jesus does not need anyone to tell him she is ill (he knows everything!). Here again, we have a Matthean principle: Jesus never asks questions which might suggest that he is less than omniscient.[94]

Thirdly, according to Mark, Jesus goes over to the mat where the sick woman is lying, takes her by the hand, and helps her up. According to Matthew, however, he simply touches (*hēpsato*) her hand. In the same way he touches the leper (Matthew 8:3 par.), the eyes of the blind (Matthew 9:29), the tongue of the deaf-mute (Mark 7:33). The gesture is equivalent to an imposition of hands. In Mark 10:13 we read that people brought their children to Jesus "to have him touch them," but Matthew 19:13 tells us it was "so that he could place his hands on them in prayer."

Fourthly, in Matthew as in Mark the sick woman immediately gets up. The verb used for her action, *egeirein*, is the verb used for resurrection: the mother-in-law gets up as though she were rising from the dead!

Finally, Mark ends his account by saying: "She immediately began to wait on them." The verb *diakonein* can mean to wait on table or perform some other material service. Thus the women of whom Luke speaks in 8:2-3 *served* Jesus and the Twelve, and assisted them with what goods they had. Martha busied herself with many things in order to *serve* Jesus. The same is true of the mother-in-law. We can almost hear her saying: "Good! Now I'll give you something to eat." But the verb *diakonein* can also mean the spiritual service of God. In this sense Jesus came not to be served but to *serve* (Matthew 20:28 par.). The spiritual sense is not excluded in the present passage of Matthew. In any case, he departs once again from Mark by saying that "she got up at once and began to serve *him*," that is, Jesus.

In the light of these various details we can ask: What meaning is Matthew trying to make us see in this event?

> In the account of the sick woman whom Jesus cures and who then "rises up" to serve him, the community could see the story of the grace they themselves had received: Jesus had cured them of their sins, and they then began to serve him. Thus, the story of a cure becomes in Matthew a symbol of the history of salvation.[95]

After this detailed analysis of the text, let us look at the *context* of our pericope.

Mark integrates the cure of the mother-in-law into a literary whole which we might entitle "the day at Capernaum." The day includes: (a) Jesus' teaching in the synagogue, on the sabbath, "with authority, and not like the scribes" (Mark 1:21-22); (b) the cure of a demoniac, in which Jesus, "the holy One of God," confronts "an unclean spirit" (Mark 1:23-28); (c) the cure of Simon's mother-in-law (Mark 1:29-31); and (d) when evening comes, many cures and expulsions of demons (Mark 1:32-34).

From a literary viewpoint, the connection between these various pericopes is only superficial. No claim is made that the linking represents a historical connection between events. In fact "'the day at Capernaum' is a theological construction."[96] But it does act as a powerful confirmation of the message which is prefixed to this entire section and which, in Mark, is the first word Jesus speaks: "This is the time of fulfillment. The reign of God is at hand! Reform your lives and believe in the gospel!" (Mark 1:15).

The message is meant for all men of all times. For Mark, all men become hearers of Jesus. In his first chapter the evangelist shows mankind how this voice which will dominate the ages began to preach the Good News.

The context in Matthew, as we would expect from so fine a catechist, is more complex. In 9:35 Matthew gives a summation which forms an inclusion with that of 4:23 and makes a literary unit of the whole section therein embraced. The two summaries are almost identical:

Matthew 4:23	*Matthew 9:35*
Jesus toured	Jesus continued his tour
all of Galilee.	of all the towns and villages.
He taught in their synagogues,	He taught in their synagogues,

proclaimed	he proclaimed
the good news of the kingdom,	the good news of God's reign,
and cured the people	and he cured
of every disease and illness.	every sickness and disease.

In between we find two sections which illustrate the summations: (a) Jesus taught: Matthew 5–7, the Sermon on the Mount; and (b) Jesus cured: Matthew 8–9, the narrative section which deals chiefly with cures. But these two sections, 5–7 and 8–9, are themselves part of a larger composition which can be diagrammed as follows:

A	Imprisonment of John the Baptist (4:12)
B	Call of the first disciples and promise to send them out (4:18-21)
C	Summation: Jesus taught and cured (4:23)
D	Jesus taught: Sermon on the Mount (5–7)
D^1	Jesus cured: Narrative section (8–9)
C^1	Summation: Jesus taught and cured (9:35)
B^1	Fulfillment of promise: sending of the disciples (10:2)
A^1	Message from John the Baptist: Are you the Messiah? (11:3)

What of the mother-in-law? She comes at an especially important point in this whole composition — after the proclamation of the charter of the kingdom (in the Sermon on the Mount) and in the first cycle of miracles, in which Jesus cures a leper, a pagan, and a woman. "Jesus is gathering his messianic assembly. The first members of this holy and healed people are not the Pharisees and teachers of the law, who thought of themselves as the first to be invited by their very office. No, the first are a leper, a pagan officer, and a woman — three people who had hardly any standing in the eyes of the jurists." [97] That is how Jesus fulfills the prophecy concerning the Servant of Yahweh, which is cited right at the end of this section on the three miracles: "It is our infirmities he bore, our sufferings he endured" (Matthew 8:17 = Is. 53:4).

This more profound reading of the cure of Simon's mother-in-law is not an isolated instance. On every page of the Gospels we find the faith of the community transforming the Gospel stories into a history of salvation. An especially important area, in this respect, is that of the petitions and professions of faith addressed to the Jesus of history by persons in the Gospels. These become prayers to the Christ of faith and proclamations of his divinity.

b) The calming of the storm: Matthew 8:23-27; Mark 4:35-41; Luke 8:22-25

We will recall how precisely Mark "films" for us certain details of the scene: They took him, "just as he was" (Mark 4:36 JB), in the boat with them. A bad squall blew up; the waves kept breaking over the boat, and the boat began to ship water. Jesus was asleep "on a cushion" in the stern, and they woke him up: "Teacher, does it not matter to you that we are going to drown?" (Mark 4:38). The anxious question is reproachful.

Matthew thinks he cannot retain the question in this form, and so he turns it into an almost liturgical prayer: "Lord, save us! We are lost!" (Matthew 8:25). "Lord" is the title of the risen Christ. "Save us" and "We are lost" can have a double meaning: "Save us from the waves that threaten to drown us" and "Save us for your kingdom." In other storms, Matthew's Church will be able to take this prayer and actualize it in their present need.

c) The walking of Jesus on the water: Matthew 14:22-33; Mark 6:45-52

The account is quite similar to the preceding. The disciples' boat "was being tossed about in the waves" (Matthew 14:24). Seeing Jesus walking toward them on the water, they are terrified and cry out, "It is a ghost!" Matthew 14:28-31 introduces into the story an episode involving Peter, who tries to walk on the water himself. The point of the episode that catches the reader's attention is the Apostle's prayer: "Lord, if it is really you. . . . Lord, save me!" (Matthew 14:28, 30).

Here is how the story ends in Matthew and Mark:

Matthew 14:32-33	*Mark 6:51-52*
Once they had climbed into the boat, the wind died down. Those who were in the boat showed him reverence, declaring: "Beyond doubt you are the Son of God."	He got into the boat with them and the wind died down. They were taken aback by these happenings, for they had not understood about the loaves. On the contrary, their minds were completely closed.

Mark is rather hard on the disciples. As is his custom, he emphasizes their failure to understand:[98] literally, "their hearts were hardened," that is, as we would put it today, their minds were closed. In Matthew's account the disciples are notably more understanding and seem to have grasped the mystery of Jesus. They prostrate themselves before him; the verb Matthew uses, *proskynein*, means to prostrate oneself in adoration, and it is a verb Matthew likes to put into his narratives.[99] Then the disciples assert their faith: "Beyond doubt you are the Son of God!" In other circumstances too the faithful might prostrate themselves before Christ and adore him as Son of God.[100]

Yet here, in 14:33, at this point in the Gospel of Matthew, the profession of faith in the divinity of Jesus comes rather unexpectedly. Two chapters later (16:15), moreover, Jesus will ask the disciples: "And you, who do you say that I am?" They could have answered: "Lord, we have already told you!" and Matthew could have then added ("See chapter 14"). But Matthew is not, on that account, a mere victim of the procedure which projects onto the earthly Jesus the later statements made of the Christ of faith. He knows that any future community which receives Jesus into its boat can acclaim him as Lord, and be saved thereby.

d) Peter's profession of faith: Matthew 16:13-20; Mark 8:27-30; Luke 9:18-21

Peter's profession of faith at Caesarea is recorded in several ways. Mark 8:29 has the shortest text; Peter's answer is simply: "You are the Messiah!" Luke 9:20 has an archaic formula that may be earlier than Mark's: "[You are] the Messiah of God," that is, the Messiah sent by God. Matthew 16:16 offers the formula that is the most complete, theologically speaking, and reflects a more mature tradition: "You are the Messiah, the Son of the living God."

e) The paralytic at Capernaum: Matthew 9:1-8; Mark 2:1-12; Luke 5:17-28

As is his habit, Matthew has once again pruned the original account; he has even risked shortening it to the point where it might become unintelligible. He keeps the words: "When Jesus saw their faith he said to the paralytic" (9:2), but the scene is less clear, for he has omitted mention of the four men who carried the sick man, of their climbing onto the roof of the house, making an opening in it, and lowering the sick man down in front of Jesus. We have to read Mark 2:2-4 or Luke 5:18-19 to see how the faith of the four played a role. And yet Matthew's account is of great value for the conclusion of this episode in which Jesus cures the sick man while forgiving his sins.

Here is the ending as Mark has it: "The man stood and picked up his mat and went outside in the sight of everyone. They were awe-struck; all gave praise to God, saying: 'We have never seen anything like this'" (Mark 2:12).

The parallel passage in Luke emphasizes the praise (a favorite theme of the Third Gospel). Rather than have the people say they had never seen anything like this, he has them say: "We have seen incredible things today!" The statement is a more positive one and offers a new subject for praise to the glory of Jesus: "At once the man stood erect before them. He picked up the mat he had been lying on and went home praising God. At this they were all seized with astonishment. Full of awe, they gave praise to God, saying, 'We have seen incredible things today!' " (Luke 5:25-26).

Here, finally, is Matthew's version: "The man stood up and went toward his home. At the sight, a feeling of awe came over the crowd, and they praised God for giving such authority to men" (9:7-8).

God had given "such authority to men": because to forgive sins is possible for God alone. But that power, after the Lord's resurrection, was given to the community itself (cf. Matthew 18:18; John 20:23). Until the parousia, the community continues this work of divine forgiveness and healing that Jesus exemplified in his cure of the paralytic. This is why, when it reads this account and celebrates this miracle, the community today glorifies God "for giving such authority to men."

f) Luke's narrative of the Passion

Let us take as our last example the Passion narrative. According to Matthew 27:46 and Mark 15:34, Jesus dies in an utter aloneness that is as mysterious as that of the persecuted just man of Psalm 22, "My God, my God, why have you forsaken me?" He dies with an inarticulate cry (Matthew 27:50; Mark 15:37), so frightening that Luke has not preserved mention of it for his readers. Luke, as we know, does not like distressing scenes. He prefers to emphasize rather the messianic joy which enters the world with Christ, despite all the latter's sufferings. Therefore he omits mention of Psalm 22, which is the prayer of a man who feels forsaken, and reveals another facet of the Passover mystery in Psalm 31 (Ps. 31:6 = Luke 23:46). Now Jesus dies after commending himself to his Father's tender love: "Father, into your hands I commend my spirit."

The ascent to Calvary, under blows from the soldiers and insults from the Pharisaic rabble, becomes in Luke the first "way of the Cross" of the Christian community. For the community is present at the scene, part of the "great crowd of people . . . including women" (Luke 23:27) who followed him and shared his distress. Even the solitude of the Cross is filled with the presence of "all his friends and the women who had accompanied him from Galilee" (Luke 23:49).[101] To the good thief he speaks words which every Christian would like to hear when his turn comes to die: "I assure you: this day you will be with me in paradise" (Luke 23:43). Jesus' death is a direct promise of eternal life; at the same time it is a model for how every upright person should die. That, certainly, is how the centurion understands it: "Surely this was an innocent man." (Luke 23:47).

We can see the model at work in the death of Stephen, the first martyr of the Christian community. His stoning is bathed, as it were, in the light of the dying Jesus' prayer, as though Christ were present at this moment. "He fell to his knees" (as Jesus did in Gethsemani: Luke 22:41) and prayed:

Acts 7:59–60	Luke 23:46, 34
Lord Jesus,	Father,
	into your hands
receive my spirit.	I commend my spirit.
Lord,	Father,
do not hold this sin	forgive them; they do not know
against them.	what they are doing.

It is possible, therefore, to actualize the Passion of Christ.[102] Stephen does it up to and including death. His dying prayer is that of the dying Christ.

Without at all wishing to give excessive importance to the results of our study, we can surely say that a reading of the Gospel story which would make it purely and simply a historical record would not do full justice to the text. A reading that determines just what the text explicitly says is, of course, an absolute necessity. The saving event is, after all, part of history, and history is part of the object of faith. But this very reading of what the text explicitly says shows us that the faith of the community plays a part in the redaction, appropriating the text for its own use and actualizing it to meet present needs.

The examples given, which are based on an analysis of different redactional stages, allow us to see the process of actualization at work in other passages as well. With the leper the community prays: "Sir [*Kyrie* = Lord], if you will to do so, you can cure me" (Matthew 8:2). With the centurion it implores him: "Sir [Lord], I am not worthy to have you under my roof. Just give an order. . . ." (Mat-

thew 8:8).[103] With the Canaanite woman it petitions the merciful
Lord: "Lord, Son of David, have pity on me. . . . Help me, Lord!"
(Matthew 15:22, 25). With the father of the epileptic boy it asks: "I
do believe! Help my lack of trust!" (Mark 9:24). With blind Bar-
timaeus on the road to Jericho it cries out: "Jesus, Son of David,
have pity on me!" (Mark 10:47). With the disciples it acclaims Jesus:
"Hosanna to the Son of David! Blessed is he who comes in the name
of the Lord!" (Matthew 21:9). "Peace in heaven and glory in the
highest!" (Luke 19:38).

In all these texts the words of Jesus are fulfilled: "I am with you
always, until the end of the world" (Matthew 28:20). "A worthy
ending to the Gospel, and the most beautiful in the four lives of
Jesus preserved for us by ecclesiastical tradition."[104] Indeed, for it
shows us that the Gospels are only beginning at the point when
Jesus leaves his disciples.

[1] Justin Martyr was the first to apply the term "Gospel" to the evangelical writings
(in his *Apology*, 66, written around the middle of the second century).

[2] G. Friedrich, "euaggelion," *TDNT* 2:731.

[3] On these opening verses of Hebrews cf. A. Vanhoye, *Situation du Christ* (Lectio
divina 58; Paris, 1969), pp. 9–17, 51–61.

[4] Cf. Vatican II, *Dogmatic Constitution on Divine Revelation*, no. 4: "The Christian economy, therefore, since it is the new and definite covenant, will never pass
away; and no new public revelation is to be expected before the glorious manifestation of our Lord, Jesus Christ" (Flannery, p. 752).

[5] Mark's notation in 7:19: "Thus did he render [i.e., declare] all foods clean,"
shows how bold Jesus was in this matter. The reaction of Peter in Acts 10:9-48 shows
how hesitant the apostles were to follow the example of Jesus.

[6] Cf. P. Grelot, *Le Bible, Parole de Dieu* (Paris, 1965), pp. 239–41; X. Léon-
Dufour, *The Gospels and the Jesus of History*, translated and edited by J. McHugh
(New York, 1968), pp. 274–76.

[7] This is the title of H. Conzelmann's book on St. Luke: *Die Mitte der Zeit*
(Tübingen, 1954). [In English: *The Theology of St. Luke*, translated by G. Buswell
(New York, 1961).]

[8] The dialogue between Jesus and John in Matthew 3:14-15 is almost certainly
supplied by Matthew, who tells us in this way that, although Jesus submits to baptism
by John, he is nonetheless superior to John.

[9] G. Bornkamm, *Jesus of Nazareth*, translated by I. and F. McLusky with J.M.
Anderson (New York, 1960), p. 56.

[10] Cf. O. Michel, "Jesus der Jude," in *Der historische Jesus und der kerygmatische
Christus* (Berlin, 1961), pp. 310–16.

[11] Cf. Strack-Billerbeck, *op. cit.*, 2:438.

[12] Cf. F. Gils, *Jésus prophète d'après les évangiles synoptiques* (Orientalia et Biblica Lovaniensia 2; Louvain, 1957). On the titles of the Lord and their religious
significance, cf. L. Sabourin, *The Names and Titles of Jesus: Themes of Biblical
Theology*, translated by M. Carroll (New York, 1967); O. Cullmann, *The Christology*

of the New Testament, translated by S.C. Guthrie, and C.A.M. Hall (revised edition; Philadelphia, 1963).

[13] The apocalyptic genre was held in high esteem in later Judaism, as is evident from the *Book of Enoch*, the *Book of Jubilees*, the *Testaments of the Twelve Patriarchs*, and the *Sibylline Oracles*, to name but a few that seem pre-Christian. Cf. J.-B. Frey, "Apocalyptique," *DBS* 1:326–54; P. Grelot, "Le Messie dans les Apocryphes de l'Ancien Testament: Etat de la question," in *La venue du Messie: Messianisme et eschatologie* (Recherches bibliques 6; Bruges, 1962), pp. 19–50.

[14] Jesus "argues against the idea that the Messiah must be of the physical lineage of David. . . . The Messiah whom David calls his Lord must be greater than David" (O. Cullmann, *op. cit.*, p. 131). On the title "Son of David," cf. E. Lohmeyer, *Gottesknecht und Davidssohn* (2nd ed.; Göttingen, 1953), especially pp. 64–84; B. van Iersel, "Fils de David et Fils de Dieu," in *La venue du Messie*, pp. 113–32.

[15] As a matter of fact, in the Gospels Jesus never applies the title to himself: "Quite apart from the word, it is striking that the cultus and the figure of the priest are found so little in the sayings of Jesus. Jesus does not call either Himself (cf. Ps. 110 and Mt. 22:44) or His disciples priests" (G. Schrenk, "hiereus," *TDNT* 3:263). O. Cullmann, however, on the basis of Psalm 110, which Christ cites in Mark 12:36 and 14:62, observes with good reason: "We cannot conclude from Jesus' critical attitude toward the priesthood that he therefore would not have included the idea of the High Priest in his conception of his task. . . . Jesus considered it his task to fulfill the priestly office" (*op. cit.*, pp. 87–89). On this whole question, cf. A. Feuillet, *The Priesthood of Christ and His Ministers*, translated by M.J. O'Connell (New York, 1975), especially pp. 19–120.

[16] The old eschatological hymn which Luke has used in the canticle of Zechariah still thinks of salvation as rescue "from our enemies and from the hands of all our foes" (1:71).

[17] Luke's text plays on the name "Jesus," which means "savior" (2:30).

[18] Cf. R. de Vaux, *Ancient Israel*, pp. 103–6 (anointing of kings) and p. 347 (anointing of priests).

[19] Cf. 2 Sam. 7:14; 1 Chron. 22:10; Pss. 2:7; 89:27 (the king); Wis. 2:15-18; Sir. 4:10 (the just man). On the divine sonship, cf. J. Lebreton, "Jésus-Christ," *DBS* 4:1025–34; G. Fohrer, "huios," *TDNT* 8:349–53; P. Benoit, "Jesus' Divinity in the Synoptic Gospels," in *Son and Saviour*, translated by A. Wheaton (Baltimore, 1960). pp. 50–85. [A translation of *Lumière et vie*, no. 9 (1953).]

[20] Origen, *Commentaria in Matthaeum* 14:7 (*PG* 13:1197B). K.L. Schmidt cites, along with Origen, a text from Marcion which Tertullian has preserved in his *Adversus Marcionem*, IV, 33, 8: "The kingdom of God is Christ himself (*Dei regnum, Christus ipse*)." But the text as such is not certain, since the words *Christus ipse* come from another line (cf. *CCL* 1:634). Cf. also M. Albertz, *Botschaft des Neuen Testaments* I/1 (Zürich, 1947), p. 170: "The Gospel is Christ himself."

[21] Cf. 1 John 1:16-17. Cf. M./E. Boismard, *St. John's Prologue*, pp. 133–45.

[22] The heresy of Marcion was to reject the Old Testament without any qualification. He was excommunicated in June, 144. The Church has in fact always had to defend itself against this insidious heresy, since some of the faithful, while accepting the Old Testament in principle, ignore it in practice and thus behave — materially — like Marcionists.

[23] Cf. J. Dupont, *Etudes sur les Actes des Apôtres* (Lectio divina 45; Paris, 1967), pp. 50–54. On the biblical background of the discourse, cf. A.-M. Dubarle, "Le discours de l'Aréopage," *Recherches de science philosophique et théologique* 57 (1973), pp. 576–610.

[24] We might say that the first example seems to fit the mind of the redactor of Mark's Gospel, the second that of Matthew. (Yet we should bear in mind that Mark too uses the argument from prophecy, especially in the account of the Passion; cf. L. Deiss, *Synopse* 1:38.)

[25] The pattern of the prayer in Dan. 3:24-45 is also found in Neh. 9:5-39 and in the Psalms of national lament, such as Pss. 79:1-5; 89:47-52.

[26] On the theme of "possessing the earth," cf. J. Guillet, *Themes of the Bible*, pp. 191–206.

[27] Vatican II, *Dogmatic Constitution on Divine Revelation*, no. 14 (Flannery, p. 759).

[28] P. Grelot, *La Bible, Parole de Dieu*, p. 256.

[29] Pascal, *Pensées*, fr. 205 (New York, 1958), p. 200.

[30] *Commentaria in Isaiam Prophetam, Prologus (PL* 24:17B).

[31] X. Léon-Dufour, preface to C.H. Dodd, *Conformément aux Ecritures* (Paris, 1968), p. 12. [This is a translation of *According to the Scriptures: The Sub-Structure of New Testament Theology* (London, 1952).]

[32] Pascal, *Pensées*, fr. 757 (New York, 1958), p. 257.

[33] Cf. J. Kremer, *Das älteste Zeugnis von der Auferstehung Christi: Eine bibel-theologische Studie zur Aussage und Bedeutung von 1 Kor. 15, 1-11* (3rd ed.; Stuttgart, 1970). The words "the third day" are not intended as a chronological notation but are part of a theological statement about the salutary character of the event (with a probable allusion to Hos. 6:2); cf. K. Lehmann, *Auferweckt am dritten Tag nach der Schrift: Früheste Christologie, Bekenntnisbildung und Schriftauslegung im Lichte von 1 Kor. 15, 3-5* (Quaestiones disputatae 38; Freiburg im Breisgau, 1968).

[34] Cf. G. Schrenk, "graphē," *TDNT* 1:758: "The thought of fulfillment [is] the heart of the early Christian understanding of Scripture."

[35] In John 5:45-46, Jesus alludes to the popular belief that Moses will come on the day of judgment to speak in defense of his disciples. Jesus tells the unbelieving Pharisees that not only will Moses not defend them but he will accuse them because he had told them of the Messiah. — In the Gospel of John, the Scriptures are explicitly cited in 1:23, 45; 2:17; 6:31, 45; 7:37, 42; 8:17; 10:34; 12:15, 38-40; 13:18; 15:25; 17:12; 19:24, 28, 36, 37. On the use of Scripture in the Fourth Gospel, cf. F.-M. Braun, *Jean le théologien* 2 (Paris, 1964), pp. 3–45, 49–149.

[36] For example: What was the name of Cleopas' companion? Where was Emmaus? (Its location has not been determined with certainty; cf. L. Pirot, "Emmaus," *DBS* 2:1059–63.) How did the tradition of the early community lose the memory of Emmaus? Why does the account speak of "two of them," when the two belong neither to the apostles nor to the holy women of whom the preceding passage was speaking?

[37] Cf. A. George, "Les récits d'apparitions aux Onze à partir de Luc 24, 36-53," in P. de Surgy *et al., La résurrection du Christ et l'exégèse moderne* (Lectio divina 50; Paris, 1969), pp. 75–104; C.H. Dodd, "The Appearances of the Risen Christ: An Essay in Form-Criticism of the Gospels," in D.E. Nineham (ed.), *Studies in the Gospels: Essays in Memory of R. H. Lightfoot* (Oxford, 1955), pp. 9–35. — The account in Luke 24:36-49 shows numerous points of contact with John; cf. P. Benoit, "Marie-Madeleine et les disciples au tombeau selon Joh 20, 1-18," in *Judentum, Urchristentum, Kirche: Festschrift für Joachim Jeremias* (Berlin, 1960), pp. 141–52. But verses 44-45, with which we are mainly concerned here, bear the marks of Luke's editing (cf. A. George, *art. cit.*, p. 79).

[38] Cf. P. Benoit, "L'Ascension," *Revue biblique* 56 (1949), pp. 161–203; reprinted in his *Exégèse et théologie* 1:363–411. Cf. also H. Schlier, "L'ascension de Jésus d'après les récits de saint Luc," in his *Essais sur le Nouveau Testament*, translated by A. Liefooghe (Lectio divina 46; Paris, 1968), pp. 263–78.

[39] Cf. Acts 13:5, 14; 14:1; 16:13; 17:2, 10, 17; 18:4, 19; 19:8.

[40] Cf. Acts 13:16-43. On the use of the Scriptures in Acts, cf. J. Dupont, *Etudes sur les Actes des Apôtres*, pp. 245–390.

[41] The discourses in Acts are all the more important because "they are offered as an overall view of the apostolic preaching. All have more or less the same orientation. The sermon on Pentecost shows us the substance of the earlier catecheses, while the later sermons illustrate rather the ways in which the Gospel was usually preached by

the 'Twelve' to their Jewish and Gentile listeners in Palestine and by Paul to his mixed audiences in the Diaspora" (J. Schmitt, *Jésus ressuscité dans la prédication apostolique: Etude de théologie biblique* [Paris, 1949], pp. 18–19).

⁴² The translation of the Psalm is made from the Greek (LXX) text. Italics indicate the Greek words repeated verbatim by the evangelists.

⁴³ Cf. L. Deiss, *Synopse* 1:48–49.

⁴⁴ This is the title of Chapter 3 in C.H. Dodd, *According to the Scriptures*. The existence of such anthologies was maintained as early as 1889 by E. Hatch (*Essays in Biblical Greek* [Oxford, 1889]), then occasionally denied, and finally confirmed by the discoveries at Qumran. The text of *4 Q Testimonia* brings together in a connected series Deut. 5:28-29; 18:18-19 (quoted from the Samaritan Pentateuch); Num. 24:15-17; Josh. 6:27, along with a text from the *Psalms of Joshua*, an apocryphal book used at Qumran; cf. A. Dupont-Sommer, *The Essene Writings from Qumran*, translated by G. Vermes (Gloucester, Mass., 1973), pp. 315–18; and *Les textes du Qumrân traduits et annotés* 2 (Paris, 1963), pp. 273–78. The script of this Qumran text belongs to about a century before Christ. Some two centuries later, toward the beginning of the second century A.D., the *Letter of Barnabas* shows the community still using citations in this fashion; cf. P. Prigent, *Les Testimonia dans le christianisme primitif: L'Epître de Barnabé I–XVI et ses sources* (Paris, 1961), and the remarks of J.-P. Audet, "L'hypothèse des Testimonia," *Revue biblique* 70 (1963), pp. 381–405. Moreover, since the *Letter* uses composite citations and even makes erroneous attributions, it shows that it is relying on earlier anthologies. It is therefore quite reasonable to assume that such anthologies could also have been used in the redaction of the Gospels.

⁴⁵ Here is a list of these prophecies: the virgin birth of Jesus (Matthew 1:22-23, citing Is. 7:14); the return from Egypt (Matthew 2:15; Hos. 11:1); the massacre of the children at Bethlehem (Matthew 2:17-18; Jer. 31:15); the settling of the family of Jesus at Nazareth (Matthew 2:23, referring to an unspecified prophecy); Jesus' taking up residence in "heathen Galilee" (Matthew 4:14-16; Is. 8:23; 9:1); Jesus, the Servant of Yahweh, takes upon himself our infirmities (Matthew 8:17; Is. 53:4); Jesus, Servant of Yahweh, proclaims true faith to the Gentiles (Matthew 12:17-21; Is. 42:1-4); Jesus announces in parables the mysteries of the kingdom of heaven (Matthew 13:35; Ps. 78:2); Jesus, the messianic king, meek and humble (Matthew 21:4-5; Is. 62:11 and Zech. 9:9); Jesus is arrested as a criminal (Matthew 26:56; Zech. 13:7?); Jesus is sold for thirty pieces of silver (Matthew 27:9-10; Zech. 11:12-13 and Jer. 32:6-15).

The list of citations differs for various modern scholars. Lagrange, *Evangile selon Matthieu* (Paris, 1948), p. 15, has eleven citations. By adding Matthew 26:54, G. Delling, "plēroō," *TDNT* 6:295, gets twelve. Loisy, *Les Evangiles Synoptiques* 1 (Paris, 1907), p. 335, note 4, has fourteen. On the subject, cf. P. Nepper-Christensen, *Das Matthäusevangelium, ein judenchristliches Evangelium* (Aarhus, 1958), pp. 139–43. On the use of the Old Testament in the "school" of Matthew, cf. K. Stendahl, *The School of Matthew* (2nd ed.; Lund, 1967).

⁴⁶ A. Schlatter, *Der Evangelist Matthäus* (Stuttgart, 1957), p. 21.

⁴⁷ Cf. Strack-Billerbeck, *op. cit.*, 1:74.

⁴⁸ These prophecies, says L. Vaganay, *Le problème synoptique* (Paris, 1954), "in all probability were part of a collection of *testimonia*" (p. 238).

⁴⁹ *Op. cit.*, p. 30. Dodd ends with a list of fifteen texts which, when read in their context, served as the scriptural basis for the kerygma of the early Church. The texts are: Pss. 2, 8, 110, 118; Is. 6:9-10; 28:16; 40:3-5; 53:1; 61:1-2; Gen. 12:3 (and 22:18); Jer. 31:31-34; Joel 3:1-5; Zech. 9:9; Hab. 2:3-4; Deut. 18:15-19.

⁵⁰ Cf. J. De Fraine, *Adam and the Family of Man*, translated by D. Raible (Staten Island, N.Y., 1965), pp. 212–33 ("The 'I' of the Psalms").

⁵¹ The Psalm is here translated from the LXX Greek version, which was the text used by the New Testament writers. The italicized words appear both in the Psalm and in the New Testament.

[52] Ps. 22:2 = Matthew 27:6; Mark 15:34. Ps. 31:6 = Luke 23:46.

[53] Pss. 31:8; 35:9; 89:11; 98:3; 103:13-17; 107:9; 111:9; 118:15; 147:6. On the *Magnificat*, cf. L. Deiss, *Mary, Daughter of Sion* (Collegeville, Minn., 1972), pp. 99–126.

[54] On this point, cf. R. Laurentin, "Traces d'allusions étymologiques en Luc 1–2," *Biblica* 37 (1956), pp. 435–56.

[55] Cf. W. Zimmerli, *The Law and the Prophets: A Study of the Meaning of the Old Testament*, translated by R.E. Clements (Oxford, 1965), pp. 5–16, 46–60.

[56] "If you [Peter] who are a Jew are living according to Gentile ways rather than Jewish, by what logic do you force the Gentiles to adopt Jewish ways?" (Gal. 2:14).

[57] John 1:17 JB. Cf. Exod. 34:6. On this subject, cf. M-E. Boismard, *St. John's Prologue*, pp. 135–49. And yet St. John cannot be accused of anti-Judaism; cf. F.-M. Braun, *Jean le théologien* 2 (Paris, 1964), p. 31.

[58] P. Grelot, in his *Le Bible, Parole le Dieu* (Paris, 1965), p. 16, note 1, rightly observes that Jesus' opposition was chiefly to the halakah with its legislative rules, not to the haggadah, which Christian tradition accepted more readily. We have already spoken of these two forms of midrash (Chapter 7, section II/2).

[59] Cf. Mark 3:1-6 and the parallels (Matthew 12:9-14; Luke 6:6-11); Luke 13:11-17; 14:1-6; John 5:1-19; 9:1-41. To these texts which relate cures done on the sabbath we must add two other passages of controversy: Mark 2:23-28 (=Matthew 12:1-8) and Luke 6:1-5. The large number of such texts shows the importance of the problem in Christ's day. — Note that the practice of Qumran was stricter than that which Christ proposes in Matthew 12:11-12 (=Luke 14:5). The *Damascus Document*, XI, 13-14, prescribes that "if [a beast] falls into a cistern or into a pit, let it not be lifted out on the Sabbath" (Dupont-Sommer, *op. cit.*, p. 153). On other relations between the texts cited and the Qumran literature, cf. H. Braun, "Qumran und das Neue Testament," *Theologische Rundschau* 29 (1962), pp. 97–234.

[60] Cf. Mark 7:1-23. Only priests, according to Exod. 30:17-21, had to clean their hands before liturgical services.

[61] Mark 10:5-9 and Matthew 19:4-6; Matthew 5:31-32; Luke 16:18.

[62] Cf. L. Deiss, *Synopse* 1:70, for a list of the sayings that have been added to the original Sermon on the Mount.

[63] At the time Jesus spoke, people did not yet suspect, of course, how thoroughly the foundations of Judaism would be shaken. We are still far from the statements of Paul, who says that the Law was crucified in the body of Jesus and slain in his death and resurrection so that we might serve "in the new spirit, not the antiquated letter" (Rom. 7:6). But the Christian seed was being sown in Jewish earth when Jesus spoke as he did in Matthew 5. Despite the fierce opposition of the Judaizers, the seed would flower into the Gospel. — On Paul and the Law, cf. A. Demann, "Moïse et la loi dans la pensée de saint Paul," in *Moïse, l'homme de l'Alliance*, pp. 189–242; G. Baum, *The Jews and the Gospel: A Re-examination of the New Testament* (Westminster,Md., 1961); J. Cambier, *L'Evangile de Dieu selon l'Epître aux Romains* 1 (Studia Neotestamentica 3; Paris, 1967), pp. 299–311.

[64] On Matthew 5:17, 20, cf. especially W. Trilling, *Das wahre Israel: Studien zur Theologie des Matthäus-Evangelium* (Studien zum Alten und Neuen Testament 10; 3rd ed., Munich, 1964), pp. 167–86.

[65] On the "I have come" sayings, cf. L. Deiss, *Synopse* 1:183.

[66] There is a considerable literature on the theme of the fulfillment of the Law. We have made use especially of the following: C. Larcher, *L'actualité chrétienne de l'Ancien Testament d'après le Nouveau Testament* (Lectio divina 34; Paris, 1962), pp. 199–284; G. Delling, "plēroō," *TDNT* 6:292–95; R. Schnackenburg, *The Moral Message of the New Testament*, translated by H. Holland-Smith and W.J. O'Hara (New York, 1965), pp. 56–81, with bibliography; G. Barth, "Matthew's Understanding of the Law," in G. Bornkamm, G. Barth, and H.J. Held, *Tradition and Interpretation in Matthew*, translated by P. Scott (Philadelphia, 1963), pp. 58–164; J. Dupont, *Les*

Béatitudes 1 (Paris, 1969), pp. 130–45; A. Descamps, "Moïse dans les Evangiles et dans la Tradition Apostolique," in *Moïse, l'homme de l'Alliance*, pp. 171–87; *idem, Les justes et la justice dans les évangiles et le christianisme primitif hormis la doctrine proprement paulinienne* (Louvain-Gembloux, 1950), pp. 123–32; J. Schmid, *Das Evangelium nach Matthäus* (3rd ed.; Regensburg, 1956), pp. 89–94; R. Hummel, *Die Auseinandersetzung zwischen Kirche und Judentum im Matthäusevangelium* (Munich, 1963), pp. 66–75; J. Schildenberger, "Fulfillment," SV 1:289–95; J. Obersteiner, "Messianism," *SV* 2:575–82; P. Nepper-Christensen, *Das Matthäusevangelium: Ein judenchristliches Evangelium?* (Aarhus, 1958), especially pp. 136–62 ("The form and role of the concept of fulfillment in the Gospel of St. Matthew"); H. Cazelles, "Loi Israélite," *DBS* 5:497–530; L. Cerfaux, "L'exégèse de l'Ancien Testament par le Nouveau Testament," in *L'Ancien Testament et les chrétiens* (Paris, 1951), pp. 132–48, reprinted in *Recueil Lucien Cerfaux* (Gembloux, 1954), 2:205–17; H. von Campenhausen, *The Formation of the Christian Bible*, pp. 1–20.

[The simplest and yet the most orthodox presentation of this topic of the relationship of the old covenant to the new covenant is presented in *The Major Old Testament Theme*, no. 30 in the *Old Testament Reading Guide* series (available from the Liturgical Press, Collegeville, Minn.).]

[67] A. Descamps, *op. cit.*, p. 131.

[68] Cf. Rom. 9:12 = Gen. 25:23; Rom. 9:25 = Hos. 2:25.

[69] Deut. 6:4; 11:13-21; Num. 15:37-41.

[70] R. Schnackenburg, *The Moral Teaching of the New Testament*, p. 73.

[71] The law of talion was taken over from the ancient Code of Hammurabi, nos. 196–197; cf. *ANET*, p. 175. Cf. also A. Alt, *Kleine Schriften* 1:341–44.

[72] P. Lestringant, *Essai sur l'unité de la révélation biblique: Le problème de l'unité de l'Evangile et de l'Ecriture aux deux premiers siècles* (Paris, 1942), p. 48. R. Schnackenburg, *The Moral Teaching of the New Testament*, writes: "A great deal of trouble has been taken . . . to test the novelty of Jesus' 'new' commandments. The result has not been unfavourable to Judaism. It is possible to find in the utterance of the rabbis parallels to all these moral commandments formulated so provocatively by Jesus, some of them saying more or less the same thing and in many points attaining the same heights of morality, others at least coming close to them. To acknowledge this is no more than just. But such comparisons miss the point. It was part of the tradition of the Jewish schools to collect the most diverse utterances of the rabbis so that alongside opinions of the highest merit we can find others confirming how right Jesus was to be scandalized" (p. 76).

[73] Cf. *Adversus haereses*, IV, 2, 3; 9, 1. Cf. L. Deiss, *Printemps de la thélologie*, p. 171; A. Rousseau, *Irénée de Lyon, Contre les hérésies*, Livre IV (Sources chrétiennes 100), p. 847.

[74] F. Prat, *The Theology of St. Paul*, translated by J.L. Stoddard (London, 1926), 1:227, comments: "One thing is certain; it is that the Law is dead for the Christian, and that the Christian is dead for the Law. In other words, there is nothing common between the Law and the Christian." Similar statements are made by H. Schlier, *Der Brief an die Galater* (12th ed.; Göttingen, 1962), pp. 98–99. E. de Witt Burton, *A Critical and Exegetical Commentary on the Epistle to the Galatians* (Edinburgh, 1921), p. 132, observes that we must be careful about the precise meaning of "law" in this passage.

[75] Cf. Amos 1–2; Is. 1:14-17; Jer. 9:2-5; Ezek. 18:5-9; Mal. 3:5; etc.

[76] Cf. Prov. 14:21; 1:8-19; cf. Sir. 25:1; etc.

[77] See above, Chapter 7, section III/3.

[78] H. de Lubac, *Histoire et esprit: L'intelligence de l'Ecriture d'après Origène* (Paris, 1950), p. 277. Cf. C. Larcher, *op. cit.*, p. 27.

[79] "Jesus acts with great independence of the letter of the Law, and his behavior

matches his teaching on the relation between the Law and the Gospel. His consciousness of being the Messiah enables him to promulgate a new law which is not
dependent on the letter of the Mosaic prescriptions. In his new law Jesus reflects
more fully than Moses did the real thought of God" (A. Descamps, "Moïse dans les
Evangiles et dans la Tradition Apostolique [note 66, above], p. 175).

[80] G. Barth, *art. cit.*, p. 158.

[81] See this chapter, beginning of section III.

[82] J. Cambier, *op. cit.*, p. 299. Cf. p. 301: "The Jewish people retained the temporary divine institution and made of it a human institution by which man could effect
his own salvation; Paul's attacks are directed against this human legalistic religion that
wrongly claims to be divine."

[83] Although provisional, these laws were "holy and just and good" (Rom. 7:12),
because they were a way to Christ.

[84] J. Moltmann, *Theology of Play*, translated by R. Ulrich (New York, 1972), pp.
48–49. Cf. St. Thomas Aquinas, *Summa theologiae*, I–II, q. 106, a. 1: "The most
important thing in the new law, and that on which its whole power depends,
is the grace of the Holy Spirit, which is received when a man believes in Christ."

[85] St. Irenaeus, *Adversus haereses*, IV, 2, 3 (*PG* 7:977B); cf. L. Deiss, *Printemps de
la théologie*, p. 160. On Christ as contemporaneous with every generation, Kier-
kegaard observes: "One can be a contemporary without being a contemporary . . .
the real contemporary is not the real contemporary by virtue of an immediate contemporaneity. . . . [This is] a privilege enjoyed only by the believer" (in *Kier-
kegaard: The Difficulty of Being a Christian*, edited by J. Collette, translated by
R.M. McInerney and L. Turcotte [Notre Dame, 1968], pp. 234, 236).

[86] L. Deiss, *Synopse* 1:30.

[87] Among the traditions used in the composition of the Gospels the exegetes
include a Q source (Q for the German word *Quelle*, which means simply "source"),
which contains only words of Jesus. "Q is simply a written collection of words of the
Lord that had been orally transmitted" (M. Albertz, *op. cit.*, 1:176). Q contains the
discourses and sayings which are found in both Matthew and Luke, but not in Mark.

[88] The Sermon on the Mount (chs. 5–7), the missionary discourse (10), the parables
(13), the discourse on the Church (18), and the eschatological discourse (24–26).

[89] In Mark the discourse in parables occupies a whole day, but the audience and
locale frequently change. In 4:1 Jesus is in a small boat facing a crowd gathered on the
shore; in 4:10 he is with his disciples apart from the crowd; in 4:21-35 the audience
and locale are not clearly indicated, and each parable is an autonomous entity with its
own introductory formula (4:21, 24, 26, 30); in 4:35 Jesus is again in the small boat.
Evidently this grouping of the parables does not correspond to any historical situation.

[90] Cf. L. Deiss, *Synopse* 1:45. There is a booklet on prayer (11:1-13), two on wealth
and poverty, a favorite theme of Luke's (12:13-34 and 16:1-31), a short eschatological
discourse (12:38-59), four parables artificially linked with meals (14:1-24), three parables on God's mercy (15), and a booklet on the true follower of Jesus (14:25-35).

[91] F. Prat, *op. cit.*, 2:19, writes: "Our mystical union with Christ does not extend
to the mortal life of Jesus; it originates only at the time of the Passion, when Jesus
Christ inaugurates his redemptive work. . . . It is realized, in fact and indeed, in
every one of us, when faith and baptism graft us upon the dying Christ and make us
participate in his death."

[92] Cf. S. Schulz, *Komposition und Herkunft der johanneischen Reden* (Stuttgart,
1960), especially pp. 150–87.

[93] L. Deiss, *Synopse* 1:30.

[94] *Ibid.*, 31.

[95] *Ibid.*, 68.

[96] X. Léon-Dufour, *Etudes d'Evangile* (Paris, 1965), p. 135.

⁹⁷ Deiss, *op. cit.*, 1:80.

⁹⁸ On the Matthean narratives, cf. the excellent article of H.J. Held, "Matthew as Interpreter of the Miracle Stories," in *Tradition and Interpretation in Matthew* (note 66, above), pp. 165–299.

⁹⁹ Cf. Deiss, *op. cit.*, 1:39–40.

¹⁰⁰ Cf. *ibid.*, 155, under entry *"adorer."*

¹⁰¹ Mark 15:40 and Matthew 27:55-56 mention only the presence of the women.

¹⁰² Th. de Kruijf, *Der Sohn des lebendigen Gottes: Ein Beitrag zur Christologie des Matthäus-Evangeliums* (Analecta Biblica 16; Rome, 1962), writes: "This actualization of the proclamation is not consciously elaborated; often we can deduce it only from secondary details, but it is certainly there" (p. 154).

¹⁰³ Luke 7:6 has a version that is less striking but closer to historical reality: "Sir, *do not trouble yourself*, for I am not worthy to have you enter my house." In Luke, moreover, it is the centurion's friends, not the centurion himself (as in Matthew), who actually speak the words to Jesus.

¹⁰⁴ A. Loisy, *Les Evangiles Synoptiques* 2 (Paris, 1908), p. 754.

Chapter 11

GOD ENTERS INTO A COVENANT WITH HIS PEOPLE

Like the assembly at Sinai under Moses, at Shechem under Joshua, and at Jerusalem under Josiah and later under Ezra, the all-embracing assembly convoked by Jesus terminates in the celebration of a covenant. After the proclamation of the word (the Gospel), the Father seals the new covenant through the mediation of his Son, Jesus Christ.

1. Jesus, "mediator of a new covenant" (Heb. 9:15)

The first thing we must do is make clear the unparalleled position of the mediator of this new covenant.

The history of Israel saw many covenants; the mediators or beneficiaries of these were Noah (Gen. 6:18; 9:12), Abraham (Gen. 15 and 17), Isaac and Jacob (Exod. 2:24), Moses (Exod. 24:1-8), Aaron (Num. 18:19), Phinehas (Num. 25:12-13), Levi (Mal. 2:4-5), Joshua (Josh. 24:25), David (2 Sam. 23:5), and the "Servant of Yahweh" (Is. 42:6). Moses, of course, had a privileged role among all these personages,[1] and the glory of the Sinai covenant undoubtedly illumined all the other covenants of the Old Testament. Moreover, these various covenants were simply special moments within the history of Israel, for it was the entire life of God's people that was favored by the graces of the covenant and that also stood under God's judgment, as the prophets liked to remind their hearers.[2] Israel, as an eternal people, was a covenanted people (cf. Rom. 9:4), and its God was the "God of favours, who hast kept the Covenant with our fathers."[3] In the last analysis the mediators were less important than the existential relation between God and his people.[4]

But this last statement is no longer wholly true when we come to

232

Jesus Christ, "mediator of a new covenant." (Heb. 9:15; 12:24). If he is to carry out his work, a mediator must be linked to both parties in the covenant, and the quality of his mediation will depend on the quality of these connecting links. Jesus is both Son of God and Son of Man.

He is the mediator *appointed by God*. "Even Christ did not glorify himself with the office of high priest; he received it from the One who said to him, 'You are my son'" (Heb. 5:5, citing Ps. 2:7).[5] The controlling idea of his entire life will be: "Father, it is true. You have graciously willed it so" (Matthew 11:26; Luke 10:21). This sentence is undoubtedly the most perfect expression of Jesus' religious attitude toward his Father, an attitude compounded of love and adoration for the Father's will. Christian tradition has seen Christ first uttering his "Yes, Father!" at the moment of the Incarnation: "On coming into the world, Jesus said: 'Sacrifice and offering you did not desire, but a body you have prepared for me; holocausts and sin offerings you took no delight in. Then I said, "As is written of me in the book, I have come to do your will, O God"'" (Heb. 10:5-7; Ps. 40:6-9).

Jesus is also *accepted by men*. He does not force his way into the human family or usurp the name of brother among brothers (Heb. 2:11) and first-born of the human race (Rom. 8:29). Rather, human hands, those of the Virgin Mary, were extended to him in welcome. It was a welcome inspired by faith and love, and Mary conceived Jesus more perfectly in her soul than she did in her body,[6] through her attitude of humble obedience (Luke 1:38). All the tender love that can accompany the conception and birth of a human being was present in Mary as she welcomed Jesus, but in her it was purified and it rendered sublime her ardent, loving faith. Her "yes," moreover, was a "yes" from mankind as a whole, for at the Annunciation she answered as the Daughter of Sion. At this moment in the history of salvation she was, "in the fullness and purity of the mystery of her own person, the living embodiment of the mystery of the Church — both the Church of the Old Testament, which prepared for the coming of Christ, and the Church of the New Testament, which perpetuates the presence of Jesus in our midst under the dimensions of space and time."[7]

Appointed by God and accepted by men, and being both Son of God and Son of Man, Jesus is the mediator beyond compare. He is so proclaimed by the first Letter to Timothy, in words probably taken from a liturgical acclamation used by the early community:[8]

"God is one. One also is the mediator between God and man, the man Christ Jesus, who gave himself as a ransom for all" (1 Tim. 2:5-6).

The celebration of the new covenant occupies the whole life of Jesus, which in its entirety, from the joyful "yes" of the Incarnation to the abandonment of the Cross, was a hymn of love to the Father. It has its climax, nonetheless, at the Last Supper, which was the sacrificial meal of the new covenant and was in turn directed toward the death on the Cross. These mysteries form, as it were, the heart of Christ's life. What a vast subject! [9] In analyzing the texts, we shall, of course, dwell only on what is directly relevant to our purpose.

2. *"On the first day of Unleavened Bread, when it was customary to sacrifice the paschal lamb" (Mark 14:12).*

The Synoptic tradition introduces the Supper with an account of the preparation for the Passover (Matthew 26:17-19; Mark 14:12-16; Luke 22:7-13). Here is Mark's account:

> On the first day of Unleavened Bread, when it was customary to sacrifice the paschal lamb, his disciples said to him, "Where do you wish us to go to prepare the Passover supper for you?" He sent two of his disciples with these instructions: "Go into the city and you will come upon a man carrying a water jar. Follow him. Whatever house he enters, say to the owner, 'The Teacher asks, Where is my guest room where I may eat the Passover with my disciples?' Then he will show you an upstairs room, spacious, furnished, and all in order. That is the place you are to get ready for us." The disciples went off. When they reached the city they found it just as he had told them, and they prepared the Passover supper.

Thus, as far as the evangelists were concerned, the supper during which Jesus would break the bread of the new covenant was celebrated in the context of the Jewish Passover.

The context reminded them of more than just the departure from Egypt and the covenant at Sinai. The Exodus was considered to be the supreme symbol of all God's marvelous deeds. [10] The "Poem of the Four Nights," which offers a kind of paschal theology in Targum style, celebrates the four nights which dominate the whole history of the world. [11] The first night is the one during which God called the world from nothingness into existence. The second is that during which Abraham made ready to sacrifice Isaac. The third is the night of the departure from Egypt. The fourth will be the night when the world ends.

The poem concludes with these words: "This is the night of the

Passover to the name of the Lord: it is a night reserved and set aside
for the redemption of all the generations of Israel." Thus the memory of God's past glorious deeds and the hope of the eternal banquet
to come created the atmosphere in which Jesus celebrated the Passover for the last time.

3. "During the meal" (Matthew 26:26).

In the Bible (and still today in the East), sitting together at table
was a special sign of friendship and mutual trust among the guests.[12]
They shared the same bread and thus gave evidence of mutual love.

We must recall, too, that meals were preceded by blessings such
as this: "Blessed are you, Yahweh our God, King of the universe;
you bring forth bread from the earth."[13] Those at table ratified the
blessing with their "Amen." Consequently, those who ate together
did not think of themselves simply as friends meeting in God's presence; they also offered their friendship to him and praised him. The
common meal became a shared prayer.

Throughout his public life Jesus shared meals with his disciples.
They had accepted him as Messiah and "Son" of God (Matthew
16:16); by sharing bread with them, he in turn accepted them into
his friendship and into his prayer as Messiah and Son. The God of
Sinai, in whose presence Moses and the seventy elders of Israel
celebrated the covenant meal (Exod. 24:11), had taken human form
in Christ. And when the "Lord and Master" waited on his disciples at table as their servant, he was foreshadowing the messianic
banquet at which joy and love would be the servants. This Passover
meal of Jesus, though completely unique because it is a farewell
meal, should not be thought of as an isolated event. It is to be seen
rather as a link in the long chain of communal meals that began on
Sinai, includes all the countless covenant meals of the Old Testament, the meals of Jesus with his disciples before and after the
resurrection, and the celebrations in which bread was broken in the
early Christian community, and acts as man's preparation for the
eternal banquet of the kingdom.[14]

The meals Jesus took with the Twelve did not create a family
turned in upon itself. His table is open to all mankind until the end
of time. At the same time, however, from the very beginning of his
public life the Lord loved to receive at table various privileged
guests whose presence was a proclamation in deeds, rather than in
words, of the Good News. By eating the bread of Matthew the
tax-collector, Jesus made it plain that he had "come to call, not the

self-righteous, but sinners" (Matthew 9:13). By welcoming the re-
pentant sinner as he sat at the table of the Pharisee who had invited
him, and allowing her to wash his feet with her tears and dry them
with her hair, he showed that he welcomed into his family those
who sought forgiveness and made their peace with him (Luke
7:49-50). By multiplying the loaves and fishes for the hungry crowd
in the wilderness (Mark 14:15-21), he created a joyous banquet for
the poor and thereby symbolized the abundance of the messianic
banquet to come. By accepting the invitation to eat with Zacchaeus,
he made it clear that "the Son of Man has come to search out and
save what was lost" (Luke 19:9-10).

The Pharisees, then, were telling the truth when they accused
Jesus of eating with tax-collectors and sinners (Mark 2:16). They
were simply noting those who became members of Jesus' family,
those who were willing to acknowledge their sins so that they might
be saved. The bread broken with sinners pointed to the bread of the
new covenant "for the forgiveness of sins" (Matthew 26:28).

4. The Last Supper and the Jewish Passover ritual

We know, at least in its essentials, what the Jewish Passover ritual
must have been like in the time of Christ.[15]

a) Preliminary ritual

The preliminary ritual included a blessing of the feast day and of
the wine (first cup); a rite of cleansing, which symbolized interior
purification and which the Lord expanded into the washing of the
feet and its accompanying catechesis (John 13:2-15; cf. Luke
22:24-27); and finally the eating of bitter herbs dipped in a spicy
sauce.It was probably during the last-named rite that Jesus spoke of
Judas' betrayal (Matthew 26:20-25; Mark 14:17-21; Luke 22:21-23)
and gave the traitor the morsel to eat (John 13:21-30).[16]

b) Homily and prayers

This part of the ceremony may be regarded as a liturgy of the
word, intended to recall and give a deeper understanding of
the spiritual significance of the meal. At the request of one of
those at the table, the father of the family explained the meaning of
the celebration and the symbolism of some elements in it (the Passover haggadah).[17] Passover means "passage," because the Lord
"passed over the houses of the Israelites in Egypt; when he struck
down the Egyptians, he spared our houses" (Exod. 12:27). The

bread was unleavened, because in their hurry to be on their way "the people . . . took their dough before it was leavened" (Exod. 12:34). The Passover lamb recalled the first Passover sacrifice, when the victim's blood, smeared on the lintel and doorposts, protected the Israelite homes against the destroying angel (Exod. 12:21-23). Finally, the bitter herbs reminded the guests of the bitterness of captivity.[18] It was in this context that Jesus pronounced the discourses recorded in John 14–17. These can be regarded both as a farewell message and as Jesus' paschal homily to his Church.[19] This part of the ritual ended with the singing of the first part of the Passover Hallel (Psalm 113 or Psalms 113-114).

c) Passover meal

This was the heart of the celebration. It included a second ablution rite; the blessing that the father of the house spoke over the bread which he then broke and distributed; the eating of the Passover lamb; and, after the meal, the blessing which the father spoke over the third cup of wine, called "the cup of blessing" (cf. 1 Cor. 10:16). The words of consecration that Jesus speaks over the bread come just before the eating of the Passover lamb, while the words over the wine come "after eating" (Luke 22:20; 1 Cor 11:25).

d) Conclusion

The entire celebration ended with the singing of the second part of the Hallel, which Jesus sang with his disciples, as we are told in Matthew 26:30 and Mark 14:26.

In schematic form, a comparison of the Passover meal and the Last Supper looks like this:

Ritual of Jewish Passover	Last Supper
A. Preliminary ritual	
Blessing of the feast day and of the first cup	
Rite of purification (ablution)	Washing of feet and catechesis (John 13:2-15; cf. Luke 22:24-27)
Eating of bitter herbs	
	Announcement of Judas' betrayal (?)
B. Homily and prayers	
Passover haggadah by the father (in Aramaic)	Discourse of Jesus (John 14–17)
First part of the Hallel (Ps. 113) or Pss. 113–114, in Hebrew)	
Second cup (haggadah cup)	

Ritual of Jewish Passover	Last Supper
C. Passover meal	
Rite of purification (ablution)	
Blessing over bread by father	Jesus' words over the bread ("This is my body")
Eating of Passover lamb	
Third cup, cup of blessing	Jesus' words over the wine ("This is my blood")
D. Conclusion	
Second part of the Hallel (Pss. 114–118 or 115–118, in Hebrew)	Singing of Psalms (Matthew 26:30; Mark 14:26)
Fourth cup (?)	

The account of the institution of the Eucharist, as presented to us in the Synoptic and Pauline tradition, has been shortened somewhat. The writers did not think it worthwhile to recount the steps in the Passover meal; they probably assumed their readers would be familiar with these. All reference especially to the eating of the Passover meal has disappeared; it was the heart of the Jewish festival meal, but the Jewish feast has now been replaced by a Christian one. Consequently, the Synoptic account by no means describes the Last Supper in its entirety. What it gives us instead is a liturgical narrative for use in the Christian celebration of the Eucharist. At the same time, however, this narrative can be interpreted only in the light of the Jewish Passover.

5. *The accounts of the institution*

It will be helpful if we have before us the text of the account of the institution. It has come down to us in four different traditions, which, however, fall into two main groups: one comprising Mark and Matthew, the other Paul and Luke.

The Mark-Matthew tradition undoubtedly was the tradition followed in Palestinian circles; the texts provided by these two evangelists resemble each other closely.

a) Tradition of Matthew and Mark

Matthew 26:26-28	Mark 14:22-24
v. 26 During the meal Jesus took bread, blessed it, broke it,	v. 22 During the meal he took bread, blessed and broke it,

and gave it to his disciples. "Take this and eat it," he said, "this is my body."	and gave it to them. "Take this," he said, "this is my body."
v. 27 Then he took a cup, gave thanks, and gave it to them. "All of you must drink from it," he said,	v. 23 He likewise took a cup, gave thanks, and passed it to them, and they all drank from it.
v. 28 "for this is my blood, the blood of the covenant, to be poured out in behalf of many for the forgiveness of sins."	v. 24 He said to them: "This is my blood, the blood of the covenant to be poured out on behalf of many."

The other group of texts consists of Paul in 1 Cor. 11:23-25 and Luke in 22:19-20.[20] What Paul gives us is perhaps the tradition followed in the Church of Antioch. He himself refers to it as already traditional: "I received from the Lord what I handed on to you" (1 Cor. 11:23).[21] His stay at Corinth (Acts 18:1-18) was from the end of 50 to the middle of 52; consequently his testimony takes us back to the very first years of Christianity.[22]

b) Tradition of Paul and Luke

Luke 22:19-20	1 Corinthians 11:23-25
v. 19 Then, taking bread and giving thanks, he broke it and gave it to them, saying "This is my body to be given for you. Do this as a remembrance of me."	v. 23 The Lord Jesus on the night in which he was betrayed took bread, and v. 24 after he had given thanks, broke it and said, "This is my body, which is for you. Do this in remembrance of me."
v. 20 He did the same with the cup after eating, saying as he did so: "This cup is the new covenant in my blood, which will be shed for you."	In the same way, after the supper, he took the cup, saying, "This cup is the new covenant in my blood. Do this, whenever you drink it, in remembrance of me."

Attempts have been made to get back to the orignal text of the institution. Any such attempt must, of course, be only a conjecture, but is nonetheless of great interest. Here is the text J. Coppens reconstructs: "And while they were eating, Jesus, having taken bread and spoken the blessing, broke [it] and gave [it] to them and said: 'Take and eat. This is my body [which is] given for you. Do this in my memory.' In the same way, having taken the cup after the meal, having given thanks, he gave [it] to them, saying: 'All of you, drink this cup, the new covenant, my blood shed for many. Do this in my memory.' "23

6. "Covenant in my blood"

Jesus clearly predicts his coming death. He speaks of his body as *given* for his disciples and of his blood as *shed* for sins. As bread is broken so that brothers may share it, so his body will be rent by suffering; as the wine is pressed like "the blood of grapes" (Gen. 49:11; Deut. 32:14),24 so his blood will well from his body under the bruising pressure of the Passion.

His death is connected with a covenant. Matthew and Mark translate the original Aramaic words awkwardly but literally: "This is my blood of the covenant." Paul and Luke give the words a better literary form, and add the idea that the covenant is a new one: "This cup is the new covenant in my blood."

In the Bible a covenant normally involves the immolation of a victim; the covenant is concluded or sealed "in blood," which literally becomes "the blood of the covenant." "Without the shedding of blood there is no forgiveness" (Heb. 9:22). The covenant which Jesus makes new is the covenant of Sinai. Moses took "the book of the covenant" and read it aloud to the people, then sprinkled the blood of a victim on both the altar and the people to signify the union God is establishing between himself and his people; as Moses did this, he said: "This is the blood of the covenant" (Exod. 24:5-8).25 His words are echoed in those of Jesus: "This is my blood, the blood of the covenant."

We must note, further, that Christ is the Passover lamb of this new Passover. The words over the bread and wine are, as we have seen, like two hands holding between them the rite of eating the Passover lamb and thereby suggest that Jesus is the new Lamb. Paul will say outright: "Christ our Passover has been sacrificed" (1 Cor. 5:7), and John 19:36 will apply to Christ on the Cross a text that refers directly to the Passover lamb: "You shall not break any of its bones" (Exod. 12:46). This typology, so important in the Christian tradition, is undoubtedly muted in the Gospel text,[26] but Jesus may have developed it more fully in his Passover haggadah.[27]

Jesus may have emphasized especially the spiritual meaning of the offering of his blood for the sealing of the new covenant. The Jewish Passover indeed transformed Jerusalem into a huge slaughterhouse, and the Passion of Jesus himself was marked by a trail of blood, but, for all that, God is not a bloodthirsty God who gorges himself on victims. He derives no profit from our offerings, as he scornfully tells "those who have made a covenant with me by sacrifice" (Ps. 50:5): "Do I eat the flesh of strong bulls, or is the blood of goats my drink?" (Ps. 50:13).

In other words, it is not the victim offered that constitutes a sacrifice but the offering of the victim, that is to say, the interior sentiments of the one who makes the offering. Even in the case of Jesus, it is not the blood shed that seals the covenant but the gift of the blood, that is, the unreserved interior self-offering of Jesus to his Father. God does not love the bloodshed of the Cross, nor does he take pleasure in the cries of pain uttered by the crucified Jesus; what he accepts is the heart of his Son, who offers himself to the Father "through the eternal spirit" (Heb. 9:14). His interior attitude was one of supreme love for the Father: "Into your hands I commend my spirit" (Ps. 31:6; Luke 23:46). It was also one of immense love for men: "Before the feast of Passover, Jesus realized that the hour had come for him to pass from this world to the Father. He had loved his own in this world, and would show his love for them to the end" (John 13:1). *That* is the meaning of Jesus' blood, the blood of the new covenant.

7. *The Servant of Yahweh, "a covenant of the people"*

The figure of the Servant of Yahweh as described in the four Servant Songs of Isaiah[28] fascinated the early Christian community. In the story of this just man who is crushed by suffering, shattered by the sins of his brothers, and then raised up and glorified by God, the community saw represented the very mystery of Jesus, the "holy servant" (Acts 4:27, 30; 3:26), who was abased to the point of death on the Cross but then "was made Son of God in power according to the spirit of holiness, by his resurrection from the dead" (Rom. 1:4). The community was also sure of the ecclesial aspect of Jesus' mission: Just as the Servant of Yahweh is sometimes an individual person, sometimes a collective person, so the calling of Jesus concerns not only himself but also the whole community of believers whom he takes with himself in his suffering and his resurrection.

The prophecies concerning the Servant manifest Jesus to us and describe his life. He is the light of the nations of whom the elderly Simeon speaks (Luke 2:32; Is. 42:6). Upon him rests the Spirit of Yahweh and the Father's favor (baptism: Matthew 3:17; Mark 1:11; Is. 42:1; transfiguration: Matthew 17:5; Mark 9:7; Luke 9:35; Is. 42:1). He takes our infirmities and sufferings on himself (Matthew 8:17; Is. 53:4). He is the Servant who proclaims the true faith to the nations and does not crush the bruised reed or quench the smoldering wick (Matthew 12:18-21; Is. 42:1-4). He is the persecuted just man who was counted among the wicked (Matthew 27:38; Mark 15:27; Luke 23:33, 37; Is. 53:12) and handed over to be insulted and spat upon (Matthew 27:26, 30; Mark 15:15, 19; Is. 50:6).

The tradition had a special affection for the fourth Servant Song of Isaiah (52:13-53:12) and used it in describing the Passion of Christ.

Isaiah 53	New Testament citations
4 It was our infirmities that he bore, our sufferings that he endured.	Matthew 8:17
5 He was pierced for our offenses, crushed for our sins; Upon him was the chastisement that makes us whole,	2 Corinthians 5:21 Romans 4:25
by his stripes we were healed.	1 Peter 2:24
6 We all had gone astray like sheep . . .	1 Peter 2:25
But the Lord laid upon him the guilt of us all.	2 Corinthians 5:21
7 Though he was harshly treated, he submitted and opened not his mouth; Like a lamb led to the	Matthew 26:63
slaughter . . .	Acts 8:32-33
9 A grave was assigned to him among the wicked and a burial place with evildoers.	Matthew 27:60
10 . . . He surrendered himself to death and was counted among the wicked; And he shall take away the sins of many, and win pardon for their offenses.	Mark 15:28; Luke 22:37

The sad song of Jesus' sufferings has evidently drawn its descriptions of pain from the prophecy of Isaiah. But several notes in the same prophecy are also to be found in the account of the institution of the Eucharist.

New Testament	Isaiah
The night *he was handed over*	He surrendered to death (53:12)
This is my blood of the *covenant*	I set you as a *covenant* of the people (42:6)
poured out	he *poured out* (Hebrew text) his soul in death (53:12)
for *many* for the forgiveness of *sins*	He shall take away the *sins* of *many* (53:12)

The prophecy in Is. 42:6, in which God establishes his Servant as "a covenant of the people," sheds a special light on the mystery of Jesus.[29] Not only does Jesus seal the covenant, but also, in an infinitely truer way than the Servant, he is this covenant in his very person.

How is this to be understood? We must bear in mind that his being, in which humanity and divinity are united in a single person, does not derive from his mission; rather, his mission derives from his being. He enlightens the nations because he is the Light. He effects a universal reconciliation, "making peace through the blood of his cross" (Col. 1:20), because he joins in his flesh and blood the clay of mankind with the gold of the divinity he receives from his Father. So too, he seals the covenant between God and men because he combines divinity and humanity in himself; his body is, as it were, a dwelling place of love wherein mankind, once hatred has been slain (cf. Eph. 3:16), may regain intimate union with God and peace among its members.

8. *The universal covenant*

According to the tradition of Matthew and Mark, the blood of the covenant is shed "for many." A more accurate translation is: "for the multitude." The original Greek text does indeed read "for many," but, as is well known, it is itself a translation of the Aramaic words Jesus spoke. In Aramaic (and Hebrew), however, "many" can be used in an exclusive sense ("many," therefore not all) and in an inclusive sense as well (truly "many," that is, all).[30] This Semitism explains many passages which cause difficulty if "many" is taken in an exclusive sense.[31] In the account of the institution we must

understand that the blood shed "for many" is in fact shed "for all."
This last meal of Jesus with his disciples is in fact the first universal
meal, the first ecumenical Passover, to which the whole world is
invited and at which the whole world is mystically gathered. It is
that banquet of the whole vast human family that Yahweh had promised for the day when "he will wipe away the tears from all faces" (Is.
25:6-8).

The universality of the covenant is not opposed to the special
election of Israel and the preferential love God has for her. On the
contrary, the universality is grounded in the particularity. The calling given to Israel is a service to the nations, and Jewish particularism is a gateway of hope for all peoples. When God concludes
a covenant with one man (Noah or Abraham) or with one people
(Israel), he does so for the sake of all men, who are called to become
brothers before him. Thus the covenant with Noah extends to his
whole posterity, i.e., in the mind of the storyteller, the whole of
mankind; it even extends to the animals that live in brotherly fashion with him in the house of the ark, and it has its repercussions in
inanimate creation as well (cf. Gen. 9:13). So too, the covenant with
Abraham is a call to all the nations that are blessed in his name (Gen.
12:3).

The new element in the universality of the covenant sealed by the
Supper comes from the person of the mediator (cf. Heb. 8:6-13).
The brotherhood of all men, who are invited to the table of the one
Father, is no longer based simply upon the unity of the human race
(as in the case of Israel) nor upon the sameness of the call (as in the
case of the nations), but upon the fact that all mankind has been
adopted by God in Jesus Christ and that every man has become a
son of God in the only Son. The unity in the universality is no longer
based on the oneness of the human race that is "born" of Adam's
body and shares the same nature, but on the unifying grace of
Christ, the Son of Man, who calls all his brothers to make up his
"body" as Son of God.[32] "Is not the bread we break a sharing in the
body of Christ? Because the loaf of bread is one, we, many though
we are, are one body, for we all partake of the one loaf" (1 Cor.
10:16-17).

The new covenant also extends to material creation and illumines
it with its grace. This grace bestows a splendor which the new
heavens and new earth given to Noah after the deluge cannot claim.
For Christ, who was begotten in the infinity of eternity before time
was created, is also, in time, "the first-born of all creatures. In him

everything in heaven and on earth was created . . . all things created through him, and for him" (Col. 1:15-16). At the Supper Christ takes creation in his hands and sheds eternal light upon it. The bread which comes from the grain of wheat dropped into the earth, and the wine which flows from the grape, while continuing to belong to the present creation, become the body and blood of the Son of God! Creation had been groaning as it waited for the glory of the sons of God to be revealed (Rom. 8:21); here it shares the joy of the Son of God, for it becomes "eucharist," that is, thanksgiving. It is no longer simply a sign of God, "declaring his glory" (cf. Ps. 19:2); it is no longer simply a channel for God's grace as in the sacraments. In the Eucharist it becomes the body and blood of the Son of God. Such is the glory the new covenant bestows on creation.

What is the role of the Twelve at this banquet of the new covenant? They represent the twelve tribes of Israel which, according to tradition (Exod. 24:4), were present when the Sinai covenant was ratified. They also represent the Church of the New Testament, which is the new Jerusalem built upon twelve courses of foundation stones that bear the names of the twelve apostles of the Lamb (Apoc. 21:14). "The Twelve [are] the living symbol of the new people of God."[33] As the priestly and kingly people that was born when the Sinai covenant was made (Exod. 19:6) and is now fully sanctified in the suffering of the Cross (Apoc. 1:6; 5:10; 1 Peter 2:9), the Church, in the persons of the apostles, receives for the first time the eucharistic bread and wine, the body and blood of Christ, and transmits this memorial to all future ages.

9. "The new covenant"

To indicate the full richness of the covenant sealed by Christ, the Scriptures call it a "*new* covenant" (Luke 22:20; 1 Cor. 11:25; 2 Cor. 3:6; Heb. 9:15) or even a (literally) "*young* covenant" (Heb. 12:24). The New Testament origin of this phrase, with its emphasis on the "youthfulness" and "newness" of the covenant, is the account of institution according to the tradition represented by Paul and Luke. "This cup is the new covenant in my blood." The word "new" was probably not spoken by Jesus himself (the Palestinian source used by Matthew and Mark shows this) and originates, not in Paul and Luke, but in the Antiochene source used in Hellenistic circles.[34]

The theme of a new covenant, however, is not peculiar to what we today call the "New Testament," as if the time of the Gospel was regarded as the time of the new covenant, while the Law and the

Prophets were relegated to the darkness of the "old" Testament.
No, the term "new covenant" came ultimately from the "old" Testament, from Jer. 31:31-34. This prophecy, one of the most famous,
is evidence that the Old Testament did not turn inward in loving
contemplation of the Sinai covenant as though it were the end-all
and be-all; rather, the Old Testament looked to move beyond the
Sinai covenant. The yearning for a new covenant was like an open
wound in Israel's flesh and would be healed only when Jesus
satisfied that yearning.

We know that Jeremiah's prophecy was very dear to the early
community, which made it one of the "testimonies."[35] The Letter to
the Hebrews cites the prophecy in order to establish the superiority
of Christ:

> *Jesus has obtained a more excellent ministry* now, just as he is
> mediator of a better covenant, founded on better promises. If that
> first covenant had been faultless, there would have been no place for
> a second one. But God, finding fault with them, says: "Days are
> coming, says the Lord, when I will make a new covenant with the
> house of Israel and with the house of Judah. It will not be like the
> covenant I made with their fathers the day I took them by the hand to
> lead them forth from the land of Egypt; for they broke my covenant
> and I grew weary of them, says the Lord. But this is the covenant I
> will make with the house of Israel after those days, says the Lord: I
> will place my laws in their minds and I will write them upon their
> hearts; I will be their God and they shall be my people. And they shall
> not teach their fellow citizens or their brothers, saying, 'Know the
> Lord,' for all shall know me, from least to greatest. I will forgive their
> evildoing, and their sins I will remember no more." When he says, "a
> new covenant," he declares the first one obsolete. And what has
> become obsolete and grown old is close to disappearing (Heb. 8:6-13;
> citing Jer. 31:31-34).[36]

The most important elements in the prophecy of Jeremiah, which
the Letter to the Hebrews reads in the light of the new covenant
itself, are the following:

a) New covenant

The covenant here declared obsolete is expressly that of Sinai. If,
in the view of the prophets, the Exodus is Israel's birth, then the
covenant is the love that brought it to birth and sustains its life. This
is the covenant, haloed in the glory of Sinai and dominating popular
piety for century after century, that Jeremiah attacks with
unheard-of boldness (this is the only passage in the Hebrew Bible
that speaks of a *new* covenant!). He declares it to be no longer in

force, since it has been broken by Israel's infidelity (Heb. 8:9). The Letter to the Hebrews will insist on its inadequacy by calling it "obsolete," "grown old," and "close to disappearing" (Heb. 8:13), while the covenant of Jesus is "eternal" (Heb. 13:20).

b) The law written in men's hearts

On Sinai the law was written on tablets of stone; in the new covenant it is written in men's hearts. Doubtless, we should not lay too much stress on this difference, since the law of Sinai was written on stone in order that men might then take it into their hearts. The point being made here is that the new covenant no longer needs to be written on stone because it is so very much a divine word of love put into men's hearts. If it were put on stone, men might forget it, as the Israelites did. Once it is written on the heart, one can never lose sight of it. You can forget a stone tablet, but you cannot "forget" your heart.

c) Mutual belonging

The new covenant involves a mutual dedication of Israel to God and of God to Israel, as expressed in the traditional formula: "I will be their God and they shall be my people" (Heb. 8:10). Such a mutual belonging was already the ideal in the old covenant.[37] Now, however, this mutual belonging is lived in communion with Christ. Between himself and the faithful the Father has set his Christ. Christ is now the place where the Father and mankind meet. It is precisely this mutual belonging, in Christ, that the Eucharistic banquet celebrates: "I myself am the living bread come down from heaven. . . . The man who feeds on my flesh and drinks my blood remains in me, and I in him" (John 6:51, 56).

d) Taught by God

Since they have the law written in their hearts, the faithful are no longer dependent on external teaching: "And they shall not teach their fellow citizens or their brothers, saying, 'Know the Lord,' for all shall know me, from least to greatest" (Heb. 8:11). Or, to state it more accurately, the truth of teaching received from without ("He who hears you hears me") will be seen as in harmony with what each person discovers in the depths of his own heart. The prophets had foretold that knowledge of the Lord would fill the earth "as water covers the sea" (Is. 11:9). In the messianic age Jesus is the divine teacher who fulfills the prophecy: "They shall all be taught by God" (John 6:45; Is. 54:13).

e) *The forgiveness of sins*

The covenant offers sinners reconciliation with God: "I will forgive their evildoing, and their sins I will remember no more" (Heb. 8:12). When recounting the celebration of the new covenant at the Supper, Matthew (26:28) notes that Christ's blood is shed "for the forgiveness of sins" (cf. Heb. 9:11-14).

f) *Conclusion*

As we reflect on the new covenant and its implementation in ways beyond men's wildest dreams, we must face up to two questions.

One has to do with Jeremiah's prophecy. Isn't the new covenant he foretells so new that it is not a covenant at all, that is, not a juridical arrangement based on law and binding two contracting parties? Does it not represent rather a completely new type of relation — the relation of love that unites God with his people? [38]

Yes, of course, in declaring the Sinai covenant obsolete, Jeremiah is not attacking the relation between God and his people but the juridical and legalistic elements in the covenant that threatened the relation. The temptation for Israel was to think that because of the contract its good deeds gave it a hold on God, that its merits put God at its disposal. The prophet is protesting against this commercialized religion in which grace becomes an obligation and love a matter of calculation. "The prophet broke free from the covenant theory. Yet he did not despise its known and well-loved garment. He thus spoke of a new covenant, though in reality this is no longer a covenant." [39]

This first question leads to the second: Is not the covenant of the New Testament also so new as no longer to be a covenant? Is it possible to speak of a contract when God offers an infinite love and men can only extend their hands like beggars to receive it? "God is rich in mercy; because of his great love for us . . . salvation is yours through faith. This is not your own doing, it is God's gift" (Eph. 2:4, 8). What possible contract can cover such a situation? What man has the right to sit at Christ's table, receive his body, and share his kingdom? For the new covenant is the gateway into the kingdom.

In conclusion, we can say that just as God's word proclaimed by Christ Jesus to the messianic community is in fact Christ Jesus himself, so the new covenant which he enters into with those who believe in his mystery is likewise Christ Jesus himself.

¹ Cf. R. le Déaut, *La nuit pascale*, pp. 122–23.

² Cf. Is. 54:10; 55:3; 61:8; Jer. 31:31-34; Ezek. 16:60-62; 34:25; 37:26. In Dan. 11:28 and Mal. 3:1 the term "covenant" is for practical purposes identical with "religion."

³ *The War Rule*, XIV, 8–9 (Dupont-Sommer, *op. cit.*, p. 190).

⁴ A. Jaubert, *La notion d'alliance dans le Judaïsme aux abords de l'ère chrétienne* (Paris, 1963), writes: "The religious life of the Israelite community was based entirely on the covenant with God. Everything dear to the Israelite heart — possession of the land, national greatness, hope of a great king who would be a descendant of David and master of the earth's peoples, the holiness of the Jewish priesthood and the whole Israelite people — all this was promised in the covenant" (p. 55). Cf. O. Procksch, *Theologie des Alten Testaments:* "The Sinai covenant stands like a 'rock of bronze' at the beginning of the history of God's people. . . . The Old Testament, like the New, springs from God's covenant. The two Testaments are documents created by the covenant in the course of its history. The history of the covenant is the history of Israel, which is nothing else than the history of the people of the covenant" (pp. 521–22).

⁵ On the priesthood of Christ according to Hebrews, cf. C. Spicq, *L'Epître aux Hébreux* 2:140–299; A. Vanhoye, *Situation du Christ*, pp. 359–87; J. Colson, *Ministre de Jésus-Christ ou le sacerdoce de l'Evangile: Etude sur la condition sacerdotale des ministres chrétiens dans l'Eglise primitive* (Paris, 1965), pp. 97–110. Cf. also C. Spicq, "Médiation dans le Nouveau Testament," *DBS* 5:1020–83.

⁶ "Prius mente quam ventre," says St. Augustine, *Sermo 215: In redditione symboli*, 4 (*PL* 38:1074). For the witness of tradition, cf. L. Deiss, *Mary, Daughter of Sion*, p. 15.

⁷ L. Deiss, *op. cit.*, p. ix. Cf. R. Laurentin, *Court traité sur la Vierge Marie* (5th ed.; Paris, 1967): "Jesus and Mary are not only son and mother but Savior-God and redeemed mankind. They are the Church established, in germ and in hidden form, in its first two members: the redeemer and the first of the redeemed" (pp. 139–40).

⁸ Cf. C. Spicq, *Les Epîtres Pastorales* 1 (4th ed.; Paris, 1969), p. 366.

⁹ As the reader is aware, the New Testament accounts do not provide the precise historical data we would like to have. We do not know for sure if the Last Supper was a Passover meal in full conformity with the Jewish ritual, nor if Jesus died at the very hour when the Passover lambs were being slaughtered. For a good account of these questions, cf. E.J. Kilmartin, *The Eucharist in the Primitive Church* (Englewood Cliffs, N.J., 1965), pp. 37–48. The historical obscurities do not affect the interpretation of the events as transmitted to us by the early Church.

¹⁰ Cf. above, Chapter 1, Introduction, section 1.

¹¹ Cf. A. Díez-Macho, *Neophyti 1: Targum Palestinense, Ms de la Biblioteca Vaticana*, vol. 2: *Exodo (Exodo 12:13-42)* (Madrid-Barcelona, 1970), pp. 441–42 (English translation).

¹² To break bread as Judas did was an especially hateful form of betrayal; cf. Ps. 41:10; John 13:18.

¹³ Cf. Strack-Billerbeck, *op. cit.*, 4:216–21.

¹⁴ On the question whether the Eucharistic meal may have signified only the permanent communion between Jesus and his disciples (and not — also — a memorial of his death), cf. H. Conzelmann, *An Outline of the Theology of the New Testament*, translated by J. Bowden (New York, 1969), pp. 50–59.

¹⁵ Cf. Strack-Billerbeck, *op. cit.*, 4:210–39; J. Jeremias, *The Eucharistic Words of Jesus*, translated by N. Perrin (London, 1966), pp. 84–88.

¹⁶ Cf. P. Benoit, "Les récits de l'institution de l'Eucharistie et leur portée," in his *Exégèse et théologie* 1:215.

¹⁷ For the ritual now in use, cf. A. Szyk, *The Haggadah* (Jerusalem, 1960), or J. Bloch, *La Haggadah de Pâque* (Paris, 1970).

[18] It is evident that tradition had added symbolic value to the elements. The unleavened bread was originally just the bread baked by desert nomads, and the "bitter" herbs were the aromatic plants of the desert with which the Bedouin seasoned their food (and still do so today). Cf. R. de Vaux, *Studies in Old Testament Sacrifice*, pp. 10–11.

[19] Cf. N. Lazure, *Les valeurs morales de la théologie johannique* (Paris, 1965), pp. 125–26.

[20] There is a special problem with Luke's text. Some manuscripts omit the end of verse 19 (19b) and the whole of verse 20. On the other hand, Luke prefaces his account of the institution with verses 15-18, in which he speaks of the Jewish Passover (mentioning explicitly the cup of wine), thus making the latter an introduction to the Christian Passover. Today the authenticity of verses 19b-20 is generally admitted, and the omission of them in some manuscripts is regarded as a mutilation of the text. "Such a mutilation would be understandable in a post-apostolic community which recognized the eucharistic coloring associated with the cup of verses 17-18 and wished to avoid having two eucharistic cups in the one account" (E. J. Kilmartin, *op. cit.*, p. 26). On the text of Luke, cf. H. Schürmann, *Le récit de la dernière cène* (Le Puy, 1966) and P. Benoit, "Le récit de la Cène dans Luc 22, 15-20," in his *Exégèse et théologie* 1:163–203. Cf. also J. Coppens, "Eucharistie," *DBS* 2:1169.

[21] L. Cerfaux, *The Church in the Theology of St. Paul*, observes: "Everything indicates that this was an apostolic tradition and not a revelation which Paul himself had received" (p. 257).

[22] E. J. Kilmartin, *op. cit.*, suggests "around A.D. 40" (p. 35).

[23] J. Coppens, "L'Eucharistie: Sacrement et sacrifice de la Nouvelle Alliance, Fondement de l'Eglise," in J. Giblet *et al.*, *Aux origines de l'Eglise* (Recherches bibliques 7; Bruges, 1965), p. 145.

[24] According to Jewish tradition, red wine was used at the Passover meal; cf. J. Jeremias, *op. cit.*, p. 52.

[25] These are the words of Moses which Heb. 9:20 quotes when speaking of Christ as mediator of the new covenant.

[26] Cf. R. de Vaux, *op. cit.*, p. 25, and the remarks of C. Spicq on 1 Peter 1:19 in his *Les Epîtres de Saint Pierre* (Paris, 1966), p. 68.

[27] Cf. J. Jeremias, *op. cit.*, p. 219.

[28] Is. 42:1-9; 49:1-6; 50:4-11; 52:13–53:12. Cf. L. Deiss, *Synopse* 1:181–82.

[29] Note that Moses, the mediator of the Sinai covenant, is also described as a servant of Yahweh (Exod. 4:10; 14:31; Num. 11:11; 12:7; Deut. 3:24; 34:5). Cf. R. Bloch, "Moïse dans la tradition rabbinque," in *Moïse, l'Homme de L'Alliance*, pp. 153–56 (on Moses and the Servant of Yahweh).

[30] Cf. J. Jeremias, *op. cit.*, pp. 179–82.

[31] Some examples (with the word "many" restored, if need be, where it occurs in Greek): Rom. 5:15: "For if by the offense of the one man [Adam] *many* [i.e., all] died, much more did the grace of God and the gracious gift of the one man, Jesus Christ, abound for *many* [i.e., all]."

Rom. 5:19: "Just as through one man's [Adam's] disobedience *many* [i.e., all] became sinners, so through one man's [Christ's] obedience *many* [i.e., all] shall become just."

Mark 10:45 and Matthew 20:28: The Son of Man has come "to give his life in ransom for the *many* [i.e., for all]."

Matthew 22:14: "The invited are *many* [i.e., all the Jews], the elect are few."

Mark 1:32-34 and Matthew 8:16: All the sick are brought to Jesus (Mark), and he cures *many*, according to Mark 1:34 (i.e., all, as Matthew 8:16 explains).

Luke 7:47: "Her *many* [i.e., all her] sins are forgiven — because of her great love."

[32] Cf. L. Cerfaux, *The Church in the Theology of St. Paul*, pp. 237–39 (the unity of Christians through the [Eucharistic] body of Christ); J. A. T. Robinson, *The Body: A*

Study in Pauline Theology, chapter on "The One and the Many." On the Church as the body of Christ, cf. W. Goosens, *L'Eglise Corps du Christ d'après Saint Paul* (Paris, 1949).

[33] J. Jeremias, *op. cit.*, p. 207.

[34] Cf. J. Jeremias, *op. cit.*, pp. 171–72.

[35] Cf. C.H. Dodd, *According to the Scriptures*, pp. 44–46. — The covenant theme was very important in the Qumran community, which claimed to be "the Community of the everlasting Covenant" (*Rule* 5:5-6) and called its members "those who cling firmly to the holy Covenant" (*Damascus Document* 1:2). Texts in A. Dupont-Sommer, *op. cit.*, pp. 83 and 110.

[36] Hebrews cites Jeremiah rather faithfully according to the LXX. On the new covenant according to the Letter to the Hebrews, cf. C. Spicq, *L'Epître aux Hébreux* 2:238–45, 285–99, 310–13. On Jeremiah 31:31-34, cf. P. Buis, "La Nouvelle Alliance," *Vetus Testamentum* 18 (1968), pp. 1–15.

[37] Cf. Deut. 7:6 and the expanded statements in Jer. 24:7; 32:38; Ezek. 11:20; 36:28; 37:27.

[38] The ideas presented in Jer. 31:31-34 are also found not only in Jer. 32:37-41 but in Ezek. 11:17-20; 34:24-31; 36:24-27; 37:23-28; Bar. 2:29-34; and, in a lesser degree, in Jer. 24:5-7; Ezek. 16:53-63; Is. 54:10; 55:3. Cf. P. Buis, *art. cit.*, and L. Krinetski, *L'Alliance de Dieu avec les hommes* (Paris, 1970), pp. 68–88. Jer. 31:31-34 is not a unique passage in Scripture; what is unique about it is that it speaks of a new covenant and contrasts it with the covenant of Sinai.

[39] G. Quell, "diathēkē," *TDNT* 2:124.

CONCLUSIONS

Our inquiry has led us from the celebration of the Sinai covenant to the celebration of the new covenant in Jesus Christ. We could carry it further by studying the Christian celebration from the early community down to our own day. In such a study we would see how Christians of all rites have understood and experienced the liturgy of the word and the liturgy of the Eucharist. We would try to extract from the historical material the basic laws which, above and beyond the various particular traditions, constitute tradition as such and connect each celebration, via the supreme moment which is the new covenant sealed by Jesus, with the great festival of Sinai.

Yet even though we stop our inquiry at the point we have now reached, we can point to some conclusions that seem quite evident. As a matter of fact, we really want, not so much to "conclude" to anything, as to take a look at current problems. The study of the past becomes really valuable only when it enables us to look to the future. The man who has climbed a high mountain spends his time, there on the top, not in marveling at the path he has struggled up, but in seeing in a new light and from hitherto unknown vantage points the landscape stretched below him.

We cannot take up all the problems and all the solutions implied in the subject of our study. We shall therefore look at those we think specially important, namely, to begin with, the connection between the celebration of the word and the covenant (Chapter 12), between the word and the ecclesial community (Chapter 13), and between the word and history (Chapter 14). We shall then speak of the homily, which actualizes the word or makes it relevant to the here and now (Chapter 15). Finally, we shall turn to the gathering of the nations, that is, to the Church's mission in our day (Chapter 16).

Chapter 12

THE CELEBRATION OF THE
WORD AND THE COVENANT

We are concerned here with the important role of the word in the concluding of the covenant and especially in the celebration of the Mass. After emphasizing the "paramount importance" of the word in the liturgy, as well as the table of the word and the table of the Eucharist, we will show that the word, proclaimed in God's name and accepted by the people, is a constitutive factor in the sealing of the covenant.

1. The "paramount importance" of the word

Vatican II's *Constitution on the Sacred Liturgy* emphasizes the "paramount importance"[1] of the word of God in liturgical celebrations. This "paramount importance" already finds expression in the simple fact that the signs used in the sacraments, as well as the prayers and songs used in liturgical celebrations, are all firmly grounded in the word of God. This is so true that if someone unfamiliar with the language of Scripture were to attend a Christian celebration, he would feel as though he were in a foreign country listening to people speaking a foreign language. This very situation creates problems, of course, for a liturgy that seeks to proclaim the faith and yet, by taking refuge in a purely material fidelity to the letter of Scripture, becomes unintelligible to those not already initiated.

The "paramount importance" of the word of God is also indicated by the rites that accompany the proclamation of the Gospel at Mass and are intended to highlight the dignity of God's word. All the liturgies, Eastern and Western, introduce the solemn proclamation of the Gospel with a procession involving lights and incense. At

Rome, in the seventh century, seven torches were carried in the procession (the seven lampstands of Apoc. 1:12, 20) and the Trisagion was sung. The liturgists tell us that all this was intended as "a representation of Christ's triumphal coming."[2]

As a sign of veneration the evangeliaries containing the sacred text were richly decorated with bindings of gold, silver, or ivory.[3] Thus in 1379 Charles V made an offering of a golden evangeliary from the tenth–eleventh centuries, on which there were 35 sapphires, 24 rubies, 30 emeralds, and 104 pearls. In Byzantine churches the evangeliary was often the greatest treasure possessed. Sometimes the manuscripts were written in letters of gold on a purple background and richly adorned with miniatures. In addition, the evangeliary could be exposed on the altar, a privilege it shared only with the Eucharist itself; this custom has been preserved in the Greek Church down to the present time. At councils, such as the Council of Ephesus in 431, the evangeliary was set on a throne to symbolize the presence of Christ who was presiding over the assembly of his Church.[4] Vatican II has restored the enthronement of the Gospel. All these rites and signs express the interior veneration the Church has for God's word.

The "paramount importance" finds its fullest expression in the Mass itself, in the readings which, as it were, preface the celebration of the Eucharist proper, for all of these readings are from the Bible. Ever since the first modest beginnings of Christian liturgy, the Church has always thought, and still does today, that only God's word was worthy to have a place in the Eucharistic liturgy.[5] The proclamation of that word in the liturgy was quite extensive. Thus, in the Church of Antioch during the fourth century there were four readings: the Law and the Prophets (as in the synagogue), the New Testament letters (or Acts), and the Gospel. The Jacobites had as many as six, with three from the Old Testament (Law, Prophets, Wisdom books) and three from the New (Acts or Catholic letters, Pauline letters, and Gospel). The Chaldeans had four readings: Law, Prophets, Pauline letters, and Gospel. The Armenian, Gallican, Mozarabic, and Ambrosian liturgies, and probably the Roman as well, had three readings, one from the Old Testament and two from the New.

We all know how formalistic, despite the accompanying liturgical rites, the reading of God's word had become in the solemn liturgy of the Roman rite. The word was proclaimed with the reader's back to the people (for the epistle) or his face to the wall (for the Gospel), in a dead language, and from a text which represented only a small part of the whole word of God.[6] The Churches which sprang from the Reformation were, despite the scriptural riches they so jealously championed, not necessarily in a better situation, since the celebration of God's word usually was made a matter of words alone and rarely led to the celebration of the Supper.

With reason, then, did the Council determine that "in sacred celebrations a more ample, more varied, and more suitable reading from sacred scripture should be restored."[7] The new lectionary for the Roman rite is a response to the challenge and represents the most courageous effort made in fifteen centuries of Church history to give the Christian people greater access to the treasures of Scripture.[8]

But the introduction of a new book, even if it be the best of lectionaries, does not magically guarantee a reform of hearts and minds. The "paramount importance" of the word of God is something that must also be realized in our liturgical celebrations and in daily life itself.

2. The table of the word and the table of the Eucharist

How is this importance of the word manifested? We are thinking here of the word as part of the Mass. There are other types of celebration, of course, focused entirely on the word; in these the word is evidently the most important element. In studying the Mass, however, we raise the problem at its highest level and in its fullest form, since the Mass is "the true center of the sacred liturgy, and indeed of the whole Christian life."[9]

In point of fact, it is safe to say that Christians in most of the Eastern and Western rites and in the confessions produced by the Reformation (except for certain Protestant Churches that do not celebrate the Supper) celebrate the word chiefly in the course of the Eucharist. Reading by the individual or the family is certainly desirable, of course. But nothing can substitute for the ecclesial celebration of God's word, that is, a celebration of it along with the entire Christian community, under the leadership of the priest in charge of the Eucharist.

In practice, the knowledge which the vast majority of the faithful have of God's word is what they have learned during the Eucharistic liturgy. It is there that they celebrate God's word. Their situation is really not much different than that of people in times when printing had not yet made Bibles available for private use, and yet people did know the word of God! In any case, the ecclesial celebration does not prevent but rather encourages the private reading of Scripture and provides the believers with ways and means of reading it.

The paramount importance of the word in the framework of the Mass can be stated briefly by saying that it has the same importance as the Eucharist itself. Vatican II asserts: "The Church has always venerated the divine Scriptures as she venerated the Body of the Lord, in so far as she never ceases, particularly in the sacred liturgy, to partake of the bread of life and to offer it to the faithful from the one table of the Word of God and the Body of Christ."[10] The word of God is thus no less "venerable" than the body of the Lord. The table of the word and the table of the Eucharist offer the faithful one and the same Lord. He who communicates in the word and he who communicates in the bread of life both share in Christ Jesus.

The text adopted in the *Dogmatic Constitution on Divine Revelation* makes up for the *Constitution on the Sacred Liturgy*, but it was not voted in without a struggle.[11] Several amendments were proposed, on the grounds that the text went too far in assimilating the word to the Eucharist. But, whereas the conciliar commission on the liturgy had allowed itself "to be too quickly intimidated"[12] by the criticisms, the commission on revelation resisted. More accurately, it refuted the criticisms in the name of tradition itself. For the comparison of word and Eucharist comes to us from the Fathers. In his *Homilies on Exodus* (preached probably after 232, at Caesarea in Palestine), Origen had already given an explanation, as he commented on Moses' command: "(Make offerings to the Lord) everyone, as he conceives in his heart" (Exod. 35:5):

> See whether or not you "conceive," that is, retain the words of God lest they slip from your hand and you lose them.
>
> I want to urge you to this by examples drawn from your religious practices. If you are habitually present at the divine mysteries, you know how carefully and respectfully you protect the Lord's body when it is given to you, lest a fragment of it fall and a bit of the consecrated treasure be lost. You would think yourself guilty, and with good reason, if some of it were lost through your negligence. Now if you rightly take such precaution when it is a question of the Lord's body, how can you think that neglect of God's word will be less severely punished than neglect of his body?[13]

And here is St. Caesarius of Arles (d. 542) bearing witness to the same belief:

> I have a question for you, brothers and sisters. Which do you think more important — the word of God or the body of Christ? If you want

to answer correctly, you must tell me that the word of God is no less important than the body of Christ! How careful we are, when the body of Christ is distributed to us, not to let any bit of it fall to the ground from our hand! But we should be just as careful not to let slip from our hearts the word of God that is addressed to us, by thinking or speaking of something else. He will be no less guilty who listens negligently to the word of God than he who by his negligence allows the Lord's body to fall to the ground.[14]

Word and Eucharist, then, are equally important, equally "venerable." And the veneration due them is the adoration we offer the Lord who is present in the word and present in the Eucharist. In the Eucharist he is present under the veil of bread and wine; in the word he is present under the veil of human words. We can therefore speak of a "real presence" of Christ in the Scriptures, a presence no less real than his presence in the Eucharist, although the latter is sacramental.[15]

The liturgy of the word can no longer rightly be called the "fore-Mass" or the "liturgy of the catechumens." There is no denying, of course, that listening to the word is an excellent way of learning, over and over again, to live according to the Gospel, nor that it is an effective, and even the best possible, preparation for the celebration of the Eucharistic liturgy proper. But it is infinitely more than a mere way of turning the earth of our souls, as it were, so that the Eucharist may bear fruit in it. It is infinitely more than a school of Chistian life. Above and beyond these things, it is essentially a celebration of Christ who is present in his word. It is a communion with Christ who "is present in his word, since it is he himself who speaks when the holy scriptures are read in the Church."[16]

3. Celebration of the covenant

There is a final point to be made about the celebration of the word. We can make it by harking back to the results of the analyses already made of the covenants of Moses at Sinai, of Joshua at Shechem, and of Josiah and Ezra at Jerusalem.[17] We just made the statement that the celebration of the word at Mass is as important as the celebration of the Eucharist proper. Now we must add that *this celebration of the word — the word proclaimed in God's name and accepted by the community — is constitutive of the covenant*. It is not simply a condition whose fulfillment gives access to the Eucharistic banquet where we eat the body of Christ and drink the blood of the covenant. No, it is itself already a celebration of the covenant.

Consider first the assembly at Sinai. We have pointed out that Exod. 24:1-11, which relates the event, is composed of texts from various sources. Undoubtedly, Exod. 24:9-11, which speaks only of a communion meal, is the oldest part of the whole text.[18] But the mosaic of texts that immediately precedes, namely 24:1-8, as inherited by Israel, closely connects the proclamation of the word or "preaching of the covenant"[19] with the sacrificial ritual, to such an extent that the "blood of the covenant" is inconceivable apart from the proclamation of the word and its acceptance by the people: "Moses came to the people and related all the words and ordinances of the Lord" (24:3). The people with one voice shouted their acceptance. Then "Moses wrote down all the words of the Lord" (24:4). Finally, when the altar had been readied and the victims immolated,

> taking the book of the covenant, he read it aloud to the people, who answered, "All that the Lord has said, we will heed and do." Then he took the blood and sprinkled it on the people, saying, "This is the blood of the covenant which the Lord has made with you, in accordance with all these words of his" (Exod. 24:7-8).

The celebration of the word is thus a constitutive element of the Sinai covenant. The altar upon which the "blood of the covenant" flows receives its full meaning from the word that is proclaimed; the covenant is concluded "in accordance with all these words of his."

We should also recall the formula "I am the Lord your God" which is so characteristic of the covenant formulary and, in particular, prefaces the Decalogue (Exod. 20:1) and, later, the great commandment: "Hear, O Israel! The Lord is our God, the Lord alone!" (Deut. 6:4). The word spoken by God and accepted by Israel is the foundation upon which the covenant is built. In turn, the covenant sheds a new light upon this word. The word is now seen as the law which God gives to *his* people and the word which the Father speaks to his children (cf. Deut. 32:5-6). When, in an evidently anachronistic fashion, the tradition connects a vast collection of laws with Sinai, it is undoubtedly ignoring the passage of time, but on the other hand it is also giving splendid expression to something that happened once at Sinai and was then engraved forever in the heart of Israel: There can be no covenant without accepting God's word, and every law is also an invitation to enter more deeply into the covenant.

The reader will remember how important the word was in the assembly at Shechem (according to Josh. 24): how the long profession of faith, with its recall of the events of Israel's history (24:2-13), and the demand for a clear choice for or against Yahweh and the people's positive response (24:14-24) turned this covenant gathering into a pure celebration of the word. Summing up the Shechem covenant, the author writes: "So Joshua made a covenant with the people that day and made statutes and ordinances for them at Shechem, which he recorded in the book of the law of God" (Josh. 24:25-26).

The text says nothing of a communion meal; [20] doubtless such a meal was taken for granted, and yet the omission is significant, for it implies that the sealing of the covenant is wholly contained in the proclamation of the word in God's name and in the acceptance of it by the people.

The word has a similar important role in the assembly of Josiah:

> He [the king] had the entire contents of the book of the covenant that had been found in the temple of the Lord, read out to them [the people]. Standing by the column, the king made a covenant before the Lord that they would follow him and observe his ordinances, statutes, and decrees with their whole hearts and souls, thus reviving the terms of the covenant which were written in this book. And all the people stood as participants in the covenant (2 Kings 23:2-3).

Even though this celebration of the law is climaxed by Josiah's famous Passover in which the communion meal recalled the Sinai covenant, the celebration was really enough for purposes of covenant renewal, since the people listened to the law, promised to "follow" Yahweh, and "stood as participants in the covenant." The communion meal was important only to the extent that it gave joyous festive expression to the covenant concluded between God and his people.

We are now in a position to say that the distinction we have been making throughout this book between the proclamation of the law to the people and the concluding of the covenant is valid only to the extent that it facilitates the analysis of elements which it distinguishes in order then to unite them. The distinction does not accurately express the reality as experienced by God's people. In that experience, the covenant was concluded as soon as the word was accepted; the communion meal only gave expression to a grace already received.

We can apply this conclusion to the Mass, which celebrates the new covenant mediated by Jesus Christ. For ease in talking about the Mass, we can distinguish between the liturgy of the word and the Eucharistic liturgy proper. But these are not two parts which follow one upon the other logically (and chronologically), with one of the two (the word) being a prior condition for the other (the Eucharist). We must rather maintain that the celebration of the word is constitutive of the covenant. Even though the bread and wine of the covenant meal are offered in the Eucharistic liturgy proper, the covenant itself is concluded in the proclamation and acceptance of the word. The Council says: "The two parts which in a sense go to make up the Mass, viz. the liturgy of the word and the eucharistic liturgy, are so closely connected with each other that they form but one single act of worship."[21] But *this one single act of worship is the celebration of the covenant.*

The clearest example of this union of word and Eucharist is undoubtedly the narrative of institution as celebrated in the Mass. Here we have, on the one hand, a proclamation of the word, and specifically the account of Jesus' last meal with his disciples, and, on the other hand, the Eucharist, the bread and wine of the new covenant. The proclaimed word is so powerful that it creates the Eucharist, that is, the presence of the dead and risen Christ, and reactualizes his covenant. But the Eucharist in turn proclaims the word: "Every time, then, you eat this bread and drink this cup, you proclaim the death of the Lord until he comes!" (1 Cor. 11:26). After the fashion of a Christian haggadah, the Eucharist explains that the body "given" and the blood "shed" recall the sacrificial death of Christ Jesus.[22] Thus the word creates the Eucharist, and the Eucharist in turn proclaims the word.

4. Pastoral perspectives

The unity of word and Eucharist, as manifested by tradition, becomes obligatory for the celebration of Mass and provides an ideal that may be formulated under the following two headings:

a) No celebration of the Eucharist without a celebration of the word

A community that is content to read the sacred texts as though it were carrying out a rite that leads to the Eucharist is still far from the full reality. The community may be observing the rubrics perfectly, but it is at odds with the true tradition of God's people. The community must learn to "celebrate" the word, that is, to receive it, with faith and love, as a covenant word and therefore a rule of life.

The readings at each Mass are a preaching of the covenant. God is, as it were, saying to the community: "If you wish to enter into my covenant and to receive the bread and festive wine in the form of Eucharist, here is the contract I offer for your loving acceptance. Upon the word proclaimed at this Mass I base today's renewal of the covenant." And the celebrating assembly must be ready to answer as the assembly did at Sinai: "All that the Lord has said, we will heed and do." Only then will the priest be able to take the "cup of blessing" and say with Moses: "This is the blood of the covenant which the Lord has made with you in accordance with all these words of his" (Exod. 24:7-8).

A corollary to this first point is that only the *word of God* is valid in celebrating a *covenant with God*. No merely human words, be they a text from the tradition, a document of the magisterium, or something current from the newspapers or magazines, can rival the word of God. Those other texts can certainly be very useful for illustrating the word and showing how it fits into the present life of men; sometimes they are even indispensable. But in no event can they replace God's word. We cannot substitute man's word for God's any more than we can substitute ordinary bread for the Eucharistic bread.[23] We can sum up the situation thus: The proclamation of human words goes with a human covenant, while a covenant with God requires the proclamation of God's word.

Communities which too readily substitute a newspaper article for the sacred text should ask themselves what religion they are celebrating — the religion reflected in the newspaper or the religion proper to the covenant with the God of Jesus Christ.

b) No celebration of the word without reference to the covenant

The proclamation of the word is not an end in itself. Its purpose is rather the communion of men with God, their entry into the covenant of love of which the Eucharist is the pledge. Every word of God throughout the history of the chosen people was preparing for God's great act: the coming of Jesus Christ into the human family so that he might enable the human family to become, through the covenant, the family of God. So too, today, every word of God has the same wonderful purpose and is meant, via the covenant, to open the doors of the Father's house.

Thus it is from the covenant that the word receives its full clarification. If the word proclaims laws, the latter will be expressions of a covenant morality.[24] If it proposes truths to be believed, the faith will be a covenant faith. In short, every word that is in the service of the covenant is ennobled by it.

This constant reference to the covenant clearly does not imply that every celebration of the word must end with the sacramental Eucharist. But it does tend, at least virtually, toward the Eucharist. Let us say that it is oriented toward the grace of the Eucharist or, if you prefer, to a "spiritual communion" when sacramental communion is not to be available. No one is in a position to give advice on how often the Eucharist should be celebrated in any given place; each community must "examine itself," as St. Paul says (1 Cor. 11:28) and determine before the Lord what is right and fitting. Each of the great rites in the Church has its own traditions, and the Eastern rites, which, by and large, celebrate the Eucharist less frequently during the week, are no less venerable than the Roman rite, in which daily Mass is the custom. What can be said is that every celebration of the word tends, in virtue of its inherent dynamism, toward the grace of the Eucharist.

The two principles we have been presenting shed some light on the question of the essence of priestly ministry.[25] As we know, little progress is being made on this question at the moment, yet the question is an important one, and there is some urgency about answering it. Until we can say clearly what a priest is, we would be naive to expect a rise in the number of vocations. No one commits himself to something foggy and difficult to pin down. Moreover, the question of the priesthood is closely linked to the preaching of the Gospel, which is the Church's primary task.

The Council of Trent made the celebration of Mass the priest's most important function. Vatican II gives priority to the preaching of the word.[26] We may be tempted therefore to construct a dilemma: word or Eucharist. Here we would be setting over against one another a priesthood focused on the liturgical celebration of the Eucharist and a prophetic priesthood ordered to the proclamation of the Good News.

The opposition would be misconceived. It is clear that the priesthood cannot be defined solely by the liturgical power to preside over the Eucharist, but neither can it be understood without reference to that power. Just as clearly, the priesthood cannot be defined solely in terms of the preaching of the word, but neither can it be understood without reference to such preaching. As a matter of fact, the intimate connection we have seen to exist between word and Eucharist is the basis of the unity of priestly ministry. The proclaimed word includes the preaching of the death and resurrection of Christ, that is, the mysteries which effect the new covenant and which the Eucharist celebrates. Just as the proclamation of the word is constitutive of the celebration of covenant and Eucharist, so too it is constitutive of the priestly ministry and especially of the Eucharistic celebration of the covenant. The priest "has the mission to preach the Gospel in the name of the Church. He does this at the highest level at which this Word can operate in the anamnesis of Christ's death and resurrection through the celebration of the Eucharist."[27]

[1] *Constitution on the Sacred Liturgy*, no. 24 (Abbott, p. 147). On the word of God in the liturgy, cf. J. Lécuyer, *Le sacrifice de la nouvelle alliance* (Le Puy, 1962), pp. 227–39; H. Schmidt, *Constitution de la sainte liturgie: Genèse et commentaire* (Brussels, 1966), pp. 181–92; J. Jossua, "La Constitution 'Sacrosanctum Concilium' dans l'ensemble de l'oeuvre conciliaire," in *La liturgie après Vatican II* (Unam Sanctam 66; Paris, 1967), pp. 141–46; A.G. Martimort *et al.*, *The Liturgy and the Word of God* (Collegeville, 1959); *La Maison-Dieu*, no. 82 (1965): *Ecriture sainte et parole de Dieu*.

[2] J.A. Jungmann, *The Mass of the Roman Rite: Its Origin and Development (Missarum Solemnia)* 1, translated by F.A. Brunner (New York, 1951), p. 445.

[3] Cf. A. Croegaert, *Les rites et prières du Saint Sacrifice de la Messe* 1 (2nd ed.; Malines, 1948), pp. 552–58. [There is an abridged English translation by J. Holland-Smith, *The Mass: A Liturgical Commentary*, 2 vols. (London, 1958–59).]

[4] Cf. St. Cyril of Alexandria, *Apologeticus ad Imperatorem (PG* 76:472B).

[5] Fluctuations in this practice concerned chiefly the inclusion of the acts of the martyrs (cf. J.A. Jungmann, *op. cit.*, 1:393, note 1). In the difficult days of persecution such readings could be a valuable encouragement to the Christian community. Other writings, such as the *Letter to the Corinthians* of St. Clement of Rome or the *Shepherd of Hermas* were also read in the churches (cf. Eusebius of Caesarea, *History of the Church*, III, 3, 6; 3, 15) because they were regarded as inspired. On the formation of the New Testament canon, cf. H. von Campenhausen, *The Formation of the Christian Bible*, pp. 210–68.

[6] The first reading was taken chiefly from St. Paul, at the expense of the Old Testament (cf. A. Croegaert, *op. cit.*, pp. 576–80); the Gospel was taken chiefly from John and Matthew (*ibid.*).

[7] *Constitution on the Sacred Liturgy*, no. 35.1 (Flannery, p. 12).

[8] Cf. N. Denis-Boulet, "The Liturgy of the Word," in A.G. Martimort (ed.), *The Eucharist (The Church at Prayer 2)*, English edition by A. Flannery, O.P., and V. Ryan, O.S.B. (New York, 1973), pp. 98–100.

[9] Instruction *Eucharisticum Mysterium* of the Sacred Congregation of Rites, May 25, 1967 (Flannery, p. 100); cf. no. 5.

[10] *Dogmatic Constitution on Divine Revelation*, no. 21 (Flannery, p. 762). The idea recurs in the *Decree on the Ministry and Life of Priests*, no. 18, and the *Decree on the Appropriate Renewal of Religious Life*, no. 6. Cf. also the *Decree on the Church's Missionary Activity*, no. 6.

[11] Cf. A. Grillmeier, "La sainte Ecriture dans la vie de l'Eglise," in Y. Congar (ed.), *La Révélation Divine* (Unam sanctam 70; Paris, 1968), pp. 438–45.

[12] Grillmeier, *art. cit.*, p. 440, note 10.

[13] Origen, *Homiliae in Exodum*, XIII, 3; French translation by P. Fortier in *Origène: Homélies sur l'Exode* (Sources chrétiennes 16; Paris, 1947), p. 263.

[14] St. Caesarius of Arles, *Sermo* 78, 2 (*CCL* 103:323–24).

[15] The Instruction *Eucharisticum Mysterium* speaks (no. 9) of Christ as present in the assembly, in the word, and in the Eucharist, and adds: "This presence of Christ under the species 'is called "real" not in an exclusive sense, as if the other kinds of presence were not real, but *par excellence*' " (Flannery, p. 109). The document is quoting Pope Paul VI, Encyclical Letter *Mysterium Fidei*, no. 29 (*The Pope Speaks* 10 [1964–65], p. 319).

[16] *Constitution on the Sacred Liturgy*, no. 7 (Flannery, p. 5).

[17] Cf. M. Noth, *The Laws in the Pentateuch*, in his *The Laws in the Pentateuch and Other Studies*, translated by D. R. Ap-Thomas (Philadelphia, 1967), pp. 1–107, especially pp. 20–59 on " 'Covenant' and Law." Cf. also P. Grelot, *Sens chrétien de l'Ancien Testament*, pp. 168–69.

[18] M. Noth, *op cit.*, p. 39.

[19] P. Buis, "Les formulaires de l'Alliance," *Vetus Testamentum* 16 (1960), p. 402.

[20] Only Josh. 8:30-35 mentions the building of an altar, the offering of holocausts, and the immolation of peace offerings.

[21] *Constitution on the Sacred Liturgy*, no. 56 (Flannery, p. 19).

[22] Cf. F. Godet, *Commentaire sur la Première Epître aux Corinthiens* 2 (2nd ed.; Neuchâtel, 1965), p. 174.

[23] Some flexibility is required in applying this rule which follows from the unity between word and Eucharist. The liturgical celebration of a community is to be defined, not by a single act of worship (a single Sunday Eucharist, for example), but by all the celebrations that establish the rhythm of its prayer life. A liturgical community is like a family, and the quality of the family's life is to be judged, not by a single gesture of love, but by its life as a whole. Consequently, a community that worthily celebrates the word throughout the year is not destroyed if occasionally it reads some other text in its celebrations. The general orientation, not the exception, is what counts.

[24] Cf. J. L'Hour, *La morale de l'Alliance*.

[25] They shed light on the problem but cannot completely resolve it. A complete solution depends on the conception one has of the structure of the Church.

[26] *Decree on the Ministry and Life of Priests*, no. 4.

[27] K. Rahner, "What is the Theological Starting Point for a Definition of the Priestly Ministry?" in K. Rahner (ed.), *The Identity of the Priest* (Concilium 43; New York, 1969), p. 85.

Chapter 13

WORD AND COMMUNITY

The importance we are giving to the word may rouse fears that the Christian community might be led astray into a kind of "biblicism." In other words, Christians might come to think of the study of the Bible as the supreme Christian activity, and the diffusion of the Bible by modern methods as the essential apostolic ministry. They would thus incorrectly avoid the real problems every baptized person must face because he lives in this world, in the universal human community, and in the stream of history.

Now, there can be no denying that every believer, every community, every confession may be subject to such temptations and that the temptations may be all the more insidious because they wear the mask of dedication to God's word and can obscure the need of an authentic conversion of heart. But the very study of the Bible, as the latter emerged from the history of God's people and was lived by that people, shows us that the service of the word demands far more than the mere study of the word. To put it another way: The very study of the Bible teaches us to avoid "biblicism," since in learning to base our lives on God's word, we discover the real dimensions of that word. We shall now consider the links between God's word and community (Chapter 13) and between God's word and history (Chapter 14).

1. Word and community

Theologians assert that the *Church* is itself, in a sense, *God's word*, and that the Church is in a way identical with the message she proclaims.[1] The *Gospel lived* by the Christian community becomes a *living Gospel* for the world. This is true not only of the Church as a whole but of each individual community that is a particular incarnation, in time and space, of the universal Church.

2. *The community, servant of the word*

The links between word and community are numerous and profound. On the one hand, the word of God, as we said earlier, creates the ecclesial community. Having been born from the word,[2] the particular Churches continue to exist only if they are continuously grounded in the word. Just as the creation of the universe is unending, in the sense that God continues to maintain the universe in existence at every instant of time and, as Scripture puts it, to hold it in his hands (cf. Ps. 95:4), so the building of the Church is never complete inasmuch as God must constantly call to Christian life those who are meant to become the "living stones" (1 Peter 2:5) of the edifice.

On the other hand, while the word creates the ecclesial community, the community can also be said to "create" the word. The Church was initially the cradle, as it were, that received the message of God at Sinai, then at Shechem, then at Jerusalem (cf. Chapters 1–4, above). The Church then tested the books inherited from the past, judging them in the light of her faith; she decided, in the light given by the Spirit, which of these books were for her the authentic voice of God (cf. Chapter 5, above). She has also watched over the deposit, that is, the revelation God has laid in her weak hands, so that she might pass it on to future ages. She proclaims the word in her liturgical celebrations and actualizes it in her homilies; now that the prophets and evangelists have fallen silent, she comments on the word in every part of her teaching. All these relations between word and community can be called entirely normal. They are to be explained by the fact that the believer is, in the magnificent phrase of Luke 1:2, a "minister of the word."

3. *Creation, God's "word"*

We can even say that in a sense the whole of creation is God's word. The humble grain of sand lost in the immensity of the oceans "cries out" God's glory as intensely as the infinite heavens with their countless stars. Since the radiant creative intelligence of God called the universe into being, the universe reflects the face of God.[3] To read the word which creation is, we need only the eyes of God's children or, better, the eyes of God's Son. The Son, himself the source of all the world's beauty, could stop to marvel at the splendor of the lily and discover his Father's name inscribed in it (Matthew 6:28-30). He listened to the singing of the birds of the air which "do not sow or reap, they gather nothing into barns; yet your heavenly Father feeds them" (Matthew 6:26). He saw the heavens as God's throne and the earth as his footstool (Matthew 5:35); the lightning that flashes from east to west was for him an image of the kingdom's sudden coming (Matthew 24:27); a bird's nest reminded him of the comfortable home which he, as Son of Man, did not have (Matthew 8:20); and the wheat ripening through the hours of day and night mirrored the certainty of the kingdom's coming (Mark 4:26-29).

The Son of God loved the caress of the evening breeze that swept in from the sea to Jerusalem, and he saw in the breeze a symbol of the Holy Spirit (John 3:8). He marveled at the joyous outpouring of a spring of water from the earth and spoke of "a fountain . . . leaping up to provide eternal life" (John 4:14). He also admired — thereby scandalizing the Pharisees with their cramped piety — the line and color of a wedding garment, finding it to be beautiful like the robe of grace; everyone must have such a robe if he is to enter the banquet hall of the kingdom (Matthew 22:11-12). Finally, in the morning star as it rose above the ending night he saw an image of his own vocation: "I am . . . the Morning Star shining bright" (Apoc. 22:16).

For Jesus, as a true son of Israel, creation was always God's temple in which everything cried "Glory!" (Ps. 29:9). But the glory is not yet the glory of the Gospel; it only hints at it, as dawn hints at day. When Jesus came upon the stage of creation, men would learn how fully the Creator is also a Father. Then creation, as God's "word," will have nothing more to say to us, because we will be able to see the Father's tender love written upon the face of Jesus Christ.

4. The Church, God's word

The Church is in a way identical with the message she proclaims. She first receives the word that reveals to her God's face and his loving will for all men; then she herself becomes God's word for men.

The Israel of the Old Testament was conscious of the relationship it had both to the word from on high and to the community of men. The wisdom of the chosen people finds expression when Chief Rabbi Alexander Safran writes:

> *God commissioned Israel, a community of men, to be the incarnation of the Torah among men. . . .*
> He made the Torah Israel's soul; he made the "soul of the Torah the ground of Israel's soul," so that Israel's will might be, not only

freely but necessarily as well, one with the will of the Creator. God
made the Torah Israel's soul, while Israel in turn is the soul of the
world, the "breath of the world," so that the Torah may serve the
world and those who dwell in it and help them become good as God
intended them to be when he created them, "the work of his hands,"
and when he created the Torah, "the work of his fingers". . . .

As mediator of this good in the world, *Israel must* not only be
attached to the Torah at the experiential level but *identify itself exis-
tentially with the Torah* through an active faith; *each Israelite must
live according to the Torah and become, as it were, a light-diffusing
letter of the Torah.* The whole people of Israel must act so that the
Torah spreads its light abroad, and must be clad as it were in a
luminous Torah scroll, thus being transformed into a *Sefer-Torah*, a
Torah scroll.[4]

Paul has something extraordinary to say on this very point. Writing to the quarrelsome Corinthians about his own vocation as an
apostle, he asks them good-humoredly whether he needs letters of
recommendation to or from them as others do (probably those he
ironically calls "super-apostles" in 2 Cor. 12:11). He then continues:
"You are my letter, known and read by all men, written on your
hearts. Clearly you are a letter of Christ which I have delivered, a
letter written not with ink but by the Spirit of the living God, not on
tables of stone but on tablets of flesh in the heart" (2 Cor. 3:2-3).

Here we have a kind of identification of the message as Paul
preaches it with the community that receives it. The community,
being now the bearer of God's word, becomes in its turn a word of
God. Like the message of the word, the message of the community
aims at a universal audience, being "known and read by all men,"
which is a rhetorical hyperbole for all who have occasion to come in
contact with the community. This word that is incarnated in, and
identified with, the community is also like the new covenant
foretold by Jeremiah (31:33), in which the law will be written not on
stone tables but on hearts of flesh.

No one, of course, would claim that there is a complete identity of
word and community. It is better to say that the community is a
sacrament of the word — in other words, that it reveals the word it
has received. Consequently, it shares in the mystery of the Church,
for although the Church is the body of Christ (Eph. 1:22-23; 4:15-
16; Col. 1:18, 24), she cannot be simply identified either with the
Lord or with the kingdom she proclaims, but is rather the sacrament
of both.[5] By living the word the Church, which is sacrament of the
word, proclaims it, and the proclamation, no matter how perfect,

will always be imperfect by comparison with the fullness of the message.

5. *The proclamation of the Good News*

The spread of the Good News with the help of the communications media is certainly much to be desired. Press, radio, television, film, theater — in short, all the media now at our disposal — are "means devised under God's Providence. . . . During his life on earth, Christ showed himself to be the perfect Communicator, while the Apostles used what means of social communication were available in their time. It is now necessary that the same message be carried by the means of social communication that are available today." [6] "Faith comes through hearing," St. Paul reminds us, "and what is heard is the word of Christ" (Rom. 10:17).

But preaching, whether oral or written, though highly desirable, is not the best nor the most convincing proclamation of the Good News. If preaching were the only form of proclamation, it would be in danger of becoming simply sectarian propaganda. The Church that is most biblical and most according to God's heart is not the Church with the best orators, the best printing establishments, and the best television networks. It is the Church whose life is most fully in accord with the message — not the Church that speaks the Gospel but the Church that lives it.

To make the point even clearer, let us give an example. The heart of the Gospel message is the resurrection of Christ. We might print thousands of copies of the words "Christ is risen," sing them on every stage throughout the world, repeat them unendingly on radio and television, celebrate them in all the liturgies of the entire world, and yet the resurrection would not thereby be proclaimed in a fully evangelical way. If we accept that Christians are to be the Lord's witnesses "even to the ends of the earth" (Acts 1:8) and that "those who have committed themselves to God [must] be careful to do what is right" (Titus 3:8), then they must fervently live the paschal life of the Lord and be truly "raised up in company with Christ" (Col. 3:1).

In other words, the real proclamation of Jesus' resurrection takes shape in men who live as though they were truly risen from the dead. Then, witnessing this new kind of life, the world will ask itself: "What makes these Christians live this way? What is the secret of their peace and joy which nothing in this world can lessen? 'See how they love one another! How ready they are to die for one another!' "[7] And Christians will be able to answer: "Christ is our life! (cf. Col. 3:4). But Christ is risen, and therefore we live the new life of the risen Christ, with his Spirit of love dwelling in our hearts to help us. Besides, this whole mystery is described in a book which we call the Gospel. Here it is, if you want to read it."

A simple verbal or written proclamation can never replace the living witness borne by the community. The faithful of the Old Testament, like the Christians of the new covenant, could not really be "the people of the book," as the Koran (Sura 5) calls them; they were rather a people who lived the message given by their God before they wrote it down in a book. The Christian community must be a living Gospel. Like the Servant of Yahweh, it must be "a light for the nations" (Is. 42:6). And what people require of a light is not that it proclaim its brightness but that it really, effectively shine forth. When outsiders looked at the first Christian communities, they did not say, "See how well they talk!" but "See how they love one another!" There is thus an indissoluble bond between word and community. The community is not only bearer of the word (and the proclamation is evidently indispensable, for God needs our mouths in order to speak to the men of our day), but is also made identical by its life with the word it brings to the world.

In his *History of the Church*, Eusebius of Caesarea (d. 399) has a characteristic story on this point. Appealing to the testimony of Clement of Alexandria (d. ca. 215) that Mark's Gospel originated in the preaching of St. Peter, Eusebius says:

> When, at Rome, Peter had openly preached the word and by the spirit had proclaimed the gospel, the large audience urged Mark, who had followed him for a long time and remembered what had been said, to write it all down. This he did, making his gospel available to all who wanted it. When Peter heard about this, he made no objection and gave no special encouragement.[8]

Peter's attitude is somewhat bewildering to us. He seems to be unconcerned about his Gospel in its *written* form, the very form in which, as he must have been aware, it would survive him and reach later generations. Perhaps Peter, with his Semitic reliance on the spoken word, was somewhat distrustful of the written word. Was he fearful that the Gospel, which is the power and strength of God, might be distorted by being written down and might lose something of its God-given energy? The important thing in Peter's view was the testimony of his own life. He was a man who could bare a back covered with whip marks and say that he was "a witness of Christ's sufferings" (1 Peter 5:1).

6. Credibility of the Church as word of God

A final remark is called for. We say that the community is a word of God. But we can say with equal justice that the community must try to be a word of God, for a Church whose life is not in harmony with its message will lose its credibility. Thus a community closed in upon itself and living a comfortable life must condemn itself as soon as it proclaims: "Blest are you poor; the reign of God is yours. But woe to you rich!" (Luke 6:20, 24). A community that has never felt the pangs of hunger or thought of sharing its bread cannot becomingly preach to the hungry: "Blest are you who hunger; you shall be filled. Woe to you who are full!" (Luke 6:21, 25). The first requirement laid upon the Church by "the ministry of the word" (Acts 6:4) to the nations is that the Church make the word believable through the testimony of her own life.

We can say of the Church as word what we say of the "notes" of the Church, such as holiness or apostolicity: they are both a privilege and a duty. The Church is holy, and therefore must become even holier. The grace given her is the grace of rendering visible the holy face of Christ. Her duty is to make it even more visible, and her sin is not to make it visible enough.

Given this perspective, we can see why it is difficult to spread the Good News. The difficulty is not any lack of the means of communication. In our day the most important news is broadcast almost instantaneously throughout the entire world, and mankind is coming more and more to resemble a single family in which all news is immediately shared. Even though there may be areas or human groups not reached by these communications networks, we can safely say that never since the beginning of history has the world been smaller (because distances have been so reduced), more in touch with the news, or better informed. And yet the Christian community is getting relatively smaller! What is lacking? Not words, declarations, instructions, decrees, etc., etc.; never before has there been so much talking about God's word! Unfortunately, what counts in the world's eyes is not what the Church says, but what she is.

[1] Cf. O. Semmelroth, *The Preaching Word: On the Theology of Proclamation*, translated by J.J. Hughes (New York, 1965), pp. 91–100: "The Church and the Word of God."

[2] Vatican II, *Decree on the Church's Missionary Activity*, no. 6, (Flannery, p. 819).

[3] Theologians prefer to distinguish and say that material creation is not an "image" of God but only his "trace" (*vestigium*); cf. St. Thomas Aquinas, *Summa theologiae* I, q. 93, a. 6. Only adoptive sonship (through grace) effects in the justified person a certain likeness of the natural sonship of Christ (III, q. 23, a. 3). Material creation can, however, be regarded as a distant extension of the eternal generation of the Word (St. Thomas, *In librum primum Sententiarum*, dist. 15, q. 5, a. 1, qla. 1, obj. 3).

[4] "Le peuple de Dieu dans la tradition juive ancienne et moderne," in *Rencontre Chrétiens et Juifs* (10, rue de Jura, Paris 13), nos. 25–26 (1972), pp. 7–8. Cf. *Vav: Revue du dialogue*, nos. 11–12 (1972).

[5] Cf. R. Coffy, *Eglise, signe du salut au milieu des hommes* (Paris, 1972): "The Church is not Christ but the servant of Christ and the sacrament of his mystery. She is not the kingdom of God but proclaims the kingdom. She is not mankind in its perfect state but mankind consciously living by the promise of a completion to come. . . . To say that the Church is a sacrament of Christ is by that very fact to acknowledge that *there can be no identification of Christ with the Church.* The Church as sacrament of Christ tries to live the mystery of her Lord and to proclaim it thereby, but *no expression she may give to the mystery can be exhaustive*" (pp. 66 and 50).

[6] Pontifical Commission for Social Communications, Pastoral Instruction *Communio et progressio*, January 29, 1971, nos. 12 and 126 (Flannery, pp. 297 and 334).

[7] The interior quotation is from Tertullian, *Apologeticum*, 39 (*PL* 1:471; *CCL* 1:151).

[8] *The History of the Church from Christ to Constantine*, VI, 14, 7, translated by G.A. Williamson (Baltimore, 1965), p. 254.

Chapter 14

WORD AND HISTORY

It is a commonplace to say that the religion of the Old and New Testaments is a historical religion, that is, a religion based upon historical events. We have in fact been seeing in this book how the assemblies of Moses at Sinai, Joshua at Shechem, Josiah and Ezra at Jerusalem, and finally Jesus as he brings into existence the messianic community were all bearers of God's word. The point we intend to go into more fully here is the relation between word and history.

The point is not unconnected with the theme of the previous chapter. We said there that creation is in a way a word of God. Creation is also, however, a kind of prologue to history; the work of the seven days (Gen. 1–2) is a prelude to the history of the human race (Gen. 3–11) and the history of the people of Abraham (Gen. 12). Is it possible, then, to claim that history, like creation, is also a word of God?

This problem suggests important and very relevant questions about liturgy, which aims at being a celebration of life. The history of God's people did not stop with the coming of Jesus, but continues on until his return, taking shape in all the events that mark our daily lives. The question we ask in the liturgy and, even more, in our daily lives is this: Should we celebrate the events of the biblical past or the events of the present time? Should we proclaim words that recall the history of the patriarchs or words that tell of the joys and cares of our contemporaries? Should we proclaim the Gospel or read the newspapers? Should we prefer a liturgy external to us in which the (Good) News comes to us from on high or a liturgy that is part of our lives because it is grounded in our experience and in which the news, good or bad, tells us of the joys and sorrows we feel and take with us into our celebrations and convert into prayers?

273

1. History, locus of God's revelation

"It is in history that God reveals the secret of his person."[1] History is the stage God has set up in the vast immensity of the ages and on which his wisdom guides the faithful. It is a book for men in which God writes his wonders before transcribing them into the Bible. God's dominion is not limited to the narrow area in which Israel lives, but extends to all the nations. Just as he rules over the ages and not merely the time in which the family issuing from Abraham lives, so too he rules not only over the history of the chosen people but also over the history of all the nations that are or have been. He weighs them all in his scales, and they are as dust or a grain of sand (cf. Is. 40:15). Even the foreign kings who claim jurisdiction over other gods are under his control. Nebuchadnezzar is called his servant (Jer. 27:6), and Cyrus his anointed one (Is. 45:1). Despite the sins that snare men in wretchedness, God never withdraws from history. Popular wisdom says that he knows how to write straight with crooked lines.[2] The fool sees in history only a succession of accidents or whims, but the believer sees an unbroken series of encounters with God. At every moment Israel can hear the cry that Amos uttered upon the hills of Samaria: "Prepare to meet your God, O Israel!" (Amos 4:12).

The proof that Yahweh directs history is, the prophets tell us, the fact that he can reveal it in advance; he predicts the future because he holds it in his hands. No idol can claim to do that. Idols are "nothings" and have no power to intervene in history; they cannot create history and are completely ignorant of the future (cf. Is. 41:23; 43:8-12).

The certainty that Yahweh is present in events is essential to the Yahwist faith. A favorite theme of the prophets is that the world in which human freedoms act and crisscross, are in conflict or harmony, is always subject to God. What creates problems for men is not the belief that God intervenes in history; their difficulties arise because they think of his intervention as frustrating human freedom. But, as a matter of fact, God guides man in such a way that man is really free and yet acts in the way God wishes. The Scriptures, however, sometimes so strongly affirm the divine action that man's freedom is somewhat obscured.[3] Yahweh whistles for the king of Assyria as a man whistles for his dog (Is. 7:18-19). The prophets are astonished at Israel's inability to see God present at every turn of the road, as Amos writes in poignant verses:

Though I have made your teeth
  clean of food in all your cities,
  and have made bread scarce in all your dwellings,
Yet you returned not to me,
  says the Lord.
Though I also withheld the rain from you,
  when the harvest was still three months away. . . .
Yet you returned not to me,
  says the Lord.
I struck you with blight and searing wind;
  your many gardens and vineyards,
  your fig trees and olive trees the locust devoured;
Yet you returned not to me,
  says the Lord.
I sent upon you a pestilence like that of Egypt,
  and with the sword I slew your young men . . .
Yet you returned not to me,
  says the Lord.
I brought upon you such upheaval
  as when God overthrew Sodom and Gomorrah;
  you were like a brand plucked from the fire;
Yet you returned not to me,
  says the Lord (Amos 4:6-11).

The refrain "Yet you returned not to me" underscores the guilt of Israel in not recognizing the presence of God who came to her in each of these events.[4]

2. *History, a profession of faith*

History is pervaded by the presence of God. But there is something more that must be said: Some events of history are so closely bound up with revelation that they themselves become objects of faith. Then the simple statement of historical fact becomes a profession of faith (cf. above, Chapter 6, I, B/1).

Such was the ancient creed (Deut. 26:5-9) recited when offering the first fruits of the harvest:

My father was a wandering Aramean who went down to Egypt. . . .
When the Egyptians maltreated and oppressed us, imposing hard labor upon us, we cried to the Lord, the God of our fathers, and he heard our cry and saw our affliction, our toil and our oppression. He brought us out of Egypt with his strong hand and outstretched arm, with terrifying power, with signs and wonders; and bringing us into this country, he gave us this land flowing with milk and honey.

Here we have the historical basis of the Israelite religion. To state these facts, which represent history with a minimum of theological interpretation, was to state one's faith in Yahweh.

This history, as an object of faith, continues on to the New Testament. "When the designated time had come" (Gal. 4:4), a time that was in fact the time designated by God's love (men had not improved nor become worthy of salvation), Jesus Christ came: "He entered world history."[5]

The earliest confession of faith in the resurrection, like the creed in Deuteronomy, simply recounts the saving events on which the Christian faith is based: "Christ died for our sins in accordance with the Scriptures; . . . he was buried and, in accordance with the Scriptures, rose on the third day; . . . he was seen by Cephas, then by the Twelve" (1 Cor. 15:3-5; see above, Chapter 10, II/1).

To believe in this history of Jesus is to believe in Christ and share in the salvation he brings.

It can be said, therefore, not only that history is the place where God reveals himself, but also that certain historical events are the basis of faith. "If Christ has not been raised, our preaching is void of content and your faith is empty too" (1 Cor. 15:14). "Christianity . . . is a living tradition, a historical movement."[6]

3. History, a word of God

If "word" means a factor in language, we can say that the events of sacred history are God's words inasmuch as they form part of the vast dialogue that God has been carrying on with mankind since the beginning. Evidently this kind of revelation in and through history is extremely important, even decisive, for Christian faith. Evidently the call of Abraham and the kingship of David are words of God. Evidently the fall of Jerusalem in 587 is likewise a word of God, and as important for the history of salvation as any prophetic book! Evidently the birth of Jesus, his Passion and his resurrection are words of God intended for all mankind. Does not Paul speak of the "message [*logos*] of the cross" (1 Cor. 1:18), meaning not simply the preaching of the Cross[7] but the very historical fact of Jesus' crucifixion?

4. "Deeds and words"

If historical events are words revelatory of God, then is the other "word," the kind spoken by the prophets in God's name, still necessary? Does it not simply repeat the facts "which speak for themselves"? In short, cannot historical events do away with any need for discourse about history?

In fact, revelation comes to us not through deeds alone nor through words alone, but through deeds and words together. Vatican II has brought out quite well the twofold path taken by the one revelation:

> It pleased God, in his goodness and wisdom, to reveal himself and to make known the mystery of his will (cf. Eph. 1:9). His will was that men should have access to the Father, through Christ, the Word made flesh, in the Holy Spirit, and thus become sharers in the divine nature (cf. Eph. 2:18; 2 Pet. 1:4). . . . This economy of Revelation is realized by *deeds and words*, which are intrinsically bound up with each other. As a result, the works peformed by God in the history of salvation show forth and bear out the doctrine and realities signified by the words; the words, for their part, proclaim the works, and bring to light the mystery they contain.[8]

The history that reveals God is not a conglomeration of brute facts welded into juxtaposition under the pressure of vast time, but a series of events guiding us toward God. The events are like stones incorporated into a building — it is not the piling up of stones that constitutes the building (a mere heap of stones is not a house), but the ordering of them according to the architect's plan. The quarries provide the stones, but only the architect can build the house. In our case, the long centuries provided the materials, but only the thought that ordered them could make of them a history of salvation.

5. *Need of the word*

Evidently the need of interpretation is not the same for all events.

—Some facts, as we said above, really speak for themselves. Thus, as the ancient priestly narrative tells us, when the plagues came upon Egypt, Pharaoh's magicians were forced to acknowledge that "This is the finger of God" (Exod. 8:15). Again, when Jesus expelled demons, every honest man was forced to acknowledge that he did his marvelous work "by the finger of God" and that "the reign of God is upon you" (Luke 11:19-20).

—In other situations the evidence is less constraining. Several interpretations of the event are possible and even plausible. God does not always throw the account books of history wide open. Even though the goal may be clear, there can be doubts about the way leading to it. To understand the event, therefore, one must be familiar with God's ways. When two lovers smile at each other, a bystander may have difficulty in interpreting its meaning; only the two, knowing and loving each other, are aware of the past tenderness and the hope for the future that lie behind the smile. Now, every event is like a tender, loving gaze of God toward men. But to decipher the meaning of the event, we must be familiar with God's smiles. Here is where the prophet has a part to play; he is the official exegete or interpreter of God's ways (cf. above, Chapter 6, II B). And just as love requires not only gestures but words to make it explicit and fully aware of itself, so the events through which God expresses his love are explained by the prophets' words.

Evidently, then, one and the same event will be interpreted in different ways by those who base their outlook on faith and by those who disregard or deny faith. When the Chaldean battering rams leveled the walls of Jerusalem in August, 587, and the city went under in fire and blood, Jeremiah saw in the event God's judgment on a people whom he continued nonetheless to hold dear. The Chaldeans who wielded the battering rams interpreted the event quite differently, seeing in it a proof of the superior methods used by the Babylonian sappers against the Jewish fortifications. Only a man who believed in Yahweh would accept Jeremiah's judgment.

—Finally, there are cases in which it is humanly impossible to read and properly interpret the event. History reveals God, but it can also hide him from us. The event can be so completely insignificant or even so utterly lacking in meaning that it becomes opaque. A child is born blind, or without hands or feet, or with a minimal intelligence — who can explain such a mystery of suffering? In the face of such a "word," who can repeat the words of the Psalm: "All the paths of the Lord are kindness and constancy" (Ps. 25:10)?

There are worse things than a child born blind. There are people born with two eyes, who then have them put out (as was done to Zedekiah by the lovely banks of the Orontes — 2 Kings 25:7). There was a Man more richly capable of love than any other man who has ever lived, a Man whose two hands blessed the children and the poor, but his enemies nailed his hands to a cross — who can understand this mystery of the Son of Man? At such moments the wisdom of God seems foolishness, and the history he controls seems a scandal. Absurdity to pagans, a stumbling block to the Jews, but supreme wisdom to those who believe (cf. 1 Cor. 1:23-24).

6. *Priority of event over word*

The event has an evident priority over the word. Before the Book of Exodus was written, there was the historical fact of the Exodus; before Gospels bore witness to the Lord, Jesus lived his life. The priority, however, is not so much chronological as it is a matter of "primordial importance."[9] Vatican II rightly speaks of "deeds and words," and the sequence of words is deliberate, having been kept in the conciliar text despite some opposition.[10]

But this evident priority will be deceptive if we do not add the following considerations. First of all, though history comes first inasmuch as it is the basis for our faith (if Christ did not rise, our faith is without an object!), it is possible for us to grasp it today only through the words and faith of the one who recorded it. Thus we can say that the word too has a priority, at least at the level of interpretation. We should not however think that we are caught, as it were, in an unending back-and-forth, with deeds referring us to words and words to deeds, like two mirrors reflecting each other and leaving us in the last analysis with nothing but an image. No, for if history is directed by God, so is the interpretation of history. Deeds and words come to us from the same source. It remains true, however, that the words refer to the deeds.

Second, we cannot think that the faith of the narrator is an impenetrable screen set up between us and the events. The events, after all, can also be the object of a historical study that is fully valid at the scientific level. In fact, such an approach is highly desirable, and sometimes even absolutely necessary. "Historical study of the Bible is a theological necessity."[11] In implementing this approach, we must not, however, forget the light that faith sheds upon events. Faith does not create the events, any more than the light creates the objects it illumines, but it does shed light upon them.

Third, what God accomplishes in history is recorded in his word, and what he announces through the word of the prophets ("Indeed, the Lord God does nothing without revealing his plan to his servants, the prophets" — Amos 3:7), is accomplished in history. Thus "history becomes word, and word becomes history."[12] It does not follow, however, that the word acquires the same rank as history, for history is the basis of the word and gives it its new meaning.[13]

7. Today

These considerations are extremely important for the contemporary history which we are in the process of writing and which is our own sacred history. At every moment of his Church's existence, the Lord continues to speak to her through the events of her life. Because he is "the first-born of all creatures" (Col. 1:15), he is also the first-born of that greatest of creations, the history of mankind: "The

Church . . . believes that the key, the center and the purpose of
the whole of man's history is to be found in its Lord and Master";
"The Lord is the goal of human history, the focal point of the desires
of history and civilization, the center of mankind, the joy of all
hearts, and the fulfillment of all aspirations."[14]

Through all its dark and splendid moments, history is entirely
oriented toward its Lord; we might even say that history is fascinated by him, even when it does not know him! Every step men
take on their journey is also a step Christ takes toward them. Every
event carries in its heart the seal of God. Consequently, we can say
that the sacred history now going on, like the sacred history set
down in the Scriptures, is, within limits, God's word to men.

But what precisely are the limits that are set to this parallel? The
sacred history set down in Scripture has several special marks. For
one thing, it enjoys the privilege of the canon of Scripture. By this is
meant that the interpretation of the events and the discernment of
God's presence within events are guaranteed by the Holy Spirit.
The voice we hear in the Scriptures is not the voice of an especially
competent historian, but the authentic voice of God himself; the
judgment that voice pronounces is infallible.

Secondly, this history is unique. It is true enough, of course, that
since any history is irreversible, it is also in a way unique. But the
same events can nevertheless recur in similar conditions: "What has
been, that will be; what has been done, that will be done. Nothing is
new under the sun" (Eccles. 1:9).

The reflections of a Qoheleth bring home to us the boredom of
history and its repetitions. But what he says does not apply to the history of salvation recorded in Scripture. In this history everything is
new, and what is new is unique. The history of Abraham is unquali-
fiedly unique — it will never be repeated. Unique, too, are the histories of Moses and of David. Unique, likewise, are the birth of Jesus,
his Passion, and his glorification; these are written forever in the account books of history and will never be seen again. Jesus offered
himself "once for all" (Heb. 7:27); once for all, he entered into the
heavenly sanctuary (Heb. 9:12); once for all, we have been sanctified
by his self-offering (Heb. 10:10).

The New Testament puts an end to the period of public revelation. ". . . no new public revelation is to be expected before the
glorious manifestation of our Lord, Jesus Christ."[15] For this reason
we cannot put contemporary sacred history and the sacred history
recorded in Scripture on the same level without running the risk of

"giving a uniform and undifferentiated, flattened-out and monoton-
ous vision of revelation and thereby doing away with its trans-
historical character, its newness, and its irreducibility to the general
categories of history."[16]

Having said this, we must straightway add that the privileged
character of biblical history does not detract from the real value of
contemporary sacred history, or, to put it another way, that the end
of public revelation has not prevented God from speaking further.
Through the deeds he once did in human history God speaks to us
now and gives us signs; his voice resounds in our ears *today* (cf. Ps.
95:7-8). "The passage of the centuries ceases to be an obstacle."[17]

God's word is needed for the understanding of words spoken now,
and the history recorded in the Old and New Testaments becomes a
criterion for interpreting contemporary history. The Spirit's judgment, which is guaranteed by the canon of Scripture, "provides an
anticipatory commentary, written well in advance."[18] Sacred history in the Scriptures does not, therefore, devalue our own history
but on the contrary gives it its true meaning before God. Current
events are not, as it were, orphans but are rather brothers to the
saving events in the Bible. We must not let these contemporary
events go astray in the desert of our private interpretations but
rather bring them before the transcendent word of God, as before a
mirror, so that we may read God's name written in them.

Looking at the relationship from the other end, we should say that
our reading of the Bible should not be a disembodied reading,
unrelated to our own time with all its good and evil. "*Everything*
written before our time was written *for our instruction*, that we
might derive hope from the lessons of patience and the words of
encouragement in the Scriptures" (Rom. 15:4).[19]

A truly biblical celebration, then, is not one concerned solely with
the past. It is rather one that lays hold of our life as it flows by, and
confronts that life with the word of God so that we may hear the
words God is speaking to us now. His present words are not part of
biblical revelation and therefore are not valid for all men of all times
as the words of the Bible are, but they do continue the personal
dialogue God carries on with the heart of every individual. No one
can evade them by saying, "What share have we with David?" (1
Kings 12:16), as the Israelites did when they set themselves up in
opposition to Rehoboam, for God speaks not simply to David but to
you, even though he does it through the history of David.

We asked earlier: Should we proclaim words that recall the history of the patriarchs or words that tell of the joys and cares of our contemporaries? We can now answer confidently: We should celebrate both! There can be no opposition between a liturgy centered on the word and a liturgy centered on life, since God's word is a word meant for people in the today of their lives; conversely, the today in which men live will reveal God's face to them only if they see that today in the light of the word.

In the delightful little book *Children's Letters to God*, Emily says: "Dear God, could you write us some more stories? We've read all the ones you wrote."[20] The new stories in God's new book are the stories we write today in the book of our lives.

---

[1] G. von Rad, *Old Testament Theology* 2:338. L. Alonso Schökel, *The Inspired Word: Scripture in the Light of Language and Literature*, translated by F. Martin (New York, 1967), speaks of three ways in which revelation occurs: creation, history, and the word (pp. 19–48). Cf. also E. Lipinski, "Révélation et histoire," in his *Essais sur la Révélation et la Bible* (Lectio divina 60; Paris, 1970), pp. 11–43; H. Urs von Balthasar, "The Word and History," in his *Word and Revelation* (Essays in Theology 1), translated by A.V. Littledale and A. Dru (New York, 1964), pp. 31–56; P. Grelot, *Sens chrétien de l'Ancien Testament*, pp. 267–75.

[2] A Portuguese proverb used by P. Claudel as exergue to his *The Satin Slipper*.

[3] Semitic thought prefers to concentrate on the transcendent divine causality without mentioning second causes. Consequently, a Semite will say that Yahweh hardens the heart of Pharaoh (Exod. 4:21; cf. 7:13), whereas in fact the hardening is due to the plagues sent upon Egypt.

[4] In the New Testament, the long discourse which Luke puts into the mouth of Stephen as he stood before the Sanhedrin (Acts 7:1-53) bears witness to the same belief. The discourse is a lengthy historical description of how history leads from Abraham to the Messiah (cf. J. Dupont, *Etudes sur les Actes des Apôtres*, p. 89). The discourse manifests less the thoughts of Stephen (the vocabulary is Luke's) than the faith of the community. Some scholars suggest that the discourse may be the kind of sermon on Israel's history used in synagogue worship; such historical panoramas could well serve as introductions to the Christian kerygma; cf. E. Haenchen, *Die Apostelgeschichte* (15th ed.; Göttingen, 1968), p. 239.

[5] Vatican II, *Pastoral Constitution on the Church in the Modern World*, no. 38 (Flannery, p. 937). In Luke 3:1-2 the evangelist situates the ministry of Jesus by reference to secular history, without intending to introduce any "theology of history"; cf. H. Conzelmann, *The Theology of St. Luke*, p. 168.

[6] Bishop Charue, "Comment parler aujourd'hui de Jésus-Christ et de la révélation divine," *Documentation catholique* 69 (1972), p. 826.

[7] As the phrase is interpreted by, for example, A. Robinson and A. Plummer, *First Epistle of St. Paul to the Corinthians* (2nd ed.; Edinburgh, 1914), p. 17 ("The preaching of the cross"). On the sense of the Greek word *logos* and the Hebrew *dabar*, cf. above, Introduction.

[8] *Dogmatic Constitution on Divine Revelation*, no. 2 (Flannery, pp. 750–51; italics added).

[9] O. Cullmann, *Le salut dans l'histoire* (Neuchâtel, 1966), p. 89.

[10] Cf. the commentary on the conciliar text in *La Révélation Divine* (Unam sanctam 70), 1:175–79.

[11] O. Cullmann, *op. cit.*, p. 120.

[12] G. von Rad, *Old Testament Theology* 2:358.

[13] There is a great difference between "the world of prediction" and "the world of fulfillment," to use the terms of G. Closen, *Clefs pour la Sainte Ecriture* (Bruges, 1954), pp. 83 and 87.

[14] Vatican II, *Pastoral Constitution on the Church in the Modern World*, nos. 10 and 45 (Flannery, pp. 910–11, 947).

[15] Vatican II, *Dogmatic Constitution on Divine Revelation*, no. 4 (Flannery, p. 752).

[16] G.-Ph. Widmer, in K.E. Skydsgaard *et al.*, *Ecriture et tradition* (Chevetogne, 1970), p. 31.

[17] Ch. Hauret, *Notre Psautier* (Paris, 1964), pp. 45–46.

[18] F.-J. Leenhardt, *L'Epître de Saint Paul aux Romains* (Neuchâtel, 1957), p. 204.

[19] Cf. Rom. 4:23: God was speaking to us when he addressed Abraham; 1 Cor. 9:10: "Does he [God] not say this for our sakes? You can be sure it was written for us."

[20] *Children's Letters to God*, ed. by E. Marshall and S. Hampel (Pocket Books, 1966).

Chapter 15

THE HOMILY

INTRODUCTION

In an earlier chapter (7) we spoke at length of the homily in synagogal worship. It is time now to organize the results of our inquiry into the Jewish homily and apply them to the Christian homily.

We shall be using the word "homily" here in the strict sense of *a discourse that explains and actualizes the word of God in the liturgical celebration.*[1] Many other kinds of discourse, having nothing to do with the homily, are possible during our liturgical gatherings: sermons, panegyrics, funeral eulogies, and all sorts of "ferverinos." We have nothing but respect for these, of course. And if a community likes that kind of bread, then it should be baked to allay their hunger. Why refuse to give a panegyric or a funeral eulogy to those who want one? In fact, such discourses may at times be a pastoral necessity, since it may be urgent to explain a disputed point of doctrine or morality or to take up some other current problem. Such discourses should, however, be called "sermons." They are not homilies in the proper sense of the term, since the true homily always has God's word for its sole object; it explains the word and actualizes it for the benefit of the celebrating community.

It must be admitted that in some circles "pious" discourses have fallen into discredit; people are bored by them. Clerics have sometimes forgotten to preach the word[2] and have wearied themselves talking about everything and anything.[3] Exhausted by their other pastoral labors, they have not always had the time for serious preparation of the substance of their homily, still less for careful polishing of its form. Discourses during the liturgy have been a kind of lukewarm sugary potion that the faithful drank out of habit, while expecting no help from it.

As a matter of fact, the homily has always been a current problem in the Church, since men have always been liable, unconsciously and frequently with the best of intentions, to substitute their own words for the word of God. The new lectionary represents the most important step taken in this area of the Roman liturgy for the last fifteen centuries. Now the pressing need is to actualize the word provided in the lectionary so that the community may profit by it. In other words, *our great need is for genuine homilies.* This, I believe, will largely determine the success of the current liturgical reform. Renewal depends on it; the homily is for us a kind of lofty mountain pass we must cross in order to enter the new promised land.

1. From translation to actualization

We said earlier (Chapter 7, section I) that the homily, in its simplest form, is a translation of the word. The archetypal example of this is to be seen in the assembly of Ezra, where the text was read in Hebrew and then translated into Aramaic. In its most perfect form, the homily is the actualization of the word in terms of the community. The archetypal example here is Jesus' homily in the synagogue of Nazareth, where, after reading Isaiah, Jesus began his homily by saying: "Today this Scripture passage is fulfilled in your hearing" (Luke 4:21).

Despite the four centuries that separate them, these two homilies are of the same type, inasmuch as to translate is already to reinterpret and to "actualize" God's ancient words for the community that listens to them today. "There can be no translation of a text from the past without some reinterpretation of it."[4] Nonetheless, it sometimes requires a long and difficult journey to go from the bare, austere splendor of a literally translated text to the living wealth contained in the actualization of such a text. We may point out three privileged stages of the journey.

a) Literal sense

The first step is to look for the literal meaning. Any other starting point is arbitrary and leads everywhere and nowhere. The essential question to be asked first is always this: What do we find written here? What is being said by the text? Vatican II observes: ". . . the interpreter of sacred Scriptures, if he is to ascertain what God has wished to communicate to us, should carefully search out the meaning which the sacred writers really had in mind, that meaning which God had thought well to manifest through the medium of their words."[5]

This is the task of the exegete. He must be humble enough to apply textual criticism (If there are variants, which is most likely to be inspired by the Spirit of God?); literary criticism (What do the words mean? Do we find literary patterns peculiar to the language of the original text?); historical criticism (At what redactional stage is the text to be located?); and theological criticism (How does the text fit into the history of revelation? What is original about it?).[6] The interpretation of the Bible is a strict science, not a game of pious riddles. A scientific approach is needed; exegesis is an operational science, "in the sense that each reader can repeat for himself all the operations that led the exegetes to their conclusions."[7]

In exegesis, then, there can be no scamping of (serious) study of the Bible (that kind of study is also a form of praise and prayer!). Many communities suffer from underdevelopment as far as the Bible is concerned. We are not saying, of course, that every page of the Bible is full of traps and requires exhaustive study. The Bible is, after all, the book of the poor and the simple, even though it provides matter for those with technical training. Nor is there any question of presenting the community, in the homily, with the immediate results of the scholar's exegetical work and parading one's esoteric knowledge before the congregation. All we are saying is that intellectual honesty requires each Christian to study the Bible according to his capacities for such study and to have some idea of what he is talking about.

Ordinarily, and quite rightly, we are reminded that we must be prudent and not broadcast to the general public ideas that are simply working hypotheses used by exegetes and that have not been submitted to the test of time.[8] Origen was already conscious of this problem:

> I pass on to you something a wise man and true believer said to me; I think of it often. He said: It is dangerous to talk about God, even if what you say is true. And, in fact, it is not only false ideas that are dangerous; even true ones are if they are not put forth at the right time.[9]

But prudence works in two directions. It is dangerous to speak too soon, but it may be even more dangerous to keep silence and avoid difficulties by smothering them in commonplaces or, even worse, sugarcoating them with pious trash. It is quite possible to be cowardly in our dealing with Scripture. Yet the faithful ask questions about the historical character of the infancy narratives and about what really happened at the baptism or temptation or transfiguration or resurrection of Jesus (to mention only some New Testament problems). They do not accept the idea that there is a paradise in which the elect have free access to the springs of living water, i.e., knowledge of the Bible, while the ordinary believer must be content with the stagnant water in the old cisterns. Such questions are healthy, and they should receive clear answers. The first and foremost virtue to be practiced in this area today is, I believe, the honesty of the real exegete. There should be no sense of shame in saying, when confronted with this or that difficulty, "I don't know the answer," or "No generally accepted solution has yet been found." What is intolerable is the lie calculated to make others believe you do know when you don't.

We must add here, along with the whole of Christian tradition, that if we are to achieve our goal and find God in his word, we must pray to the Holy Spirit. A joyful, serene piety is a good companion on the exegetical journey. Origen advised Gregory Thaumaturgus: "Do not be content to knock [at the door] and to seek. It is absolutely necessary that you also ask, if you are ever to understand the things of God."[10] One principle accepted by the Fathers as they endeavored to interpret the Scriptures was this: "Those who utter a prophecy and those who wish to understand it need the same grace; no one can understand a prophecy unless the Spirit who inspired it enables him to understand the words."[11]

Gregory's words are a little extreme, since the grace of uttering prophecy is not quite the same as the grace of interpreting it. But he is right in saying that we cannot find God unless the Spirit leads us to him. When faced with a more than usually difficult passage of Scripture, Origen himself did not hesitate to stop in the middle of his homily and ask his hearers: "Help me with your prayer so that I may really speak God's word to you."[12]

b) Christological sense

The second stage or step is the Christological meaning. As we indicated at length earlier (Chapter 10, sections II and III), Christ fulfills the Scriptures; his life and message were written down in advance "in the law of Moses and the prophets and psalms" (Luke 24:44). We must therefore discover the face of Jesus on every page of the Bible, look for his presence at every stage of history, and see how, as Irenaeus puts it, "the writings of Moses are the words of Christ."[13]

All this applies first of all to the texts of the Old Testament. Without the presence of Christ, the Old Testament remains a Jewish book; which is not to deny that the Jewish tradition itself, throughout its history, marveled to discover the riches yielded by a messianic interpretation of the texts. With the presence of Christ, however, the Old Testament becomes a gospel; Christ transfigures every page with his divinity; his mystery shines through the letter of the Bible as it later shone through his risen body. Origen gave the name "spiritual" understanding to this Christological reading of Scripture and observed:

> I cannot call the Law an *Old* Testament if I understand it spiritu-
> ally. The Law becomes an *Old* Testament only for those who under-
> stand it only according to the letter. For such people the law has
> evidently become *old*; it has aged because it has lost its power. But
> for us who understand and explain it spiritually and in the light of the
> Gospel, it is always new; the two Testaments together form a New
> Testament for us, not new in date but new because of the new mean-
> ing we find.[14]

The search for the Christological meaning must also be carried on in the New Testament, including the Gospels. There are moments, of course, when Christ is evidently present, as for example in such sayings as "I am the good shepherd," where Christ himself is speaking. But many sayings can be understood without reference to him and thus go astray; they need to be brought back to their true place by an authentically Christological interpretation of them. Take, for example, the beatitude "Blest are the poor in spirit: the reign of God is theirs" (Matthew 5:3). We must bear in mind as we read this that Christ is the archetypal poor man who most perfectly lives this beatitude, and that Christians are to live it, not as stoics, but in imitation of the Lord, who, as St. Paul says, "made himself poor though he was rich, so that you might become rich by his poverty" (2 Cor. 8:9).

Finally, we must emphasize the unity of the Bible as a whole, the ecclesial symphony played by the two orchestras of the Old and New Testaments. The New Testament is unintelligible apart from the Old, since it is the flower and fruit produced by the Old. But the Old Testament is just as mysterious without the New, for it remains a bare tree that produces no flowers and fruit. Without the resurrection of Jesus, the longing of the Old Testament is like an unfinished symphony made up of sadness and weeping. Vatican II rightly says that the Old Testament sheds light upon and explains the New Testament, while the New Testament gives the Old its full meaning.[15] The two Testaments are two melodies that harmonize; each has its own beauty, but only both together yield the splendid hymn that is Jesus Christ.

c) Actualization

The third step or stage is actualization. Each community must make its own the words Jesus spoke to the Nazarenes in their synagogue: *"Today* this Scripture passage is fulfilled *for us."* Each community must ask itself: "What is God saying to us today in his word?"·

Actualization is the heart of the homily. Every age must hear the word in its own way. It cannot, of course, ignore the help offered by tradition, which is the rich treasure of the wisdom of the past. But neither can it deprive itself of the grace, and the dangers, of actualizing the word in accordance with its own personality, so as to enrich the past with the discoveries of the present. Each age must experience and live the mystery of the contemporaneity of the word to all times and places. Revelation is complete, but the time for listening to God is not yet over. The complete meaning of the word will have been penetrated only when God at the end of time closes the book of history and reveals himself no longer through the word but face to face. Then the contemporaneity of the word will give way to the eternity of God.

Actualization forces us to raise once again the difficult problem of translation. What does it mean to translate a text? Sometimes people have thought it simply means passing from Hebrew, Aramaic, and Greek to French or English or German. Such a passage is necessary, of course, and even relatively easy. In principle, every good Bible makes this passage, and the experts in translations are always trying to improve their work, so that their text is as faithful as possible to the language used by the Spirit of God.

The translation of which we speak in connection with the homily, however, makes other kinds of demand. It inserts God's message into the life of the community. It transposes the message and causes it to enter into the sensibility, understanding, concerns, joys, and troubles of the community or, in short, into all that makes up this community with its special treasures, the individual face that the word fashions for it, the special accent with which it responds to the word in prayer. To translate God's word is to incarnate it, to a certain extent, in a particular community.

At times a priest or other believer will say that this or that passage of the Bible is not adapted to their community. In proposing such an impossible position, these unfortunate people are simply admitting that there has been no homily. Their task, after all, is precisely the daunting but joyful one of *translating* the word for the profit of their community! Christ needs their words if he is to address their community, just as he needs the priest's hand in order to break the Eucharistic bread and divide it among the faithful.

For a good homily, more is needed than simply to repeat the words of the Bible; if that is all one does, one is by no means sure of transmitting the authentic word of God. Moreover, a simple repetition of the same formulas does not even guarantee that the message is preserved in its integrity. The divine truths themselves, of course, are eternal and stand apart from time by reason of their changelessness. But the words that express these truths to me are living things, subject to the ebb and flow of history and carried along on the changing tides of fashion.

There are times, then, when fidelity to the message will require that the homilist express it in a different way. If, for example, we repeat with Matthew 16:18 that "the gates of hell will not prevail against the Church" (a word-for-word translation of the Greek), we risk causing the community to misunderstand the message. For in today's language, "hell" (Hades) no longer means simply the abode of the dead; it means the abode of the devil. But what Matthew is saying is that the gates of death will never prevail against the Church or that the Church will forever remain the eternal kingdom of God. Similar instances can be found on almost every page of the Gospels. In practice, therefore, if we are properly to "translate" the messages for the community, we must read it with the eyes of those who wrote it, and hear it with the ears of the community we are addressing.

We also hear it said at times that the word of God is not relevant, in the sense that it is concerned with the ancient problems of two or three thousand years ago. At that time the problems were current, but today the community is involved in problems about which the word says nothing. It has nothing to say about the wars that eat like cancers at our world, about the terrible problems of the Third World, about apartheid, and certainly nothing about birth control. But this objection, even more than the preceding, is invalid. It completely mistakes the nature of the homily, the function of which is precisely to bring all the cares and joys of the community into the presence of the word, to confront them with it, and to submit them to its judgment. In the homily the whole community, weighed down by its troubles or exalted by its joys, stands in the presence of the word, looks at itself in the word as in a mirror, and discovers there the features of Jesus Christ.

To actualize the word, then, means to show the community what this word has to say to it today, how God is speaking to it in *the today that is its life*.

The homily, consequently, cannot be a matter simply of giving historical explanations of the text; these may be quite useful, but they do not constitute a homily. Nor does a homily consist in explaining Palestinian geography, though information about that may be quite relevant. Nor does it consist in explaining Semitisms or biblical vocabulary or scriptural themes or the moral exhortations of the Bible, however serviceable all such explanations may be. All these explanations are only crutches to help us enter into the presence of Christ, whereas the homily is an encounter with Christ.

We must add that neither is the homily to consist in theological explanation. Just as God has no intention of playing the historian for us (even though he creates history) or the geographer (though he creates the universe) or the philologist (though he invented all of man's languages and created all their knowledge), neither does he intend to act as our theologian, even though he is God! No, he is calling us to share his life! He is giving us his life! Consequently, a homily does not consist in explaining to the community that there are three persons in God (a point of theology) or, more in detail, that God is a Father, that he has sent his Son among men, and that this Spirit has descended upon our world (these three statements are the scriptural way of expressing the Trinity). All that can be a fine introduction, of course. But the real homily begins only at the point when we understand that "this passage has been fulfilled today, *for us*," and that the God who is Father of our Lord Jesus Christ is also *our* Father, that his Son Jesus Christ is *our* brother, and that the Spirit of Father and Son has been given *to us*.

The three steps or stages — literal meaning, Christological meaning, and actualization — yield a tripartite structure that is basic. It will always be necessary to determine just what the text is saying, then to discover Jesus in it, and finally to hear what he has to say to the community today. However, according to need, the emphasis may be placed on one or the other of the three points. Sometimes the text is so readily understood that no exegetical preparation of the congregation may be needed; in other instances the Christological sense will be the clearest thing about the passage. The homily therefore can never be a ready-made affair, but must be tailored to fit the needs of the congregation. Of the three stages, the third will undoubtedly allow of the widest variation. The literal and Christological senses will often be evident, whereas the actualizations can be as numerous as the communities the homilist faces, with their varying situations and needs. Flexibility is very much in place, to the extent that it serves the word.

2. A *homily at every celebration*

We may formulate a principle: Every time the word is proclaimed to a community, it should be actualized. In practice this means that there should be a homily at every Mass and at every celebration of the word. The community present need not be large; a homily, unlike the great occasional discourses of a former day, does not require great throngs to come and listen to the "great preacher." We should recall that according to the Gospel, two or three people form a fine community: "Where two or three are gathered in my name, there am I in their midst" (Matthew 18:20).

If the word is not actualized, it will "fall to the ground" and not be received as it should. It was said of Samuel that "the Lord was with him, not permitting any word of his to be without effect" (1 Sam. 3:19). In the same way, the community must not let any words God speaks to it to fall to the ground or to be without effect. If the word of God is not actualized for the community, the Bible becomes simply a library in which Israel and the apostles are the librarians. A library, however, becomes a source of knowledge only when the books speak to us; otherwise it is a cemetery. The homily, however, is what makes the Bible speak.

The homily need not be long. Two or three minutes can be quite enough. In fact, we may say that, as a general rule, if the homily is well prepared, it will last only two to three minutes. If it is not well prepared, it may last twenty (and I am hardly exaggerating).

Evidently no one can preach a daily sermon or a daily panegyric. He would quickly exhaust his range of knowledge, and having worked through all his notes, he would literally have nothing more to say. But a daily homily, a real homily, is the simplest thing in the world. No one need fear he will be worn out by the effort. No one grows tired by daily seeking and gazing upon the face of Jesus Christ, any more than he is wearied by eating every day. The word, after all, is a kind of food: "Not on bread alone is man to live but on every utterance that comes from the mouth of God" (Matthew 4:4).

The real probem is not with simply having a daily homily, but with its quality. Even the priest who, due to special circumstances, celebrates alone, facing the wall, should deliver a daily homily to himself. Nothing forbids, and everything urges him to sit down for a short period after the readings and to ask himself in the silence of his heart: "What is God saying to me today in his word?"

3. *All the texts?*

The lectionary of the Roman Rite now provides four passages from the Bible: three readings, the third of which is the Gospel, and the responsorial psalm. The four make a good deal of reading. Are all four to be explained?

The same question can arise even with regard to a single reading. Sometimes there is enough in a passage to provide material for several homilies. Must we be exhaustive and speak of everything?

The word is like a kingly table, marvelously laden, to which God invites the beggars whom he loves. To do honor to the host, each guest need not fill his plate at every course. The result would be indigestion rather than the honoring of God. Therefore, eat what you please and as much as you please. God wants you to experience delight, not fatigue. The same applies to the homily. You need not speak of all the texts; the important thing is to speak *for the sake of* the community and to allay its hunger.[16] The same text can inspire a short homily on a particular point to a particular community or a longer homily on another point to another community. The important thing is the community.

In making such choices we are following authentic biblical tradition. Jesus made such a choice for his homily at Nazareth; Luke 4:18-19 ends the citation for Is. 61:1-2 right after the words "to announce a year of favor from the Lord," and omits the words that immediately follow, "and a day of vindication by our God." He wants to show the mystery of the Lord as a day of joy and salvation, not as a day of vengeance. Such choices are legitimate and sometimes account for differences in the Synoptic accounts of the same events.

We must immediately add, however, that every word of God is food for us. It is legitimate to adapt the text to the needs of the

community, but it would be contrary to the whole of biblical tradition systematically to neglect certain revelations in favor of our personal choice. The important thing, after all, is not what you think
and say about God, but what God thinks and says and reveals about
himself. We must therefore achieve a balance: The word is to be
adapted to the community, but the community must also adapt itself
to the word (cf. above, Chapter 6, section I A/2). The community
must be on the lookout, sometimes even in very rough passages and
arid texts, for the traces of its God.

4. The homily as word of God

The homily is not simply a human discourse about God, but is
itself a word of God. It does not, of course, have the universal value
of the word in which the Church, according to its canon of Scripture, recognizes God's authentic voice addressing all mankind. A
homily to one community may not necessarily be deliverable to all
other communities. Nonetheless, the homily is a word of God to the
community celebrating here and now. Why can this be said? Because the homily should be simply a kind of broadcasting of the
eternal word into the specific time in which we now live (the most
wonderful time of all, since it is the time God gives us and since it
permits us to live today in God's presence). "The one who speaks is
to deliver God's message" (1 Peter 4:11). And he who hears what is
said should accept it as God's word. "In receiving the message from
us," St. Paul says to the Thessalonians, "you took it, not as the word
of men, but as it truly is, the word of God" (1 Thess. 2:13).[17]

The "few words" and the long sermon, like the panegyrics and the
other occasional discourses (we have pointed out their value already), represent a great danger to the homily. These literary
genres had their hour of glory, and past generations paid them the
tribute of their admiration. But they are completely out of place
after the proclamation of God's word. They are like a barren wilderness of words stuck right in the middle of the celebration,[18] and if
they claim a lion's share of the time available, they become cancers
destroying the health and balance of the liturgy, no matter how
much they may claim to be broadcasting "important truths." The
important truth conveyed in the homily is quite different and very
simple. It comes down to this: "This is what God is saying to you
today; here is how his word lays claim to you today. If you hear his
voice today, harden not your heart!"

5. Literary genres and forms

The homily has no set literary form. It may take the form of ardent poetry, like Melito of Sardis' splendid paschal homily,[19] or it may take the form of catechetical instruction, as Origen's homilies do. Its basis, however, is the literary form of the biblical text; the latter provides the "linguistic architecture"[20] that influences the construction of the homily.

It is well known that Israel used a large variety of literary genres, even those which were cultivated in the literatures of her neighbors and of which splendid examples have been recovered in the hieroglyphic writings buried in the sands of Egypt and the cuneiform writings from the Mesopotamian ruins. The oldest literary genre is surely the myth;[21] the best biblical examples of it are the creation accounts in the opening chapters of Genesis. The historical genre must be subdivided into documentary history, based on the royal archives or the temple archives as in 1 Kings; epic history, as in the matriarchal narratives; and thematic history, as in the work of the Chronicler. The lyric genre is to be found especially in the Psalms, the didactic genre in the Wisdom literature, the juridical genre in the legislative codes, the prophetic genre in the oracles of the prophets, the apocalyptic genre in the apocalyptic discourses of the Synoptics, and the epistolary genre in the letters of St. Paul.

These various genres are rarely to be found in a pure state in a single book; for the most part they intermingle and enrich one another. Critical study shows how a book that presents itself as a lapidary unit is in fact a conglomeration of disparate parts. Even a letter of St. Paul may be put together from several letters and make use of various literary genres.

And what diversity we find even within the same genre! There is a world of difference between the prayer of Psalm 88, in which fear is overcome, and the confessions in which Jeremiah shouts his despair; and yet both texts are laments. There is also a world of difference between the Letter to Philemon, in which Paul intercedes so tenderly for a fugitive slave, and the Letter to the Romans, which is a theological treatise.

The homily is a human echo of God's word. Therefore it adopts to some extent the literary genre of the text it is actualizing. But whatever the literary genre of the text, the aim of the homily is always to reach the basic question: What is God saying today to the community? The homilist must be familiar with all the literary genres, so that he will not mistake poetry for history (Jonah or Judith), or, far worse, history for poetry (the accounts of the Lord's resurrection). He can also make use of them all, since we can take as a general principle that the literary genres and symbols that God uses in his word are adapted to our mentality; at the very least, the homilist must be prejudiced in favor of the biblical genres. It is by no means to be taken for granted that the homilist has to "clean up" the parable of the sower or the allegory of the Good Shepherd, get rid of the images, and end up with "clear" (!) concepts, on the pretext that we do not meet sowers or shepherds on the streets of our cities. Like every work of art, images and symbols are far richer than any conceptual translations of them.

To attain his goal, the preacher may use the three kinds of preaching found in the New Testament: kerygma, instruction, and exhortation.

Kerygma (proclamation) is the announcement of the reign of God (Matthew 4:23) which we accept through repentance (Matthew 4:17), of the Messiahship of Jesus (Acts 2:36), and of his death and resurrection as mysteries of salvation (1 Cor. 1:23-24). The kerygma "came gradually to be recognized as the centre not only of the Gospels, but also of primitive Christianity itself."[22] True enough, not all the sermons we read in the Acts of the Apostles are purely kerygmatic;[23] all, nonetheless, do have the kerygma as their main focus and tend to be proclamations of the kingdom of God in Jesus Christ.

Didascalia (instruction, catechesis, teaching) proposes the other truths relating to faith. Kerygma and *didascalia* collaborate to bring the believer into the presence of Jesus Christ and lead him to the kingdom. It is written of Jesus that he "toured all of Galilee. He taught (*didaskōn*) in their synagogues [and] proclaimed [*kēryssōn*] the good news of the kingdom" (Matthew 4:23; 9:35). Like Jesus, the preacher is a herald who proclaims the good news, and a teacher who instructs the community.

Parainesis (advice, recommendation, exhortation) is moral exhortation. We find good examples of it in the latter part of various Pauline letters, as in Phil. 4:8: "Finally, my brothers, your thoughts should be wholly directed to all that is true, all that deserves respect, all that is honest, pure, admirable, decent, virtuous, or worthy of praise." The best kind of exhortation is the one the homilist does not need to make explicitly, because it flows directly out of the kerygma and the instruction.

We need not dwell on the need of balancing these various functions of the homily and adapting them to the congregation, which will need now kerygma, now instruction, now exhortation. A homily that is to take root in the lives of the faithful must spontaneously mingle kerygma, instruction, and exhortation, being more concerned to nourish the faith of the hearers than to follow a schema for preaching.

A word, finally, about the literary form of the discourse. If only we had the literary skill and could present God's words to the community as on a golden platter! Literary beauty is also a creature of God and should be drafted into the service of the word. Think of the fierce beauty of Amos, the limpid splendor of Isaiah, the passionate tenderness of Jeremiah, the sweetness of the Song of Songs! Above all, think of Jesus and how his words drew men! In our own day his parables still seem as fresh and natural as if they were being uttered for the first time; no one can ever forget them. Excessive concentration on literary effect is, of course, just as blameworthy as neglect of literary form. But since the homily tends to be a kind of friendly talk, there is more danger today of its becoming excessively unpolished rather than excessively elaborate. The goal should be the beauty of simplicity and transparency.

6. Homily by the minister or shared homily

The canon law of the Roman Church gives clerics a monopoly when it comes to preaching in the church.[24] The monopoly has produced the monologue homily. The question to be raised at this point is the following: May — should — the participation of the laity, which finds expression in the sharing of the Eucharistic bread, also find expression in the sharing of the word? Will the time come when, after the reading of the word, the presiding minister will address the congregation in the words once used in the synagogue of Antioch in Pisidia: "Brothers, if you have any exhortation to address to the people, please speak up" (Acts 13:15)? Will we ever carry out in the liturgy Paul's advice: "In wisdom made perfect, instruct and admonish one another" (Col. 3:16)? Is the time not gone forever when we can adhere to an aristocratic conception of the homily in which the priest alone speaks and the faithful have no function but to listen? Has the time not come for allowing the assembly to share in the homily?

The arguments in favor of reapportioning the ministry of the word are the following:

a) The whole Church — and not merely the ordained priesthood or the hierarchy — shares in the priestly, prophetic, and kingly function of Christ.[25] The Christian people, having this prophetic role, should proclaim the word of God not only by their lives but also by their words, in accordance with their understanding of it.[26] Christ entrusted the Scriptures and the understanding of them to the entire Church and not simply to the hierarchy, and the hierarchy has no mission to gag the faithful. On the contrary, the role of the hierarchy is to stir up the charisms and keep them alive: "Do not stifle the Spirit. Do not despise prophecies. Test everything; retain what is good" (1 Thess. 5:19-21).

The proclamation of the kingdom should be understood to include not only the word of God itself but also the actualization of the word in the homily. The proclamation should be the work of God's people and not merely of an intellectual caste whose mission it would supposedly be to secrete the word, as it were, and then pass it on for the admiration and acceptance of the people.

Let there be no misunderstanding here. It would be false to claim that until now the Christian people has never exercised its prophetic gift. The whole of Church history before Vatican Council II proves the opposite. The great movements that, like a series of springtimes, have marked the Church's course through history, that have illumined and warmed the Church on her often difficult journey through the world, and that were in part responsible for Vatican II itself (I am thinking of the biblical and liturgical movements and of Catholic Action) — all these started among the people and did not owe their existence to the hierarchy. The hierarchy did not initiate them (such is not necessarily its role), but it did authenticate them.

In the past, however, the people's exercise of its prophetic mission took place apart from the celebration of the liturgy. At the door of the church the laity were stricken dumb; more accurately, the only right they had was to sing and say "Amen." A barrier had been erected between life and liturgy, between prophetism and worship.

We are justified then in asking what form the ministry of the word should take in our liturgical celebrations. There can be no objection to maintaining that the Roman liturgy will evolve to the point where Christians generally, not just the clergy, take charge of the homily. The priesthood in the Roman rite has become a jack-of-all-trades, monopolizing especially the ministries proper to apostles, prophets, and teachers. It is time to distinguish the various ministries from one another and to redistribute them throughout the Christian community — not in order to deprive the priesthood or hierarchy of them but simply to allow the Christian people to exercise the charisms they possess.[27]

b) Actualization of the word can be better adapted and made more relevant. After all, the homily, as we have already pointed out, is not to be a handing out of exegetical scholarship (the homilist's role is not to answer his neighbor's difficulties with the text of Scripture); its purpose is rather to relate the word to the present situation of the community. But the congregation knows its own joys, troubles, and concerns far better than the priest does, especially since in the Roman rite he often lives apart from them. This claim is especially valid for Masses at which the congregation consists of a well-defined group. Nothing can improve upon a homily by the mother of a family at a Mass for children; her actualization of the word is quite likely to hit home! It is likewise clear that a student, who really knows what life among his fellows is like, can effectively incarnate the word once more for other students.

Objection: A priest must do a lot of serious study of Scripture if he is to speak knowledgeably of it; so why ask the laity to talk of something they know nothing about, something they have neither the time nor perhaps the desire to study? The objection is not valid. The laity are being asked to speak precisely of what they do know very well! Their function is not to trot out before the congregation some tattered rags of semi-clerical erudition, but to speak from where they stand, that is, to speak from where they encounter the word and in accordance with their understanding of it. The objection can in fact be turned against the exegetes themselves: "If the bread of the word is to be shared in such a way that all can assimilate it, there is need of kinds of competence and experience which are not always and necessarily those of the presiding minister alone."[28] The homily can only be enriched if each homilist attacks it from within his own situation in the Church.

7. Role of the presiding minister

Entrusting the homily to the congregation does not mean excluding the minister, still less stripping him of his function. On the contrary. As the one who presides, he is responsible, first of all, for the good order of the celebration. It is very difficult to direct properly the sharing of the congregation in the homily. Rarely does any group lack its "exhibitionist" who talks on and on to the congregation when he should be still; every group will also have some member who has found the precious pearl but forgets to show it to others. The Corinthians ran into these problems, and Paul's advice to them is still good: "All well and good, so long as everything is done with a constructive purpose. If any are going to talk in tongues let it be at most two or three, each in turn" (1 Cor. 14:26-27); "God is a God, not of confusion, but of peace" (14:33); "Set your hearts on prophecy, my brothers, and do not forbid those who speak in tongues, but make sure that everything is done properly and in order" (14:39-40).

This does not mean that the presiding minister must himself direct the course of the homily. He can delegate this function to someone in the congregation who has a gift for this kind of direction. But the minister does retain final responsibility.

This responsibility is really for the celebration as a whole and includes the homily as part of the whole. Can we say more specifically what the responsibility of the presiding minister is, that is, the responsibility proper to his presidential role? (We are speaking here only of the homily.) He authenticates the homily spoken while he is presiding. He thus proposes it to the congregation as an authentic interpretation and actualization of the Gospel for his community. Making the proper allowances, we can apply to him what the Council says of the Church's teaching office: "The task of giving an authentic interpretation of the Word of God, whether in its written form or in the form of Tradition, has been entrusted to the living teaching office of the Church alone. Its authority in this matter is exercised in the name of Jesus Christ. Yet this Magisterium is not superior to the Word of God, but is its servant."[29]

His act of authentification can take various forms:

—He can, in his function as presiding minister, introduce and conclude the homily. But he must be careful, as he does this, not to play the role which some of the congregation might want him to play ("the priest, who knows it all"). Rather, he must help the community express its mind (and not just what he would like to hear the people say), and then gather together the riches discovered in the word by the community.

—He can also speak his piece during the homily, since he is, after all, a member of the community. He *must* intervene if it seems to him that the message conveyed by the word is being improperly interpreted or actualized.

> The hierarchy has its own proper charism which it cannot surrender to anyone else: it is the teacher that guarantees the Christian authen-

ticity of every service of the word in the Church. The hierarchy is the final court of appeal for deciding whether or not the way the word is actualized is valid and in conformity with the essential data of tradition.[30]

—He may also avoid intervening at all if the homily seems good and he has nothing to add. He then authenticates it by his silence, which in this case is equivalent to approbation. To continue the comparison made just above, that is how the magisterium ordinarily authenticates the progress made in biblical studies and in all other areas. Popes and bishops are not usually professional exegetes; their charism is to lead the Church, and so they authenticate that which, after study, discussion, and debate, becomes the common belief of the whole community.

8. Everyone's business

Some readers may be inclined to say: "What you're saying concerns the ministers who preside at our liturgical meetings and those who have the charism of words. It doesn't concern me; my charism is silence."

That turns the truth upside down! In a sense, the homily is everyone's business. Those who are ministers of the word do what they can; some days, as they are well aware, their homily never quite gets off the ground, and they are the first to acknowledge it. They also know that for the community a good homily is a grace from God. But if they do what they can, you too should do what you can. And what you can do is actualize the word, not letting it "fall to the ground," but asking yourself each time you hear the word: "What is God saying to me today?" There is a threshold in the consciousness of the hearer that no one can cross but himself. It is the threshold beyond which the noise of human words has stopped and each individual can say within himself: "Speak, Lord, your servant is listening." Thus there is a homily which no one else can preach in your stead. It is a homily you must listen to in silent adoration.

9. Conditions for effectiveness

The first condition for the fruitful practice of the dialogue homily is, I think, the existence of a true community, one that is alive and receptive. There must be a degree of warm friendliness, a sense of genuine humanness and genuine Christianity. A successful dialogue homily, like the successful answer to most other problems in liturgy, supposes that the community is not simply a mass of people sitting side by side, each one locked up in himself; the community must be a family whose members are open to one another.

The ideal community for a dialogue homily is the one described in Acts: "They went to the temple area together every day, while in their homes they broke bread. With exultant and sincere hearts they took their meals in common" (Acts 2:46-47); "The community of believers were of one heart and one mind" (Acts 4:32). The liturgy itself, of course, fosters the growth of such community, but it will develop it all the more effectively if something of it is there to start with.

There are also some material conditions: the arrangement of the church and the acoustics. Some churches and chapels are built like long tunnels, so that all the individual sees is the back of the person in front of him. Dialogue then becomes almost impossible.

Other conditions, finally, are simply a matter of group dynamics. Here, as elsewhere, grace does not suppress nature. "The usefulness of spirituality is unlimited" (1 Tim. 4:8). Undoubtedly. But it is not a substitute for anything else.

When we come to the actual homily itself, we should distinguish between small homogeneous communities and large gatherings.

In the first case, the participation in the homily should be a simple and easy matter, whether at the Office or at Mass or at any other celebration. After the presiding minister's homily (if he gives one), those who wish can share with the community their knowledge of Christ and their understanding of the contemporaneity of the word just read. Isn't it completely normal that Christians who are ready to share their lives with their brothers should also be ready to share the best of themselves, namely their knowledge of the mystery of Christ Jesus?

There is no need that everyone should say something. There is no need that an individual say something on every occasion. One thing we must avoid at all costs, and that is that, after having expelled the demons of the old rubricism, we substitute a new torment — the unconditional obligation to say something! No! Let a person speak when he or she has something to say.

The case of the large gathering (at Sunday Mass, for example) is more difficult. If everyone spontaneously speaks out, the Mass will sound like an Oriental bazaar. Sharing in the homily will be possible, however, if the homily has been prepared in collaboration with the liturgical committee or other groups, even if it be actually delivered by a single individual. Those who spontaneously get up to speak should show the maturity of their faith. The effort of the presiding minister to keep the celebration peaceful and dignified will be decisive. He must keep his eyes on the essential thing, which is not participation in the homily but the discovery of the treasures of the word. "All well and good, so long as everything is done with a constructive purpose" (1 Cor. 14:26).

It is hard to offer any further concrete advice than this, since practical solutions will depend in part on the traditions of each community and even of each people. One community will prefer a well-organized, Western-style exposition; another will prefer approaching the truth Eastern-style, through a series of narrowing concentric circles; another will prefer to spread out the wares of the word like a merchant's goods, African-style, to the accompaniment of a lot of back-and-forth.[31] No type of dialogue can be excluded in principle as long as it is suitable for a given community and provides a way of asking the key question: "What is God saying to us today in his word?"

10. *The whole Mass a homily*

The homily normally comes after the last reading, which, in all liturgical traditions, is the reading of the Gospel. But the word of God cannot be imprisoned within one part of the Mass, the part we call "the liturgy of the word." The whole celebration, that of the word and that of the Eucharist, is a celebration of the covenant, as we noted earlier. It is therefore entirely natural that the word should be present throughout the Mass, from the entrance rite to the rite of dismissal.

The point is not to talk ceaselessly. It is far better, on the contrary, to proceed with discretion and reserve than to sin through verboseness. Nor is there any question of scattering "mini-homilies" throughout the Mass; there is no surer way of devaluating the homily than to have too much of it, no matter what varied forms it might take (whether lector's exhortations or celebrant's comments). In speaking of the whole Mass as a homily, we are referring rather to the diffusion throughout the Mass of the homily's most important function: the actualization of the word for the community which is celebrating the covenant.

We shall simply indicate some possibilities. To make the suggestions concrete, we shall take as an example the Mass of Easter

Sunday, for which the readings, in the Roman rite, are Acts 10:34, 37-43; Ps. 118:1-2, 16-17, 22-23; Col. 3:1-4 or 1 Cor. 5:6-8; John 20:1-9.

a) Opening exhortation

This can be attached to the formula of greeting and can present in biblical terms the mystery the community is about to celebrate: "Christ is our Passover that has been sacrificed! Let us rejoice in this Mass at the banquet table of the Lord!" (cf. 1 Cor. 5:7-8)..

b) Penitential rite

Instead of mechanically using ready-made formulas which become boring to even the most fervent, we can turn to that part of the word that provides petitions for forgiveness. Here is an example, based on Col. 3:1-4 and attached to the *Kyrie*:

> Paul tells us: "You have been raised up in company with Christ. Set your heart on what pertains to higher realms" (Col. 3:1). Because we do not set our hearts enough on those spiritual realities, Lord, have mercy. *Lord, have mercy.*
>
> Paul tells us: "Be intent on things above, rather than on things of earth" (Col. 3:2). Because we often remain too engrossed with the things of earth, Christ, have mercy. *Christ, have mercy.*
>
> Paul tells us: "Your life is hidden now with Christ in God" (Col. 3:3). Because we often forget to live fully the life of the risen Christ, Lord, have mercy. *Lord, have mercy.*

c) Introduction to the readings

The introductions can serve as listeners' guides and thus prepare the congregation for a more fruitful reception of the word.

d) General intercessions.

These will quite naturally be a response to the word that has just been proclaimed.[32] Here are some intentions suggested by the readings in the Mass of Easter.

> For the Church of Jesus Christ, that she may bear witness in the world to her Lord's resurrection (cf. Acts 10:42), let us pray.
>
> That she may continuously rid herself of the old yeast and become a fresh dough (cf. 1 Cor. 5:7), let us pray.
>
> For our community, that it may imitate Jesus Christ, who went about doing good (cf. Acts 10:38), let us pray.

That we may set our hearts chiefly on what is above and live the life of the risen Christ (cf. Col. 3:1), let us pray.

That all men may come to believe in the Lord's resurrection and receive forgiveness of their sins (cf. Acts 10:43), let us pray.

e) Preface

The theme given at the beginning of the various prefaces in the Sacramentary may be expanded.

f) The Lord's Prayer and the "Lamb of God"

While preserving the traditional formulas, the invitation to these two prayers can also be enriched with elements drawn from the word of God. In introducing the Lord's Prayer, the celebrant might say, for example: "Let us pray with confidence to the Father in the words our Savior gave us, that the kingdom of the risen Christ may truly come upon our earth."

For the "Lamb of God," the following formula of introduction might be used: "Behold the risen Christ! Behold the Bread of the new Passover (cf. 1 Cor. 5:7)!

g) Thanksgiving[33]

A series of thanksgiving acclamations may be inserted after Communion and the period of silent thanksgiving, and before the closing prayer of the celebrant. Here is an example based on the responsorial psalm, with a refrain for the community.

Let us thank the Lord, for his hand has done wonders (Ps. 118:16); in raising Jesus from the dead, he raises us as well (Col. 3:1).

Glory to you forever!

Let us thank the Lord who urges us to proclaim by our lives that his love is everlasting (Ps. 118:1).

Glory to you forever!

Let us thank the Lord for this day that he has made, a day of joy and gladness (Ps. 118:24), a foretaste of the everlasting Pasch.

Glory to you forever!

h) Formula of dismissal

The formula of *dismissal*, "Go in the peace of Christ," can be extended and transformed into a *mission mandate*: "Go in the peace of Christ and let your lives proclaim that Christ is risen!"

Thanks to the word, each Mass takes on a special cast. The traditional formulas are freed from the corruption that time causes and continually revitalized by contact with the Scriptures.

11) *The vocation of the homilist*

The dignity of the homilist's vocation derives from the dignity of the homily. If the homily is God's word, as we have maintained, then the preacher is a "prophet," a spokesman for God. And if the community takes part in the homily, the whole community exercises its prophetic vocation.

The preacher has the awesome responsibility of speaking no word that God cannot accept as his own. He must "follow a straight course in preaching the truth" (2 Tim. 2:15). He must apply to himself the Apostle's words that seem so intolerably presumptuous and yet do express very well the mystery of the homily: "Christ . . . speaks in me" (2 Cor. 13:3).

Humility is required for this ministry. Humility before the word, first of all. "There are too many mysteries in Scripture."[34] In addition, there is too much darkness in our minds. The believer who searches for the God of the Scriptures is a sinner whose powers of understanding are wounded. If he yields to vanity and preaches a showy homily, he "trades on the word of God" (2 Cor. 2:17).

Humility before the community as well.[35] Anyone who accepts the ministry of actualizing the word for his brothers also accepts the obligation of first listening to the word himself. He must humbly gauge the abyssal distance between the message he proclaims and the manner in which he actualizes it in his own life. The *Didache* say that "every prophet who teaches the truth without putting it into practice is a false prophet."[36] The statement is extreme, of course, since if the Church had always first to practice what she teaches, she would be reduced to teaching very little; if she had to be perfectly holy before she spoke, she would have remained silent since the very first day. There is no doubt, too, that the word can be preached even by someone moved by vanity and ulterior motives, as St. Paul noted even in his day (Phil. 1:15-18).

But the statement from the *Didache* nonetheless does say something quite true: that if one is to speak in the name of God, he must to some extent live according to God. Paul is not afraid to say: "Imitate me as I imitate Christ" (1 Cor. 11:1; cf. 4:16; Phil. 3:17; 4:9; 1 Thess. 1:6). No one will be naive enough to take these words completely at face value, nor presumptuous enough to speak them as his own. Paul did not imitate Christ Jesus perfectly, for we know that he had his faults, and he thought of himself as the foremost of sinners (1 Tim. 1:15). What the words mean is that the preacher must set out on the road to holiness as Paul did when he began his apostolate of preaching the Lord. Preaching is a school of humility. The gold of the Gospel is carried in an earthen vessel (cf. 2 Cor. 4:7). Is the vessel to preen itself because of the gold it contains?

Here we see the paradox in the preacher's vocation: he proclaims salvation to the world, and yet his ministry does not necessarily sanctify him (cf. Phil. 1:15-18); he carries the burden of his own wretchedness and yet becomes God's co-worker (1 Cor. 3:9); like his brothers in this world, he gropes in the darkness, and yet his face must reflect the light of Christ; he preaches God's freely given mercy on the world and must first implore it for himself; he speaks with authority and yet has no authority over the message he transmits; he is only a steward, yet it is the very treasures of God that his lips reveal to the world! We are "ambassadors for Christ, God as it were appealing through us" (2 Cor. 5:20)!

---

[1] "The homily is the explanation, during a liturgical gathering, of a text of Scripture that has been read or sung during the same service," according to P. Rouillard, "Homélie," *Catholicisme* 5:829. "In the Greek Fathers from the beginning of the third century 'homily' is a term for a talk on Scripture" (*ibid.*). On the homily, cf. L. Fournier, *L'homélie selon la Constitution de la Sainte Liturgie* (Brussels, 1964); *Présence et dialogue*, no. 6 (June–July, 1968), pp. 22–25; L. Maldonado, *Vers une liturgie sécularisée* (Paris, 1971), pp. 97–110; L. Della Torre, "La prédication dans la liturgie," in J. Gelineau (ed.), *Dans vos assemblées* (Paris, 1971), pp. 169–98, with bibliography on p. 169; *Paroisse et liturgie*, no. 54 (1972), pp. 323–25; J. Kahmann, *The Bible and the Preaching of the Word*, translated by T.J. Holmes (De Pere, Wis., 1965); Cl. Geffré, "La révélation hier et aujourd'hui," in J. Audinet *et al.*, *Révélation de Dieu et langage des hommes* (Paris, 1972), pp. 95–121. On the preaching of St. Paul, cf. J. Murphy-O'Connor, *Paul on Preaching* (New York, 1964), and H. Conzelmann, *An Outline of the Theology of the New Testament*, translated by J. Bowden (New York, 1969), pp. 265–68.

[2] Not too long ago, A. Croegaert, *op cit.*, had an excursus entitled "Friend, be original! Preach the Gospel!" (p. 584).

[3] See the resentful pages J. Sulivan wrote on preaching in his *Provocation ou faiblesse de Dieu* (Paris, 1959), pp. 41–52. In point of fact, the limitations of preaching derived from the limitations of the liturgy itself, to the extent that the latter was regarded as the carrying out of inconsequential stereotyped rites. It is significant that the highly respected *Dictionnaire de théologie catholique*, the sourcebook for anyone serious about the Church, has 213 columns on "Predestination" and 46 on "*Praemotio physica*," but not a line on "Preaching," which should have come in between these other two articles [French: "Prédestination," "Prédication," "Prémotion physique."] There is nothing on "Homily" either.

⁴ Cl. Geffré, *art. cit.*, p. 97.

⁵ *Dogmatic Constitution on Divine Revelation*, no. 12 (Flannery, p. 757). In distinguishing here between what the sacred writers meant and that "which God had thought well to manifest through the medium of their words," the Council had no intention of taking a position in the debate over the "fuller meaning" (*sensus plenior*); cf. P. Grelot, "L'inspiration de l'Ecriture et son interprétation," in *La révélation Divine* 2 (Unam Sanctam 70; Paris, 1968), pp. 370–71. On the *sensùs plenior*, cf. P. Grelot, *Sens chrétien de l'Ancien Testament: Esquisse d'un traité dogmatique* (Tournai, 1962), bibliography on p. 449, note 4.

⁶ Cf. H. Cazelles, *Ecriture, Parole et Esprit* (Paris, 1970), pp. 119–74 and L. Desrousseaux, "Un itinéraire exégétique," in *Le langage de la foi dans l'Ecriture et dans le monde actuel* (Lectio divina 72; Paris, 1972), pp. 29–42. Cf. also H. Schlier, "Was heisst Auslegung der Heiligen Schrift?" in his *Besinnung auf das Neue Testament* (Freiburg im Br., 1962), pp. 35–62.

⁷ H. Cazelles, *op. cit.*, p. 108. Cf. L. Alonso Schökel, "Is Exegesis Necessary?" and B. Dreher, "Exegesis and Proclamation," in R.E. Murphy (ed.), *Theology, Exegesis, and Proclamation* (Concilium 70; New York, 1971), pp. 30–38 and 56–66 respectively.

⁸ C. Wiéner makes the following comparison: "One of my friends is having a house built; in front of the rising structure is the usual placard, 'No admission except to workmen.' If I do get in, there will be nothing to hint to me of the warm domesticity that will reign there a few months from now. All I will see is debris. I'll catch cold because there are no panes in the window; I may fall into the basement and break a leg because there is no stairway, only an open hole. An exegete's workroom is just as dangerous for the uninitiated" ("Exégèse et annonce de la Parole," *La Maison-Dieu*, no. 82 [1965], p. 66).

⁹ *Homiliae in Ezechielem*, I, 11 (*PG* 13:677A).

¹⁰ *Letter to Gregory*, 4; French translation by H. Crouzel in *Grégoire le Thaumaturge: Remerciement à Origène suivi de la Lettre d'Origène à Grègoire* (Sources chrétiennes 148; Paris, 1969), pp. 192–94.

¹¹ Gregory Thaumaturgus, *Encomium of Origen*, 15 (*PG* 10:1094D; cf. Crouzel, *op. cit.*, p. 171).

¹² *Homiliae in Genesim*, III, 5 (*PG* 12:179A).

¹³ *Adversus haereses*, IV, 2, 3. Cf. IV, 9, 1: "One and the same father of the family, the Word of God, our Lord Jesus Christ, established both covenants. He spoke with Abraham and Moses, and in these last times has given us freedom and abundant grace." Cf. L. Deiss. *Printemps de la théologie*, pp. 160–61.

¹⁴ *Homiliae in librum Numerorum*, IX, 4; French translation by A. Mehat, in *Origène: Homélies sur les Nombres* (Sources chrétiennes 29; Paris, 1951), p. 172. Cf. H. de Lubac, *The Sources of Tradition*, translated by L. O'Neill (New York, 1968), pp. 113–29), for other patristic passages on the "harmony of the two Testaments."

¹⁵ *Dogmatic Constitution on Divine Revelation*, no. 16 (Flannery, pp. 759–60).

¹⁶ The *General Instruction of the Roman Missal* (April 3, 1969) explains that the homily should be adapted to the needs of the celebrating community (no. 41).

¹⁷ Cf. Hippolytus of Rome, *Apostolic Tradition*, 45 (written ca. 215): "If there is an instruction on the Word of God, everyone will go to it gladly, with this thought in mind, that it is God whom he hears speaking through the mouth of the man giving the instruction" (in L. Deiss, *Early Sources of the Liturgy*, translated by B. Weatherhead [2nd ed.; Collegeville, Minn., 1975], p. 69).

¹⁸ Cf. L. Bouyer, "The Word of God Lives in the Liturgy," in A.G. Martimort *et al.*, *The Liturgy and the Word of God* (Collegeville, Minn., 1959): "[The sermon] was no longer a part of the Mass, but an *entre-acte* between two parts of the Mass. Anything could be spoken of as well as and besides the Gospel, and no allusion was ever made, ordinarily, to the other Scriptural texts of the liturgy. Moral exhortations,

political comments, financial appeals, and sometimes, but less frequently, a sort of catechism lesson for adults had long since taken the place of the homily; while in large parishes or on great occasions this was the time for one of those rhetorical exercises (with appropriate gestures and vocal inflections) which have always delighted the crowd and which, like some works of art, exist 'for art's sake' — that is, in this case, for the pleasure that good people take, as they say, in listening to 'a man who can speak well' " (p. 55).

19 Cf. L. Deiss, *Printemps de la théologie*, pp. 91–106.

20 H. Cazelles, *op. cit.*, p. 141.

21 "Myth is an undifferentiated literary genre, being poetry by reason of its images, history by reason of its sense of lived experience, philosophy by reason of the human problems it faces, theology by reason of its appeal to the divine world in the midst of human life, and sociology and liturgy as well" (Cazelles, *op. cit.*, p. 142).

22 J.M. Robinson, *A New Quest for the Historical Jesus* (Studies in Biblical Theology 25; Naperville, Ill., 1959), p. 38.

23 The chief kerygmatic discourses in Acts are the three sermons of Peter (2:14-39; 3:12-26; 10:34-43), the discourse of Stephen (7:2-53), and the two discourses of Paul (13:16-41; 17:22-31).

24 *Code of Canon Law*, can. 134: "Laymen, even though they be religious, are forbidden to preach in church."

25 Vatican II, *Dogmatic Constitution on the Church*, no. 31: ". . . the faithful [the laity] who by Baptism are incorporated into Christ, are placed in the People of God, and in their own way share the priestly, prophetic and kingly office of Christ" (Flannery, p. 388). Cf. the Report of the International Theological Commission (October, 1970), *Le ministère sacerdotal* (Paris, 1971), pp. 35–37.

26 *Dogmatic Constitution on the Church*, no. 35: "Christ is the great prophet who proclaimed the kingdom of the Father both by the testimony of his life and by the power of his word. Until the full manifestation of his glory, he fulfills this prophetic office, not only by the hierarchy who teach in his name and by his power, but also by the laity. He accordingly both establishes them as witnesses and provides them with the appreciation of the faith and the grace of the word" (Flannery, pp. 391–92).

27 It is sometimes said that laymen can speak *at the time of* the homily but that their words do not constitute the homily (cf., e.g., *Présence et dialogue*, no. 6 [June–July, 1968], p. 23). But does such a distinction reflect what really goes on? Does it express the community's perception of what is happening?

28 L. Della Torre, *art. cit.*, p. 175.

29 *Dogmatic Constitution on Divine Revelation*, no. 10 (Flannery, pp. 755–56).

30 L. Maldonado, *op. cit.*, p. 104.

31 L. Della Torre rightly observes (*art. cit.*, p. 192) that a *dialogue homily* is not a *debate homily*. But if a debate leads to a homily, i.e., to a search for what God's word is saying, why reject it? The peoples of the Third World, who live outside Western civilization, usually display less Cartesian rigidity (which is not to say "less intelligence"!) in their thinking. A debate may often be the best approach to an understanding of the word.

32 Cf. L. Deiss, *Concile et chant nouveau* (Paris, 1969), pp. 186–92.

33 Cf. L. Deiss, "L'action de grâce après la communion," *Assemblée nouvelle*, no. 10, pp. 8–10.

34 St. Pamphilus, *Apologia pro Origene* (*PG* 17:543).

35 Cf. J. Murphy-O'Connor, *op. cit.*, ch. 5: "The Preacher and His Audience."

36 *Didache* 11:10; cf. J.-P. Audet, *La Didachè: Instruction des Apôtres* (Paris, 1958), pp. 447–51.

Chapter 16

THE GATHERING OF THE PEOPLES, OR MISSION TODAY

1. The problem

The reader is asked here to recall the conclusions we reached in our analysis of the gathering of peoples that God effects in the messianic age (above, Chapter 9). These conclusions were: Jesus devotes himself, as a "gatherer," exclusively to Israel; he does not make any attempt to recruit from among pagans; instead, the other nations, having discovered the wonderful deeds God does for those who belong to him, hasten to Jerusalem and beg membership in the chosen people; the mission to the nations does not consist first and foremost in going out to them but in living God's salvation in such a way that the nations will come seeking the Church: "Let us go with you, for we have heard that God is with you" (Zech. 8:23).

This image of mission does not resemble the one people sometimes have of missionary activity; the two may even be in opposition to each other. For contemporary practice consists rather in going off "to the missions" in order to win the nations for Christ. This practice can appeal to the example of Paul and his missionary journeys. It can also appeal to the Lord's command at the end of Mark's Gospel: "Go into the whole world and proclaim the good news to all creation" (16:15).

We have every right, therefore, to ask how we are to reconcile the words of the risen Christ, "Go into the whole world" with the command he gave when sending his disciples on their journey through Galilee, "Do not visit pagan territory" (Matthew 10:5). Or to put it another way: How are we to reconcile the missionary viewpoint of

310

the Old Testament, according to which the nations come to the Church, with that of the New Testament, according to which the chosen people go out to the nations?

These problems are not simply scholastic puzzles. On the contrary, they are extremely important for the Church today. I mean for the Church, not as a human society (at this level people can always manage to find opportunistic survival techniques), but as the community of Christ, that is, the community as the Lord in his love wants it to be. At times — even too frequently — the Church allows herself to get absorbed in problems of internal organization and in matters of purely ecclesiastical discipline or even of liturgical ritual. She yields to the temptation of adolescent narcissism. She likes at times to admire herself in the mirror instead of looking outward to the world.

Yet the Church's primordial duty is the preaching of the Gospel, and her only right to exist derives from fulfillment of that basic duty. Just as the Word became flesh "for us men and for our salvation," as the Creed puts it, so the Church was created and can continue truly to exist in Christ only if she works "for us men and for our salvation." Today the "us men" means the whole of mankind. The Church is the servant of over two billion men who do not yet know Christ or who have the wrong conception of him (which is probably the worse way of not knowing him). She cannot go on much longer indulging in the luxury of devoting her time and energies to the contemplation of herself and her internal problems. These problems are small indeed when compared with the evangelization of so many human beings. Isn't she likely to resolve these internal problems much more easily if she devotes herself to her missionary task?[1]

The observations we shall offer here are only a partial approach to the problem.[2] But what we have established thus far in this book remains a solid acquisition. On the basis of it, we hope to advance a little in reflection on the Church's mission and its present situation.

2. The Church, sacrament of salvation

"Between the nations and himself Yahweh set Israel."[3] In the New Testament "the Israel of God" (Gal. 6:16) is now the Church of Jesus Christ. Between the nations and himself God today sets the Church. And the salvation the Church announces, the kingdom she proclaims, is that of the risen Christ who by his resurrection has set all mankind in motion toward the shores of eternity.

The Church's first duty is to live fully the rich life thus made possible and to reflect in her face the resurrection of her Lord. There is no point in her scurrying along the roads of the world or setting up her platform in the public square and shouting to the pagans: "Come with us! Enter the Church!" They might well answer us: "What for? Why should we?" No, the Church's most pressing missionary obligation today is to make herself more beautiful, more radiant, more attractive, so that those outside may see her and come asking: "We want to go with you because we have come to realize that *God is with you!*" When that happens, they will also have recognized Jesus present in the Church. For he is *Emmanuel*, that is, *God-with-us*.

We may well maintain that the slow progress of evangelization is not due exclusively to the ill will of non-Christians, but is attributable in part to the shortcomings of the baptized. Bishop Frétellière has written: "We must admit that the Church nowadays does not seem very attractive. In her present state not many of our contemporaries think of her as a great beacon of light and hope in the world of today."[4] Was it not a work of housecleaning and beautification that Pope John XXIII was beginning when he convoked the Second Vatican Council? We have found indeed that what we thought of as a housecleaning turned out, in some areas, to be a restoration or even a rebuilding. But no effort should be felt excessive, no work too difficult, when the goal is to enable the Church to fulfill her vocation of being the *universal sacrament of salvation*.

We know how many of the conciliar texts stress this point. The *Dogmatic Constitution on the Church* says in its very first number: ". . . the Church, in Christ, is in the nature of sacrament — a sign and instrument, that is, of communion with God and of unity among all men."[5]

J. L. Witte writes:

> The Church is not missionary solely because of Christ's positive command. Apostolicity has been made an element of her very nature by him who came on earth as an *efficacious sign*, to all mankind, of God's universal salvific will. The Church in turn is a *sign of Christ* and his universal mission, and by that very fact she is also *the sacrament* of the unity of all mankind. The Church is thus missionary to the very depths of her being.[6]

3. *Local community and mission*

Each local community is, as it were, an incarnation of the universal Church in time and space. "Those who, under the authority of the bishop, sanctify and govern that portion of the Lord's flock assigned to them render the universal Church visible in their locality."[7]

Since the local Church shares in the grace of the universal Church, it also shares in her mission. Thus the theology of the Church as universal sacrament of salvation is played out, as it were, on the local scene, since each local Church must manifest the salvation of Jesus Christ that has come to it, and must by its beauty robe itself in the universal beauty of the Lord.

This duty is evidently incumbent in a special way on those who are officially dedicated to missionary work.[8] But it also affects all members of the Local Church. The entire community is a Christ-bearer and forms the kingly, priestly, and prophetic people that God has set between the nations and himself. Since Vatican II, no one can limit mission to missionaries.

The demonstrative power of the signs given must also be examined. Signs are not necessarily valid anywhere and everywhere, since their meaning is always relative to those who perceive them. Perhaps people in the past paid more attention to the sign as given (i.e., the sign the missionary gives) than to the sign as received (i.e., as perceived by someone who does not know Jesus Christ). This is not at all meant as a criticism of the social or caritative works of a former time, but is simply an invitation to exercise critical judgment with regard to the contemporary situation, and, if necessary, to adapt the signs used so that they may point more clearly to the salvation of Jesus Chirst.

4. "Go, make disciples of all nations"

Because of these words with which St. Matthew's Gospel ends, countless missionaries through the ages have left everything so that they might proclaim the Good News to the peoples of the world. We must now try to determine the precise meaning of Christ's words. Here is an accurate translation of the Greek text:

> Full authority has been given to me both in heaven and on earth; go, therefore, and make disciples of all the nations. Baptize them in the name
> of the Father,
> and of the Son,
> and of the Holy Spirit.
> Teach them to carry out everything I have commanded you. And know that I am with you always, until the end of the world! (Matthew 28:18-20).

The authenticity (though not the canonicity) of these words has been strongly criticized.[9] "They should be regarded as a *saying in* the Lord rather than as a *saying of* the Lord."[10] In any event, they bear Matthew's mark, since the generalizations — *full* authority, *all* the nations, *everything* I have commanded you, *always* — are characteristic of the First Gospel.[11] But the fact that the end of Luke and of Mark also have missionary mandates shows that the idea of apostolate was the normal conclusion to the Gospel narrative and pointed forward to the age of the great missionary adventure.[12]

The true disciple of Jesus brings his Master new disciples. Beyond a doubt, that is the principal affirmation made in the missionary command. In other words, the emphasis is on winning other disciples and not on "going," i.e., "departing" for the missions. The translation "go and make disciples" really does not do justice to the text, since the verb *poreuō*, "go," when used in the aorist participial form (Matthew 28:19 reads, literally, "having gone, make . . ."), is often a simple pleonasm;[13] this is true of Hebrew as well as Greek.[14] Thus, when Luke writes in the parable of the banquet, "What you should do when you have been invited is go and sit in the lowest place" (Luke 14:10), he does not mean that the invited person must depart or set off to take the lowest place. An example even closer to our text is to be found in Matthew 9:13: "Go and learn the meaning of the words, 'It is mercy I desire and not sacrifice.' " The two texts are parallel: "Go and learn . . . ," "Go and make. . . ." Just as the point is not that a person must go off somewhere to learn what mercy is, neither is it the point that one must go off somewhere to make disciples for Jesus.

To be sure, the text is in no sense opposed to the idea of setting out for other places in order to proclaim the Good News there. Mission normally does demand sacrifices of that kind: "The good news must first [before the parousia can take place] be proclaimed to all the Gentiles" (Mark 13:10; cf. 14:9).[15] God needs our lips if he is to speak to the nations, and our hands if he is break the bread of friendship as well as the bread of the Eucharist. Paul can boast that in the service of the Lord he "traveled continually, endangered by floods, robbers . . . imperiled in the city, in the desert, at sea" (2 Cor. 11:26). He gives forceful expression to the need of preachers: "How can they believe unless they have heard of him? And how can they hear unless there is someone to preach? And how can men preach unless they are sent?" (Rom. 10:14).

In any event, mission cannot be identified with the movement from one place to another. What makes the missionary is not the distance he travels but the testimony he gives. Consequently, there can be no opposition between the missionary perspective of the Old Testament, according to which the nations come to Israel when they see the light of salvation shining upon her (cf. Is. 60), and the missionary perspective of the New Testament, according to which the disciples go to bring this light to the ends of the earth. What we must keep in mind is that the important, indeed the only really necessary thing is not to go but to have the light.

We should also note that the missionary mandate is part of what we might call a hymn for the enthronement of the Son of Man.[16] By his resurrection Jesus has been appointed universal Lord, and it is this resurrection that intervenes between the mandate for the Galilean mission, "Do not visit pagan territory," and the missionary mandate at the end of Matthew. The resurrection is now the essential content of the preaching concerning Jesus.[17] It is also the door that gives the pagans access to the kingdom; it overthrows the wall of separation between Jews and Gentiles; it reconciles all in one body; it puts an end to the hatred between them and gives access to the Father (cf. Eph. 2:14-18). Mission is thus a logical consequence of the resurrection.

There is a final point to be made. The missionary mandate ends with an allusion to Emmanuel. The prophecy "With us is God!" of Is. 8:10, which Matthew placed at the beginning of his Gospel (1:23), is fulfilled by Jesus' promise, "I am with you always, until the end of the world!" (Matthew 28:20), which marks the end of his ministry and the beginning of his disciples' work. More than ever, the time of mission is the time of Christ's presence in the ecclesial community. Nearness in space to the pagan peoples would be of no avail if there were not also a spiritual nearness of heart. And this spiritual presence in the midst of the nations is in turn sustained by the presence of the risen Jesus with the missionary. What the missionary is really proclaiming is that the Lord is always with him.

5. The missionary practice of the early community

a) From the beginnings to Paul's first missionary journey (ca. 45–49)

On the first Pentecost the apostles were gathered at Jerusalem; there they received the Holy Spirit, proclaimed the Lord's resurrection, and brought home the first fruits of the apostolic harvest (some three thousand, according to Acts 2:41). They divided the known world into missionary fields, then, leaving behind them the women and children, set out each for his own territory and established local Churches. That is how popular piety, with a trace of ecstatic wonder mixed in it, sometimes imagines the beginnings of the early Church's missionary activity.[18] Such an image bears no relation, however, to the historical evidence; it is a pleasant figment of the imagination but tends to obscure the reality. It will be quite useful for us to see how, in fact, the early community, as presented in the Acts of the Apostles, went about carrying out the missionary mandate left them by Jesus.[19] We shall learn from this how they understood the mandate.

There is no basis for maintaining that after the resurrection of Jesus, the Twelve immediately undertook a ministry of preaching such as Jesus had carried on during his public life. The only thing the documents tell us for sure is that Peter returned to fishing in the sea of Tiberias, along with some companions whose names tradition has preserved — Thomas, Nathanael, James and John (the sons of Zebedee), and two others (John 21:1-2).

Nor does anything suggest that the situation changed radically after the first Pentecost, the official foundation date of the Church, and that the apostles immediately set out "for the missions." On the contrary. Luke's idyllic descriptions of the first Christian community (Acts 2:42-47; 4:32-35; 5:12-13) suppose it to be rather sedentary. The same is suggested by the appointment of the seven "deacons"[20] (Acts 6:1-6), to assure equitable material help to the widows of the Greek-speaking disciples. Luke writes that "the Twelve assembled the community of the disciples" (Acts 6:2), which supposes that the community, or the major part of it, was to be found in Jerusalem.

About the year 36 Stephen underwent martyrdom. The violent persecution of the Church which ensued caused the disciples to disperse "throughout the countryside of Judea and Samaria" (Acts 8:1). This also meant, of course, the spreading of the Good News. Such ways of sowing the seed are typical of divine Providence! Luke expressly observes: "The members of the church who had been dispersed went about preaching the word" (Acts 8:4). Thus it was in consequence of the ill will of men that Philip was led to evangelize Samaria (Acts 8:5). But the apostles, as Luke explicitly notes (8:1), remained in Jerusalem. From this we must conclude that six or seven years after the resurrection of Jesus, the apostles seemed unworried about how they would become his witnesses "to the ends of the earth" (Acts 1:8). Evidently they had put themselves in the hands of divine Providence and were more disposed to let God guide them than to dash out to distant missions.

For the next period our information is rather fragmentary. There is no trace of any departure of the Twelve for the missions. Much less, then, can any date for a departure be pinpointed. The tradition we find in Clement of Alexandria (d. ca. 215), Eusebius of Caesarea (d. 339), and the apocryphal *Acts of Peter* would have it that on the orders of Jesus himself the apostles stayed in Jerusalem for some twelve years.[21] Possibly. We are sure, according to Acts, that Peter went on apostolic journeys. Luke records that "Peter was making numerous journeys" (Acts 9:32),[22] including those to Lydda (Acts 9:32-35) and Joppa (Acts 9:36-43), but also that Peter ministered exclusively to Jews. In this connection Luke tells us that "those in the community who had been dispersed by the persecution that arose because of Stephen went as far as Phoenicia, Cyprus and Antioch, making the message known to none but Jews" (Acts 11:19). Peter would leave Jerusalem only after the execution of James, the brother of the Lord (cf. Acts 12:17), which must have occurred in 43–44, or about fourteen years after the resurrection.[23]

We can see a comparable slow development in the case of Paul, the missionary *par excellence*. His conversion on the road to Damascus (Acts 9:1-19) dates from 36–37.[24] He then preached at Damascus, spent some time in Arabia, and went to Jerusalem to see Peter. Three years had passed since his conversion (Gal. 1:17-18). He returned to Tarsus, his native city, where Barnabas sought him out as a fellow-worker for a year (Acts 11:25-26). Only then did his first missionary journey take place between 45 and 49; it was ten years since he had received baptism from Ananias. Once again, in the case of Paul as in that of the Twelve, we cannot speak of a hasty departure for the missions.

The impression we receive is rather that the apostles responded to events and left God the responsibility of going before them and preparing the way. Sometimes they even followed up on work done by others: "When the apostles in Jerusalem heard that Samaria had accepted the word of God [brought there by Philip, after the dispersal of the Jerusalem community], they sent Peter and John to them" (Acts 8:14).

The preaching of the Gospel to the pagans will be undertaken even more slowly and prudently. It will take a vision from God to force Peter to address himself to pagans like Cornelius, the centurion of Caesarea, and it will take a minor domestic Pentecost[25] and the gift of tongues before Peter is willing to baptize Cornelius and his household (Acts 10). Peter thought it necessary to justify his ministry among the pagans to "the apostles and the brothers in Judea" (Acts 11:1 JB).

We have a typical case in the foundation of the Church at Antioch (Acts 11:19-26),[26] which was to become the missionary capital and the source of evangelization for the whole Mediterranean basin, and where the faithful were to be called "Christians" for the first time. This city was itself evangelized almost by accident by believers who were originally from Cyprus and Cyrene and had been forced to leave Jerusalem by the persecution that followed upon Stephen's martyrdom. Only when the Church of Jerusalem heard what was going on in Antioch did it send Barnabas to strengthen the communion of the two Churches in the faith.

In summary, if we consider the whole period from the death of Jesus (Passover in the year 30) to the first missionary journey of Paul (between 45 and 49), we cannot but conclude that the first community, and especially the Twelve, showed no great enthusiasm for missionary work, despite the mandate for a universal mission.[27] In straightforward language, the community did not work directly for the spread of the Good News, or, if it did, the texts do not tell us about it. It was not the Twelve but Philip the deacon who evangelized the Samaritans; it was not the Twelve but Greek-speaking Jews from Cyprus and Cyrene who brought the Good News to Antioch. According to Gal. 2:7, and therefore in 49 or in 56–57, according to the date adopted for the writing of this letter, Peter was still a Jewish apostle serving only Jews.

b) Missionary expansion

And yet the Church described in Acts did experience an intense missionary development and an extraordinary expansion during this same period. Luke is careful to make us aware of the numerical growth:

    —Acts 1:15: Before the Ascension the community has one hundred and twenty members.

    —Acts 2:41: Some three thousand are added on Pentecost.

    —Acts 2:47: The Lord adds daily to the numbers, and, in Acts 4:4, the community has reached five thousand.

—Acts 5:14: "More and more believers, men and women in great
numbers, were continually added to the Lord."

—Acts 6:1: "The number of disciples grew."

—Acts 6:7: "The number of the disciples in Jerusalem enor-
mously increased. There were many priests among
those who embraced the faith." [28]

—Acts 9:31: "The church. . . . was being built up."

—Acts 9:42: At Joppa "many came to believe in the Lord."

—Acts 11:21: At Antioch "a great number of them believed and
were converted to the Lord."

—Acts 11:24: "Large numbers were added to the Lord."

—Acts 12:24: "The word of the Lord continued to spread and
increase." [29]

How is this expansion to be explained? First of all, Luke evidently does not tell us everything. He imposes a pattern on the
events narrated, telling us first about Jerusalem (Acts 1–6), then
about Judea and Samaria (6–12), and finally about other areas of
the world (13–28). The sequence is prompted by the words of the
risen Christ: "You are to be my witnesses in Jerusalem, throughout Judea and Samaria, yes, even to the ends of the earth" (Acts
1:8). But there may have been other missionary journeys well
before Paul and Barnabas set out for "the ends of the earth." For
this was a time when the Church was missionary without having
missionaries, that is, without having believers who were specifically dedicated to this task; every Christian was a missionary.

Jerusalem, moreover, being as it was the heart of the chosen
people and a religious center with a vast influence, was an ideal
place from which to spread the Gospel. Every pilgrimage brought
throngs of visitors to the Holy City and, as at the first Pentecost,
could bring many of them home as converts to Christianity. The
end of every pilgrimage was like a new departure for the missions!

Luke emphasizes the universalist aspect of the first Pentecost.
He finds delight in the vast panorama of the Peoples present: "We
are Parthian, Medes, and Elamites. We live in Mesopotamia,
Judea and Cappadocia, Pontus, the province of Asia, Phrygia and
Pamphylia, Egypt, and the regions of Libya around Cyrene.
There are even visitors from Rome — all Jews, or those who have
come over to Judaism; Cretans and Arabs too" (Acts 2:9-11). The
list was probably added later to the original text.[30] It is not an
especially clear list, and the best explanation is that Luke took it
from another source.

The list begins with four peoples: Parthians, Medes, Elamites, and Mesopotamians, who are scattered over the map from east to west. The mention of Judea is surprising — perhaps it is in the middle of the list because Jerusalem is the center of the world? We then get lost in a maze of unimportant provinces, like Pamphylia, which is mentioned alongside the vast province of Asia. Greece is omitted, but not the sands of Cyrenaic Libya. Syria is not mentioned, which might indicate that the list originated in Syria. The geographical list is followed by a short religious classification: "Jews, or those who have come over to Judaism," i.e., proselytes. Finally, there is a brief recapitulation: "Cretans and Arabs"; today we might have said "Westerners and Easterners." Twelve peoples in all, with the Romans added and bringing up the rear.

The purpose of the list is evident. It tells us that the whole world (or almost the whole world!) — "every nation under heaven," says Luke (Acts 2:5) — was present at the Christian Pentecost, and the news of the Lord's resurrection thus reached out-of-the-way places like Pamphylia and Cyrenaica. The twelve peoples may be meant as an allusion to the twelve apostles, each people receiving its own apostle to bring it the Good News. As for the Romans, who make thirteen, their evangelization will be Paul's task, as Luke will show at the end of Acts (28:17-31). So then, if the Church was born on Pentecost, it was born as a universal Church.

Universality was also a mark of the feast of Pentecost in the biblical tradition.[31] Pentecost was like a Tower of Babel in reverse; at Babel the peoples spoke the same language but ended up unable to understand one another, and so they dispersed; at Pentecost they spoke different languages but were at one in praising together the great deeds of God. The feast was marked, not by unification through a religious esperanto, but by unity of praise that drew upon the varied riches of many peoples and their languages.

In Jewish tradition Pentecost was also regarded as a feast that celebrated the gift of the Law and the renewal of the covenant. It was thought that the Law of Sinai had been proclaimed in seventy different tongues; the seventy tongues are an evident allusion to the seventy peoples listed in the catalogue of nations in Gen. 10. Moreover, Moses was accompanied on Mount Sinai by seventy elders (Exod. 24:9), who represent the peoples. Tradition also maintained that the Septuagint, the Greek translation of the Hebrew Bible, was written by seventy wise men, each nation thus having its own translator. At the time of the Galilean mission the Lord sent out seventy missionaries (Luke 10:1), as though to signify that every people should have its own missionary. Such is the universalist background against which Luke writes his account of the Christian Pentecost.

But the greatest missionary power during the early years was the witness given by the community itself. Three times (Acts 2:42-47, 4:32-35, and 5:12-14) Luke introduces summaries which describe in idyllic terms the community of Christians at Jerusalem.[32] This community is faithful to the teaching of the apostles, to fraternal communion, to the breaking of bread, and to prayer; it is "of one heart and one mind"; it bears witness in a powerful way to the Lord's resurrection; it is the source of signs and wonders among the people. Especially significant is the statement: "Nor was there anyone needy among them" (Acts 4:34), which is a direct reference to the Septuagint text of Deut. 15:4: "There shall be no needy among you." Luke seems to be saying: "The Christian community is indeed the messianic community! See, among us no one is in need!"

A naive admiration has no doubt led to some idealization of the picture. But Luke achieves what he wants to achieve — to make credible the missionary expansion of the Jerusalem community. He shows us a community whose spotless beauty wins upright souls to faith in the risen Christ. The first summary ends with a reference to the "missionary" God who recruits believers for the Church: "Day by day the Lord added to their number those who were being saved" (2:47). The third summary emphasizes the fascination the early community had for outsiders. It does so in a remarkably heavy way that highlights the awkwardness of the editing. For after observing that "no one dared to join them," it nonetheless goes on to say that "more and more believers, men and women in great numbers, were continually added to the Lord" (5:13a and 14). This evidently means that despite fear of persecution by Judaizers, many declared themselves followers of Jesus. In joining the Christian believers, they "joined the Lord," so clearly did the community mirror the risen Christ.

The missionary power of the early Church and the secret of its growth amid persecution was the attraction its beauty had for all who approached it and the ideal life it lived with Christ: "The community of believers were of one heart and one mind." We have every reason for thinking that when the Catholic Church of our day begins to look again like the original community, it too will experience a comparable missionary expansion.

6. *Mission — God's work*

Our consideration of the missionary activity of Jesus, together
with the conclusions we can draw from it for missionary activity in
our own time, is a source both of humility and of joy. For it turns out
that the mission for the sake of which some people have offered
themselves body and soul to God and for which they have sacrificed
all their energies and their dearest hopes is not primarily their work
at all. It is not man but God who carries the work through. It is God
who calls, God who converts, God who saves. He is the real
"missionary." Other "missionaries" are simply witnesses, among the
peoples of the earth, to the salvation God effects. Mission is God's
work, not simply in the sense that he who works at it does so for the
sake of God, but in the sense first and foremost that God himself is
the one who is at work, carrying out his plan of universal salvation
by means of his Church.

Christ himself, as we pointed out, did not go "to the missions."
But he did give the supreme testimony of offering his life "in ransom
for the many" (Mark10:45), that is, for all men without exception.
These "many" are also the multitude that is invited to the feast of
the covenant which Jesus seals with his blood. He has made his
resurrection the center of reality, and to every man who believes he
offers the grace of escaping death and rising with him. What he asks
of the missionaries is not primarily to "convert souls" any more
than to heal bodies, but simply to be a witnesses by their lives to the
stupendous fact that God is with them and saves them. "It is written
that the Messiah must suffer and rise from the dead on the third
day. In his name, penance for the remission of sins is to be preached
to all the nations, beginning at Jerusalem. *You are witnesses of this*"
(Luke 24:46-48). "*You are to be my witnesses* in Jerusalem, throughout Judea and Samaria, yes, *even to the ends of the earth*" (Acts 1:8).

Mission is not primarily a matter of activities, undertakings, sermons, and the spread of the Gospel by word of mouth and in writing. It is a matter first and foremost of bearing witness to Christ. Or
to put it more accurately, all the other activities are valuable to the
extent that they bear witness to God's presence in our lives and to
his salvation.

At a time when missionary vocations are on the decrease, the
extent of the missionary task may discourage us. In the hundred
years just ending, the old Christian countries exported a great
wealth of tender love and dedication to the mission areas of the

world. And yet the religious picture of the world has not been changed in the direction of Christianity. On the contrary — the disproportion between Christians and non-Christians is increasing. If the present situation continues — and is there any reason why it will not? — we may wonder whether Christians will at some point become nothing more than a very minor sect and be relegated to the museum of mankind's religious history. And yet, the future cannot dismay us nor take our joy from us. We are toiling at a task that is beyond our strength. And what the Lord asks of us is "Be my witnesses." That is the mission we must carry out. It is for him to accomplish his mission at the time he decides upon, in accordance with his own blessed will, which is one of tender love for each and every human being.

[1] We have an almost tragic illustration of the truth of this statement in problems concerning the priesthood. Questions of the priestly status (work, marriage, politics) are to the fore on the ecclesiastical scene, while the problem of the missions is pushed into the background or even simply forgotten! Even in our day, a very small number of priests — perhaps less than ten percent (cf. J. Comblin, *La résurrection* [Paris, 1958], p. 28; cf. also A. Ageneau and D. Pryen, *Chemins de la mission aujourd'hui* [Paris, 1972], p. 77) — devote themselves to the evangelization of two and a half billion non-Christians. Ninety percent of the priests for the established Church, ten percent for the missions!

[2] The reader will profit by referring constantly to Vatican II's *Decree on the Missionary Activity of the Church*. For an overall view from the Protestant side, cf. J. Blauw, *The Missionary Nature of the Church: A Survey of the Biblical Theology of Mission* (New York, 1962). In 1959 Blauw was asked by the International Missionary Council and the World Council of Churches to do "a survey and appraisal of recent work in Biblical theology having any bearing on the nature and necessity of the Church's mission to the world" (p. 7). His survey is based on the work done in the last thirty years. Cf. also M. Spindler, *La mission, combat pour le salut du monde* (Neuchâtel, 1967); J. Giblet, "Le sens de la mission dans le Nouveau Testament," *Assemblées du Seigneur*, no. 98 (1967), pp. 42–53.

[3] R. Martin-Achard, *op. cit.*, p. 70.

[4] In *Préparation au ministère presbytéral*, reports presented to the meeting of the French bishops at Lourdes in 1972 (Paris, 1972), pp. 66–67. Cf. also A. Ageneau and D. Pryen, *op. cit.*, pp. 42–43.

[5] Flannery, p. 350. The statement is quoted in the *Pastoral Constitution on the Church in the Modern World*, no. 42 (Flannery, p. 942). The *Dogmatic Constitution on the Church*, no. 48, speaks of the Church as "the universal sacrament of salvation" (Flannery, p. 407), a phrase quoted in the *Pastoral Constitution . . .*, no. 45 (Flannery, p. 947) and in the *Decree on the Church's Missionary Activity*, no. 5 (Flannery, p. 817). Cf. also *Dogmatic Constitution on the Church*, no. 9, and *Constitution on the Sacred Liturgy*, nos. 5 and 126. On this subject, cf. P. Smulders, "L'Eglise, sacrement primordial," and J.L. Witte, "L'Eglise, sacrement de l'unité," in *L'Eglise de Vatican II* (Unam sanctam 51; Paris, 1966), pp. 328–38 and 457–91 respectively.

[6] J.L. Witte, *art. cit.*, p. 490.

[7] Vatican II, *Dogmatic Constitution on the Church*, no. 28 (Flannery, p. 385).

[8] In Acts 13:1-3 we see the community of Antioch setting apart Paul and Barnabas, two of its "best" members, and sending them as missionaries.

[9] Cf. D. Bosch, *Die Heidenmission in der Zukenftsschau Jesu*, pp. 184–92.

[10] Cf. D. Bosch, *op. cit.*, p. 188.

[11] Cf. L. Deiss, *Synopse* 1:27.

[12] In Matthew, the missionary mandate is given in Galilee, without any reference to the Ascension. In Luke it is given either on Easter day (Luke 24:47-48), which in the Gospel seems to be the day of the Ascension as well, or else forty days later, according to the tradition in Acts 1:8.

[13] Cf. F.W. Blass and A. Debrunner, *A Greek Grammar of the New Testament and Other Early Christian Literature*, translated and revised by R.W. Funk (Chicago, 1961), no. 419. W. Bauer, *A Greek-English Lexicon of the New Testament and Other Early Christian Literature*, translated and revised by W.F. Arndt and F.W. Gingrich (Chicago, 1957): "The aor. ptc. of *por.* is oft. used pleonastically to enliven the narrative" (p. 698). F. Zorell, *Lexicon Graecum Novi Testamenti* (Paris, 1931), has a similar comment: "The participle *poreutheis* is often used pleonastically to make a description more vivid" (col. 1105).

[14] Some examples (with the Greek form of "go" translated literally): "The Pharisees, having gone off, began to plot how they might trap Jesus in speech" (Matthew 22:15); "Immediately the man who received the five thousand, having gone, invested it" (Matthew 25:16); "So they [the chief priests and the Pharisees], having gone, kept it [the tomb] under surveillance of the guard, after fixing a seal to the stone" (Matthew 27:66); "Having gone, tell that fox" (Luke 13:32). Even when used by itself, the verb can have a very weak meaning, as in the expressions "Go in peace" (Luke 7:50; 8:48) or "Go and do the same" (Luke 10:37).

[15] Even if these words, presented by the Gospel as spoken before the Passion, are really sayings of the risen Christ (cf. J. Schmid, *Das Evangelium nach Markus* [4th ed.; Regensburg, 1958], p. 241), and even if we prefer the view that they express the missionary situation of the community around 50–70 A.D., it is difficult to see in them pure creations of the community, without any basis in words the Lord himself had spoken. Given the Judaizing and particularist tendencies of the early community, it is hard to see how such sayings could simply have been made up. We may also observe with J. Schmid (Excursus "The Command of the Risen Christ concerning Mission and Baptism," in his *Das Evangelium nach Matthäus* [3rd ed.; Regensburg, 1960]) "the undeniable fact that none of the universalist sayings of Jesus expressly mentions the mission to the pagans" and that "the real basis for the universalism of Jesus is his teaching on the subject of God as Father of all mankind" (p. 395).

It would thus be imprudent for the exegete to base the whole missionary duty on one or other saying of the Lord, the authenticity of which can be challenged. It would be equally imprudent for him to reject completely and in principle the authenticity of these sayings. It is exegetical wisdom, on the contrary, to acknowledge that the missionary obligation is rooted directly in the Good News the Lord had preached. Mission, then, does not create his words but simply makes explicit the truth they contain.

[16] "Full authority has been given to me" reminds us of the Son of Man in Dan. 7:13-14; cf. E. Lohmeyer, *Das Evangelium nach Matthäus* (Göttingen, 1958), pp. 416–17.

[17] Cf. J. Schmitt, *Jésus ressuscité dans la prédication apostolique* (Paris, 1949), and J. Comblin, *op. cit.*, p. 29: "Preaching to the pagans is based on the resurrection of Jesus."

[18] Some missionary congregations used to celebrate a feast of the "Dispersal of the Apostles" (July 11).

[19] Cf. F. Gils, "Vers la mission universelle," *Evangile*, no. 82, pp. 3–36; J.-P.

Audet, *Structures of the Priesthood: Home, Marriage and Celibacy in the Pastoral Service of the Church*, translated by R. Sheed (London, 1967), pp. 72–76.

[20] On the ministry of the Seven, cf. A. Lemaire, "From Services to Ministries: 'Diakoniai' in the First Two Centuries," in B. van Iersel and R. Murphy (eds.), *Office and Ministry in the Church* (Concilium 80; New York, 1972), pp. 35–49; *idem, Les ministères aux origines de l'Eglise* (Lectio divina 68; Paris, 1971), pp. 49–58.

[21] Cf. Clement of Alexandria, *Stromata*, VI, 5, 43; Eusebius of Caesarea, *Historia Ecclesiastica*, V, 18, 14; *Actus Petri cum Simone*, in A. Lipsius (ed.), *Acta Apostolorum Apocrypha*, Pars Prior (reprinted, Darmstadt, 1959), p. 49.

[22] Literally, "when Peter was passing through all," i.e., all places or all the believers. Translators vary in their interpretation; e.g., "Peter went here and there among them all" (RSV) and "Peter was making a general tour" (NEB).

[23] Cf. E. Haenchen, *Die Apostelgeschichte*, pp. 54–55. This was the date when the Twelve ceased to be important as a group, since no effort was made after James' death to complete the number twelve, as there had been after the death of Judas, when Matthias was chosen to replace him (Acts 1:15-26). The reason for this change of outlook was that the Twelve represented a specifically Jewish structure (the Twelve were at the service of the twelve tribes of Israel). Once the pagan "tribes" were admitted to the Church, the Jewish structure was no longer relevant.

[24] Cf. F. Prat, "Chronologie biblique," *DBS* 1:1283; A. Strobel, "Zeitrechnung," *Biblisch-historisches Handwörterbuch* 3:2223.

[25] This "mini-Pentecost" of the *pagans* (Acts 10:44-46) is very important in Luke because it corresponds to the first Pentecost, which, despite its universalism, was nevertheless immediately meant for Jews and proselytes.

[26] It is possible that the conversion of the "Greeks" of Antioch (Acts 11:20) took place before the conversion of Cornelius. Dislocations in temporal sequence are not contrary to Luke's methods (cf. L. Deiss, *Synopse* 1:48). When such shifts do occur, they usually have, in Luke, a theological purpose: he "deliberately rearranges the sequence in order to make Cornelius be the first Gentile received into the Christian community. . . . According to the account in Acts, Peter has the honor of opening the doors of the Church to the Gentiles; once they have been opened, Paul can do the rest" (J. Dupont, *Etudes sur les Actes des Apôtres*, pp. 409–10, 411).

[27] Quite diverse factors may have been responsible for this attitude. A. Wikenhauser, *Die Apostelgeschichte* (3rd ed.; Regensburg, 1966), remarks: "If the apostles and the whole Church of Jerusalem were slow and hesitant about accepting a mission to pagans, the reason is that it was difficult for them to overcome their Jewish past with its vibrant hope of the restoration of the kingdom to Israel" (p. 162).

[28] There was a rather large number of priests in Jerusalem in the days of Jesus; J. Jeremias, *Jerusalem in the Time of Jesus*, thinks there must have been about 7,200 (cf. pp. 198–207).

[29] For the remainder of Acts, cf. 13:48-49; 14:1, 21; 16:5; 17:4, 12; 18:8; 19:10, 20.

[30] This would explain the awkward repetitions in vv. 6-7 and 11b-12.

[31] On this tradition, cf. J. van Goedoever, *Fêtes et calendriers bibliques*, pp. 303–11; R. le Déaut, "Pentecôte et tradition juive," *Spiritus*, no. 7 (1961), pp. 127–44, reprinted in *Assemblées du Seigneur*, no. 51 (1963), pp. 22–38; J. Dupont, "La nouvelle Pentecôte," *Assemblées du Seigneur*, no. 30 (1970), pp. 30–34; J.-P. Charlier, *L'Evangile de l'enfance de l'Eglise: Commentaire de Actes 1–2* (Etudes religieuses 772; Brussels, 1966) pp. 109–41; J. Potin, *La fête juive de la Pentecôte* (Lectio divina 65; Paris, 1971).

[32] Possibly Luke is citing Judeo-Christian documents to which a redactor has made some further additions. In the first summary, 2:42 and 46-47 are original, 2:43-45 secondary. In the second, 4:32 and 34-35 are original, 4:33 secondary. In the third, 5:12a and 15-16 are original, 5:12b-14 secondary. Cf. P. Benoit, "Remarques sur les sommaires des Actes II, IV et V," in his *Exegèse et théologie* 2:181–92.

INDEX OF SCRIPTURE TEXTS

INDEX OF NAMES

TOPICAL INDEX